MERTON & THE TAO

MERTON &
THE TAO

DIALOGUES WITH JOHN WU
AND THE ANCIENT SAGES

Edited by Cristóbal Serrán-Pagán y Fuentes

FONS VITAE

The Fons Vitae Thomas Merton Series

Merton & Sufism: The Untold Story, 1999
Merton & Hesychasm: The Prayer of the Heart, 2003
Merton & Judaism: Holiness in Words, 2003
Merton & Buddhism: Wisdom, Emptiness,
and Everyday Mind, 2007
Merton & The Tao: Dialogues with John C. H. Wu
and the Ancient Sages, 2013

Fons Vitae is deeply grateful to Nina Bonnie, without whose
support this volume would not have been possible.

First published in 2013 by
Fons Vitae
49 Mockingbird Valley Drive
Louisville, KY 40207
http://www.fonsvitae.com

Library of Congress Control Number: 2013941908

ISBN 978-1887752-992

See pages 404-405 for Acknowledgments
and Permissions Notices.

Cover photograph of John C. H. Wu.

This book was typeset by Neville Blakemore, Jr.
Printed in Canada

Dedicated to

Judi Rice

Jonathan Montaldo

CONTENTS

THE FONS VITAE THOMAS MERTON SERIES

Professional theologians and lay readers, scholars and spiritual seekers in a broad spectrum of religious practice regard the Cistercian
monk Thomas Merton (1915-1968) as one of the most important
spiritual writers of the last half of the twentieth century. The writing
impelled by his monastic life's interests in the world's religious
traditions are recognized as a seminal and continuing catalyst for
inter-religious dialogue in the twenty-first century.

Ewert Cousins, a distinguished Professor of Religion and
the General Editor of both the World Spirituality Series and the
Classics of Western Spirituality Series of Paulist Press, has called
Merton an "axial figure" who bridges within his own experience
and theological work the contemporary estrangements between
religious and secular perspectives. Dr. Cousins has publicly shared
his opinion that Thomas Merton means almost more today to many
than he actually did in his lifetime. He is becoming an iconic figure
who models inter-religious dialogue for those who are seeking a
common ground of respect for the varied ways in which human
beings realize the sacred in their lives. Merton's life and writing,
especially when it focuses on the contemplative practices common
to the world's major religions, have indeed become a forum, or
a bridge in Cousins' term, upon which those engaged in inter-
religious dialogue can meet and engage one another.

In his reaching out to living representatives of the world's various religious traditions by correspondence, and by his immersing
himself in the study of religious traditions other than his own Roman Catholicism, Merton models the inclusivity of intellect and
heart necessary for fruitful inter-religious dialogue. His personal
journal for April 28, 1957, witnesses to his zeal for a unity of learning and living as a method of personal "inner work" for ensuring
communication and respect among religious persons:

> If I can unite in myself, in my own spiritual life, the thought of
> the East and the West, of the Greek and Latin Fathers, I will
> create in myself a reunion of the divided Church, and from that

unity in myself can come the exterior and visible unity of the church. For, if we want to bring together East and West, we cannot do it by imposing one upon the other. We must contain both in ourselves and transcend them both in Christ.

The Fons Vitae publishing project for the study of world religions through the lens of Thomas Merton's life and writing brings Merton's timeless vision of all persons united in a "hidden ground of Love" to a contemporary audience. The first four volumes of the Fons Vitae Thomas Merton Series—*Merton & Sufism, Merton & Hesychasm, Merton & Judaism, and Merton & Buddhism*— featured essays by international scholars who gathered in three academic conferences in Louisville, Kentucky to assess the value of Merton's contributions to inter-religious dialogue. Each volume includes Merton's own writing across various genres: essays, poetry, and transcriptions of his lectures to the novices at Gethsemani that highlighted Merton's interest in contemplative traditions other than his own.

The scholars' articles in this fifth volume of the series, *Merton & The Tao*, study Merton's encounters with two Taoist "masters," one of them ancient, the other his contemporary. Merton cited his work of translating the poetry of Chuang Tzu in his volume, *The Way of Chuang Tzu*, as his favorite book. This volume studies Merton's identification with Chuang Tzu and his poetry as crucial for understanding dimensions of the Christian monk's consciousness in his final years. Merton met the second Taoist master, John Wu, Sr., with whom he collaborated in his translations of Chuang Tzu, both in person and by correspondence. John Wu, a many-faceted and realized human being as lawyer, professor, autobiographer, and devout Roman Catholic, incarnated and made real Merton's simultaneous encounters with the thought of both the East and the West. This volume presents the complete and annotated correspondence between Merton and John Wu.

The next volume in this series will include studies in *Merton & World Indigenous Cultures*. We hope that the Fons Vitae Thomas Merton Series will find a place in the libraries of those who promote the study and practice of contemplative religious traditions.

Jonathan Montaldo and Gray Henry
General Editors
for the Fons Vitae Thomas Merton Series

THOMAS MERTON'S PRAYER

The following prayer was offered by Thomas Merton at the First Spiritual Summit Conference in Calcutta. It appears as part of Appendix V in *The Asian Journal of Thomas Merton.* We offer it again here as the context from which this book arose and in which it has been prepared for publication.

> Oh God, we are one with You. You have made us one with You. You have taught us that if we are open to one another, You dwell in us. Help us to preserve this openness and to fight for it with all our hearts. Help us to realize that there can be no understanding where there is mutual rejection. Oh God, in accepting one another wholeheartedly, fully, completely, we accept You, and we thank You, and we adore You, and we love You with our whole being, because our being is in Your being, our spirit is rooted in Your spirit. Fill us then with love, and let us be bound together with love as we go our diverse ways, united in this one spirit which makes You present in the world, and which makes You witness to the ultimate reality that is love. Love has overcome. Love is victorious. Amen.

PREFACE

Merton & The Tao will make a major contribution to those interested in Merton studies, in the interfaith dialogue between East and West, and in the comparative study of world religions and mysticism. Additionally, the unpublished correspondence between Thomas Merton and John C. H. Wu will bring more awareness about the more scholarly and humanistic side of Merton after his lengthy collaboration with one of the brightest Chinese minds in the twentieth century. The letters are full of humorous exchanges and contemplative assertions. They shed new light on Merton's later years in the sixties covering an array of topics from his contacts with D. T. Suzuki to his love affair with M to his trip to Asia. Without doubt, the new edited collection of unpublished letters of Merton-Wu and the excellent essays written by some of the best Mertonian and Taoist scholars in the field will serve us well by bringing together religious humanism and rigorous scholasticism. Over the last few decades there has been a growing demand and renewed interest in global spirituality inside and outside Academia. In the context of globalization there is no better time to introduce this new East-West study than now.

For historical reasons I have preferred to use "Taoism" rather than "Daoism" when referring to Merton's time, since the usage of the word was commonly accepted in his own days by scholars. I might also add that I chose to keep the many different languages intact for pedagogical reasons. Instead of standardizing their styles I have respected each scholar's unique perspective on these essays and the way they cited their sources. However I try to standardize the use of italics or punctuation when it was most needed.

Part I opens up with a short history of Taoism. I invited Livia Kohn to write this overview of Taoism because she is one of the leading experts in the American Academy of Religion and a former professor of mine at Boston University. Also I collaborated with an article on the central Taoist mystical teaching of *wu-wei*. Both Merton and Wu understood how important this Chinese philosophy is to Lao Tzu and Chuang Tzu. Without it we cannot fully appreciate the mystical insights and sense of humor of Merton and Wu in their poetic renderings on Chuang Tzu. Part II combines the lucid commentaries of Merton scholar and sinologist Lucien Miller (University of Massachusetts in Amherst) with the critical appraisal of Bede Bidlack (St. Anselm College). Additionally, I was delighted to obtain a copy of Donald P. St. John's (Moravian College) study on Merton's eco-theology and spirituality using *Chuang Tzu* as its framework. Part III focuses on the spiritual friendship between Tom Merton and John Wu during the seven years of their correspondence. Both John Wu, Jr. (Chinese Culture University in Taiwan) and Lucien Miller introduce us to this great relationship that was made in heaven and contextualize for us how the process of writing together *The Way of Chuang Tzu* came into being. We learn that Wu as a Chinese translator helped Merton with getting the style of language right while Merton helped Wu with his book *The Golden Age of Zen*. Both trusted each other's work and insights and built a solid foundation for future scholarly projects. Part IV and Part V are at the heart of this volume containing the collected letters between Merton and Wu, Sr. (1961-1968) and Merton and Wu, Jr. (1967-1968). Each part includes annotations produced by John Wu, Jr. and the editor of this volume to contextualize the names of authors, schools of thought, teachings and sources throughout the correspondence. Part VI offers a series of meditations by John Wu, Jr. in memory of his father John C. H. Wu. The volume ends with a list of contributors, acknowledgments, and an index.

According to Chinese scholar Lucien Miller, the hitherto unpublished manuscript of the letters between Thomas Merton and John C. H. Wu (Ching-hsiung Wu, 1899-1986) marks a hidden yet seminal movement among the religious encounters between East and West in the twentieth century. Writing to Thomas Merton at the midway point of their six and a half year correspondence, March 14, 1961—August 18, 1968, John C. H. Wu observes: "Between true friends the Lord Himself serves as the postman." Wu's comment epitomizes the consciousness that he and Merton came to share regarding the true nature of the ninety-one letters they exchange. Theirs is a threefold encounter between self and other, Christianity and Asia, the human and the divine. Throughout their correspondence both Merton and Wu cultivated a strong spiritual bond based on mutual respect and love for each other. There is no doubt in my mind that their shared interest in the comparative study of Eastern and Western mysticism brought Merton and Wu together. Merton's interest in Asia landed him in Bangkok, Thailand where he died after experiencing an aesthetic illumination in front of Polonnaruwa's giant Buddha statues. Wu found the Unknown Christ of Taoism and Confucianism in ancient China and came to America to teach at Seton Hall. Both agreed that the spirit of *aggiornamento* during the Second Vatican Council would bring an up-dating to the Christian Church by looking at the East. In Merton's case, he went to Asia as a pilgrim to learn from their spiritual traditions. Wu came to the United States and helped Merton to see Asia more clearly. In the last analysis, John Wu gave Thomas Merton the titles of *Mei-Teng* (or "Silent Lamp") and *Tao-Jen* (or "The Man of Tao"). Interestingly, former President of the International Thomas Merton Society (ITMS) Monsignor William Shannon adopted the title of "Silent Lamp" for one of his biographies on Merton.

As the editor of the new volume on *Merton & The Tao: Dialogues with John Wu and the Ancient Sages* by Fons Vitae, I must say how grateful I am to the General Editors of these series, Gray Henry and Jonathan Montaldo and to Neville Blakemore for typesetting the text. They have been very patient with me while I was teaching and doing research at Valdosta State University before I was finally able to put my hands to finishing this volume. I owe my special thanks to Gray for her vivid illustrations and for formatting the text, to Jonathan for his editorial skills and annotated comments. I have learned a great deal in the past three years of editing this volume from having multiple conversations with him. I would like to also give a special thanks to Danielle Costello the Secretary of the Philosophy and Religious Studies Department at Valdosta State University for typing my article.

Cristóbal Serrán-Pagán
Thomas Merton's birthday
January 31, 2013

PART I
INTRODUCTION TO TAOISM

DAOIST TRADITIONS

Livia Kohn

Daoism is the indigenous organized religion of traditional China. Best known in the West as "Taoism" (using an older mode of transliterating Chinese), it is a multifaceted, complex combination of traditions that can be divided according to three types of organization and practice: literati, self-cultivation, and communal.

Literati Daoists are members of the educated elite who focus on Daoist ideas as expressed by the ancient thinkers Laozi and Zhuangzi, whose works were classified as the "Daoist school" (*daojia*) in the Han dynasty. Literati Daoists use the ancient concepts of Dao, yin-yang, sage, nonaction, and spontaneity to create meaning in their world and hope to exert some influence on the political and social situation of their time, contributing to greater universal harmony, known as the state of Great Peace. Literati lineages and legitimation come from a fundamental dedication to the classical texts, which they interpret in commentaries and essays, and whose metaphors they employ in stories and poetry. Literati Daoists may live a life of leisure or be active in society as local officials, poets, writers, or teachers, but in all cases their self-identity derives from ideas centered on the Dao. They have been part of the tradition since its inception, and the ancient thinkers Laozi and Zhuangzi may well be considered their first example (see Kohn and Roth 2002). But they also appear among commentators to the texts, patriarchs of religious schools, thinkers of Confucian or Buddhist background, and academics today.

Daoist practitioners of self-cultivation or "nourishing life" (*yangsheng*), too, come from all walks of life, but rather than the understanding of universal principles and the creation of social harmony, their main concern is the attainment of personal health, longevity, peace of mind, and spiritual immortality, defined as mystical oneness with the Dao, a sense of eternal existence, and close communication with otherworldly realms and entities. Seekers of long life pay little attention to political involvement and their organization depends strongly on the master-disciple relationship.

1

Groups can be small and esoteric with only a few active followers (as in certain Taiji quan lineages), large and extensive with
leanings toward organized religion (as in some Qigong groups),
or vague and diffuse with numerous people practicing a variety of
different techniques (as for the most part today). Historical continuity is strong, and the earliest descriptions of self-cultivation
practices are found before the Common Era, tentatively ascribed to
distant followers of Laozi and Zhuangzi and quite evident among
Han-dynasty immortality seekers. The successors of these early
activists, moreover, gave rise to several organized Daoist schools
when they had inspiring visions and received divine instructions
from the gods.

These organized schools, moreover, formed the backbone
of communal Daoism, the third major form of Daoism. Called
the "Daoist teaching" (*daojiao*), communal Daoism has priestly
hierarchies, formal initiations, regular rituals, and prayers to the
gods. Some of its organizations are tightly knit fraternities with
secret rites and limited contact to the outside world. Others are
part of ordinary society, centered on neighborhood temples and
concerned with the affairs of ordinary life—weddings and funerals,
protection and exorcism. Their expression tends to be in liturgies,
prayers, and moral rules (see Kohn 2004). Historically, they have
been documented since the second century C.E. and shown a high
degree of continuity over the millennia. While specific rites and
organizational patterns changed, there is a distinct line from early
groups to Daoist organizations today, and one can see a clear link
between the ritual of medieval China and contemporary liturgies
(see Dean 2000).

Today, communal Daoists can be either lay or monastic. The
dominant lay school is called Orthodox Unity (Zhengyi) or Celestial Masters (Tianshi), while the monastic school is known as
Complete Perfection (Quanzhen). The Celestial Masters transmit
their teachings in family lineages from father to son. Their headquarters are located in Taiwan, and they focus on rituals of cosmic
harmony, purification, healing, and burial. Monastic Daoists of
Complete Perfection follow the Dragon Gate (Longmen) branch
and have their headquarters at the White Cloud Temple (Baiyun
guan) in Beijing. Its members practice joint daily rituals as well
as individual cultivation that involve the transformation of the
body's energy into pure spirit through a practice known as inner

alchemy (*neidan*). They also pursue the longevity techniques of self-cultivation, such as Qigong and Taiji quan, in preparation of more spiritual endeavors.

Interconnected from the beginning, these three types of Daoism—literati, self-cultivation, and communal—although distinct in their abstract description, are not mutually exclusive in practice. On the contrary, as contemporary practitioners often emphasize, to be a complete Daoist one must follow all three paths: studying ancient philosophy and being socially responsible, undertaking self-cultivation for health and spiritual advancement, and performing rituals and prayers to the gods.

Historically, too, the tendency was to integrate all forms, so that certain literati Daoists were also ordained priests and masters of meditation, followers of organized groups which studied the classics and engaged in gymnastics, and self-cultivation practitioners who wrote poetry and prayed to the gods. But there is no norm, and one cannot categorically state that *only* those people are Daoists who exhibit the clear presence of *all* three kinds of religious activity. Even someone dedicated to only one aspect, a marginal or informal member of the religion, might still consider himself a Daoist and may well have an important contribution to make. To do justice to the Daoist tradition, one must therefore examine its different aspects on all the different levels, as several recent survey works have done quite successfully (see Kohn 2001; Miller 2003; Kirkland 2004).

LITERATI DAOISM

THE *DAODE JING*. Literati Daoism goes back to two classical, philosophical Daoist texts, the *Daode jing* (Book of the Dao and Its Virtue) and the *Zhuangzi* (Book of Master Zhuang). Associated with the sage Laozi, the Old Master who later came to be venerated as a creator deity under the name Lord Lao (Laojun; see Fig. 1), the *Daode jing* is a short text in about five thousand characters, divided into eighty-one chapters and two parts, one on Dao (1-37), and one on De (38-81). It is written in verse—not a rhyming, steady kind of verse, but a stylized prose that has strong parallels and regular patterns—and contains sections of description contrasted with tight punchlines. The text has been transmitted in several different editions, three of which are most important today. The first is the so-called standard edition, also known as the transmitted edition.

Fig. 1. The deified Laozi or Lord Lao in a statue at the foot of Mount Qingcheng, Sichuan, in 2004. Author's photograph.

Handed down by Chinese copyists over the ages, it is at the root of almost all translations of the text (LaFargue and Pas 1998). It goes back to the third century C.E., to the erudite Wang Bi (226–249) who edited the text and wrote a commentary on it that Chinese since then have considered inspired (see Lin 1977; Rump and Chan 1979). It has shaped the reception of the text's worldview until today.

The second edition is called the Mawangdui edition, so named after a place in south China (Hunan) where a tomb was excavated in 1973 that dated from 168 B.C.E. It contained an undisturbed coffin surrounded by numerous artifacts and several manuscripts written on silk, mostly dealing with cosmology and longevity techniques, such as gymnastics and sexual practices. Among them were two copies of the *Daode jing*. The Mawangdui version differs little from the transmitted edition: there are some character variants which have helped clarify some interpretive points, and the two parts are in reversed order, i.e., the text begins with the section on De, and then adds the section on Dao (see Henricks 1989). The manuscripts are important because they show that the *Daode jing* existed in its complete form in the early Han dynasty, and that it was considered essential enough to be placed in someone's grave.

The third edition was discovered in 1993 in a place called Guodian (Hubei). Written on bamboo slips and dated to about 300 B.C.E., the find presents a collection of various philosophical works of the time, including fragments of Confucian and other texts. Among them are thirty-three passages that can be matched with thirty-one chapters of the *Daode jing*, but with lines in different places, and considerable variation in characters. Generally, they are concerned with self-cultivation and its application to questions of rulership and the pacification of the state. Polemical attacks against Confucian virtues, such as those describing them as useless or even harmful (chs. 18–19), are not found; instead negative attitudes and emotions are criticized. This Guodian find of this so-called "Bamboo Laozi" tells us that in the late fourth century B.C.E. the text existed in rudimentary form, and consisted of a collection of sayings not yet edited into a coherent presentation. From this find, it appears that, gradually, a set of ideas and practices was growing that would eventually develop into something specifically Daoist (see Henricks 2000; Allan and Williams 2000).

ANCIENT WORLDVIEW. Although the *Daode jing* has often been hailed as representing the core of the Daoist worldview, it is a multifaceted work that can, and has been, interpreted in many different ways, not least as a manual of strategy, a political treatise on the recovery of the golden age, a guide to underlying principles, and a metalinguistic inquiry into forms of prescriptive discourse. It can be read in two fundamentally different ways: as a document of early Chinese culture or as a scripture of universal significance (see Schwartz 1985).

Looked at in terms of Chinese culture, concepts of statesmanship, political principles, military strategy, and royal virtues become essential, and the focus is on understanding the text in the context of contemporaneous works and the social and political situation of the time. Seen as a scripture of universal significance, ideas of personal cultivation, freedom of mind, and the attainment of spontaneity and naturalness take center stage—the text's main appeal is its timeless characterization and alleviation of the human condition. Both approaches are equally important and have been proposed by readers and scholars over the centuries; both are also evident in numerous traditional commentaries and the uses of the text throughout Chinese history (see LaFargue 1992; 1994).

The basic concept in the text is Dao or "Way." It can be understood either metaphysically as the underlying source and power of the universe, practically as the way in which the world functions, or analytically as the way in which people can (or cannot) speak about reality. The text does not make its understanding easy. Rather, the first chapter of the standard edition begins by saying that Dao cannot be named or known with ordinary human senses. It may be described as lying at the root of creation and the cycles of nature, the "mother" of all that keeps nature and society in harmony.

In religious terms Dao is seen as a mystical power of universal oneness; more metaphysically, it is a fundamental ontological entity or absolute truth. Some scholars have also read it in terms of relativist thinking, as a universal way that can never be approached or described, while others see it as a supreme principle that is too deep to be properly expressed in words. The intellectual historian Benjamin Schwartz describes it as "organic order"—"organic" in the sense that it is part of the world and not a transcendent other as in Western religion, "order" because it can be felt in the rhythms of the world, in the manifestation of organized patterns (Schwartz 1998).

Although ideally at the root of a perfectly ordered cosmos, the Dao over the course of human history and the unfolding of culture has come to be buried under the complexity of social structures and lost together with the purity in human hearts. To recover the original harmony of all and thus a state of Great Peace, people should practice simplicity (ch. 19)—a message that has made the *Daode jing* very popular in alternative circles of Western societies (Hardy 1998). Simplicity is expressed in two forms. First it is the physical restraint on accumulating too many things, abstention from eating rich and fancy foods, and generally a tendency to keep one's circumstances limited to what one really needs. Second, it may involve a mental exercise of tranquility and purification, which helps clear the mind and heart from the overload of sensory inputs and the cravings and desires associated with the world.

The *Daode jing* does not spell out any meditative or self-cultivation techniques and contains no claims about physical immortality (Chen 1973). But it portrays the sage (*shengren*) as one who has realized this mind and transformed into a person of Dao: socially responsible, unassuming and nondescript in his person, yet entirely benevolent and helpful in all situations (chs. 2, 27). He does not speak or preach but acts appropriately at all times, his mind in a constant state of nonaction, i.e., free from all invasive and personally motivated tendencies (Liu 1991; 1998). The sage may have a high position in society—and ideally is even the ruler (and thus, in ancient China, usually male)—but he will not think of himself as "possessing" anything, nor will he insist on his position, his way, or his personal wishes (chs. 3, 64). On the contrary, his mind and self at one with the Dao, he sees the inherent patterns of nature and the world and thinks only of the greater good of all (chs. 22, 80). He is a representative of universal virtue, embracing all beings and developing peace within and goodness without.

THE *ZHUANGZI*. The same ideal is also strongly present in the *Zhuangzi*, compiled in the mid-third century B.C.E. and associated with the thinker Zhuang Zhou (c. 370–290 B.C.E.). According to an early biography, he was of lower aristocratic background, highly erudite, and served as a minor government official. He first worked for a local southern Chinese state, then withdrew to dedicate himself to his speculations, teaching his ideas to disciples who later wrote them down. He also included various other schools in the book, which consists of thirty-three chapters and is written in prose (see Watson 1968; Graham 1981; Mair 1994). Its many stories, fables, and fictional dialogues made it the first text of classical Chinese fiction, and its worldview and language have inspired literary works as well as religious visions over the centuries (Mair 1983).

The main body of thought in the text is associated with Zhuang Zhou (chs. 1-7, 16-27). It defines the Dao not only as the core power of the universe but also as the inherent quality all people and beings have that determines the way they are. All beings can realize their inner core of spontaneity (*ziran*) to the fullest, find an ideal state of "free and easy wandering," and attain "perfect happiness" by being who they are and accepting where they stand in life (Graham 1982).

The ideal Daoist vision here is to become a perfected (*zhenren*) in a state of complete nonaction, the mind completely concentrated and empty, the senses absorbed in the spheres of the cosmos. The perfected has gone beyond ordinary perception and sees and hears through the Dao; he or she has "done away with understanding and become one with the Great Dao" (ch. 6). There is no sense of ego-identity left in this person; the perfected is without likes and dislikes, easily goes along with life and without any fear of death. The realization of the Dao here is, therefore, less a social or historical undertaking than an inner, personal, quest—attained in perfect freedom and peace within, trust in the Dao and compassion for all creatures without. Much of this vision has later impacted the self-cultivation tradition within Daoism, encouraging practitioners to find oneness with the Dao through exercises and meditations.

OTHER SCHOOLS. Among other schools represented in the text (see Graham 1980), there are first the primitivists, sometimes also called anarchists (chs. 8-10), who hate all government and idealize the time before the arrival of iron-age technology—iron plows, wagon axles, and swords. They suggest that when there were fewer people, no communications, no governments, and no infantry-fought wars, life was simple, easy, and good. They are, in one word, the proponents of a movement back to the stone age and away from everything "modern" society has to offer. Their ideal has continued in the figure of the anti-social hermit who prefers his lonely hut and simple food to a well-appointed life in society. Pervasive in Chinese history, the hermit can still be found today (see Porter 1993).

Second come the syncretists (chs. 11-15, 33), who integrate organized cosmology with an understanding of the Dao, outlining in more technical detail and concrete instructions just how one should align oneself with the Dao—using the structure of the natural world, the movements of the stars, and the divination signs (hexagrams) of the *Yijing* (*Book of Changes*; see Wilhelm 1950). This dimension of ancient Daoist thought became dominant under the Han dynasty, when cosmology was even further formalized and adopted as a key governing tool by the new rulers. It also became the basis of much later Daoism.

Third, there are the hedonists (chs. 28-31), who emphasize ease and leisure, a life of no constraints and no restrictions, an attitude of giving in to desires and serving only one's own happiness and satisfaction. Their basis is the idea that if the individual is part of the Dao, then whatever he or she feels and wants is also part of the Dao, and therefore all one's personal desires are expressions of cosmic goodness and have to be satisfied without fail. Hedo-nist ideas have continued in Daoism in the figure of the eccentric poet and social dropout, forever drunk and in disregard of social conventions. It is also apparent in certain later immortals, such as the famous Eight Immortals, who are well known for their ease in life, their eccentric leisure activities, and their happy laughter at everything and with everyone.

Literati Daoists follow the ideas of the ancients, usually prefer-ring one or the other branch, by incorporating the concepts of Dao, nonaction, spontaneity, sage, and perfecting into their lives and thereby find a deeper understanding of themselves and the world. They hope to gain a sense of flow in their lives and endeavor to see the world as an integrated organism that ideally moves along in perfect harmony but is disturbed here and there by intentional and ego-centered actions. Their main practice is the reading and study of texts, and often they will write commentaries, essays, poems, or letters about them, praising the depth of the ancients and reinterpret-ing their visions as their personal needs demand.

SELF-CULTIVATION

THE CONCEPT OF *QI*. Many literati Daoists are also drawn to methods of self-cultivation, not only the meditations of forgetfulness and "mind-fasting" already mentioned in the *Zhuangzi* and formalized in later centuries (see Kohn 1987), but also to more physical practices that evolved in the Han dynasty under the influence of Chinese medicine. The concept of Dao, already expanded and classified through early cosmology, was made accessible in the human body as *qi* or vital energy, an invisible yet pervasive force that created health and sickness by, like the Dao, being either in harmony or deviant, buried and distorted by ego-centered concerns.

Qi in the body, then, comes in two forms: a basic primordial or prenatal *qi* that connects it to the cosmos and Dao in general; and a secondary, earthly or postnatal *qi* that is replenished by breath-ing and food and helps the body survive in everyday life. Both forms of *qi* are necessary and interact constantly with each other, so that primordial *qi* is lost as and when earthly *qi* is insufficient and earthly *qi* becomes superfluous as and when primordial *qi* is complete—as in the case of the embryo in the womb (see Maspero 1981). People, once born, start this interchange of the two dimen-sions of *qi* and soon begin to lose their primordial *qi*, especially through interaction with the world on the basis of passions and desires, sensory exchanges, and intellectual distinctions—the very same features considered most harmful for cosmic interaction in the classical texts. '

When people have lost a certain amount of primordial *qi*, they get sick and eventually die. Medicine accordingly serves to replenish *qi* with outside stimuli, such as drugs, herbs, medicated diet, acupuncture, massages, or certain exercises (see Liu 1988). Once health is established, however, *qi* can be further developed and purified through so-called longevity techniques, which include diets, breathing exercises, gymnastics, massages, sexual practices, and meditations (see Kohn 1989). These ensure not only the recovery of original *qi* and the realization of the natural life expectancy but may even result in enhanced primordial potency and lead to increased old age and vigor.

Going even beyond this, longevity techniques can become ways of transforming the *qi*-constellation of the human body/mind and thereby attain a level beyond natural life known as immortality. This is a state at one with the Dao at the core of creation, a mystical oneness and a sense of everlasting life and cosmic power, a transcendence to a divine realm at the origins of the universe. Reaching for this, Daoist self-cultivation thus aims at the attainment of immortality through methods that lead initially to good health and with prolonged practice ensures extended longevity.

To reach the highest level, ideally practitioners should live separate from society, engage full-time in techniques of physical and spiritual control, and have their mind set on the world beyond. The oldest practitioners of this kind, known from the Han-dynasty *Liexian zhuan* (Immortals' Biographies), accordingly lived in the wilderness, dressed in garments of leaves or deer skins, fasted by living on pure *qi* or ate raw food they found in the woods (see Eskildsen 1998; Fig. 2). They were said to become light in their bodies and gain various magical powers, including the ability to fly. After attaining extended longevity of several centuries, they eventually ascended to heaven in broad daylight and went to live in wondrous paradises, luscious mountains surrounded by extensive bodies of water, the most prominent of which are known as Penglai and Kunlun.

FORMS OF PRACTICE. Daoist self-cultivation has played two major roles in traditional China. First, within organized Daoist schools

Fig. 2. Daoist adepts practicing immortality techniques on remote mountain cliffs. Mural at the Temple to the Goddess of Dawn, Mount Tai, Shandong. Author's photograph.

it was used as a preparatory stage that readied the body for the pursuit of more religious activities, be they intense meditations or elaborate rituals. The concept here is that the practitioner's body has to be open and free in its *qi*-flow to allow perfect communication with the otherworld, the necessary precondition for meditation and ritual to be effective. The other major role of self-cultivation practices was within the larger society, where they were used by people of all backgrounds and social status for various reasons— health, sexual vigor, anti-aging—commonly without any particular Daoist beliefs, community affiliation, or other contact. Ordinary people, physicians, Confucian officials, and Buddhist monks all engaged in them, not unlike the work-outs people do in modern health clubs.

Although the basic pattern of self-cultivation is the same on the various levels and similar practices are applied, the exercises are not entirely the same. Take breathing as an example. When healing or extending life, natural deep breathing is emphasized, with the diaphragm expanding on the inhalation. When moving on to immortality, however, reverted breathing is advised, which means that the diaphragm contracts on the in-breath. Undertaking this kind of reverted breathing too early or at the wrong stage in one's practice can cause complications, from dizziness to disorientation or worse.

Again, the point is made clear in the case of sexual practices. In healing, sexual activity with a partner is encouraged in moderation and measured ways, with both partners reaching regular orgasms. In longevity practice, sexual activity may still be undertaken with a partner, but ejaculation and other loss of essence and *qi* is avoided and the sexual stimulation is used to raise the awareness of the positive flow of *qi* in the body, which is then redirected to relieve stress and increase vitality. Through the practice, as Mantak Chia and Michael Winn say, people "become more aware that all living things are one" (1984, 171).

In immortality, finally, sexual practices become part of inner alchemy and are undertaken entirely within one's own body and without a partner. They serve the creation of an immortal embryo through the refinement of the sexual energy *jing* first into *qi*, then into cosmic spirit *shen* (see Ni 1992). Immortality is thus the creation of an inner spirit being and means the avoidance of ordinary joys and excitements. Practices associated with it are not only unsuitable (and probably impossible) for people on the levels of healing and longevity, but may even be harmful if attempted improperly.

The same point can also be made for diets and fasting. Eating for health and long life involves the abstention from heavy foods such as meat and fat, as well as from strong substances such as alcohol, garlic, and onions (Lu 1986). Instead, practitioners are encouraged to eat lightly and in small portions. As their *qi* increases, they will need ever less food, until—in immortality practice—all main staples can be cut out and food is replaced by the conscious intake of *qi* through breath in a technique known as *bigu* or "avoiding grain" (Eskildsen 1998).

QIGONG. The modern application of these techniques is found equally among medical, martial, and Daoist circles, from where they are rapidly spreading into the wider populace and also to the West. The most common practices are Qigong (Qi Exercises) and Taiji quan (Great Ultimate Boxing), which both use slow, gentle body movements that open the *qi* channels, provide a free flow of energy, help in healing, create strength and well-being, and lead to a greater awareness of cosmic energies and the Dao. They have their roots in ancient breathing techniques, gymnastics, self-massages, and meditations but develop them in unique and modern ways.

Qigong in particular is of quite recent origin. It begins in 1947, when the communist party cadre Liu Guizheng (1920-1983), suffering from a virulent gastric ulcer, was sent home to recover or die. He went home but refused to die—he was only 27 years old at the time! Instead, he took lessons in gymnastics and breathing from the Daoist Liu Duzhou. After 102 days of faithfully undertaking these practices, he was completely cured. He returned to his job and described his healing success to the party, which appointed him as a medical research leader in Hebei province with the task to study the effects of breathing on healing. In 1948, he created the term *Qigong* to indicate the methods which focused largely on breathing at the time. He then began to teach party officials and repeated his success with various ailments (Lin 2000).

Qigong is undertaken in all postures of the body. Always connected with deep, abdominal breathing and encouraging a state of inward absorption and letting go (*fangsong*), it consists for the most part of short exercises that are geared toward *qi*-activation and specific medical problems. A few are stationary, such as certain seated meditations where attention is focused in the elixir field (*dantian*) in the lower abdomen or the common practice called "standing like a pine tree." For this, practitioners stand with their feet hip-width apart and their hands loosely facing the abdomen. They remain without movement for ten to twenty minutes while envisioning themselves being rooted in Earth and growing toward Heaven, stable and strong yet swaying slightly as the *qi* passes through them (Cohen 1997).

The vast Qigong practice is in motion. Typically simple gymnastic moves are combined in sequences and matched with cosmological entities, such as Heaven and Earth, the five phases, and the eight trigrams (see Jahnke 1997). In all cases, the mind is used to visualize the *qi*-flow to specific areas in the body or its absorption from Heaven and Earth. Qigong for the most part is self-administered in these daily exercises, but it can also be activated through *qi*-infusion by a trained practitioner in a form of therapeutic touch or sent by a master over long distances by the mere power of thought.

TAIJI QUAN. In contrast to Qigong, Taiji quan, also spelled T'ai Chi Ch'uan, is a more cosmic and martial practice which can be traced back to the seventeenth century when it arose from a combination of philosophy, gymnastics, and martial arts training. An integrated flow of moves, stretches, squats, and kicks, it also combines with breathing and a deep inner focus. All moves are executed while standing; they are often quite complex and take regular, long-term practice to master. The knees are bent, the stomach is pulled in, the back is straight, the head is up, and the hands and feet move from the abdomen rather than from the shoulders and hips. The eyes see straight ahead without looking at anything in particular. The mind is empty but attentive, relaxed but alert, open to outside stimuli but without reaction. From a calm mind, focused intention arises which in turn leads to the harmonious flow of *qi* in the body, moving along the key meridians and into the extremities (Delza 1996).

Historically, Taiji quan has its roots among healing gymnastics, Daoist philosophy, and martial training. Its gymnastic roots are obvious in the emphasis on deep, abdominal breathing, the gentleness of the moves, and the rhythmic alternation of bends and stretches. Its philosophical vision involves the Great Ultimate (*taiji*), a name for the universe at the time of creation, when yin and yang are present but not yet differentiated into the five phases, symbolized in the commonly known black-and-white circle (see Chan 1963). Practitioners harmonize the *body's qi*-flow and make their minds one, thus reuniting with the state of creation.

In its martial roots, finally, Taiji quan goes back to the need for self-defense among Chinese communities and temples. The most famous warrior monks were those of the Buddhist Shaolin Temple (near Luoyang), associated with Bodhidharma, the sixth-century founder of Chinese Chan. As documented in historical records, monks of the temple—and thus presumably also members of other institutions as well as villagers and peasants—practiced fighting skills to ward off bandits and marauding armies. However, they did not fight unarmed, but used poles, staffs, cudgels, and pickaxes for most of Chinese history. This changed only in the seventeenth century, when the incoming Qing dynasty prohibited all use of weapons among non-military fighters. Both monastic and civil militias accordingly developed styles of unarmed combat, combining their defensive moves with the age-old practices of longevity breathing and gymnastics (see Shahar 2000).

Through its martial roots, Taiji quan not only became a practice that furthered strength, discipline, and willpower, but which also inherited the two main lineages of martial thinking of traditional China. They are the tradition of chivalry of ancient Confucianism, which encouraged the practice of archery and charioteering as tools for aristocratic self-cultivation and which emphasized honor, respect, good manners, precise timing, balance, and composure in all actions; and the tradition of bending and softness of ancient Daoism, expressed most clearly in Sunzi's *Art of War*, which stressed flexibility, yielding, humility, nonviolence, inner focus, and wisdom (Rodell 2003). Taken together, Taiji quan can be described as a body-focused moving meditation which has distinct health benefits, enhances long life, and leads to a sense of union with the Dao.

DAOIST PRACTICE IN AMERICA. Today Daoist self-cultivation is widely practiced both among religious Daoists and the general populace. It is becoming increasingly popular in the West, so that in the U.S. there are three major institutions of Complete Perfection background. The Fung Loy Kok Temple in Denver is a branch of a Hong Kong organization, whose most prominent and prolific member is Eva Wong. The Temple of the Mysterious Pivot (Xuanji guan) and the Taoist Studies Institute in Seattle are run by Harrison Moretz, offering training in a variety of practices, including both Taiji quan and Qigong. And the Center for Traditional Taoist Studies, originally called the New England Center of Tao, near Boston, was founded by Alexander Anatole. It holds classes in Daoist philosophy and provides training in meditations and Chinese health techniques (see Siegler 2001).

Three other self-cultivation schools are run by individually trained masters who derived their methods from various teachers and do not follow a specific lineage. The best-known among them is Mantak Chia, originally of Thailand, who was trained in Hong Kong, Singapore, and Thailand, and subsequently founded the Healing Tao Center in upstate New York. The Center offers training in complex and advanced systems of inner alchemy, aiming at the spiritual expansion of consciousness, not only for leading a better life in the here and now but also to attain immortality upon death. It is a highly personal goal, undertaken with others insofar as we are all spiritually interdependent, but ultimately an individual effort, guided by the master and learned in workshops (see Chia and Chia 1993).

Another prominent Daoist master in the United States who presents a similar program is Ni Hua-ching. Working out of southern California, he presents an extensive philosophy of inner alchemy and detailed methods for the attainment of immortality in numerous books and in workshops held at the Shrine of the Eternal Breath of Tao in Malibu, and the College of Tao in Prado (New Mexico). In addition, there is an American-run organization that supports Daoist practice both in China and the West, known as the Taoist Restoration Society. Centered in Colorado and led by Brock Silvers, it organizes projects to repair and restore temples on Daoist mountains in China, is concerned about religious freedom of Daoists, and supplies Westerners with guidance for practice and the material implements necessary for Daoist practice.

Beyond these, there are numerous masters of Taiji quan, Qigong, gymnastics, massage, Chinese medicine, martial arts, and *Feng Shui*, who claim a more or less close relationship with Daoism and offer ways to self-cultivation and perfection along Daoist lines. They all use the methods traditionally associated with the self-cultivation branch of the Daoist religion and apply them in various ways to the symptoms and life conditions of the modern world. It is due to their efforts that this form of Daoism is by far the best known and the most active aspect of the religion today.

COMMUNAL DAOISM

THE EARLY CELESTIAL MASTERS. Unlike the other two, the communal dimension of the religion is studied least yet has produced the most voluminous resources. Begun in 142 C.E. with the revelation of Daoist teachings by the divinized Laozi, or Lord Lao, to the immortality seeker Zhang Daoling, the first Celestial Master, the practice has brought forth several large schools, complex ordination hierarchies, elaborate rituals and monastic organizations, as well as numerous scriptures, commentaries, treatises, liturgies, and hagiographies, which for the most part are collected in the about 1500 bound booklets of the Daoist Canon (*Daozang*) of the year 1445. It is not possible to detail the complexity of communal Daoist history here, so we will focus on the nature and development of the two schools still dominant today, the Celestial Masters and Complete Perfection.

The school of the Celestial Masters grew from Zhang revelation of the Dao in 142. Arising at a time when many disasters—floods, droughts, locust plagues, famines, epidemics, and corrupt government—hit the country, they represented a millenarian vision of a new age and quickly rose to great popularity. Their home ground was Sichuan in southwest China, and they were closely parallel to another millenarian Daoist movement in Shandong (east China), known as the Dao of Great Peace (Taiping dao). The two had much in common, but saw their roles in the new age differently. Great Peace followers believed that they should replace the ruling dynasty and, in 184, rose in rebellion, were defeated, and became extinct as a Daoist school. The Celestial Masters saw themselves as advisers to whatever new ruler would arise, submitted to a local warlord, spread throughout China, and became the leading lay school of Daoism (see Seidel 1969).

Only fragmentary information has come down from the Great Peace movement, but we know of the followers of the Celestial Masters that they were hierarchically ranked on the basis of ritual attainments, with the so-called libationers at the top. They served as leaders of the twenty-four districts and reported directly to the Celestial Master himself. Beneath them were meritorious household leaders who represented smaller units in the organization and who guided the demon soldiers, the lowest level of initiates. Members came from all walks of life and included many non-Chinese. At the bottom were the common followers, again organized and counted according to households. Each of these had to pay a rice tax or equivalent in silk, paper, brushes, ceramics, or handicrafts. In addition, each member, from children on up, underwent formal initiations—sometimes in the form of stylized ritual intercourse known as the "harmonization of qi"—and was equipped with a list of spirit generals for protection against demons: seventy-five for an unmarried person and one hundred fifty for a married couple. The list of spirit generals was called a register and was carried, together with protective talismans, in a piece of silk around the waist (see Kleeman 1998).

In terms of doctrines and practices, the Celestial Masters believed in the Dao at the center of creation, represented by the personal creator god Lord Lao, who appeared to special seekers (and virtuous rulers) as the need arose. Although described in the texts as a person with special attributes and features, Lord Lao does not appear in human form in the Daoist art of the period. Rather, in accordance with the doctrine that the Dao cannot be described, he is shown as an ornate canopy or an empty throne. The belief was that he created and ruled the universe, assisted in this task by a celestial administration which kept records of life and death, and consisted of the Three Bureaus of Heaven, Earth, and Water. These three were celebrated at the major festivals of the year, known as the Three Primes, held on the fifteenth day of the first, seventh, and tenth months, when all participated in banquets known as kitchen-feasts. The Three Primes were also the occasion of general assemblies and tax management: in the first month, the tax was set according to the number of people in the household; in the seventh and tenth months, it was collected as the harvest was brought in.

Throughout the year, followers went about their business and delivered certain amounts of community service, repairing roads and bridges and maintaining so-called lodges of righteousness where travelers could stay on their journeys. They were also held to practice regular recitations of Laozi's *Daode jing* and observe a set of twenty-seven precepts based on the text. The rules prohibited socially disruptive behavior and prescribed an austere and disciplined lifestyle. Should anyone deviate from the norm and commit a sin, his or her body would forthwith be invaded by demons, thought to hover everywhere around the living in large numbers. The demons would then cause the person to get sick. As a consequence, all healing among the early Celestial Masters was undertaken through ritual and magic; acupuncture, herbs, and other medical treatments were expressly prohibited.

Treatment began with the sick person being isolated in a so-called quiet chamber or oratory where he or she had to think of all sins going back to childhood. Once certain sins had been identified, a senior master would come to write them down—in triplicate and together with a formal petition for their eradication from the person's divine record. The three copies would then, in a formal ceremony, be transmitted to Heaven (by burning), Earth (by burying), and Water (by casting into a river), whose officials supposedly set the record straight and restored the person's good health (see Tsuchiya 2002).

This formal ritual of confession and petition goes back to another local cult that flourished at the same time and was run by Zhang Xiu. Under the third Celestial Master Zhang Lu, the two organizations merged, creating a more stringent organization and controlling a large territory in southwest China. This lasted until 215, when the warlord Cao Cao conquered the area and decided not to tolerate a separate organization in his domain. As a result, large numbers of Celestial Masters followers were forcefully evacuated and had to migrate to different parts of the empire, spreading their cult as they went and laying the foundation for the strong Daoist school they later became.

Modern practice. Today the Celestial Masters are the dominant lay organization of Daoism, with headquarters in Taiwan. They include two major types of Daoists, known as red-head and black-head because they wear red kerchiefs and black headdresses, respectively. Red-head Daoists tend to be more shamanistic and popular, using magical implements such as the buffalo horn and learning their rites by word of mouth. Their main activities involve ceremonies to grant protection for residences, pregnancies, children, health, and good fortune, as well as exorcisms to dispel evil spirits, droughts, dangers, and diseases. They are often involved in trance states and mediumistic séances. Black-head Daoists, on the other hand, are more scripturally oriented, work with written liturgies, and use elaborate implements such as formal vestments and sacred staffs, and often employ a troupe of acolytes and an orchestra of music. Typically involved in large-scale ceremonies, they perform funerary and memorial services for the dead and conduct the festivals of renewal for the living (see Saso 1971).

Most rituals begin with the establishment of a sacred space either by erecting a special altar platform or by placing five cosmic talismans of the five directions around the altar. Next, the space is purified and sealed, and a nocturnal announcement is made, stating the inception of a grand ceremony to the universal forces. On the next morning, the leading officiant or Master of High Merit visualizes the various deities while chanting incantations, engaging in sacred hand gestures (mudras) and performing a ritual dance that imitates the movement of the cosmos. He will envision first the host of local and directional gods, then the immortals and deities of the pure Dao, and end with the Three Pure Ones, the three central powers of all—rulers of the highest Daoist heavens and representatives of the major kinds of scriptures, who also include Lord Lao. As he visualizes them, he invites them to take up their reserved seats in the sacred space. Upon their arrival, they are offered incense and tea.

The highlight of the ritual sequence is reached when the priest, and through him the sponsors and supporters of the rites, enter into a formal audience with the gods and present the gods with a memorial to explain the purpose of the rites, which tend to include thanksgiving for past boons and prayers for future good fortune. This presentation, as the initial invitation of the gods, is accompanied by the performance of spells, hand signs, and dance steps. The master goes on an ecstatic excursion to the heavens, renewing himself as much as the entire universe in the process. Once this is completed, the gods are celebrated in a formal banquet, the successful conclusion of the audience is announced, and the gods are sent back to their celestials spheres. At the final conclusion, the sacred space is released or the special platform demolished. Rites such as these are called festivals of renewal and take place only once in sixty years. They may last from three to seven days and usually involve more than one local community (see Saso 1972; Dean 2000).

Monastic Daoists. All these are key activities of the Celestial Masters. Unlike them, monastic Daoists of the school of Complete Perfection engage in smaller, daily rites to the gods and focus their activities on self-cultivation, notably through the method of inner alchemy. The school of Complete Perfection is not the first monastic group in Daoism (see Kohn 2003), but it is dominant today. It was founded in the twelfth century by Wang Chongyang (1112–1170), a member of the local gentry in northwest China (Shaanxi) who first served as a military official, then retired to become an immortality seeker. He had various revelatory experiences, in which he was being taught by Lü Dongbin, the leader of the Eight Immortals, and on this basis started an ascetic, monastic movement of Dao-realization which spread very quickly (see Yao 2000).

His main disciples were six men and one woman, known as the Seven Perfected. After Chongyang's death they observed the standard three-year mourning period, then spread his teaching all over China and founded various branches or lineages. The most important among them is Qiu Chuji (1148–1227), better known as Master Changchun, the founder of the leading Longmen lineage. When he was 72 years old and patriarch of the school, he was summoned to see Chinggis Khan in his Central Asian headquarters in 1219. He went on the three-year journey (see Waley 1931) and established good communications with the Khan who promptly appointed him the leader of all religions of China and exempted his followers from taxes and labor. This made the Complete Perfection school the most powerful religious group in north China and contributed greatly to its continued popularity.

As the school grew, it integrated more and more popular gods into its pantheon. Not only did its followers venerate the Eight Immortals, Seven Perfected, and Three Pure Ones, but they also adopted popular figures such as the God of Wealth (Guandi) and the God of Literature (Wenchang), both very efficacious for merchants and officials alike, as well as a number of female goddesses, well known for rescuing sufferers and helping women. Among them are the Celestial Consort (Tianfei or Mazu), the protectress of fishermen and merchants and a great slayer of demons; the Goddess of the Morning Clouds (Bixia yuanju), the daughter of the Lord of Mount Tai, a deity of celestial radiance whose acolytes help in distress and bring children; the Mother of the Dipper (Doumu), originally a Tantric goddess named Marîcî, the daughter of Brahma and mother of the seven stars of the Northern Dipper, a personification of light and life, who rules human destiny and saves people from peril (see Fig. 3).

Fig. 3. The goddess Doumu or Mother of the Dipper, an adaptation of the Buddhist goddess Marici, with her ten arms. Statue in the White Cloud Temple in Beijing. Author's photograph.

赤松子

Fig. 4. A Complete Perfection Daoist in regular garb. Temple to the Goddess of Dawn, Mount Tai, Shandong, 2004. Author's photograph.

Complete Perfection followers live in same-sex communities and adhere to a strict schedule. A typical day begins at 3:00 A.M. and ends at 9:00 P.M. It consists of several periods of seated meditation, worship, meals, and work, including work in the gardens and the fields. Numerous rules specify details of body control and behavior. Monks and nuns should guard their eyes by not raising their gaze to look at natural phenomena, unwholesome views, or sensually stimulating sights. They should also guard the ears and not listen to news, gossip, jokes, chatter, music, or drama. Loud or boisterous vocalization as much as gossip and idle chatter is strictly prohibited. Speech should be calm, quiet, circumspect, and about wholesome topics. Sleep periods, meals, and hours of rest are times of complete silence, and only words of prayer and recitation are to be uttered in the halls of worship. One's master has to be addressed with utmost softness and politeness, and only in words suitable to the holy and honorable occasion (see Kohn 2004).

All Complete Perfection followers, whether monks or nuns, dress in dark-blue pants and top coats, and wear their hair in a top-knot, surrounded by a dark blue cap (see Fig. 4). Their main goal is to attain immortality through inner alchemy, for which they practice meditation. After a thorough physical preparation with the help of longevity techniques, notably Qigong and Taiji quan, the practice begins with becoming aware of an inner force known as essence (*jing*). Defined as sexual energy, this manifests when arousal takes place, but this arousal does not lead to sexual intercourse. Instead essence is consciously moved through the body and circulated around the torso, up along the spine, across the head, and down along the front. Through this circulation, essence becomes subtler and faster and is transformed into energy (*qi*).

This renewed energy is then collected in the elixir field of cinnabar field (*dantian*) in the lower abdomen, where it forms first a pearl, then a ball, and eventually grows into an energy being called the immortal embryo. As it grows, it becomes even purer until it consists only of pure spirit (*shen*). Eventually this spiritual double of the practitioner is born by moving up along the spine and exiting through the top of the head. Freed from the body, it makes the practitioner immortal so that he or she can travel to the heavens and otherworldly palaces (see Despeux and Kohn 2003; Skar and Pregadio 2000).

In addition, Complete Perfection followers also perform regular audience rites to the gods, notably during their morning and evening services. Typically an officiant, surrounded by a group of six to eight Daoists (both male and female), invites the gods to join them for the ceremony. Various hymns are sung and sacred texts recited. Musical instruments are used, notably flutes, cymbals, and drums (see Fig. 5). Again, the ceremony culminates in the offering of a memorial, giving thanks and asking for good fortune, then the gods are sent off and the monastery can go about its business for yet another day.

Fig. 5. A group of male and female Daoists celebrating a ritual for the protection of the community. Temple of the Three Pure Ones, Mount Heming, Sichuan, 2004. Author's photograph.

CONCLUSION

Daoism encompasses three major traditions and strands: literati concerns with concepts and the understanding of the ancient philosophers; self-cultivation activities that focus on the body and include numerous medical and martial concepts; and communal organizations with a penchant for ritual, communication with large numbers of deities, and the establishment of official hierarchies and formal rules. All three have left behind documents, for the most part collected in the Daoist canon and its supplements (see Komjathy 2002, intr.), and have created formal structures, established terminologies, and transmission lineages.

REFERENCES

Allan, Sarah, and Crispin Williams, eds. 2000. *The Guodian Laozi.* Berkeley: Institute of East Asian Studies.

Chan, Wing-tsit. 1963. *A Source Book in Chinese Philosophy.* Princeton: Princeton University Press.

Chen, Ellen Marie. 1973. "Is There a Doctrine of Physical Immortality in the *Tao-te-ching?*" *History of Religions* 12: 231-49.

Chia, Mantak, and Maneewan Chia. 1993. *Awaken Healing Light of the Tao.* Huntington, NY: Healing Tao Books.

Cohen, Kenneth S. 1997. *The Way of Qigong: The Art and Science of Chinese Energy Healing.* New York: Ballantine.

Dean, Kenneth. 2000. "Daoist Ritual Today." In *Daoism Handbook*, edited by Livia Kohn, 659-82. Leiden: E. Brill.

Delza, Sophia. 1996. *The T'ai-Chi Ch'uan Experience.* Albany: State University of New York Press.

Despeux, Catherine, and Livia Kohn. 2003. *Women in Daoism.* Cambridge, Mass.: Three Pines Press.

Eskildsen, Stephen. 1998. *Asceticism in Early Taoist Religion.* Albany: State University of New York Press.

Graham, A. C. 1980. "How much of *Chuang-tzu* Did Chuang-tzu Write?" *Studies in Classical Chinese Thought,* Journal of the American Academy of Religions Supplement 35: 459-501.

———. 1981. *Chuang-tzu: The Seven Inner Chapters* and Other Writings from the Book of *Chuang-tzu.* London: Allan & Unwin.

Graham, A. C. 1982. *Chuang-tzu: Textual Notes to a Partial Translation.* London: University of London.

Hardy, Julia. 1998. "Influential Western Interpretations of the *Tao-te-ching.*" In *Lao-tzu and the Tao-te-ching*, edited by Livia Kohn and Michael LaFargue, 165-88. Albany: State University of New York Press.

Henricks, Robert. 1989. *Lao-Tzu: Te-Tao ching.* New York: Ballantine.

———. 2000. *Lau Tzu's Tao Te Ching: A Translation of the Startling New Documents Found at Guodian.* New York: Columbia University Press.

Jahnke, Roger. 1997. *The Healer Within Using Traditional Chi-*

nese Techniques to Release Your Body's Own Medicine. San Francisco: HarperCollins.

Kirkland, J. Russell and Norman J. Girardot. 2004. *Taoism: The Enduring Tradition.* New York: Routledge.

Kleeman, Terry. 1998. *Great Perfection: Religion and Ethnicity in a Chinese Millenarian Kingdom.* Honolulu: University of Hawaii Press.

Kohn, Livia. 1987. *Seven Steps to the Tao: Sima Chengzhen's Zuowanglun.* St. Augustine/Nettetal: Monumenta Serica Monograph XX.

———, ed. 1989. *Taoist Meditation and Longevity Techniques.* Ann Arbor: University of Michigan, Center for Chinese Studies Publications.

———, ed. 2000. *Daoism Handbook.* Leiden: E. Brill.

———. 2001. *Daoism and Chinese Culture.* Cambridge: Three Pines Press.

———. 2003. *Monastic Life in Medieval Daoism: A Cross-Cultural Perspective.* Honolulu: University of Hawaii Press.

———. 2004. *Cosmos and Community: The Ethical Dimension of Daoism.* Cambridge, Mass.: Three Pines Press.

———, and Harold D. Roth, eds. 2002. *Daoist Identity: History, Lineage, and Ritual.* Honolulu: University of Hawaii Press.

Komjathy, Louis. 2002. *Title Index to Daoist Collections.* Cambridge, Mass.: Three Pines Press.

LaFargue, Michael, and Julian Pas. 1998. "On Translating the *Tao-te-ching.*" In *Lao-tzu and the Tao-te-ching*, edited by Livia Kohn and Michael LaFargue, 277-302. Albany: State University of New York Press.

———. 1992. *The Tao of the Tao-te-ching.* Albany: State University of New York Press.

———. 1994. *Tao and Method: A Reasoned Approach to the Tao Te Ching.* Albany: State University of New York Press.

Lin, Paul J. 1977. *A Translation of Lao-tzu's Tao-te-ching and Wang Pi's Commentary.* Ann Arbor: University of Michigan, Center for Chinese Studies Publications.

Lin, Zixin. 2000. *Qigong: Chinese Medicine or Pseudoscience?* Amherst, NY: Prometheus Books.

Liu, Xiaogan. 1991. "*Wuwei* (Non-Action): From *Laozi* to *Huainanzi.*" *Taoist Resources* 3.1: 41-56.

————. 1998. "Naturalness (*Tzu-jan*), the Core Value in Tao-ism: Its Ancient Meaning and Its Significance Today." In *Lao-tzu and the Tao-te-ching*, edited by Livia Kohn and Michael LaFargue, 211-28. Albany: State University of New York Press.

Liu, Yanzhi. 1988. *The Essential Book of Traditional Chinese Medicine*. 2 Vols. New York: Columbia University Press.

Lu, Henry C. 1986. *Chinese System of Food Cures: Prevention and Remedies*. New York: Sterling Publishing.

Mair, Victor H. 1994. *Chuang Tzu*. New York: Bantam.

————. ed. 1983. *Experimental Essays on Chuang-tzu*. Honolulu: University of Hawaii Press.

Maspero, Henri. 1981. *Taoism and Chinese Religion*. Translated by Frank Kierman. Amherst: University of Massachusetts Press.

Miller, James. 2003. *Daoism: A Short Introduction*. Oxford: One World.

Ni, Hua-ching. 1992. *Internal Alchemy: The Natural Way to Immortality*. Santa Monica: College of Tao and Traditional Chinese Healing.

Porter, Bill. 1993. *The Road to Heaven: Encounters with Chinese Hermits*. San Francisco: Mercury House.

Rodell, Scott M. 2003. *Chinese Swordsmanship: The Yang Family Taiji Jian Tradition*. Annandale, VA: Seven Stars Trading Co.

Rump, Ariane, and Wing-tsit Chan. 1979. *Commentary on the Lao-tzu by Wang Pi*. Honolulu: University of Hawaii Press.

Saso, Michael. 1971. "Red-Head and Black-Head· The Classification of the Taoists of Taiwan According to the Documents of the 61st Celestial Master." *Bulletin of the Institute of Ethnology of the Academia Sinica* 30: 69-82.

————. 1972. *Taoism and the Rite of Cosmic Renewal*. Seattle: Washington University Press.

Schwartz, Benjamin. 1985. *The World of Thought in Ancient China*. Cambridge, Mass: Harvard University Press.

————. 1998. "The Worldview of the *Tao-te-ching*." In *Lao-tzu and the Tao-te-ching*, edited by Livia Kohn and Michael LaFargue, 189-210. Albany: State University of New

York Press.

Seidel, Anna. 1969. "The Image of the Perfect Ruler in Early Taoist Messianism." *History of Religions* 9: 216-47.

Shahar, Meir. 2000. "Epigraphy, Buddhist Historiography, and Fighting Monks: The Case of the Shaolin Monastery." Asia Major, 3rd s., 13.2: 15-36.

Siegler, Elijah. 2001. "The Tao of America: The History and Practice of Taoism in the US and Canada." Ph. D. diss., University of California, Santa Barbara.

Skar, Lowell, and Fabrizio Pregadio. 2000. "Inner Alchemy (*Neidan*)." In *Daoism Handbook*, edited by Livia Kohn, 464-97. Leiden: E. Brill.

Tsuchiya, Masaaki. 2002. "Confession of Sins and Awareness of Self in the *Taiping jing*." In *Daoist Identity: History, Lineage, and Ritual*, edited by Livia Kohn and Harold D. Roth, 39-57. Honolulu: University of Hawaii Press.

Waley, Arthur. 1931. *The Travels of an Alchemist*. London: George Routledge & Sons.

Watson, Burton. 1968. *The Complete Works of Chuang-tzu*. New York: Columbia University Press.

Wilhelm, Richard. 1950. *The I Ching or Book of Changes*. Princeton: Princeton University Press, Bollingen Series XIX.

Yao, Tao-chung. 2000. "Quanzhen—Complete Perfection." In *Daoism Handbook*, edited by Livia Kohn, 567-93. Leiden: E. Brill.

LIST OF ILLUSTRATIONS

Fig. 1. The deified Laozi or Lord Lao in a statue at the foot of Mount Qingcheng, Sichuan, in 2004. Author's photograph.

Fig. 2. Daoist adepts practicing immortality techniques on remote mountain cliffs. Mural at the Temple to the Goddess of Dawn, Mount Tai, Shandong. Author's photograph.

Fig. 3. The goddess Doumu or Mother of the Dipper, an adaptation of the Buddhist goddess Marici, with her ten arms. Statue in the White Cloud Temple in Beijing. Author's photograph.

Fig. 4. A Complete Perfection Daoist in regular garb. Temple to the Goddess of Dawn, Mount Tai, Shandong, 2004. Author's photograph.

Fig. 5. A group of male and female Daoists celebrating a ritual for the protection of the community. Temple of the Three Pure Ones, Mount Heming, Sichuan, 2004. Author's photograph.

THE MYSTICAL TEACHING OF *WU-WEI* IN THE *DAODE JING*: A COMPARATIVE STUDY OF EAST AND WEST ON SPIRITUAL DETACHMENT

Cristóbal Serrán-Pagán y Fuentes

INTRODUCTION

The mystical teaching of *wu-wei*, literally translated as "non-action," needs to be reexamined in light of new scholarly interpretations of this ancient tradition. The notion of *wu-wei* is often translated as inaction. Particularly in Western culture inaction is a term that denotes a pejorative character in nature of idleness or abstention from involvement of any sort. Yet in ancient Daoism the philosophy of *wu-wei* is a type of action so well in accordance with the flow of things that its author leaves no trace of himself or herself in the universe. Thus the teaching of *wu-wei* could be rightly interpreted as acting without interfering with the natural course of things. Thomas Merton's letter exchanges with John Wu will help the Trappist monk to better grasp the teaching of *wu-wei* which is at the heart of Daoism. Without fully grasping the spiritual implications of this ancient teaching Merton would have failed as a trustworthy commentator on his *Way of Chuang Tzu*.

Several questions arise. Is there any evidence that the *Daode jing* is written by a quietist? What do we mean by quietism? Could there be other interpretations of this teaching of *wu-wei* different from the quietist view that some scholars refer to? If so, should we try to show some evidence that the *Daode jing* does not represent a quietist withdrawal version that neither alludes to an absolute withdrawal from society nor the world?

This paper is divided into five general sections: (I) The historical context of the *Daode jing*. (II) The philosophical study of *wu-wei* in the *Daode jing*. (III) The mystical study of *wu-wei* in the *Daode jing*. (IV) The comparative religious study of *wu-wei* and *kenosis*. (V) Some final thoughts on the teaching of *wu-wei*.

PART I: THE HISTORICAL CONTEXT OF THE *DAODE JJING*

The historical background of China plays a major role in unveiling the reasons behind why the *Daode jing* was written between the fifth and fourth centuries B.C.E. and to which audience this Chinese masterpiece of literature is speaking. Most surely the *Daode jing* was written in response to the political turmoil China was experiencing at the time. During the Warring States period unstable circumstances like a period of wars and an autocratic moral system contributed to the explanation why the *Daode jing* came into being.

The *Daode jing* is written as a direct response to the rigid morality of Confucianism. The Confucianists put more emphasis on religious rituals, codes of behavior, moral precepts, and so on. Their worldview differs from the Daoist in the degree to which the Confucianist stresses a humanistic-legalistic, moral society following the Dao. Unlike the Confucianist, the Daoist seeks to follow the Dao in harmony with and through Nature. The mystical teaching of *wu-wei*, or the ideal of creative quietude, will form the basis for a new Daoist way of life based on the contemplative practices of simplicity, spontaneity, and naturalness.

The author/s of the *Daode jing* seems to suggest that the person who lives in a moral-spiritual universe must develop an intuitive, trans-rational wisdom rather than embracing a purely rational one. This ancient text gives the reader plenty of meaningful and practical advice on how to live your day-to-day activities in harmony with the Dao. For instance, Laozi persuades the reader to learn the text by heart rather than to analyze it word by word. Thereby the Daoist text focuses on gaining intuitive wisdom rather than just focusing on acquiring rational knowledge.

Michael Page makes the following distinction between Daoism and Confucianism:

> It is easy to see that Taoism, at its best a metaphysical, mystical, light-hearted and artistic way of life, represented a complete contrast to Confucianism; it was the yin of society, counterbalancing the yang of Confucianism. . . . The debate between them can be seen as the interplay of two

forces, never ending, but always in the dynamic tension and balance. (See Page 1988, 31-32.)

The historical context of the *Daode jing* was introduced by the Chinese historian Ssu-ma Ch'ien, in his book *Shih Chi* ("Historical Memoirs"), written about 100 B.C., who narrates the meeting between Laozi and Confucius. This treatise shows the incompatibility between these two great religious figures. The historical context of this on-going debate between Confucianists and Daoists is relevant for scholars in an attempt to better understand the origins of the *Daode jing*. Opinions about the identity of the author of the *Daode jing* and the original date of the text are controversial. For instance, Laozi means "Old Master." This has led scholars to believe that the text may have more than one author. Mircea Eliade articulates four different positions that form the scholarly consensus on Laozi's life:

> (1) Lao-tzu is the same person as Lao Tan of the sixth century and hence could have been visited by Confucius; (2) Lao-tzu lived in the so-called 'Spring and Autumn' period (ca.774-4810, but he is not the author of the Tao-te-ching; (3) he lived in the Period of the Warring Kingdoms (ca. 404-221), but it is not certain that he wrote the Tao-te-ching; (4) he is not a historical personage. (See Eliade 1982, 26.)

Some scholars date the text to "the third century" (Eliade 1982, 26). However, the text contains a number of aphorisms in verse that could go back "to the sixth century" (Eliade 1982, 27). In spite of its paradoxical and multifaceted character, the *Daode jing* delivers a consistent, fundamental unity of thought.

The *Daode jing* is often translated as "the scripture of the Dao and the Virtue" or "Way and Its Power." It contains about 4,400 words, and it is the most profound and enigmatic text in all of Chinese literature. Additionally, it is generally thought to be a poetical-philosophical-mystical treatise written by Laozi.

One can conclude that the *Daode jing* contains no dates, no proper names, and nothing that could tie it to a specific historical setting. The ahistorical nature of the *Daode jing* is shared by much of the religious literature that is found in the Daoist Canon. For Merton the beauty of this timeless, mystical text has to do primarily with the spiritual and moral power that the *Daode jing* still has and reveals on a daily basis to our contemporary readers.

PART II: THE PHILOSOPHICAL STUDY OF *WU-WEI* IN THE *DAODE JING*

The Daoist philosophy of *wu-wei* has practical implications in such competent fields as morality, politics, the military, spirituality and cosmology. According to Benjamin Schwartz the *Daode jing* can be read in the following ways: "As a philosophical handbook on how to live prudently in the world; a discourse on the ways of politics; an esoteric treatise on military strategy; a utopian tract; or a text that advocates 'a scientific naturalistic' attitude toward the cosmos. (See Schwartz 1985, 192.)

The early Daoist philosophers saw the *wu-wei* principle as the supreme political philosophy of the sage-rulers. The sage is therefore a master of *wu-wei*. He will act in accordance with the Will of Heaven by following the Dao.

Wu-wei is one of the central philosophical concepts in Daoism. As Herrlee G. Creel states, "*wu-wei* as a Taoist concept has never been considered easy to comprehend" (Creel 1970, 53). However Creel identifies the Daoist teaching of *wu-wei* with "a desire to withdraw from and take no part in the struggle of human affairs" (Creel 1970, 78). As a matter of fact Creel saw the *wu-wei* principle "as a technique of government" (Creel 1970, 54) rather than as a different mode of expression of the Dao itself.

Unlike Creel, Guo Xiang, a famous Chinese commentator on the Zhuangzi, argues the following: "The ruler governs the world through perfect non-action. . . . Non-action is thus defined as action in true harmony and accordance with things. . . . The world and the Tao are there for human beings to realize themselves for what they really are" (Kohn 1992, 72).

The starting point of the *Daode jing* focuses its attention on cosmology and the political role of the sage. As Livia Kohn points out: "It [the text] was considered a work that presented a certain cosmological interpretation of the universe and provided instruction on how to live in perfect harmony with this universe to create a world envisioned as ideal. (See Kohn 1992, 45.) Let me illustrate this mystical philosophy through Laozi himself who recommends that political and military leaders practice the contemplative method of *wu-wei* by following the way of the Tao. He strongly advocates for a "government by non-interference" (Welch 1957, 28). What Laozi's timeless message seems to suggest to all type of civic and religious leaders is how to act responsibly in any given form of government without much interfering with the cosmic laws of following the Dao.

Laozi first attempts to reveal the cosmic patterns that underlie all changes in the universe, following the Motherhood of all thousand things in the *Daode jing*, namely the Dao. The importance of Laozi's work is significant, especially considering the practical benefits of finding in the everyday life stillness, peace, and joy. The timelessness of the work proves the universal character of the *Daode jing*, and yet it transcends the peculiarity of the moment due to its trans-historical nature. Consequently the contemplative is able to reconnect with the source of all life.

Even when the Dao cannot be fully described in ordinary language the mystic points time after time to the ineffable or nameless One, without conveying any kind of dogmatic position. As Rev. John R. Mabry points out in *God as Nature Sees God*, the *Daode jing* "holds no dogma, has no organizational structure, no priesthood or clergy, no scripture as such, no creedal formulas, or anything else that resembles religious trappings for us." (See Mabry 1994, 18.)

Spontaneity of action is one of the central themes in the *Daode jing*. The goal for any Daoist is to learn how to live spontaneously by letting Nature be our teacher; that is to say, the mystical philosopher must follow the course of the Dao by letting go effortlessly (*wu-wei*), without undergoing any human interference with the Will or Mandate of Heaven (*Tian*). As the modern physicist Fritjof Capra notes in his popular book, *The Tao of Physics*: "Spontaneity is the Tao's principle of action, and since human conduct should be modeled on the operation of the Tao, spontaneity should also be characteristic of all human actions." (See Capra 1983, 116.)

To follow the course of the Dao is to balance out our actions with the natural and spontaneous movement of the Dao. Such a way of acting in Daoist philosophy is called *wu-wei*, literally translated as "not doing," but a more accurate translation is "to act without acting" (i.e., to move in accordance with the natural flow of the Dao). If this natural flow is understood as water then the *Daode jing* describes it as "nothing in the world is weaker than water, but it has no better in overcoming the hard." (Chap. 78)

How does a Daoist recover this harmonious cosmic order by following the course of the Dao? Laozi asserts that one must return to a mystical simplicity of doing no-thing which paradoxically is everything. A good Daoist learns how to act without going against *Tian*. For instance, in the fields of politics a good ruler will practice *wu-wei* by detaching himself from any hidden political, economic or religious agenda so that he can benefit the majority of his subjects. As Livia Kohn explains "non-intervention is thus the key to good government, to a harmonious and peaceful world" (Kohn 1992, 50). In Merton's view the Daoist principle of non-intervention is not conducive to a total withdrawal from all worldly and political affairs. Rather the teaching of *wu-wei* can be explained metaphorically as how a good traveler leaves no track or trace behind, and yet human action is mandatory.

PART III: THE MYSTICAL STUDY OF *WU-WEI* IN THE *DAODE JING*

It seems clear to me that the teaching of *wu-wei* has definitely a mystical character, and without that mystical sensibility it would be impossible to appreciate the importance that this Daoist practice conveys to the follower of the Dao.

First, the *Daode jing* is a mystical text in the sense that its author/s is pointing to ultimate reality as the Dao, which is the mother of all thousand things. Furthermore, in the *Daode jing* there are approximately some thirty of the eighty-one chapters dealing with the mystic dimension. According to Schwartz they are "among the most poetic and rhapsodic passages in the entire text. . . . Here we find the constant paradoxical effort to speak about the unspeakable" (Schwartz 1985, 198). As the Chinese text illustrates in its first chapter any attempt to define the Dao is doomed to failure. The Dao which is spoken is no longer the Dao.

One reason why some scholars have discarded the *Daode jing* as a non-mystical text is because they define mystics as people whose goal is to withdraw from the world or to escape from it. But the healthy Daoist mystic integrated different roles within his society as ruler, shaman, and sage. As Toshihiko Izutsu states, "the man who stands behind the utterances which we have quoted above is a philosopher-mystic, or a visionary shaman turned into a philosopher." (See Izutsu 1983, 293.) Thus the genuine mystic does not withdraw entirely from the world. Instead a true contemplative is able to transcend the world in order to come back fully enlightened and share his or her wisdom with others by restoring a harmonious cosmic order with the Dao.

Another reason mentioned by some Western scholars is that the

Daode jing lacks a rigorous criteria or methodology as to how to describe the mystical experience or journey. As Kohn points out:

> In terms of contents, the Tao-te-ching expresses most of the fundamental concepts of the mystical tradition, especially regarding cosmology and the political role of the accomplished sage. It conspicuously lacks any concrete descriptions of mystical methods, physical or otherwise, nor does it emphasize the mind and development of the individual. . . . It is, however, quite definitely a mystical text as far as the tradition of Taoism is concerned. (Kohn 1991, 11)

In fact, a considerable number of mystical texts avoid giving a detailed description on how to become one with the Divine, since the mystical experience happens spontaneously and effortlessly. Consequently the use of paradoxes and mystical symbols will convey a more accurate description of the spiritual journey towards the Divine than any systematic attempt to describe that which is ineffable in its innermost reality.

Without doubt the *Daode jing* is a mystical text once we comprehend the simplicity of its message. Paradoxically, the Dao is said to be hidden in Nature and yet it reveals Herself throughout the universe. For Laozi, the Dao is both transcendent and yet immanent. The Chinese text is apophatic in nature. As Schwartz says, the Daoist principle of *wu-wei* in the *Daode jing* follows the *yin* cosmic principle:

> The non-assertive, the uncalculating, the non-deliberative, non-purposive processes of generation and growth—the processes by which the 'empty' gives rise to the full; the quiet gives rise to the active, and the one gives rise to the many. The female is the epitome of *wu-wei*. (Schwatz 1985)

> On the other hand, the systematic and careful 'scientific' observation of nature would seem to be precisely one of those highly deliberate, calculating, and intentional projects which in no way corresponds to the spirit of *wu-wei*. (Schwartz 1985, 205)

Laozi also came up with other relevant mystical symbols that relate to *wu-wei* such as the Uncarved Block (*p'u*), the Female, the Valley, and the Newborn Child. These symbols point to the ineffable reality of the Dao. Holmes Welch in his *Parting of the Way* cites such mystical symbols in the *Daode jing* as following:

> Water which, through unresisting, cuts the most resistant materials . . . towards which, when it has reached the lowest place (the Valley) all else flows; which in its lowliness, and non-resistance 'benefits the ten thousand things'; and the symbol of the Female, who like the Valley, is yin, the passive receiver of yang; who conquers the male by attraction rather than force; and who without action causes the male to act. (Welch 1957, 35)

Water represents the material substance for life and the Dao permeates the whole universe like water running through the valley. The sixth chapter of the *Daode jing* states: "The Goddess of the Valley never dies. Her name is the 'Dark Woman.'" The female is seen in Nature as a nourishing principle. Additionally the author of the *Daode jing* says, "to know the masculine and yet maintain the feminine is to become the valley of the world." (Chap. 28) For Eliade, "The image of the valley suggests the idea of emptiness and at the same time the idea of a receptacle of waters, hence of fecundity" (Eliade 1985, 29). Clearly the Daoist text stresses the interplay of these two cosmic forces, the masculine (*yang*) and the feminine (*yin*) in and through Nature.

Other symbols discussed by Welch are the doctrine of the Uncarved Block (*p'u*), which is also known as "the doctrine of the return to our original nature" (Welch 1957, 3549), and the symbol of the Newborn Child which represents the union of the individual with the Dao as the source and end of all life. We find the following passage in the *Daode jing* that alludes to this symbol of the Newborn Child by stating: "Can you return to the state of the infant?" (Chap. 10) For the Daoist the goal is to return to the state of infancy, or what mystics called a return to the state of undifferentiated Unity as the Dao. In Merton's view this return to the "state of the infant" is a reminder of the Christian message of finding our true original face which is none other than our True Self in Christ.

The principle of *wu-wei* can be easily understood in this symbolic context as water by being represented as the female cosmic energy, which unresistingly accepts the lowest level yet wears away the hardest substance. The Dao is the way the universe works often characterized by spontaneous creativity and sometimes symbolized as a child or infant in the *Daode jing*. Thus the ideal state of becoming one with the Dao is through simplicity and freedom from desire, comparable to that of the doctrine of the return to our original nature—the Uncarved Block (*p'u*). This ideal state of pure consciousness is described by Laozi as childlike, dark, nameless, and uncultured. The Daoist gains a certain degree of stillness by practicing *wu-wei*.

PART IV: THE COMPARATIVE RELIGIOUS STUDY OF *WU-WEI* AND *KENOSIS*

The paradox of *wei wu-wei* cannot be translated literally and still render its meaning. Thus, negatively, *wu-wei* means 'to act without action,' or 'to do without doing.' But positively, it means to follow the course of Nature which is to be in harmony with the Dao. Van Over refutes the Western understanding of *wu-wei* that regards non-action pejoratively. He writes that "non-action does not mean idleness, or 'doing nothing' in the Western sense of that phrase" (Van Over 1973, xix).

Comparatively, the Daoist teaching of *wu-wei* may resemble the Christian kenotic teaching of emptying ourselves in order to let God be God in us. As Mabry points out:

> In non-action we find one of the most easily misunder-stood concepts of Taoism. To Westerners—especially Americans—a line like, "when you practice not-doing, nothing is left undone" sounds like a rationalization for supreme laziness. In fact it is just the opposite. Non-action is the most efficient means of accomplishing there is. . . . *Wu-wei*, therefore, isn't inactive at all, but is activity at is most efficient, because it accomplishes without effort. (Mabry 1994, 130-131)

According to Merton, the principle of *wu-wei* "is not intent upon results and is not concerned with consciously laid plans to delib-erately organized endeavors" (Merton 1975, 13). For the Trappist monk *wu-wei* is the mode of action of the Dao itself which moves spontaneously like the Holy Spirit throughout the universe. Merton related to this Daoist sacramental, cosmological view that he found in Laozi and later in Chuangzi.

Merton also describes the true character of *wu-wei* when he writes:

> *Wu-wei* is not mere inactivity but perfect action—because it is act without activity. . . . It is not mere passivity, but it is action that seems both effortless and spontaneous. . . . It is completely free because there is in it no force and no violence. . . . It is not 'conditioned' or limited by our individual needs and desires, or even by our own theories and ideas. (Merton 1975, 14)

Thus, the Taoist ideal of *wu-wei* is a non-self-conscious reflection in the way T. P. Kasulis describes in his book, *Zen Action Zen Person*:

> The Taoist ideal of personal activity, *wu-wei* or 'non-doing,' is an unselfconscious responsiveness. The Taoist endeavors not to interfere with the patterns of change, but to contemplate and be harmonious with them as they are enacted. . . . So Lao tzu advises us to be like water—responsive and yielding, but not in a passive or fatalistic way. (Kasulis 1985, 36)

The Taoist goal is the return of the true person to its source, to Nature itself—without any effort (*wu-wei*), spontaneously. As the following text cites: "Guard emptiness, nonbeing, and the spontaneous flow of life, let your body and spirit become one with the Tao, and you can live forever as an immortal" (Kohn 1993, 219).

The *wu-wei* principle is inner activity, the ability to achieve effortlessly that which apparently causes an intentional effort. According to Laozi: "There is great beauty in the silent universe. . . . The sage looks back to the beauty of the universe and penetrates into the intrinsic principle of created things. Therefore the perfect man does nothing, the great sage takes no action. In doing this, he follows the pattern of the universe." (Chap. 8.1)

To recapitulate this point that the *wu-wei* principle is not exclusively identified with pure inaction let me illustrate it with a quote from David G. Bradley:

> A corollary to the concept of Tao as the natural way is the often misunderstood teaching of *wu-wei*, or 'not doing.' Often interpreted as 'passive,' *wu-wei* affirms that the most effective way to live and act is to follow positively the natural way which in no fashion interferes with the Tao. *Wu-wei* means 'not acting' only in the sense that one does

not himself try to influence the natural, but merely follows
Tao. (Bradley 1963, 135)

The way of Dao and the teaching of *wu-wei* are better understood if
they are apprehended mystically. The teaching of *wu-wei* can easily
degenerate into mere inactivity if it is interpreted literally. Thus
the Daoist teaching of *wu-wei* eventually may fall prey to quietism
and fatalism, whereas the original teaching of Laozi was nothing
of this kind. "This must have been," according to Blackney, "the
origin of the principle of *wu-wei*, deliberate inactivity, quietism,
by which the self was voided and the Way took over one's being
and doing" (Blackney 1955, 35).

We have also seen that much of what Laozi suggested in the
Daode jing runs parallel to the reports of other Christian mystics
elsewhere in the world. The Chinese *wu-wei* principle of the *Daode
jing* echoes the Christian kenotic principle of no-thing-ness or *la
nada* in St. John of the Cross. In the case of the Carmelite mystic
kenosis or letting go of the old self in Adam gives room to the new
self in Christ.

In the *Daode jing* the teaching of *wu-wei* is a mode of expression of the Dao itself; in the Christian mystical tradition, God and
the world are not seen as two different entities, but they are two
distinct aspects of one single reality, the Godhead. For the Daoist
mystic the cosmic interdependence between the Dao, the universe
and the self is seen as one continuum reality. As Blackney points
out: "Mysticism is not theology and Chinese mystics made no pre-
tense of being theologians. . . . God, the Way and nature together
were One" (Blackney 1955, 43).

For the Christian, then, love is the root cause of all good deeds;
for the Daoist it is acting without interfering with Nature as the
most effective way to act. It has a pragmatic character rather than
a theological one. It must be coupled with humility and compassion
together. As Archie J. Bahm describes, "the three jewels or germs
of wisdom of Taoism" are "gentleness, frugality and humility"
(Bahm 1958, 92). After all, the Daoist ideal of growing quietly in
the humility of a simple, ordinary life is analogous to the Christian
monastic ideal of simplicity and spiritual detachment. As Merton
says: "It is more a matter of believing the good than of seeing it as
the fruit of one's effort" (Merton 1975, 13).

The means by which Daoist and Christian mystics attain oneness with the Divine is through the practice of spiritual detachment on a daily basis. Spiritually, it is the art of dying to oneself every day so that we let the Dao/God be the Dao/God in us. Death and rebirth/resurrection go hand in hand. According to William Johnston, non-attachment may convey two practical points:

> The first is: let go of anxieties. This is the message of the Sermon of the Mount and it is of cardinal importance in the mystical journey. . . .The second practical point is closely related to this and it is this: surrender all attachment to thinking—that is to say, to discursive thinking, to images and concepts and knowledge of any kind. But let me again stress that one does not give up knowledge: one gives up attachment to knowledge. (Johnston 1978, 98-99)

The Daoist principle of *wu-wei* is easily misunderstood if it is not apprehended in its dynamic process which Johnston called the principle of "non-interference," "active inaction," or "creative quietude." (Johnston 19789, 100-105)

Another Christian mystic, Pierre Teilhard de Chardin, represents in my view the clearest approach to the Daoist *wu-wei* principle. For Teilhard, the notion of spiritual detachment or letting go (*kenosis*) includes a paradoxical movement of attachment and non-attachment. Teilhard's book, *The Hymn of the Universe*, resembles Laozi's cosmology. But it is in *The Divine Milieu* where Teilhard gives an account of what he means by non-attachment. Teilhard states:

> The Christian as we have described him in these pages, is at once the most attached and the most detached of men. . . . It is God and God alone whom he pursues through the reality of created things. For him, interest lies not truly in the things, but in absolute dependence upon God's presence in them. (Teilhard 1965, 70-73)

For Teilhard, attachment and detachment are not mutually exclusive. Once the Christian mystic surrenders to something greater than him/herself then God takes full possession of the person by adopting a new self in Christ through a process of pleromatization in which God is seen "all in all." (1 Cor. 15:28) Similarly, for Laozi, the union with the Dao makes the person whole again. Or as Meister Eckhart would say: "One religious practice which is ab-

solutely essential for the return to God" is "detachment" (Colledge
& McGuinn 1981, 47).

In Merton's view, *wu-wei* and *kenosis* share a powerful mystical
bond in that both Daoist and Christian mystics must renounce the
fruits one's actions and must learn to be detached from all egotisti-
cal desires if they want to live in harmony with the Dao/God. In all
mystical traditions we can find this teaching of spiritual detachment
working through their sacred texts and sages.

As we have seen the Daoist principle of *wu-wei* was never meant to
be pure inaction or total escapism from the world in spite of what
Creel has said. The Jesuit scholar William Johnston was well aware
of the danger that this word 'passivity' denotes for many Western
scholars. For this reason he states the following:

> And yet this word 'passivity' must be used with the greatest
> caution. For while it is true that one layer of conscious-
> ness is passive and empty and dark, it is also true that a
> very powerful activity is going on at a deeper layer of the
> psyche. . . . He considers the active dimension of mysti-
> cism very important and he is wary of the word "passive."
> This is because there have been in all religious traditions
> schools of so-called quietism, and their voice can still
> be heard today: "Be absolutely still! Empty your mind!
> Erase all thoughts from your consciousness! Blot out ev-
> erything! Stop thinking! And this is mysticism." But this
> is not mysticism, oriental or occidental. This is nonsense.
> (Johnston 1978, 36)

Merton adds the following: "Hence *wu-wei* is far from being in-
active. It is supreme activity, because it acts at rest, acts without
effort. Its effortlessness is not a matter of inertia, but of harmony
with the hidden power that drives the planets and the cosmos"
(Merton 1968, 76).

The perfect man of the *Daode jing* has a responsible role to
play in the political and religious context of his time. For Laozi,
the political leader must turn into a sage like in Plato's *Republic*.
The king or ruler must become the true philosopher. The perfect
man must show the Way through love, humility, and compassion,
which are the three jewels mentioned in Daoism. For Merton, each

human being must exercise the *wu-wei* principle if we want to build an enlightened society. The Daoist ideal that Merton was so interested in was that of a contemplative in action. It is no wonder why he got fully immersed in the study of Daoist mystics like Laozi and Chuangzi. These ancient sages did show us the Way before Christians claimed Jesus as the Christ is the Truth, the Way, and the Light.

WORKS CITED

Bailey, Raymond. *Thomas Merton on Mysticism.* Garden City, New York: Image Books, 1987.

Blackney, R. B. *The Way of Life.* New York: Penguin Books USA Inc., 1983.

Capra, Frijof. *The Tao of Physics.* Boulder, Colorado: Shambala Publications, Inc., 1983.

Colledge, Edmund, and Bernard McGinn. *Meister Eckhart: The Essential Sermons, Commentaries, Treatises and Defense.* New York: Paulist Press, 1981.

Creel, Herrlee G. *What is Taoism? And Other Studies in Chinese Cultural History.* Chicago: The University of Chicago Press, 1970.

De Chardin, Teilhard. *The Divine Milieu.* New York: Harper & Row, Publishers, 1980.

Eliade, Mircea. *A History of Religious Ideas.* Vol. 2. Chicago: The University of Chicago Press, 1984.

Izutsu, Toshihiko. *Sufism and Taoism: A Comparative Study of Key Philosophical Concepts.* Berkeley: University of California Press, 1984.

Johnston, William. *The Inner Eye of Love: Mysticism and Religion.* San Francisco: Harper & Row, Publishers, Inc., 1973.

Kasulis, T. P. *Zen Action, Zen Person.* Honolulu: University of Hawaii Press, 1985.

Kohn, Livia. *Early Chinese Mysticism: Philosophy and Soteriology in the Taoist Tradition.* Princeton, NJ: Princeton University Press, 1992.

———. *The Taoist Experience: And Anthology.* Albany: State University of New York Press, 1993.

———. *Taoist Mystical Philosophy: The Scripture of Western Ascension.* Albany: State University of New York Press, 1991.

Mabry, John. R. *God, As Nature Sees God*. Rockport, Massachusetts: Element, 1994.

Merton, Thomas. *Mystics and Zen Masters*. New York: The Noonday Press, 1993.

————. *Thoughts on the East*. New York: New Directions Publishing Corporation, 1995.

————. *The Way of Chuang Tzu*. New York: New Directions Publishing Corporation, 1969.

Page, Michael. *The Power of Ch'i*. Hammersmith, London: The Aquarian Press, 1994.

Schwartz, Benjamin I. *The World of Thought in Ancient China*. Cambridge, Massachusetts: Harvard University Press, 1985.

Van Over, Raymond. *Chinese Mystics*. New York: Beacon Hill, Boston: Beacon Press, 1957.

Welch, Holmes. *The Parting of the Way: Lao Tzu and the Taoist Movement*. Beacon Hill, MA: Beacon Press, 1957.

Yu-Lang, Fung. *A Short History of Chinese Philosophy*. New York: The MacMillan Company, 1960.

PART II
MERTON AND *CHUANG TZU*

MERTON'S *CHUANG TZU*

Lucien Miller

INTRODUCTION

Thomas Merton's *The Way of Chuang Tzu*, published in 1965, is a central literary work in the body of his writings.[1] Its immediate and lasting appeal lies in its literary grace and philosophical wisdom. Merton's own attraction to the Chinese text and its tradition intensifies his longing to travel to the East, and his own rendition is a gateway to his posthumous *Asian Journal*. The religious experience of the poet, monk, and pilgrim in Dharamsala, India, and Polonnaruwa, Sri Lanka, the year of his death, 1968, is illuminated by *The Way of Chuang Tzu*.

The Chinese classic, the *Zhuangzi*, is an anthology of mainly Taoist writings that evolved over the contentious Warring States period, 403-221 B.C.E., compiled by various hands and influenced by contending schools of thought. In the standard edition edited by Guo Xiang in the late third to early fourth century, C.E., the *Zhuangzi* consists of three major sections, the Inner, Outer, and Miscellaneous Chapters (*Neipian, Waipian, Zapian*),[2] made up of seven, eleven, and fifteen sections, totaling thirty-three in number. As the noted sinologist and translator, Burton Watson, observes, the Inner Chapters are traditionally considered paramount, containing the thought and style central to the whole text, and there is an original "mind, or group of minds," behind them, one which stands at the center of Chinese tradition.[3] I shall concentrate primarily on these Inner Chapters in the following discussion of Thomas Merton's *The Way of Chuang Tzu*.[4]

---

1. Thomas Merton, *The Way of Chuang Tzu*. New York: New Directions, 1965.

2. *Neipian, Waipian, Zapian* 內篇, 外篇, 雜篇.

3. Burton Watson, *The Complete Works of Chuang Tzu*. New York & London: Columbia University Press, 1968, 1-14.

4. Merton skips Chapter Five entirely, "Hallmarks of Perfect Virtue," "De chong fu" 德充符, possibly because its stories of the maimed and handicapped are replicated in selections he chooses from other chapters. Unless otherwise noted, translations of the Chinese are mine.

As to the question of authorship, there is definite historical evidence of a Zhuang Tzu (personal name, Zhuang Zhou) living in the fourth century, B.C.E., but recent scholarship by a ground-breaking team of sinologists, E. Bruce Brooks and A. Taeko Brooks, indicates the text originates in the first half of the third century B.C.E., evolves over time, and is multi-layered, as evidenced by the polemics and textual presence of contending schools of thought from the Warring States period.[5] While it is highly unlikely that Zhuangzi himself (hereafter, Chuang Tzu, following Merton's use of the standard Wide-Giles spelling) had a hand in writing the *Zhuangzi*, Merton assumes he did, and is fascinated by a mind like his own, bemused, anguished, and questioning, and while unconventional and removed from the mainstream, critically engaged and compassionate. Accordingly, in my discussion of *The Way of Chuang Tzu,* I shall adopt Merton's usage, with the understanding that while "Chuang Tzu" refers to collective authorship, for Merton it's the name of a kindred spirit and personality.

ORIGINS: MERTON AND CHUANG TZU

Just prior to the publication of *The Way of Chuang Tzu* in 1965, Merton wrote his friend, James Laughlin, the publisher of New Directions, "Looking forward to *Chuang Tzu*, that is one book I am happy about."[6] Soon after the book appeared, Merton responded to a letter of congratulations from another close friend, William "Ping" Ferry, "Glad you like Chuang Tzu. I certainly do. That is my favorite book. I mean of my own. Most of my own books I can't stand. This one I really like."[7]

---

5. The Brooks' recent redoubtable study, *The Original Analects: Sayings of Confucius and His Successors,* New York: Columbia University Press, 1998, has revolutionized understanding of the Confucian textual tradition. In the *Zhuangzi,* the Brooks find an early stratum of animal fables and metaphors of Indian origin, a late band of polemics against Confucian proto-democracy and Mician logic, as well as a conversion to the advocacy by Confucian and Mencian schools of public service fortified by meditation. E. Bruce Brooks thinks Merton is drawn by the anguish and anomaly in the *Zhuangzi,* the contending voices who resisted conventional mores and political orthodoxy. (Personal communication regarding forthcoming study, June 19, 2001.)

6. *Thomas Merton and James Laughlin: Selected Letters*, ed. David D. Cooper. New York & London: W. W. Norton, 1997, 267. Entry date: September 12, 1965.

7. *The Hidden Ground of Love: The Letters of Thomas Merton on Religious Experience and Social Concerns*, ed. William H. Shannon. New York Farrar

Why is it that *The Way of Chuang Tzu* is Merton's "favorite book?" To appreciate Merton's assertion, I think we need to understand his "Chinese" identity, his personal identification with Chuang Tzu, and, most especially, the spirituality of Merton's *Chuang Tzu* revealed in his "versions," as he called them, of the Chinese classic. Before turning to the latter, it is vital to draw the picture of Merton's Asian self that unfolds in his letters and journals.

Merton's work on Chuang Tzu starts in 1961, when he writes John C. H. Wu, a distinguished scholar and Chinese Catholic, seeking his guidance and advice studying Confucian and Taoist thought and Chuang Tzu, at the suggestion of Father Paul Chan. Father Chan had read Merton's letter to Archbishop Yu Pin in which Merton mentioned a tentative project on Chuang Tzu for New Directions.[8] Thus begins a friendship with John Wu that lasts until Merton's death, and a dialogue over Chuang Tzu that ends with the publication of *The Way of Chuang Tzu* by New Directions in 1965, and Merton's permanent "retirement" (Merton's own word) to his hermitage, August 20, that same year.[9]

Merton writes some two dozen letters to John Wu regarding the Chuang Tzu project, sometimes three times a month the initial year, 1961—a frequency rarely encountered in his correspondence. Clearly, he is excited about this collaboration. In a journal entry from *Turning Toward the World* written that same year, Merton reflects on the task before John Wu and himself:

> I know once again we are touching something real that cries out for a hearing (*Sapientia in plateis clamitat* [Wisdom cries out in the marketplace]). I can see no other way to be honest before God than to *hear* the premonitions of His wisdom in one like Chuang Tzu. . . . I think this will be a fine work, even though it may 'accomplish nothing.' (Why read Chuang Tzu and want to accomplish something?

Straus Giroux, 1985, 223. January 26, 1966.

8. Merton letter to John C. H. Wu, March 14, 1961. *The Hidden Ground of Love*, 611-612.

9. See Robert Daggy Introduction to *Dancing in the Water of Life: Seeking Peace in the Hermitage*, The Journals of Thomas Merton, vol. 5. Robert E. Daggy, ed. HarperSan Francisco, 1997, xiv; Merton letter to W. H. Ferry (July 20, 1965): "The Chuang Tzu book is finished, censored, in the hands of the lads at New Directions. A book called *Mystics and Zen Masters* has just been delivered to Farrar, Straus and Giroux. With this all off my chest, on August 20 I am officially retiring to the hermitage . . . ." *The Hidden Ground of Love*, 221.

Wisdom takes care of herself. Tao knows what she is about. She has already 'accomplished' it. . . . And I have had the first glimpse of a reservoir that is already full to the edges. It remains only for us to drink).[10]

The project belongs to what Merton considers his special vocation. In another entry from the same journal, he talks about the "task that has been given me:"

To emphasize, clarify the living content of spiritual traditions, especially the Xian, but also the Oriental, by entering myself deeply into their disciplines and experience, not for myself only but for all my contemporaries who may be interested and inclined to listen. This for the restoration of man's sanity and balance that he may return to the ways of freedom and of peace, if not in my time, at least some day soon.[11]

Writing to John Wu, Merton speaks of their joint vocation. "I have no more doubts about the project being willed by God. It has the marks of the Holy Spirit's action upon it everywhere, doesn't it? . . . So let us then proceed with love for the God Who manifested His wisdom so simply and so strikingly in the early Chinese sages, and let us give Him glory by bringing out the inner heart of that wisdom once again." The letter closes with a cheer for their mutual cause, a paean of missionary zeal and hope that is almost embarrassing in its missionary enthusiasm:

It is all-important for us to *be* in Christ what the great sages cried out to God for. May our studies help us to live what they hoped for, and may we be able to bring to the Orient hope and light, which by right is theirs: for Christ rose up in the East, and we sing to Him '*O Oriens*' in Advent. His is what William of St. Thierry called the *orientale lumen*. To that great light let us be humbly devoted and let us seek its tranquil purity in which all lights are fulfilled.[12]

In a subsequent letter, Merton encourages John Wu and himself to listen to the Holy Spirit, "in the gaiety and childlike joy of Chuang

10. *Turning Toward the World: the Pivotal Years*, The Journals of Thomas Merton, vol. 4. Victor A. Kramer, ed. HarperSanFrancisco: 1996, 102. Entry dated March 24, 1961.

11. *Turning Toward the World*, 155. August 22, 1961.

12. *The Hidden Ground of Love*, 613-14. April 1, 1961.

Tzu," whose liberty of spirit Merton sees fulfilled in St. Paul's
Epistles and in St. John.[13] This vision of scriptural linkage is ex-
emplified at the end of the second year of working on their project,
when Merton delights in quoting to John Wu the last line of "The
Useless Tree," their first selection for *The Way of Chuang Tzu*,
putting Chuang Tzu's phrase in the mouth of the Christ-child:

> The very name of Chuang Tzu restores me to sanity, at
> least momentarily. . . . It takes Chuang Tzu to remind us of
> an essential element in the Gospel which we have simply
> 'tuned out' with all our wretched concerns. The whole Ser-
> mon on the Mount, for instance. And the Discourse of the
> Last Supper. Even the central message of the Cross and the
> Resurrection. And the crib full of straw, in which the Lord
> of the world laughs and says, "You should worry!"[14]

Again and again, the Chinese text brings Merton to the heart of the
New Testament and to his own interior being.

Speaking of the latter, Merton talks about his late idea of
vocation in his correspondence with Rosemary Radford Ruether
in terms that remind us of Chuang Tzu. Merton tells her he is attracted to the way of the non-monk, the anti-monk, the marginal
person, and the tramp.[15] A part of this vocational identity lies in
a "Chinese" core that is exposed and unprotected. As far back as
1956, he had suggested to James Laughlin, "I think after all I am
innately Chinese (Zen is really Chinese—combination of Taoism
and Buddhism, reduced to its practical essence, all doctrines thrown
out, naked contact with reality)."[16] Five years later, at the beginning
of his relationship with John Wu, Merton jokes to him about their
mutual Chinese and Buddhist identities:

> If I once reached Buddhahood and redescended to my
> present state, all I can say is that I made a really heroic
> sacrifice. But I don't regret it, as the other Buddhas seem
> to have done the same. Yourself for instance. Thus we go
> along gaily with littleness for our Mother and our Nurse,

13. *Hidden Ground of Love*, 615. April 11, 1961.
14. *Hidden Ground of Love*, 623-24. December 20, 1962.
15. *At Home in the World: The Letters of Thomas Merton and Rosemary Radford Ruether*, ed. Mary Tardiff, O. P. Maryknoll, New York: Orbis Books, 1995, 66.
16. *Thomas Merton and James Laughlin*, 114. May 7, 1956.

and we return to the root by having no answers to questions. Whatever I may have been in previous lives, I think more than half of them were Chinese and eremitical.[17]

Significantly, in "A Note to the Reader" which prefaces *The Way of Chuang Tzu*, Merton, the Catholic monk, defends his turning to Chinese Taoist spirituality by identifying with Chuang Tzu. Like St. Augustine who read Plotinus, St. Thomas who read Aristotle and Averröes, "both of them certainly a long way further from Christianity than Chuang Tzu ever was!" Merton notes, and Teilhard de Chardin who used Marx and Engels in his synthesis of evolution, "I think I may be pardoned for consorting with a Chinese recluse who shares the climate and peace of my own kind of solitude, and who is my own kind of person."[18]

> For his part, John Wu immediately sees in Merton the ideal interpreter of the Taoist sage, Chuang Tzu, a Catholic monk who knows contemplative traditions, East-West. Emphasizing this point, he tells Merton, "Only a man like yourself steeped in the works of the great Christian mystics can know what Lao Tzu and Chuang Tzu were pointing at, and how utterly honest and correct they were."[19]

When the project ends, in 1965, John Wu magnifies his earlier praise, extolling Merton's unity of being, "The beautiful thing about you is that your heart is as great as your mind. Thus in you love and knowledge are united organically. Herein lies your profound significance for this great age of synthesis of East and West."[20] He gives Merton a Chinese name, Mei Teng,[21] "Silent Lamp," symbolizing Merton's new role as recluse living in a hermitage, to which Merton responds, "it was moving to be 'baptized' in Chinese with a name I must live up to. After all, a name indicates a divine demand. Hence I must be Mei Teng, a silent lamp, not a sputtering

17. *Hidden Ground of Love*, 618. May 29, 1961.

18. *The Way of Chuang Tzu*, New York: New Directions, 1965. "A Note to the Reader," 11.

19. William Shannon cites John Wu's unpublished letter (March 20, 1961), responding to Merton's March 14, 1961, invitation. *Hidden Ground of Love*, 612-613.

20. See William Shannon's citation of John Wu's letter of September 6, 1966. *Hidden Ground of Love*, 611.

21. *Mei Teng* 昧 燈 .

one."[22] Merton cannot resist making fun of his name too, signing a later letter to John Wu,

> Fr. Louis
> Old Cracked Mei Teng[23]

John Wu rejoices, seeing in Merton a poet who is, as it were, Chuang Tzu reborn. Upon receiving from Merton a signed copy of *The Way of Chuang Tzu*,[24] he delightedly declares:

> I have come to the conclusion that you and Chuang Tzu are one. It is Chuang Tzu himself who writes his thoughts in the English of Thomas Merton. You are a true man of Tao just as he is. You have met in that eternal place which is no place and you look at each other and laugh together. . . . The spirit of joy is written over all the pages."[25]

In a response in the spirit of his Taoist master, Chuang Tzu, Merton can do no less than declare his own innocence and non responsibility:

> As to what you said about the book, well, all I can say is that if Tao did the job through me, it was done in the usual way: without my knowing a thing about it. All I know is that in the beginning especially I was doing a job for which I felt no capacity whatever, and in the end, while I still felt I had no capacity, it did not make any difference, I was having a lot of fun. As to attributing it to me, well, you can do so if you like, maybe Tao is playing games and acknowledging who did the work in this particular way. Who am I to interfere with Tao?[26]

---

22. *Hidden Ground of Love,* 632. December 28, 1965. John Wu sent Merton a poem elaborating on its meaning: "Silent lamp! Silent lamp!/ I only see its radiance/ But hear not its voice!/ Spring beyond the world!" *Hidden Ground of Love,* 633. William Shannon's citation of John Wu's letter of January 10, 1966.

23. *Hidden Ground of Love,* 633. February 27, 1966.

24. "I am sending off a copy of Chuang Tzu signed for you. . . . I owe you a great debt for this. It has been a wonderful experience and something I cannot repay with a few words. I will keep you always in my prayers. And may we always live more and more in that wonderful spirit of acceptance that was his. It is of course the real key to all this talk about 'turning to the world.'" *Hidden Ground of Love,* 631. November 1, 1965.

25. *Hidden Ground of Love,* 631. November 24, 1965.

26. *Hidden Ground of Love,* 632. December 3, 1965. A few months earlier, in a similar humorous vein proclaiming John Wu's Christian spiritual gifts, Merton

"Merton's Project"

Merton initiates the Chuang Tzu project asking John Wu to tutor him in Chinese classics and early Taoist mysticism. He proposes that after he has gained some understanding, the two select passages from the *Chuang Tzu* for Wu to translate, while Merton will write an introductory essay.[27] Wu soon sends Merton a sample of his own translation (whose poetic form Merton praises), along with English, French, and German renditions by previous translators.[28] Merton finds Léon Wieger's French text "breezy" but "to some extent helpful," mainly for its inclusion of the Chinese text. He likes Richard Wilhelm's edition, but it is doubtful Merton seriously relies on Wilhelm, as Merton admits his own German is weak.[29] Among the four translations consulted, Merton concentrates on

announces that *The Way of Chuang Tzu* has been approved by the censors. "You will be pleased to hear the news: the Chuang Tzu book was not only passed with honors by both censors, but one of them even asked to keep the ms. for a good long time so that he might study it and use it more. So you must have said a good strong prayer and the Holy Spirit must have breathed over the waters of argument. In fact, though, now that I know who did the censoring, I can see they would be open to something like this. There are others who would have had seven kinds of fits." *Hidden Ground of Love,* 629. July 22, 1965.

27. *Hidden Ground of Love,* 611-12. March 14, 1961. *Thomas Merton and James Laughlin: Selected Letters,* 169. May 5, 1961.

28. In an introductory note to the correspondence between Merton and Wu, William H. Shannon lists translators whose books Wu sent Merton: James Legge, Herbert Giles, Léon Wieger, Richard Wilhelm (actually, Merton had a copy of Legge; Merton letter to Wu, *Hidden Ground of Love,* 611-12, March 14, 1961). Shannon says Wu assisted Merton "by making his own literal translation of the passages Merton selected." *Hidden Ground of Love,* 611. I have not seen Wu's translations. Merton's sources: James Legge, trans. *The Texts of Taoism: The Tao Te Ching, The Writings of Chuang Tzu.* New York Julian Press, 1959. [orig. Vols. XXXIX and XL of *Sacred Books of the East.* London: Oxford University Press, 1891]; Herbert A. Giles, trans. *Chuang Tzu: Taoist Philosopher and Chinese Mystic.* London: George Allen and Unwin, Revised edition, 1926. orig. 1889; Léon Wieger, trans. *Les Pères du Système Taoiste: Lao-tzeu, Lie-tzeu, Tchoang-tzeu.* Paris: Belles Lettres, 1975. orig. 1913; Richard Wilhelm, trans. *Dschuang Dsi: Das Wahre Buch Von Südlichen Blütenland.* Jena: Eugen Diederichs, 1920. orig. 1915.

29. Thanking Wu for sending Zen texts in German, Merton says, "but my German is slow. I shall be eager to see if they appear in English translation." *Hidden Ground of Love* 618, May 5, 1961. Merton agrees with Wu that the Wilhelm version is, "very very solid and trustworthy." *Hidden Ground of Love,* 619, August 12, 1961. Trying to get started translating himself, Merton said, "The German version is particularly helpful." *Hidden Ground of Love,* 619-20, October 11, 1961.

two English renditions by the late nineteenth century sinologists, James Legge and Herbert Giles. Merton's initial impression of the former—the 1959 Julian Press reprint (with an Introduction by D. T. Suzuki)—is erroneous: it "looks suspiciously doctored to me."[30] Gradually, while composing a list of passages that interest him, he comes to depend on it, along with Giles.[31] He praises the latter, written in "clear, idiomatic English, throwing light on Legge's more cautious and careful translation.[32]

One of Merton's keen desires for the project is to learn a few Chinese characters, or "ideograms," as he falsely calls them—a tiny proportion of Chinese words are actually ideograms or pictograms. The etymologies Wu explains help Merton "get the wonderful differences of nuance and meaning which have tremendous importance."[33] He writes Paul Sih, asking his recommendation of a character text for beginners, as he cannot approach the task of translating Chuang Tzu without learning at least a couple of hundred "fundamental ideograms." "I have to make at least some kind of gesture at thinking through the ideograms and not just through sentences in Western languages," Merton declares.[34] He tries to use Matthews' Chinese-English dictionary, confessing to Sih he "cannot make head or tail of it," nonetheless planning "to go through it and learn a hundred or so ideograms that may prove essential for this kind of text," and wishing "there was some sensible way of learning the 214 radicals."[35] After Sih visits him at Gethsemani and teaches him "the rather complex skill of reading the Chinese Dictionary," he resolves in a journal to "keep at the classics in the original (with a translation handy of course!)," and consoles himself with this thought: "Even if I only learn one or two characters, and look long at them in their context, something worth while has been done."[36]

---

30. *Hidden Ground of Love,* 611-612, March 14, 1961. Except for a change in the system of romanizing Chinese characters, the Julian Press edition is the same as Legge's 1891 original.

31. *Hidden Ground of Love,* 613-614, April 1, 1961; 614-15, April 4, 1961.

32. *Hidden Ground of Love,* 615, April 11, 1961.

33. *Hidden Ground of Love,* 617, May 19, 1961.

34. *Hidden Ground of Love,* 619, August 12, 1961.

35. *Hidden Ground of Love,* 550, October 24, 1961.

36. *Turning Toward the World,* 210, March 12, 1962. When appealing to Dom Ignace Gillet, the Father General of the Cistercian order, for permission to go to Japan for study, Merton argues: "I must add that for this work it is very important that I learn Japanese and (classical) Chinese and that is why I would

Despite his lack of knowledge of Chinese characters, in the course of that first year working on *Chuang Tzu*, 1961, Merton comes to accept Wu's idea that Merton himself should do his own translations. To my own mind, this accommodation gradually takes place as Merton interiorizes the spirit of Chuang Tzu, gleaned from his reading, while contemplating nature in the environs of Gethsemani. Sending his suggested lists of selections to Wu in May and June of that year, and looking forward to a visit when he can see Wu's translation, Merton hints towards a personal understanding of Tao: "Now I enjoy the quiet of the woods and the song of the birds and the presence of the Lord in silence. Here is Nameless Tao, revealed as Jesus, the brightness of the hidden Father, our joy and our life. . . ."[37] Receiving Wu's suggestion about how "I ought to proceed," Merton resists doing his own renditions, saying the result "will really only be a manipulation of what has already been said in English by Giles and Legge." Wu, Merton insists, gets "the real substance" of the *Chuang* Tzu, and Merton's role is "merely polishing up the English expression." He agrees, however, to "take a fling at a few passages I like just for the joy of doing it."[38]

By midsummer of 1961, Merton reluctantly agrees with Wu to experiment writing his own renditions, with the help of other published translations, but only if he "learns two hundred fundamental ideograms," as mentioned above. "It will necessarily be slow and awkward, however."[39] He writes Paul Sih, "I was scared to even think of" Wu's idea "to try my own hand at Chuang Tzu," but "did a couple of short passages the other day and found they came out all right." He elaborates on his misgivings:

> Of course it is just a matter of putting together three or four translations and then following hunches, which is what John advised me to do, saying he would go over the finished product and make all the corrections. But it is hardly a work of scholarship, and honestly if *this* is going

---

need a little time. It seems to me that a year would be the minimum." *The School of Charity*, 238, September 24, 1964. Classical Chinese and Japanese in a year? A Merton enthusiasm.

37. *Hidden Ground of Love*, 617, May 19, 1961. For Merton's anticipation of Wu's translation and his request that Wu add and subtract from the list of selections, see *Hidden Ground of Love*, 617, May 27, 1961.

38. *Hidden Ground of Love*, 617-18, Mar 29, 1961.

39. *Hidden Ground of Love*, 619, August 12, 1961.

to be the procedure, I wonder if there is any point in your publishing the book.[40]

That fall, Merton tells Wu he has been enjoying working on *Chuang Tzu*, following Wu's proposed intuitive approach and "the various translations," but complains, "it takes an enormous amount of time to do it this way. Anyone translating from the original would move much faster."[41] Continuing his grumbling about time, Merton finally bows to the wishes of both John Wu and Paul Sih. He writes the latter, "since both you and John agree, I must say I resign myself to it, and will attempt to do the work, in fact will enjoy it shamelessly: but it will certainly take time."[42]

Nearly ten months later, calling his renditions "versions," for the first time, Merton writes Wu, insisting his non-scholarly translations are mere imitations, of the "after Chuang Tzu" variety. The result "no longer even pretends to be a serious rendering. I might insert it in a collection of poems I am getting together, as an experiment."[43] In his response, John Wu flatly contradicts Merton: "You have taken him by the forelocks not by the tail. I swear that I am not flattering when I say that this is exactly what Chuang Tzu would write had he learned English."[44]

We have a new translation paradigm. In John Wu's view, Merton is not an unscholarly imitator foreign to Chinese culture. As poet and monk-hermit, Merton is the English Chuang Tzu. This standpoint is corroborated by Wu's son, John Wu, Junior, whose comments, which follow, are illuminating:

> I don't have the time just right now to give you any very concrete help which would entail my going into the correspondence and finding all the references to Merton's project but will do so in a future email if you find the following inadequate.
> Let me just say this off the top of my head.
> In the above, I deliberately wrote, "Merton's project," for that is exactly what I think it was. It was certainly not my

---

40. *Hidden Ground of Love*, 549-50, August 16, 1961. Apparently, originally Paul Sih was to be publisher, or find one.

41. *Hidden Ground of Love*, 619-20, October 11, 1961.

42. *Hidden Ground of Love*, 550, October 24, 1961.

43. *Hidden Ground of Love*, 623, July 10, 1962.

44. *Hidden Ground of Love*, 623, William Shannon quotes Wu's letter to Merton, July 17, 1962.

father's and, if he were alive, he would be the first to admit it. Of course, one of Merton's pretexts for writing to my father in the first place was to get him to become involved in a cooperative venture to do a new translation of the Chuang Tzu. Merton suggested that my father translate the text literally word-for-word and then Merton would put it into good fluent English. I don't think that my father ever really took to this idea because he thought it would be too unwieldy, and in the end, he was proven right. My father's virtue was that he understood well Merton's incredible intuitive sense both as a poet and as a contemplative monk and that these two qualities combined with the existing translations in English, French and German would be more than sufficient for Merton to produce something rather unique. This gave the monk confidence and, in time, after Merton had sent my father some completed versions of the selections he had made, my father, literally overwhelmed and thrilled by what he read, knew that his suggestion that Merton ought to go about the task alone and his intuition regarding Merton's ability to do such a project was correct and confirmed.

My father had the basic belief that no ancient classical text, East or West, can really be "translated," that, at best, the translations, no matter how well done, are mere commentaries or interpretations on the original text. This is especially true of works of a poetic nature, such as the Tao Teh Ching and The Chuang Tzu. He came to this conclusion when he was rendering The Psalms into semi-classical Chinese. So, in fact, when he made his suggestions to Merton, there was indeed a very personal basis for prodding Merton to proceed the way he did. In a way, his attitude was very Taoistic in the sense that he believed there ought to be as little interference as possible on his part. In the final analysis, it was prudent that he did not meddle with Merton's obvious genius.

I believe the only real contribution my father made was to have checked for any gross misinterpretations, of which surprisingly he found very few. In view of this, the book was a stupendous achievement in that the selections are done close to the original text and, most significantly, near perfectly caught the spirit of the Taoist sage. And why was

Merton able to accomplish this, according to my father? Because he had somehow in his own vocation breathed the spirit of the ancient Taoists at Gethsemani. In one of his letters, my father said only half-jokingly, if Chuang Tzu were writing in English, he would write exactly the way Merton wrote. I'm sure that the monk was thrilled by those words![45]

John C. H. Wu's acute self-sense of his role reminds me of the *peitong*,[46] a guide or intermediary when conducting field work in China, who introduces the foreign researcher to local sites and native storytellers, but does not fabricate the proposal, control its design, nor bring into being the results. Merton's Chinese "Master," so to speak, insists *The Way of Chuang Tzu* is Merton's work, not an unwieldy collaborative project on a classic Taoist text, which, *ipso facto*, is untranslatable. Following a Taoist approach, he does his best to get out of the way of his intuitively gifted student so that the latter can proceed freely on his own, catching the spirit of Chuang Tzu, close to the bone of the original. In Wu's view, Merton's movement from "west" to "east" happens because Merton has interiorized Asia-in-Gethsemani, through his life as mystic-monk and hermit, his sensibility as poet, and his study of translations. While this insightful understanding rings true, and Wu's modest view of his role is clarifying, I should hasten to cite Merton's assessment of Wu's major part in *The Way of Chuang Tzu*. In his "A Note to the Reader," Merton writes that if someone wants to complain about the book, "he can blame me and my friends, and especially Dr. John Wu, who is my chief abettor and accomplice, and has been of great help in many ways. We are in this together."[47]

In my opinion, if Merton can be the English Chuang Tzu because the poet-monk has "breathed the spirit of the ancient Taoists at Gethsemani," it is equally true that, for Merton, the *Chuang Tzu* is the Chinese Gospel.[48] Chuang Tzu himself interiorizes the Gospel,

---

45. John Wu, Jr., email to Lucien Miller, March 6, 2001.

46. *Peitong* 陪同 .

47. "A Note to the Reader," *The Way of Chuang Tzu*, 9.

48. At the end of the project, Merton shared his high regard for Chuang Tzu, relating the Taoist sage to a Christian faith-based perspective. He mailed Etta Gullick "some 'versions' of Chuang Tzu I have dared to do, based simply on comparisons of various translations and on some guessing of my own. Chuang Tzu seems to have been on the right track in many respects, though without the theological depth that would come with true faith: still, he grasped the nature of things and of our orientation to God in silence. Tauler liked Proclus for the same

so to speak, recalling Merton to the Gospel's sanity and simplicity. As he writes in a 1962 Christmas-time letter to Wu, Chuang Tzu reminds us "One thing is necessary." Chuang Tzu is an antidote to "Christianity as it has developed in the West, including monasteries of the West," which "has become a complex and multifarious thing." He continues, citing a famous Zen *koan*, "What is your original face before you were born?" intimating that the voices of the Christ-Child and Chuang Tzu are the answer to "they,"—the complexity, insanity, and noise of the world:

> I am proud that you should want to use my 'versions' [in your class]. By all means do so. . . . All best wishes always, and every blessing in this holy season when the animals and the shepherds show us the way back to our child mind and to Him in Whom is hidden our original face before we are born. Be of good cheer. They cannot silence either Chuang Tzu or this Child, in China or anywhere. They will be heard in the middle of the night saying nothing and everybody will come to their senses."[49]

Now proud of the quality of his versions, Merton rejoices. "Chuang Tzu is my delight," he writes Wu, midway through 1963.[50] While another translator's rendition is published, and Merton has little time for his project throughout 1964, he is not discouraged. He remains determined to stay his course, and finishes the project in the spring of 1965.[51] Receiving what he calls "your nosegay of poems called The Way of Chuang Tzu," Wu praises Merton's translations in the same voice with which he spoke when the project was

reasons as I do CT." *Hidden Ground of Love*, 370-71, June 9, 1965.
49. *Hidden Ground of Love*, 623-24, December 20, 1962.
50. *Hidden Ground of Love*, 624, June 23, 1963.
51. James Laughlin sends a new translation of Chuang Tzu by James R. Ware, *The Sayings of Chuang* Chou, New York, New American Library [Mentor], 1963, but Merton continues his work, "slowly and without trying to get anywhere special, just because I like the guy, and there might still be room for my 'versions.'" *Thomas Merton and James Laughlin,* 236, December 7, 1963. In an early 1964 journal entry, Merton promises to take up Chuang Tzu again, "but all my resolutions about work go out the window." *Dancing in the Water of Life: Seeking Peace in the Hermitage*, ed. Robert E. Daggy, HarperSan Francisco, 1997. The Journals of Thomas Merton, vol. 5, 77. February 14, 1964. By the end of the year, he writes Wu, "I still have not given up the idea of various versions of Chuang Tzu." *Hidden Ground of Love*, 626, December 23, 1964.

just underway: "I am simply bewitched. If Chuang Tzu were writing in English, he would surely write like this."[52] Merton responds graciously, full of gratitude and praise for John Wu, saying his letter "made me so happy that I had been insane enough to go ahead with the work on Chuang Tzu." While Wu sees Merton as Chuang Tzu "writing in English," Merton says he has encountered living in Wu "the spirit of Chuang Tzu himself." "The publisher (New Directions), is delighted," Merton carries on, excitedly, telling Wu that now he has completed "A great many more texts and a longish introduction." *The Way of Chuang Tzu* will need illustrations—hopefully those beloved Chinese ideograms "like Tao, *wu-wei* and so on." Waxing euphoric, Merton insists the book will be dedicated to John C. H. Wu: "then your name will appear on a good blank page and we will all fly away on the back of the same dragon."[53]

VERSIONS OF *CHUANG TZU*

Bearing in mind the vision of Merton as the English Chuang Tzu, a "Chinese" hermit whose interiorized Taoist Chinese text brings him closer to the Gospels, and whose interiorized Gospels unwrap the *Chuang Tzu*, I should like now to turn a comparative eye on *The Way of Chuang Tzu*. Of course sufficient explanation for the wonder of Merton's "favorite book" cannot be found in the hyphenated identity of "poet-monk," but ultimately remains hidden in the person of Thomas Merton. What one can do to ferret out the mystery, without resolving it, is to read closely passages from *The Way of Chuang Tzu* in light of the Chinese text. I shall do this with the English translations Merton used close at hand, by Herbert Giles and James Legge, while urging others with a knowledge of French and German equal to Merton's to continue the inquiry by comparing Merton's versions with renditions by Léon Wieger and Richard Wilhelm. As noted previously, Merton's reference to the former as "breezy" but "to some extent helpful," and his comment to John Wu that "my German is slow," suggests the significance of the French and German translations is minimal, but that remains to be seen.[54]

---

52. *Hidden Ground of Love*, 627, May 11, 1965. John Wu letter quoted by William Shannon.

53. *Hidden Ground of Love*, 627-28, June 9, 1965.

54. Of the eighteen selections Merton made from the Inner Chapters of the

Merton speaks rather apologetically of his versions which are the "the result of five years of reading, study, annotation, and meditation," as "'imitations' of Chuang Tzu, or rather, free interpretative readings," that "grew out of a comparison of four of the best translations" whose "notable differences" taught him that translators of Chuang Tzu "have had to do a great deal of guessing," revealing not only their scholarly knowledge, "but also their own grasp of the mysterious 'way.'" Merton calls his own "readings" "ventures in personal and spiritual interpretation," concluding that "*any* rendering of Chuang Tzu is bound to be very personal."[55] Merton's critical understanding of his own book is countered by Burton Watson, who wrote in the Introduction to his *The Complete Works of Chuang Tzu*, "Readers interested in the literary qualities of the text should . . . look at the 'imitations' of passages in the *Chuang Tzu* . . . by Thomas Merton. . . . They give a fine sense of the liveliness and poetry of Chuang Tzu's style, and are actually almost as close to the original as the translations upon which they are based."[56] I believe that Merton's own sense of his versions belies what he accomplishes, and that *The Way of Chuang Tzu* transcends "imitations" and "translations." Merton did not know Chinese. Astonishingly, a comparison between Merton's versions and the Chinese text reveals a reading between the lines which embodies the original *Chuang Tzu.*

In comparing Merton's versions from the seven Inner Chapters of the *Chuang Tzu* with the original, it is immediately apparent that Merton is highly selective. Merton's English sources, the Giles and Legge translations, are complete, while his renditions are segments. For example, the first piece in *The Way of Chuang Tzu*, "The Useless Tree," is a translation of approximately seven lines of the original fifty, from the end of Chapter One of the *Chuang Tzu*, "Wandering Without a Care," *Xiaoyao you.*[57] "The Fasting of the Heart" (Chap-

---

Zhuangzi, five have sections which seem closely parallel in content to Wieger's "breezy" translations: "The Useless Tree," "Great Knowledge," "The Pivot," "The Fasting of the Heart," "The True Man."

55. "A Note to the Reader," *The Way of Chuang Tzu,* 9.

56. Burton Watson, Introduction, *The Complete Works of Chuang Tzu,* 28.

57. "The Useless Tree," *The Way of Chuang Tzu,* 35-36. From "Wandering Without a Care," *"Xiaoyao you"* 逍搖遊. *Zhuangzi duben* 莊子讀本 (*Chuang Tzu Reader's Edition,* hereafter *ZZDB*) 1: 54. Huang Jinhong, ed., 黃錦宏 (Taipei: Sanmin, 1974). The *Reader's Edition* used in this study follows the standard edition edited by Guo Xiang (d. 312 C.E.), and contains helpful aides for language

ter Four, "In the World of Human Beings," "*Renjian shi*") contains
fifteen lines of the original, and drops eighty. Merton cuts and skips
about freely, weaving a tapestry about a single vista, paring details,
and cutting to the bone.[58] Generally speaking, Merton selects a single
parable, fable, dialogue or question that embodies a central theme in
the original, and gives his selection a title based on a gathering metaphor or phrase which appears in the Chinese text. Thus, "The Useless
Tree" comes from a line in the original describing a tree as, literally,
"lacking that which is usable," *wu suo keyong*.[59] "The Fasting of the
Heart" is based on Chuang Tzu's concept of "heart-mind purification," *xin zhai,* set forth in "In the World of Human Beings."

Merton's way of utilizing Giles and Legge is to move back
and forth between them, with a shifting degree of loyalty. He reads
Giles as a guide to Legge (actually, Giles' 1889 translation precedes
Legge's 1891 rendition by two years), finding Giles' prosaic style
clear and idiomatic, shedding light on Legge's more painstaking,
meticulous translation. Frequently he enriches the vocabulary he
finds in both. In Merton's "The Breath of Nature" (from Chapter
Two, "Leveling Opposites," "*Qiwu lun*"), Giles' and Legge's
"mouths" and "nostrils"—metaphors for the hollows in trees upon
which the wind plays—become "maws" and "snouts."[60] From
time to time, Merton adheres to Legge's language—the "knots,"
"crooked" branches, the "crouching wildcat" which leaps "high
and low," and the mighty Yak that "can't catch mice!" in Merton's
"Useless Tree" come close to the "knotted and crooked" branches,
the "wild cat" "crouching and low," which leaps "avoiding neither
what is high nor what is low," and the Yak which "cannot catch
mice" in Legge's *The Writings of Chuang Tzu*.[61] Again, besides
borrowing Legge's vocabulary, Merton is wont to enliven it. For
example, an illuminating footnote in Legge inspires a vivid image

---

students, including classical Chinese text, vernacular Chinese translation, tone
marks, and pronunciation of Chinese characters. While a line count depends on
the Chinese text used, the ratio between Merton's *The Way of Chuang Tzu* and
the Chinese text remains roughly accurate.

58. "Fasting of the Heart," *The Way of Chuang Tzu,* 50-53. *xin zhai* 心 齊.
"In the World of Human Beings," "*Renjian shi*" 人 閒 世, *ZZDB* 4: 83.

59. *wu suo keyong* 無 所 可 用. *ZZDB* 1: 54.

60. "Leveling Opposites," "*Qiwu lun*" 齊 物 論. *ZZDB* 2: 60. Chinese *kou*
口 and *bi* 鼻. Merton, "The Breath of Nature," *The Way of Chuang Tzu,* 38. Giles,
Chuang Tzu, 34. Legge, *The Writings of Chuang Tzu,* 222.

61. Legge, *The Writings of Chuang Tzu,* 222.

in Merton. Legge's "Ailantus" which he annotates as, "The Ailantus glandulosa, common in the north of China, called 'the fetid tree,' from the odour of its leaves,"[62] becomes the "stinktree" in Merton's "The Useless Tree." Merton loves the colloquial, naughty humor, and sheer earthiness he rightly senses in Chuang Tzu. Thus, Legge's Victorian reserve when translating Chuang Tzu's description of the weak arguments of combatants—"like their water which, once voided, cannot be gathered up again,"[63] Merton transforms into: "Their talks flows [sic] out like piss, / Never to be recovered."[64]—a reading much closer to the original Chinese, "Piss on it, that's what they do (with words) they can't take back."[65]

Occasionally, *The Way of Chuang Tzu* follows Giles closely, in the sense of the "gist" of meaning which Giles yields, but Merton's poetic, fun, free-spirit self invariably takes over, as he senses Chuang Tzu's own spirit of satire, irony and humor—a spirit Giles sorely misses. Legge's systematic approach is highly informative, but Merton must have abhorred its dry pedestrian mode. Giles' prose is smoother and less encumbered with scholarly apparatus and florid "Victorian" language, but he himself seems unaware of the poetic dimension and interior sense of Chuang Tzu. Sometimes, seemingly exasperated by Giles' and Legge's dull character descriptions, Merton adds color or interposes speech. The Prince of Wei in "The Fasting of the Heart," a noble "of mature age" (Giles) "in the vigour of his years" (Legge), Merton depicts as, "a lusty full-blooded fellow."[66] In "Two Kings and No Form" from Chapter Seven, "After the Fashion of Deities and Princes," Merton coins titles for the three divine protagonists. According to the narrative,

62. Legge, *The Writings of Chuang Tzu*, 222.
63. Legge, *The Writings of Chuang Tzu*, 227.
64. Merton, "Great Knowledge," *The Way of Chuang Tzu*, 40.
65. "qi niao zhi shuo wei zhi, bu ke shi fu zhi ye." 其溺之所為之,不可使復之也. "Qiwu lun," *ZZDB* 2: 61. Watson, *The Complete Works of Chuang Tzu*, 37, translates as: "They drown in what they do" taking the alternative reading of *niao* as "drown" rather than "urinate." Further examples of Merton's colloquial translations: "Wait a minute!" Chuang Tzu orders Hui Tzu during a debate in "The Joy of Fishes," *The Way of Chuang Tzu*, 98; "It goes like a breeze!" exclaims the cook about effortlessly dressing an animal in "Cutting Up and Ox," *The Way of Chuang Tzu*, 47. Such idiomatic expressions are not found in the Chinese text, but do reflect its conversational diction . . .
66. "Fasting of the Heart," *The Way of Chuang Tzu*, 50. "qi nian zhuang" 其年壯 ("one in the prime of life"), "Renjian shi," *ZZDB* 4: 81. Giles, *Chuang Tzu*, 51. Legge, *The Writings of Chuang Tzu*, 251.

the "God of the South Sea" and the "God of the North Sea" feel
sorry for their friend, the "God in Between" ("Chaos," Hundun),
because he lacks bodily senses, so they punch holes in his body to
enable him to see, hear, eat, breathe, and eliminate waste, where-
upon Chaos dies. Playing on the roles of the divine friends and their
descriptive names, Merton dubs "Reckless," the God of the South
Sea, "Act-on-Your-Hunch," "Impulsive," the God of the North Sea,
"Act-in-a-Flash," and "Chaos," the God in Between, "No Form."[67]
Mimicking and extending the crazy wisdom of the madman of Chu
who attacks Confucius for teaching virtue in "Confucius and the
Madman," Merton has the madman speaking words the latter never
says in either Giles or Legge:

> When I walk crazy
> I walk right:
> But am I a man
> To imitate?[68]

The essential likeness to the *Chuang Tzu* that Merton achieves in
his versions is to make them poetic, in the broadest sense, ranging
from literary form and language to tone and rhetoric. The layout of
an individual line in *The Way of Chuang Tzu* is sometimes closer to
the original Chinese than either Legge's or Giles' version. Thus, a
line in Merton's "Cutting Up An Ox," "A good cook needs a new
chopper / Once a year—he cuts," parallels the syntactical emphasis
and diction of the Chinese almost exactly, "liang pao sui geng dao
ke ye" (from Chapter Three, "Caring for Life").[69] Given Merton's
ignorance of Chinese, this uncanny likeness probably is because of
Merton's rhythmical sense and the linear simplicity of the line in
both Giles and Legge. When we look at a larger section of text from
"Cutting Up An Ox," however, Merton's eye for form is transparent. Regarding metrics, for example, while the Chinese text—and

---

67. "Reckless," *Shu* 儵, the God of the South Sea, *Nanhai zhi di* 南海之帝;
"Impulsive," *Hu* 忽, the God of the North Sea, *Beihai zhi di* 北海之帝; "Chaos,"
Hundun 渾沌, the God in Between, *Zhongyang zhi di,* 中央之帝. From "After
the Fashion of Deities and Princes," "Ying Di Wang" 應帝王, *ZZDB* 7: 122.

68. *The Way of Chuang Tzu,* 58. From "Renjian shi," *ZZDB* 4: 87.

69. "liang pao sui geng dao ge ye." 良庖歲更刀割也. "Caring for Life,"
"Yang sheng zhu" 養生主, *ZZDB* 3: 77. Legge, *The Writings of Chuang Tzu,*
247: "A good cook changes his knife every year;—(it may have been injured) in
cutting." Giles, Chuang Tzu, 48-49: "A good cook changes his chopper once a
year,—because he cuts."

the English prose translations Merton uses—is normally printed in blocks of characters, filling a page, like prose, frequently the form is in fact that of poetry, in rhythmically metered sets of characters, often set out in rhymed, parallel phrases. In Merton's version, he moves rhythmically, line by line, in a form which intimates the altering four and six character pattern of rhythmical, parallel lines in the Chinese.[70] A juxtaposition of Merton's version and the corresponding Chinese text (Mandarin transliteration) reveals an intimate metrical association:

Prince Wen Hui's	Baoding
Was cutting up an ox.	wei Wenhui jun jie niu
Out went a hand,	shou zhi suo chu
Down went a shoulder,	jian zhi suo yi
He planted a foot,	zu zhi suo lu
He pressed with a knee,	xi zhi suo ji
The ox fell apart	hua ran xiang ran
With a whisper,	
The bright cleaver murmured	zou dao huo ran
Like a gentle wind.	mo bu zhong yin
Rhythm! Timing!	
Like a sacred dance,	
Like "The Mulberry Grove,"	he yu sang lin zhi qu
Like ancient harmonies![71]	nai zhong jing shou zhi hui.

Except for two phrases—"Rhythm! Timing!" and "Like a sacred

---

70. E. Bruce Brooks has an opposite view. While noting Merton's poetic sensibility, Professor Brooks dislikes his choice of short lines, which he finds gratuitous, creating a false air of breathless piety (Personal communication). My conviction is Merton's choice fits the text in structure and tone.

71. "Cutting Up An Ox," *The Way of Chuang Tzu*, 45. Note the rhythmical movement, rhyme, and six-four character structure of the Chinese: *Baoding wei Wenhui jun jie niu* 庖丁為文惠君解牛

shou zhi suo chu	手之所觸
jian zhi suo yi	肩之所倚
zu zhi suo lu	足之所履
xi zhi suo ji	膝之所踦
hua ran xiang ran	砉然嚮然
zou dao huo ran	奏刀騞然
mo bu zhong yin	莫不中音
he yu sang lin zhi qu	合於桑林之舞
nai zhong jing shou zhi hui	乃中經首之會

"Yangsheng zhu," *ZZDB* 3: 77.

dance"—extensions of meaning which are implied in the Chinese
text, Merton's rendering is closer to the *Chuang Tzu* than the prose
translations of either Giles or Legge.

As noted, Merton's poetic sense captures the colloquial language, vivid imagery, and metrical mode of the *Chuang Tzu*. That
same sensibility discovers and echoes the tonal qualities of the
ancient Chinese text. Rhetorical questions asked at the beginning
or end of a passage, quick-paced question-and-answer dialogue
mid-way, and a simplification of detail are touches Merton uses to
embody the varied mood and ambiance of the *Chuang Tzu*, which
turns a poignant eye upon mutability and death while satirizing
human foibles and mores.

MERTON'S MUSICAL VARIATIONS

In my view, the best analogy for Merton's "versions" comes from
music, in the term, "variation." A composer writes a piece of music
which interiorizes another composer's work, but in a form—opera,
symphony, sonata—and using an instrument or instruments—voice,
violin, banjo—often different from the original. The variation is
not a "translation" in the stereotypical sense, a "pony" or "trot"
to be read side-by-side with the original as a crutch for the beginning language student, nor a "literal" or "figurative" translation by
someone with linguistic expertise, such as a sinologist, who may
translate for an audience unfamiliar with the original. Rather, a
variation is an interpretation steeped in the original that is a new
creation, marked by the informed listener's (one who knows the
original) spontaneous response, "this is it." One hears the original
and re-creation at once, absorbed by the variation.

What makes *The Way of Chuang Tzu* a work of artistic delight
are Merton's interpolations, which are not found in the English
translations by Giles or Legge, but are consistent with the spirit of
the Chinese *Chuang Tzu*. They are significant revelations of both
Merton's poetic sensibility, and his mystical understanding of the
Chinese text, three years prior to his journey to Asia and his death.
In these "musical variations," Merton grasps the original in a fresh
sense, reading between the lines and discerning an essential drift of
implied meaning. Or else, his intuitive sense causes him to project
a Western religious, cultural, or political association that amplifies
Chuang Tzu's spirit without engulfing it. Lastly, the voices of Chuang Tzu and Merton harmonize, producing a new music unknown

to one without the other. To use the Gospel metaphor—what we have in *The Way of Chuang Tzu* is old wine in new wine skins, new wine in old wine skins, and new wine in new wine skins—all variations on the *Chuang Tzu leitmotif* of change which I believe Chinese readers of antiquity would have found a delight had they been able to tune in on Chuang Tzu and Merton singing together.

A FRESH SENSE

Among the many examples of discernment of implicit meaning, those attributable to Giles or Legge are rare. In "A Hat Salesman and a Capable Ruler," Merton perceives Chuang Tzu mocking social standards of proper dress and extends the satire to ridicule ancient (and contemporary) Han Chinese prejudice against ethnic minorities. The hat salesman tries selling to "the wild men of the South" who have "shaved heads" and "tattooed bodies"—contemptible marks of savagery to Han Chinese. But "What did they want / With silk / Ceremonial hats?" Merton has Chuang Tzu ask, satirizing the "civilized," ritual-minded Chinese.[72] A combination of intuition and theological connaturality enables Merton to know how Chuang Tzu can understand the feelings of fish swimming in water. In "The Joy of Fishes," Merton has Chuang Tzu say:

> I know the joy of fishes
> In the river
> Through my own joy, as I go walking
> Along the same river.[73]

The Chinese text simply reads, "I know it beside the Hao [River]." Merton recognizes that Chuang Tzu is making an argument by analogy: while men and fish belong to different *phyla*, the former can understand the latter through connaturality, what Jacques Maritain defines as intuitive knowledge of the other through intellect, affective inclination and disposition of the will. Chuang Tzu is "co-natured" with the fish in a moment of poetic awareness.[74]

---

72. "A Hat Salesman and a Capable Ruler," *The Way of Chuang Tzu,* 37. "Xiaoyao You," *ZZDB* 1:53.

73. "The Joy of Fishes," *The Way of Chuang Tzu,* 98.

74. A knowledge through union, inclination, and congeniality. Realities closed to reason are experienced via intuitive knowledge. Jacques Maritain, *The Range of Reason,* New York: Scribner, 1952. Chapter 3, "On Knowledge Through Connaturality."

Following Chuang Tzu's "drift," so to speak, Merton says, in effect, "I am happy walking besides the river, therefore fish are happy swimming in the water."[75]

FORGING LINKS

The associative passages which amplify Chuang Tzu are a joy, containing Christian hints, Western cultural nuances, or political undertones reflecting the wry humor of the poet-monk going his own way in search for the true self. Religious ascetic practices and rituals are frequent targets of satire, and Merton has Confucius and Lao Tzu join the fun. "There is a time for putting together / And another time for taking apart," says Merton in "Metamorphosis," echoing the well-known meditation on time and human mutability in *Ecclesiastes*.[76] This Jewish interpolation from the Hebrew Bible fits Chuang Tzu's sense of the human condition and his acceptance of death. Conversely, the non acceptance of death and the vanity of clinging to life are parodied by both Chuang Tzu and Merton. Chuang Tzu mocks the over-blown mourning at Lao Tzu's funeral through a character named Chin Shih who "lets out three yelps and splits" the scene, attacking Lao Tzu for creating disciples who are too attached to their Master.[77] Merton entitles his version of the same tale, "Lao Tzu's Wake," turning the Taoist's last rites into an Irish Catholic funeral.[78] At another funeral, which Merton entitles "Three Friends," Confucius himself comes in for a pasting. In the episode, two chums chant a giddy dirge to their departed buddy,

75. "The Joy of Fishes," *The Way of Chuang Tzu*, 98. "I know it beside the Hao [River]." "Wo zhi zhi Hao shang ye" 我 知 之 濠 上 也. From "Autumn Floods," "Qiushui" 秋 水, *ZZDB* 17: 204. The English translations are more tentative and timid, lacking Merton's personal joy. Giles: "I knew it from my own feelings," *Chuang Tzu*, 171. Legge: "I know it (from our enjoying ourselves together) over the Hao," *The Writings of Chuang Tzu*, 440.

76. "Metamorphosis," *The Way of Chuang Tzu*, 63. From "The August and Revered Teacher," "Da Zong Shi" 大 宗 師, *ZZDB* 6: 108. *Ecclesiastes (Qoheleth)* 3: 1-8. Neither Giles' nor Legge's wording contains biblical overtones. Giles, 79: "I obtained life because it was my time: I am now parting with it in accordance with the same law." Legge, 296: "when we have got (what we are to do), there is the time (of life in which to do it; when we lose that (at death), submission (is what is required)."

77. *Chin Shih* 秦 失. "lets out three yelps and splits" 三 號 而 出. The yelps are probably customary laments required in funeral mourning ritual. From "Yangsheng zhu" 養 生 主, *ZZDB* 3: 78.

78. "Lao Tzu's Wake, *The Way of Chuang Tzu*, 56-57.

to the inappropriate accompaniment of a lyrical lute:

> Hey, Sung Hu!
> Where'd you go?
> Hey, Sung Hu!
> Where'd you go?
> You have gone
> Where you really were.
> And we are here—
> Damn it! We are here![79]

In the midst of their merriment, a disciple sent by Confucius to oversee the funeral rites bursts in on the two celebrants, shocked to find they are not following proper etiquette.

> May I inquire where you found this in the
> Rubrics for obsequies,
> This frivolous carolling in the presence of the departed?

The two friends looked at each other and laughed:

> "Poor fellow," they said, "he doesn't know the new liturgy!"[80]

Merton's "rubrics for obsequies" and "new liturgy" are inventions, far from the Chinese text's *li*, meaning "propriety," "ritual" or "rite," and distant from Giles' "decorum" and Legge's "rules."[81] However, these fabrications are close to the spirit of Chuang Tzu who lampoons Confucius' clinging to empty form, and surely they echo the debates within Merton's monastic community over "the new liturgy." In the liturgical reform movement which follows

---

79. "Three Friends," *The Way of Chuang Tzu*, 55. From "Da Zong Shi" 大宗師, *ZZDB* 6: 109. Giles' translation is plain: "Ah! Come back to us, Sang Hu, / Ah! Come back to us, Sang Hu. / Thou has already returned to thy true state, / While we still remain here as men,—Alas!" *Chuang Tzu*, 81. Legge coins an expression for the traditional practice of calling back the dead: "Ah! Come, Sang Hu! Ah! Come, Sang Hu! / Your being true you've got again, / While we, as men, still here remain / Ohone!" *The Writings of Chuang Tzu*, 299.

80. "Three Friends," *The Way of Chuang Tzu*, 55.

81. "Three Friends," *The Way of Chuang Tzu*, 55. The Chinese text reads: "Singing in the presence of the corpse! What about the rites?" "Lin hu er ge li hu" 臨戶而歌禮乎; "These (people) don't know the meaning of the ritual," "Shi wu zhi li yi" 是惡知禮意. "Da Zong Shi," *ZZDB* 6: 109. *li* 禮: Giles, "decorum," *Chuang Tzu*, 81; Legge, "rules," *The Writings of Chuang Tzu*, 299.

Vatican II, traditionalists and liberals often are at odds, and Merton is wont to lament or spoof their fights over ritual.[82]

In "The Man With One Foot and The Marsh Pheasant," Merton implants a theme of political ambition within a brief excerpt about theodicy. He follows Giles' and Legge's translations which say, "Heaven" (Tian) is responsible for a seemingly innocent official being maimed.[83] Chuang Tzu, says A. C. Graham (modifying a cliché about Spinoza), is a "Heaven-intoxicated man." In the *Chuang Tzu*, Heaven is an impersonal power, not a creator but a generator, towards which Chuang Tzu feels awe, and sometimes personifies as the "Maker of Things."[84] While keeping to the notion that human fate is Heaven's will, Merton inserts his own bitter modification. The officer's disfigurement is, "A penalty in the political game!" As Merton is wont to do in his satirical essays on the bombing of Hiroshima or the extermination of Jews at Auschwitz, he mocks a distorted view of divine will, and satirizes human greed for power. The person who questions innocent suffering, scoffs:

> Heaven . . .
> sent him into politics
> To get himself distinguished.
> See! One foot! This man is *different*.[85]

This radical mutation is not found in the Chinese text.[86]

---

82. Another Catholic monastic echo occurs in Merton's "Fasting of the Heart," where Confucius corrects a well-meaning disciple, Yen Hui, who thinks going without wine and meat is real fasting. "Well, you can call it 'observing a fast' if you like," said Confucius, "but it is not the fasting of the heart." *The Way of Chuang Tzu*, 52. Merton's monastic brothers would know well the phrase, "observing a fast," and would appreciate Chuang Tzu's distinctive "fasting of the heart," *xinzhai* 心齊, and its literal meaning, "heart-mind purification." *ZZDB* 4: 83.

83. A. C. Graham says commentators mistakenly assume the official has one foot. Actually, "the man is singular in appearance or character, a freak or eccentric." *Chuang-tzu the Seven Inner Chapters*. London: George Allen & Unwin, 1981. p. 64.

84. Graham, *ibid*, 15, 16, 18. "Maker of Things." "Zao wu zhe" 造物者. "Da zong shi," *ZZDB* 6: 108. Merton translates as, "the Maker." "Metamorphosis," *The Way of Chuang Tzu*, 62.

85. "The Man With One Foot and the Marsh Pheasant," *The Way of Chuang Tzu*, 48. From "Yangsheng zhu," *ZZDB* 3: 78. Giles' comment conjoins divine will and human ambition: "It was by God's will that he took office with a view to personal aggrandizement." *Chuang Tzu*, 49.

86. "Heaven did it, not man. Heaven creates uniqueness, human appearance is relative." "Tian ye fei ren ye. Tian zhi sheng shi shi du ye, ren zhi mao you yu

At the end of the selection, Merton reworks Giles and Legge, highlighting a motif found throughout his letters and journals of the 1960s: personal freedom. The little Marsh Pheasant may have to "hop ten times" for "a bite of grain," or "run a hundred steps" for "a sip of water,"

> Yet she does not ask
> To be kept in a hen run
> Though she might have all she desired
> Set before her
> She would rather run
> And seek her own little living
> Uncaged.[87]

In relation to the theme of personal freedom, the most significant associative interpolations are those that emphasize self or non-self. Merton consistently explores the meaning of "person" in his writings, and *The Way of Chuang Tzu* is an Asian document recording that quest, parallel in importance to *The Asian Journal.*[88] A holy card, "A Litany of the Person," composed by Brother Paul Quenon and distributed at Merton's Gethsemani Abbey, lists various epithets of personhood such as "image of God," "dwelling of God," and "chosen of God," identities from the Christian tradition Merton would assuredly affirm. In *The Way of Chuang Tzu,* Merton seems to incorporate Chuang Tzu's fullness-in-emptiness sense of non-self within his exploration of person, conjoining the flowering of consciousness with the disappearance of a fixed individual ego

---

ye." 天 也 非 人 也 。 天 之 生 是 使 獨 也, 人 之 貌 有 與 也. *ZZDB* 3: 78.

87. *The Way of Chuang Tzu,* 49. *ZZDB* 3: 78. Giles: "they [wild fowls] do not want to be fed in a cage. For although they would thus be able to command food, they would not be free . . . ." *Chuang Tzu,* 49. Legge: "it does not seek to be nourished in a coop. Though its spirit would (there) enjoy a royal abundance, it does not think (such confinement) good." *The Writings of Chuang Tzu,* 248,

88. The holy card was available to recent visitors to Gethsemani Abbey attending the Seventh General Meeting of the International Thomas Merton Society, Bellarmine University, Louisville, Kentucky, June 7-10, 2001. The card summarizes traditional Christian teaching: "image of God, born of God's breath, vessel of divine Love, after his likeness, dwelling of God, capacity for the infinite, eternally known, chosen of God, home of Infinite Majesty, abiding in the Son, called from eternity, life in the Lord, temple of the Holy Spirit, branch of Christ, receptacle of the Most High, wellspring of Living Water, heir of the kingdom, the glory of God, abode of the Trinity. God sings this litany eternally in his Word. This is who you are."

and body-self identity in the phrase, the "True Self." While there is no Chinese expression for "True Self" in the *Chuang Tzu*, Merton may have in mind "True Man" (*zhen ren*), a term frequently encountered in the Chinese text and the English translations, which Legge glosses as, "one whose nature is in agreement with the Tao," and one whose "most prominent characteristic" is "his perfect comprehension of the Tao and participation of it."[89] These adaptations reflect Merton's passionate quest for the fullness of truth during his life-long pilgrimage towards God.

Essentially, Merton celebrates the mystery of personal being in these associative passages from *The Way of Chuang Tzu*, a mystery illuminated by the cook in "Cutting Up An Ox." When the cook's sensate, analytical self is forgotten in a moment of absorption with his task, he acts freely and spontaneously, his spirit open to Heaven and in harmony with the Way (or as Tao, ultimate reality, absolute). After years of study and practice—the ability to act intuitively and rightly is not innate—the cook no longer sees the ox as a whole nor its individual parts:

> But now, I see nothing
> With the eye. My whole being
> Apprehends.
> My senses are idle. The spirit
> Free to work without plan.[90]

The "spirit" (*shen*) in the *Chuang Tzu* is not the Holy Spirit, soul or individual self, but may be likened to what Graham, borrowing from Goethe, terms the "daemon" or the "daemonic," a numinous force "wiser than ourselves" which infuses and dwells in one trained like the cook to be receptive to Tao and to Heaven.[91] "My whole

---

89. *Zhen ren* 真人. Legge, *The Writings of Chuang Tzu*, 83, 285. See Merton's translation, "The True Man," *The Way of Chuang Tzu*, 60-61.

90. "Cutting Up An Ox," *The Way of Chuang Tzu*, 46. "Yangsheng zhu" *ZZDB* 3: 77. "Whole being" is unknown to Merton's translators. Giles: "And now I work with my mind and not with my eye. When my senses bid me stop, but my mind urges me on, I fall back upon eternal principles." *Chuang Tzu*, 48. Legge: "Now I deal with it [ox] in a spirit-like manner, and do not look at it with my eyes. The use of my senses is discarded, and my spirit acts as it wills." *The Writings of Chuang Tzu*, 247.

91. Shen 神. *ZZDB* 3: 77. Graham admonishes readers that western notions of the daemonic as restless, anguished, or malign are "foreign to the Chinese word." *Chuang-tzu the Seven Inner Chapters*, 35, footnote 72.

being apprehends" is Merton's alteration, an attempt to embody Chuang Tzu's perception of intuitive knowing in the personal spirit of the cook acting in tune with Heaven, and to voice self-other identification, an indescribable intuitive knowledge of the person experienced through and beyond the senses. For Merton, steeped in Judaic-Christian traditions and the contemplative life, "whole being" means self-in-relation to God, the true self as person and not as an individual, and may explain why he resonates with Chuang Tzu's notions of "True Man" and "spirit."

Merton must have found the image of Lao Tzu in "Lao Tzu's Wake" amusing—in contrast to the perceptive cook in "Cutting Up An Ox," the Taoist sage is a miserable failure, criticized for neglecting the bond between his "true being," "True Self," and Heaven. Substituting "God" for "Heaven" (*Tian*), Merton explains Lao Tzu's fault:

> He weakened his true being . . .
> He forgot the gift God had entrusted to him:
> This the ancients called "punishment
> For neglecting the True Self."[92]

While "true being" and "True Self" are neither in the Chinese nor the English translations,[93] Merton correctly intuits that Lao Tzu's "punishment," according to the *Chuang Tzu* text, came from "opposing Heaven" or "hiding from Heaven" and "forgetting what he had received,"[94] that is, separating individuality from personality as a heavenly source. For Merton a self in isolation from the divine is the false self, the opposite of the True Self or non-self, which is the person in infinite relationship.

Merton's keen interest in person and self sometimes causes him to personify relations that are more objective in the *Chuang Tzu*. Thus, his version of a phrase in "The Pivot" reads: "There is nothing that cannot be seen from the standpoint of the 'Not I.' And there is nothing which cannot be seen from the standpoint of the 'I.'" In the *Chuang Tzu* the original literal sense is impersonal:

92. "Lao Tzu's Wake," *The Way of Chuang Tzu*, 56. "Yangsheng zhu" *ZZDB* 3: 78.

93. Merton may have gleaned "true being" and "True Self" from Legge's "Heaven-nature." Legge, *The Writings of Chuang Tzu*, 249.

94. "punishment for opposing Heaven," "dun tian zhi xing" 遁天 之 刑; "forgetting what he had received," "wang qi suo shou" 忘其所受. *ZZDB* 3: 78. Graham: "hiding from Heaven," *Chuang-tzu the Seven Inner Chapters*, 65.

"Every thing has its 'that,' every thing has its 'this.'" The same objectivity is found in both Giles, "There is nothing which is not objective: there is nothing which is not subjective," and Legge, "All subjects may be looked at from (two points of view),—from that and from this."[95] Nevertheless, Merton's personification of self in this particular phrase from "The Pivot" is a selection from Chapter II of the *Chuang Tzu*, "Leveling Opposites," a chapter which indeed includes self and other in its non-stop play on relations between contraries and parallels, such as Heaven and earth, life and death, heat and cold, and pleasure and pain. Merton's association with person is an appropriate amplification.

A fascinating aspect of these associative selections emphasizing person and self is a perspective echoed in Merton's famous last recorded words, spoken just before his death: "So I will disappear."[96] The disappearance in death of what might be called the ego, lesser self, or false self, is not a morbid fact in Merton's writing, but an attractive ideal, something for which he longed and hoped, as it signifies the transition to union with God. The whole of the selection, "Man is Born in Tao," is worth citing in this connection.

> Fishes are born in water
> Man is born in Tao.
> If fishes, born in water,
> Seek the deep shadow
> Of pond and pool,
> All their needs
> Are satisfied.
> If man, born in Tao,
> Sinks into the deep shadow
> Of non-action
> To forget aggression and concern,
> He lacks nothing

95. "The Pivot," *The Way of Chuang Tzu,* 42. "Every thing has its 'that,' every thing has its 'this.'" 物無非彼物無非是. Chapter Two, "Leveling Opposites," "*Qiwu lun*" ZZDB 2: 62. Giles, *Chuang Tzu,* 37. Legge, *The Writings of Chuang Tzu,* 230.

96. Merton ended his December 10, 1968, talk on "Marxism and Monastic Perspectives" at the Bangkok Conference, with these words. *The Asian Journal of Thomas Merton.* Naomi Burton, Brother Patrick Hart, and James Laughlin, eds. New York: New Directions, 1973, 343.

His life is secure.
Moral: "All the fish needs
Is to get lost in water.
All man needs is to get lost
In Tao.[97]

There is no "non-action," forgetting of "aggression," or "moral" of getting "lost" in water or the Tao in the original passage or the English translations. The point of the *Chuang Tzu* excerpt is an analogy, accurately captured in Legge's translation: "Fishes forget one another in the rivers and lakes; men forget one another in the arts of the Tao."[98] Merton's version is consistent with this analogy: just as all the needs of fish are satisfied when they are in their element, water, so people lack nothing in theirs, the Tao. Moreover, Merton's insert, non-action (*wu-wei*), the discipline of acting without attachments to our actions so the Tao may prevail, is found throughout the *Chuang Tzu*, and the monk is clearly associating it here with the ideal of non-violence directed against aggression celebrated in his writings on peace. As for the fish and men who "get lost," they embody the disappearance of ego-self at the heart of Merton's longing, and the charmed existence of the "True Man" (*zhen ren*) he admires in the *Chuang Tzu*, for whom death is no different from life:

They [*zhen ren*] did not . . .
drive grimly forward
Fighting their way through life.
They took life as it came, gladly;
Took death as it came, without care;
And went away, yonder,
Yonder![99]

The phrase, "nor drive grimly forward / Fighting their way through life," and the transcendent emphasis, "And went away, yonder, / Yonder!" are Merton's adaptations,[100] echoing perhaps Gerard Manley

---

97. "Man is Born in Tao," *The Way of Chuang Tzu*, 65.

98. Legge, *The Writings of Chuang Tzu*, 301. "yu xiang wang hu jiang hu ren xiang wang hu dao shu," 漁相忘乎江湖人相忘乎道術. "Yang sheng zhu," *ZZDB* 3: 78.

99. "The True Man," *The Way of Chuang Tzu*, 61. "Da zong shi," *ZZDB* 6: 105.

100. Giles: "Cheerfully they played their allotted parts, waiting patiently

Hopkins' rapturous paean to human immortality, "We follow, now we follow.— / Yonder, yes yonder, yonder; / Yonder,"[101] consistent with hints of transcendence we have seen in "Three Friends,"[102] and humorously embodied in "Metamorphosis." In the latter, a character who contracts a mortal illness celebrates his mutability and the eternal process of change, praising the "Maker of Things":

> If He takes me apart
> And makes a rooster
> Of my left shoulder
> I shall announce the dawn.[103]

Parts of Chapter Five, "Hallmarks of Virtue Complete," which Merton did not translate but would have read, celebrate the handicapped, maimed, or ugly person whose great virtue or power (*De*) is seen in his or her indifference to disaster, social ostracism, and death. In the chapter Confucius speaks of such a person as a "sage" (*sheng ren*) who "rules heaven and earth . . . and whose mind-heart never tastes death. Such a one selects the day for ascending. Others follow him."[104]

Disappearance is a compelling subject for Chuang Tzu, about which the Taoist master frequently waxes euphoric, whether it

---

for the end." *Chuang Tzu*, 72. Legge: "They accepted (their life) and rejoiced in it; they forgot (all fear of death), and returned (to their state before life)." *The Writings of Chuang Tzu*, 286.

101. "The Leaden Echo and the Golden Echo," *The Poems of Gerard Manley Hopkins*, fourth edition, ed. W. H. Gardner and N. H. Mackenzie, London: Oxford University Press, 1967, 91-93.

102. "Hey, Sung Hu! / Where'd you go? . . . You have gone / Where you really were . . . Damn it! We are here!" "Three Friends," *The Way of Chuang Tzu*, 55. Regarding the death of Sung Hu, the Chinese text speaks of a homecoming or going back : "[Sung Hu] returned to the true, while we are still acting as men. Alas!" "er yi fan qi zhen er wo you wei ren yi," 而 已 反 其 真 而 我 猶 為 人.

103. "Maker of Things," "Zao wu zhe" 造 物 者. "Metamorphosis," *The Way of Chuang Tzu*, 63. "If gradually in the course of change [the Maker] takes my shoulder and makes it into a cock, I'll accordingly watch the night for when (to crow), "jin jia er hua yu zhi zuo bi yi wei ji yu yin yi qiu shi re," 浸 假 而 化 予 之 左 臂 以 為 雞 予 因 以 求 時 夜. "Da zong shi," *ZZDB* 6: 108.

104. Virtue or power, *De* 德. "Sage," *sheng ren* 聖 人. He "rules heaven and earth . . . and whose mind-heart never tastes death. Such a one selects the day for ascending. Others follow him." "Guan tian di . . . er xin wei chang si zhe hu. Bi qie ze ri er deng jia ren ze cong shi ye," 官 天 地 . . . 而 心 未 嘗 死 者 乎. 彼 且 擇 日 而 登 假 人 則 從 是 也. "Hallmarks of Virtue Complete," "De chong fu" 德 充 符, *ZZDB* 5: 96-97.

means the unity of opposites, oneness with Heaven or Tao, mortal illness, the death of his wife, or his own death. In his exploration of self and non-self in the *Chuang Tzu*, Merton becomes entranced.

New Harmonies

The links Merton forges between his musical variations and the *Chuang Tzu* culminate in a new music not heard in other translations. In the five years between inception and completion of the translation project, Merton's discernment of implied meaning, cultural, political, and religious associations, and his affinity for intimations of person and transcendence, evolve into a vision unknown to Chuang Tzu, and perhaps, prior to reading *The Way of Chuang Tzu,* unknown to Merton himself.

Much of the new music has to do with a mystical sense with which Merton reworks the *Chuang Tzu*. At the end of "The Pivot," Merton inserts a paragraph long interpolation, and introduces "the still point" as a metaphor for the pivot of Tao, around which contraries revolve and converge. He breaks in with a strong affirmation of "the light of direct intuition"— Merton's new rendering of "Heaven" (*Tian*)—rejecting Legge's "Heavenly nature" and Giles' "God."[105] He drops more modest translations of *ming* as "light of the mind" (Legge) or "light of nature" (Giles), replacing them with "the true light."[106]

> He who grasps the pivot is at the still-point from which
> all movements and oppositions can be seen in their right
> relationship. . . . Abandoning all thought of imposing a limit
> or taking sides, he rests in direct intuition. Therefore I said:
> "Better to abandon disputation and seek the true light!"

The Chinese for this last phrase reads, "[in disputes] nothing is as good as clarity,"[107] implying intellectual-mystical light is vital. In Merton "the true light" echoes the *Gospel of John*'s revelation of Christ as "the true light" of the world "which enlightens

---

105. "Illuminates them [logical disputes] in relation to Heaven," "zhao zhi yu tian" 照 之 於 天. *ZZDB* 3: 62. Legge, "Heaven (-ly nature)," *The Writings of Chuang Tzu,* 230. Giles, "God," *Chuang Tzu,* 37.

106. *Ming* . Legge, "light (of the mind)," *The Writings of Chuang Tzu,* 230. Giles, "light of nature," *Chuang Tzu,* 37.

107. "nothing is as good as clarity," "ze mo ruo yi ming" 則 莫 若 以 明. *ZZDB* 3: 62.

everyone."[108] "The still point" reminds us of Louis Massignon's "le pointe vierge" and of T. S. Eliot's "still point of the turning world" in *The Four Quartets*, the absolute center of silence and light.[109] In "The Useless Tree," Merton has Chuang Tzu tell his critic, Hui Tzu, to plant the tree in "emptiness," a word Merton knows well is associated in the West with the deepest Buddhist and Taoist conceptions of reality. The same passage in the *Chuang Tzu* text is concrete, using negatives to designate infinitude, a linguistic feature common to apophatic mystical literature: "Why not plant it in a land lacking there-ness, in a limitless wild?" In Merton's rendition, "plant it in the wasteland / In Emptiness," "emptiness" is synonymous with "wasteland." It is a physical metaphor for a metaphysical reality, and thus has tangible being, unlike Giles' "plant it in the domain of non-existence."[110]

"Still point," "direct intuition," "true light" and "emptiness" are all loaded terms through which Merton intensifies his own spiritual experience of reading the *Chuang Tzu* text as word-event, expanding metaphysical realities.

There are many direct references to "God" in *The Way of Chuang Tzu,* strengthening the Western reader's impression of a God-Tao identity, unknown to the *Zhuangzi,* which so far as we are aware is not acquainted with Hindu or Jewish traditions of theism. Yet, there are good reasons for Merton's musical mutation. We have seen hints of a personal deity in Merton's "Metamorphosis," in the "Maker" who subjects creatures to mutability. The same term is found in the Chinese text: "Wow! The Maker of things has taken hold of me and made me so crookedy-crooked!" says a sick man.[111]

---

108. *John* 1: 9.

109. "After the kingfisher's wing / Has answered light to light, and is silent, the light is still / At the still point of the turning world." "Burnt Norton," First Quartet, Movement IV, *Four Quartets.* New York: Harcourt, Brace & World, 1943. p. 7.

110. "Why not plant it in a land lacking there-ness, in a limitless wild?" "He bushu zhi yu wu he you zhi xiang kuang mo zhi ye?" 何不樹之於無何有之鄉廣莫之野. *ZZDB* 1: 54. Giles, *Chuang Tzu,* 33.

111. Merton's perception of "God" as "Maker" is close to both the Chinese original and the English translations. Merton, " 'Great is the Maker,' said the sick one, 'Who has made me as I am!' " "Metamorphosis," *The Way of Chuang Tzu,* 63. Chinese text, "Wow! The Maker of things has taken hold of me and made me so crookedy-crooked!" "Wei zai fu zao zhe jiang yi yu wei ci ju ju ye" 偉哉夫造者將以予為此拘拘也. *ZZDB* 6: 108. Giles, " 'Verily God is great!' said the sick man. 'See how he has doubled me up.' " *Chuang Tzu,* 79. Legge,

In "The Breath of Nature," Merton joins Chuang Tzu in speculating on the source of wind and the "music of the earth." Merton writes, "Something is blowing . . . some power stands behind all this . . . What is this power?" A disciple in the *Chuang Tzu* text wonders, "The one who excites and stirs up this, who is it?"[112] In "Great Knowledge," Merton agrees with Chuang Tzu that there is a "True Governor" (*Zhen Zai*) in the background, an invisible source, a hidden wholeness—being the Godhead as the cosmic Tao:

> One may well suppose the True Governor
> To be behind it all. That such a Power works
> I can believe. I cannot see his form.
> He acts, but has no form.[113]

Merton's rendition, while following Giles and Legge's personification of the True Governor as a "He," is intuitively closer to the Chinese: "It seems there is a True Governor, but no trace to grasp. That it can act is readily believable, but its form is invisible. It has feeling, yet is shapeless."[114] As noted previously, in "Lao Tzu's Wake," Merton replaces "Heaven" with "God" in the phrase, "(Lao Tzu) forgot the gift God had entrusted to him." Elsewhere in the same passage, Merton, going along with Giles and Legge, writes:

> Here is how the ancients said all this
> In four words:

"'How great,' said (the sufferer), 'is the Creator! That He should have made me the deformed object that I am!'" *The Writings of Chuang Tzu,* 295.

112. Merton, "The Breath of Nature," *The Way of Chuang Tzu,* 38-39. "The one who excites and stirs up this, who is it?" "Nu zhe qi shei ye" 怒 者 其 誰 邪. *ZZDB* 2: 60. Giles does not name the source. Legge calls it an "agency." Legge, *The Writings of Chuang Tzu,* 226.

113. "Great Knowledge," *The Way of Chuang Tzu,* 41.

114. "Great Knowledge," *The Way of Chuang Tzu,* 41. "It seems there is a True Governor, but no trace to grasp. That it can act is readily believable, but its form is invisible. It has feeling, yet is shapeless." "Ruo you Zhen Zai er tuo bu de zi zhen. Ke xing yi xin er tuo bujian qi xing you qing er wu xing" 若 有 真 宰 而 特 不 得 其 朕. 可 行 已 信 而 不 見 其 刑 有 情 而 無 行. *ZZDB* 2: 61. Giles, "It would seem as though they have some True Master, and yet I find no trace of him. He can act—that is certain. Yet I cannot see his form. He has identity but no form." *Chuang Tzu,* 38. Legge, while insisting that "Governor" is a metaphor for Tao, personifies the source as "He" and "his:" "It might seem as if there would be a true Governor concerned in it, but we do not find any trace (of his presence and acting). That such a One could act so I believe; but we do not see His form. He has affections, but He has no form." *The Writings of Chuang Tzu,* 227-228.

"God cuts the thread."

Merton mistakenly concurs with Giles and Legge that the phrase is a reference to death. The word, "God" (*Ti*), does indeed appear in the Chinese—"The ancients said that this [freedom realized in transcending joy and sorrow] was God's untying the hanged"— most probably the term, *Ti*, is a vestige of an era prior to the *Chuang Tzu* as its usage is exceptional.[115] Finally, in a passage where Confucius advises a disciple who wants to reform others, that he must instead follow the difficult practice of fasting of the heart, Merton, following Giles, has Confucius say, "But easy ways do not come from God." Once again, "God" replaces "Heaven."[116]

Merton's appreciative reading of John Wu's persuasive argument about affinities between Tao, Heaven, and God in Wu's essay, "The Wisdom of Chuang Tzu," doubtlessly is one source of the "God-talk" in *The Way of Chuang Tzu*.[117] While Legge repeatedly critiques associating Tao and Heaven with Judeo-Christian "God," in Giles' translation these terms are nearly synonymous, and Giles may be an influence as well. I think, however, that the real origin is Merton's interior landscape, freshly envisioned through the meeting between himself and Chuang Tzu. As indicated earlier, Merton's "still point," "direct intuition," "true light" and "emptiness" are part of the new music. So are Chuang Tzu's "Maker," "True Governor," and "God." They are words and terms which mirror the "something," or "some power," that Merton discerns in all relationships.

To illustrate this point, I should like to close with a change in

---

115. "Lao Tzu's Wake," *The Way of Chuang Tzu,* 57. "The ancients said that this [freedom realized in transcending joy and sorrow] was God's untying the hanged," "Guzhe wei shi di zhi xian jie." 古 者 謂 是 帝 之 縣 解. *ZZDB* 3: 78. Giles, "The ancients spoke of death as of God cutting down a man suspended in the air." *Chuang Tzu,* 50. Legge, "The ancients described (death) as the loosening of the cord on which God suspended (the life)." *The Writings of Chuang Tzu,* 249-250. A. C. Graham on "Ti:" "a supreme ruler who belongs to the culture of the older Shang dynasty rather than to the Chou, which replaced him by Heaven." *Chuang-tzu: The Seven Inner Chapters,* 18.

116. The Chinese sense is different: "One who makes fasting undemanding enjoys not bright Heaven's accord." "Yi zhi zhe hao tian bu yi" 易 之 者 皞 天 不 宜. *ZZDB* 4: 82.

117. "The Wisdom of Chuang Tzu: A New Appraisal," *Chinese Humanism and Christian Spirituality: Essays of John C. H. Wu* [Wu Ching-hsiung]. Paul K. T. Shih, ed. Jamaica, N.Y.: St. John's University Press, 1965, 61-93.

metaphors. Merton's encounter with the *Chuang* Tzu gives birth to a child who belongs to neither Merton nor Chuang Tzu alone, but to both. The meaning of this metaphor is illustrated in a last excerpt from *The Way of Chuang Tzu,* "When a Hideous Man . . . ." The selection is a mere fragment from one of the Outer Chapters, "Heaven and Earth," encapsulating the dimensions of the new music we have heard in the Inner Chapters.

> When a hideous man becomes a father
> And a son is born to him
> In the middle of the night
> He trembles and lights a lamp
> And runs to look in anguish
> On that child's face
> To see whom he resembles.

The Chinese original is different in substance, "One midnight, a horrific woman bore a child. Hastily she grasped a torch to study the baby, terrified lest it look like her."[118] In the Chinese, "the hideous man" is a "li ren," someone suffering a contagious or malignant disease, such as leprosy, who gives birth to a baby, and logically is a woman.[119] The allegory is transparent. She is hoping against hope that the child does not look like her, and has not inherited her disease. In Merton's version, he makes identity a paradoxical mystery, an encounter between father and son, self and other, and, perhaps, Merton the composer of variations and Chuang Tzu the original artist. This closing fragment is immensely suggestive of Merton himself—an "ugly" father who wants and does not want his child to look like or be like him, the self who hopes yet fears the non-self is true self, and the poet-monk virtuoso who wants his musical variations approved by the Master composer, wonders whether they are too close or too far from the sounds he has heard, and exults too in melodies unknown to either artist alone.

118. "When A Hideous Man . . . ," *The Way of Chuang Tzu,* 77. "One midnight, a leprous woman bore a child. Hastily she grasped a torch to study the baby, terrified lest it look like her." "Zhi ren yeban sheng qi zi ju qu huo er shi zhi ji ji ran wei kong qi si ji ye" 厲 之 人 夜 半 生 其 子 遽 取 火 而 視 之 汲 汲 然 唯 恐 其 似 己 也. Chapter 12, "Heaven and Earth," "Tian Di" 天 地. *ZZDB* 12: 160.

119. Gender is unidentified in the Chinese, but context implies female. Giles, "ugly man," *Chuang Tzu,* 129. Legge, "ugly man," *The Writings of Chuang Tzu,* 376. In a footnote, Legge suggests "leper."

CONCLUSION

Ultimately, Merton knows composition as a mysterious unfolding, much like his own person, a lotus budding in the monk's pond of Gethsemani and *The Way of Chuang Tzu*, flowering and fading on the far side of the mountain in Asia and *The Asian Journal*. Encountering Mount Kanchenjuga, the Dalai Lama and other Tibetan monks, the Polonnaruwa statues of Buddha, and his fellow Christian monks in Bangkok, Merton experiences the Will [or Mandate] of Heaven and disappears.

MERTON'S WAY OF *ZHUANGZI:*
A CRITIQUE

Bede Bidlack

INTRODUCTION

In 1965, Merton published *The Way of Chuang Tzu*, his only book exclusively on Daoism.[1] Of Merton's many books on a variety of subjects, this one held a prominent place in his heart: "I have enjoyed writing this book more than any other I can remember."[2] Even though Merton faced several liabilities in this work, those liabilities make *The Way of Chuang Tzu* all the more remarkable for its insight into the tradition of Daoism known through Zhuangzi and its interest for Christian life.

The Way of Chuang Tzu is a condensed and rearranged edition of the thirty-three chapters of the original work, called the *Zhuangzi*, as it was handed on through Guo Xiang (252-312 C.E.), an editor and commentator. Merton took translations—two English, one French, and one German—and compared them. Then he applied his own intuitive insight into *Zhuangzi* to bring together what he calls his "imitations" or "readings."[3] Merton accurately notes the guess-work that goes into translating a difficult text like the *Zhuangzi*. The guesses are based on two sources: one's scholarship and one's experiential grasp of the mysterious Way or the Dao. Merton's strength was not his scholarly understanding of the complex and rich tradition that came to be called Daoism long after Zhuangzi. Therefore, by Merton's logic, the value of his guesses comes from his grasp of the Dao.

His intuitive understanding of what the *Zhuangzi* is trying to

---

1. I would like to thank Philip J. Ivanhoe and Patrick F. O'Connell for their valuable comments on an earlier version of this chapter.

The Pinyin form of transliteration has largely replaced the Wade-Giles system prominent in Merton's time. Words like *Chuang Tzu* will appear as *Zhuangzi* and *Tao* as *Dao*. However, all quotations will use the system adopted by the author quoted.

2. Thomas Merton, *The Way of Chuang Tzu* (New York: New Directions, 1965), 9-10.

3. *The Way*, 9.

communicate is the charm of Merton's little book, as well as its very relevance. If a reader wants a scholarly account, there are better resources. What Merton did was to introduce the tradition of an ancient mystical thinker to a Western audience separated by millennia, thousands of miles, and layer upon layer of cultural difference. To accomplish this, Merton did not need to present a complete "reading." He chose sixty-two passages that were con- sistently short tales rather than long, difficult treatises.[4]

The work gives an insight into Merton's heart—his hopes, his ideals—because Merton presents only those passages that especially appealed to him. What was the appeal? In the words of Merton, "[H]umility, self-effacement, silence, and in general a refusal to take seriously the aggressivity, the ambition, the push, and the self-importance which one must display in order to get along in society."[5] He marks the book as "ventures in personal and spiri- tual interpretation." Then he goes on to write: "Any rendering of Chuang Tzu is bound to be very personal."[6] In this respect, Merton is engaging in a religious activity that occurs throughout history. People see and take away from traditions what they recognize and need in their own spiritual development.

Before encountering Merton in *The Way of Chuang Tzu*, an introduction to Zhuangzi is in order.

THE TRADITION OF ZHUANGZI

Our knowledge of Zhuangzi,[7] "Master Zhuang," comes from the Han historian Sima Qian's *Shiji* ("Record of the Historian" 2nd century C.E.). The *Shiji* reports that his family name was Zhuang and his given name was Zhou, he held a minor position at Lacquer Garden during the reign of King Hui of Liang or Wei (370-319 B.C.E.) and Xuan of Qi (319-301 B.C.E.). According to Sima Qian: "There was nothing upon which his learning did not touch, but its essentials derived from the words of the Old Masters."[8] Lee

---

4. Ekman P. C. Tam, *Christian Contemplation and Chinese Zen-Taoism: A Study of Thomas Merton's Writings* (Hong Kong: Tao Fong Shan Christian Centre, 2002), 55; Patrick F. O'Connell, "The Way of Chuang Tzu," in William H. Shannon, Christine M. Bochen, and Patrick O'Connell, *The Thomas Merton Encyclopedia* (Maryknoll, NY: Orbis Books, 2002), 521-523.

5. *The Way*, 11.

6. *The Way*, 9.

7. Zhuang Zhou's dates, 368-286 B.C.E., are largely legendary.

8. Sima Qian's *Shiji* as translated by Victor Mair in "The *Zhuangzi* and Its

86 • Bede Bidlack

Yearly postulates that Zhuangzi could have been a former member of the Confucians and Yangists, but eventually a crisis compelled him to go his own way.[9]

Thomas Merton presents the ancient Chinese figure in several of his passages. Possibly the most well-known tale involving Zhuangzi, "The Turtle" presents him fishing in a river when he is approached by officials who invite him to a life at court, at the king's request. Zhuangzi expresses his preference for a life of simplicity, like a turtle wagging its tail in the mud, over a life of display at court. [10]

Of the *Zhuangzi* corpus, only the first seven chapters are attributed to a single author. Differences in style and language set the other chapters off as coming from other sources, possibly composed of followers of Zhuangzi, that use the terms and ideas that are in a tradition of *Zhuangzi*. The standard source for these writings come from Guo Xiang, who reduced the *Zhuangzi* corpus from a fifty-two chapter version to the extant thirty-three chapter version. By 300 C.E., he included a commentary.[11] Readers of the *Zhuangzi* classify the work into: Chapters 1-7, the Inner Chapters, as they have been called since the Han (206 B.C.E.-220 C.E.), Chapters 8-22, the Outer Chapters, as they have been known since Guo Xiang, and Chapters 23-33, the Miscellaneous Chapters.[12] Of the 62 passages Merton selected, 16 are from the Inner Chapters, 31 from the Outer Chapters, and 15 from the Miscellaneous Chapters.[13] There were several versions of the *Zhuangzi* in ancient China, which were eventually abandoned and lost in favor of Guo Xiang's version. By the twentieth century, Guo Xiang's text proliferated into over 100 versions.[14] Merton availed himself of four of these when writing *The Way of Chuang Tzu*: those of James Legge (English), Herbert Giles (English), Léon Wieger (French), and Richard Wilhelm (German).

Impact," in *Daoism Handbook* edited by Livia Kohn (Leiden: Brill, 2000), 31.

9. Lee Yearly, "Zhuangzi's Understanding of Skillfulness and the Ultimate Spiritual State," in *Essays on Skepticism, Relativism, and Ethics in the Zhuangzi*, edited by Paul Kjellberg and Philip J. Ivanhoe (Albany: SUNY Press, 1996), 153.

10. *The Way*, 93-94.

11. "*Zhuangzi* and Its Impact," 39.

12. "*Zhuangzi* and Its Impact," 36.

13. Patrick F. O'Connell, "The Way of Chuang Tzu," in *The Thomas Merton Encyclopedia*, 522.

14. Hyun Höchsmann and Yang Guorong, "Notes on Text and Translation," in *Zhuangzi*, translated and introduced by Hyun Höchsmann and Yang Guorong (NY: Pearson, 2007), xii.

MERTON'S INTERPRETATION OF DAOISM

In *The Way of Chuang Tzu*, Merton has two lines in the opening chapter, "A Study of Chuang Tzu," and one in "A Note to the Reader" that are misleading to anyone unfamiliar with Daoist studies or Thomas Merton's life.

In the first of these lines, Merton is trying to present the Daoism of Zhuangzi in a way palatable to his largely Christian readers:

> One must also see [Chuang Tzu] in relation to what followed him, because it would be a great mistake to confuse the Taoism of Chuang Tzu with the popular, degenerate amalgam of superstition, alchemy, magic, and health-culture which Taoism later became.[15]

The distancing of Zhuangzi from all later traditions of Daoism, as Merton does, is difficult to overlook by a modern scholar of Daoism. In addition, introducing Daoism as a "degenerate amalgam of superstition, alchemy, magic, and health-culture" reads as vitriol to both scholars and Daoists alike.

Here Merton reveals himself as an inheritor of a particular kind of Chinese interpretation of Daoism—that of Christian missionaries.[16] When Christian missionaries, like Matteo Ricci, arrived in China in the 17th century, they realized that they needed to influence the empowered *literati* in order to establish a foothold for Christianity. The *literati* were the Confucian government administrators and educators. Confucians at the time adopted a polemical position that viewed Daoism and Buddhism as "superstitions" unworthy of serious intellectual cultivation. The Christians, choosing not to see Confucianism as a religion but as a secular philosophy, accepted this view. Since the West understood so little of Daoism into the 20th century, no one responded to the "superstition" label. Merton's mentors in his study of Chinese thought, John C. H. Wu and Paul K. T. Sih were both Catholic Christians and were not motivated to challenge the 17th century interpretation.

Today, however, scholars recognize "superstition" as a Christian term, that suggests that Christians have miracles and faith,

---

15. *The Way*, 15. See also Thomas Merton, *Mystics and Zen Masters* (New York: New York: Farrar, Straus, Giroux, 1967), 146.

16. Anna Seidel, "Chronicle of Taoist Studies in the West 1950-1990," *Cahiers d'Extrême-Asie revue de l'Ecole française d'Extrême-Orient, Section de Kyoto* 5 (1989-1990): 223-347.

but other religions have superstitions and beliefs. Such a Christian stance suggests that the religious other is not to be taken seriously, but only reveals itself as needing saving from the darkness of its errors. Also, Merton's reference that Daoism from the Han onwards is a "degenerate amalgam" indicates his belief in some pure form of Daoism to which Zhuangzi had access. On the contrary, the *Zhuangzi* that Merton read was a collection of essays at the hands of several authors over a period of time, not the unadulterated intuition of a single author.

These two assumptions—Christians have miracles, others have superstitions and the existence of a pure Daoism—have fallen away to postmodern critique. On the one hand, Christianity does not have an exclusive vision of Truth so that whole traditions can be dismissed as superstitions (i.e. untrue), and on the other hand, the development of religions is far more complex than it was presented from the late 19th century to the mid-20th century. The notion that there is an "Ur-religion" that all religions in their purest form resemble has been largely dismissed.[17] While it is true that the *Zhuangzi* did find its way into use by Chinese shamans and longevity cults, pre-Han Zhuangzi should not be read as being religiously neutral and only later corrupted. In addition, the inheritance from which Merton was working was what Guo Xiang redacted during the 4th century C.E., when the "degenerate" influences on the *Zhuangzi* were in full swing. In many chapters there are references to mysterious yogic practices and beings with miraculous powers.

Merton's second misleading line follows directly after the first: "The true inheritors of the thought and spirit of Chuang Tzu are the Chinese Zen Buddhists of the T'ang period (7th to 10th centuries A.D.)."[18] He is following the understanding of D. T. Suzuki (1870-1966), who was not an unproblematic figure with regards to Zen Buddhism.[19] By adopting such an interpretation, Merton

---

17. This is the argument of perennial philosophy. One of the earliest theorists of perennial philosophy was Aldous Huxley, who wrote *The Perennial Philosophy* (New York: Harper & Row, 1945). Merton read Huxley's *Ends and Means* in 1938, but he did not subscribe to perennial philosophy. Here, I am merely critiquing the simplifications in the early study of religion and the degree to which Merton seems to be participating in the simplifications.

18. *The Way*, 15.

19. John P. Keenan, "The Limits of Thomas Merton's Understanding of Buddhism," in *Merton and Buddhism: Wisdom, Emptiness, and Everyday Mind*, edited by Bonnie Bowman Thurston (Louisville, KY: Fons Vitae), 118-133.

put a veil over his eyes that restricted his vision of Zhuangzi to its relation to Zen. Merton refers the ideas in the *Zhuangzi* back to Zen on several occasions in an effort to get around later Daoism.[20] In his zeal for Zen, Merton overlooks about a thousand years of religious development in Daoism and assumes that Zen Buddhism was somehow inoculated against it. The position is like the claim of some Protestants that they are the true inheritors of the message of the Gospels and St. Paul, while attempting to ignore the fifteen hundred years of Catholic Christianity before the Reformation. Merton would have a strong reaction against this, as any Daoist would demur at Merton's claim that nothing of importance happened with the thought of Zhuangzi until the Tang Dynasty.[21]

Having recognized all of this, we should not be too hard on Thomas Merton. In 1965, the year of the publication of *The Way of Chuang Tzu*, postmodern critique was over a decade into the future. The work that ushered in the awareness of religious and cultural presuppositions in the study of religion was Edward Said's *Orientalism,* which was published in 1979.[22] More recently, and perhaps more relevant to Merton's situation is Jane Naomi Iwamura's "The Oriental Monk in American Popular Culture."[23] Iwamura presents the image of "the Oriental Monk" through news media and film (e.g. the Dalai Lama, Kwai Chang Caine, and Mr. Miagi) as a gentle image that serves as a salve for the sores of modern America: materialism, technocracy, and imperialism. It expresses "disillusionment with Western frameworks, and the hope and fears attached with alternative spiritualities of the East."[24] While Merton was not influenced by the popular culture about which Iwamura writes, he was weary with his own disillusionment of American

20. *The Way,* 16; *Mystics,* 54, 73, 75.

21. There was an infusion of *Zhuangzi* into *Chan* (Japanese, "Zen") Buddhism. The convergence of their ideas includes a distrust of language, the ubiquity of Dao, and the use of a dialogue of riddles, or *gong'an* (Japanese *koan*). Likewise, there is an influence of Buddhism on the tradition of *Zhuangzi* (not on the oldest chapters, which predate Buddhism in China by two or three hundred years); see Victor Mair, "The *Zhuangzi* and Its Impact," in *Daoism Handbook,* edited by Livia Kohn (Leiden: Brill, 2000), 30-52.

22. Edward Said, *Orientalism* (New York: Vintage Books, 1979).

23. Jane Naomi Iwamura, "The Oriental Monk in American Popular Culture," in *Religion and Popular Culture in America,* revised edition, edited by Bruce David Forbes and Jeffrey H. Mahan (Berkeley: University of California Press, 2005), 25-43.

24. "The Oriental Monk," 37.

life, the nuclear threat, and Cistercian life.

For example, as he studied the Cistercian life in his office as master of novices from 1955-1965, he noted that the life at Gethsemani in his day lacked the simplicity of an earlier era; Gethsemani was "too crowded, too busy, and too successful."[25] At the same time, he was troubled as he saw so many of his confreres leave the monastic life in such numbers that it was labeled the "Dropout Phenomenon."[26] After reading Iwamura, one may see a tendency in Merton's interest in the East to operate as a salve for his own wounds. In "the Oriental Monk"—in this case, Zhuangzi—Merton imagined an ideal. Zhuangzi presented Merton with the way his monastic life should be.

As with postmodern critique, in 1965, Daoist studies were just maturing and had not yet arrived in any substantial way in the West. Only in the year of Merton's death, 1968, did Westerners organize the first international conference on Daoism attended by Joseph Needham, Nathan Sivin, Kristofer Schipper, and Anna Seidel.[27] In early twentieth century China, the traditional Confucian scholar was raised to believe that Buddhism and Daoism were superstitions and of no interest. As late as 1911, the polymath Liu Shipei freed himself from this myopia and peeked into the Daoist canon. In the West, the lone student of Daoism was Henri Maspero (1883-1945), whose work was published only after his death in 1950. Much later, Schipper and Seidel were the first to make ongoing contributions to the West's understanding of Daoism. Still, it was up to a Chinese scholar, Qing Xitai, to write the first comprehensive history of Daoism up to the twentieth century over the years of 1988-1995 (now available in English). In America, there was virtually no substantial knowledge of Daoism before the 1980s. Livia Kohn opened the world of Daoism to the English speaking world with her rich encyclopedia, the *Daoism Handbook*,

---

25. *Christian Contemplation*, 37; Michael Mott, *The Seven Mountains of Thomas Merton* (Boston: Houghton Mifflin Company, 1984), 337-468.

26. *Seven Mountains*, 388.

27. Timothy H. Barrett, "Daoism: A History of a Study," in *Encyclopedia of Religion*, second edition, edited by Lindsay Jones (New York: MacMillan, 2005), 2214; Kristofer Schipper remarked that Mircea Eliade attended, as well, "Between Eternity and Modernity: Daoism and its Reinventions in the 20th Century, An International Symposium sponsored by the Fairbank Center and the Ecole Française d'Extrême-Orient" (Cambridge: Harvard University, June 13-15, 2006).

published in 2000.[28] Yet even today, the academy is slow to catch the excitement of this rich tradition. The disinterest could be due, in part, to scholars of Daoist studies not opening the relevance of the religion to the larger interests of the academy, as Buddhism and Hinduism have done.[29]

For these reasons, we must not exaggerate Merton's understanding of Daoism or, to a lesser degree, his understanding of Zhuangzi.[30] He was reading through a number of filters in his own context—disillusionment, Christianity, Zen, and a skewed view of Daoism—while knowing too little of the context of the *Zhuangzi*.[31] It would be unfair to judge Merton's work solely on our current knowledge of Daoism and religious studies. To do so would be like judging the computers of the 1960s to those of today. They simply do not compare. Nonetheless, these two lines cast a shadow over what Merton accomplished in *The Way of Chuang Tzu.*

MERTON'S FIVE YEARS OF MEDITATION

The third line is Merton's reference to *The Way of Chuang Tzu* as being the fruit of "five years of reading, study, annotation, and meditation."[32] His audience should not think that this was all Merton was doing in his monastery from about 1960 to 1965. As Merton writes himself:

> In the contemplative life one imagines that one would spend all the time absorbed in contemplation, but alas this is not the case. There are always innumerable things to be done and obstacles to getting them done, and large and small troubles.[33]

---

28. "Daoism: A History," 2212-2216.

29. Stephen R. Bokencamp, comments at the AAR Proceedings of "Ritual, Temple, and Power," Philadelphia, PA, November 19, 2005.

30. I think Ekman Tam's book, *Christian Contemplation*, makes this exaggeration. Nonetheless, it is a fine study of the movements of Thomas Merton's inner, contemplative life. I learned much from it.

31. See Francis X. Clooney, *Seeing through Texts: Doing Theology among the Srivaisnavas of South India* (Albany, NY: State University of New York Press) for the importance of the relationship between a text and its context.

32. *The Way,* 9.

33. Thomas Merton, *The Hidden Ground of Love: Letters of Thomas Merton on Religious Experience and Social Concerns,* selected and edited by William H. Shannon (New York: Farrar, Straus, Giroux, 1985), 39.

Of the things that were done, one can note the incredible publication of many books, articles, and pamphlets.[34]

His "obstacles" and "large and small troubles" are nearly as
numerous. For the sake of brevity, I will simply list some of them
with little explanation. There was the well-known wrestling with
Abbot James Fox over a life of solitude. The volume of his business
correspondence increased due to his agent, Naomi Burton, leaving
Curtis Brown Literary Agency in December 1959 and Merton attempting to be his own literary agent. In addition, he maintained
several other wide circles of correspondence. Editors from news-
papers and journals were constantly asking him for articles: "Great
God, what have I done to make everyone believe I secrete articles
like perspiration!"[35] He struggled with his superiors over censorship
of his position on nuclear war and social justice. He was somewhat
of a hypochondriac, and suffered from: arm pains, stomach trouble,
breathlessness, and a skin disease on his hands in the fall of 1964.
These years witnessed dramatic change at Gethsemani both in the
physical plant and in its spiritual life, most markedly the use of the
vernacular instead of Latin in its liturgies. In the fall of 1964 he
had many meetings and many visitors. The most difficult of these
was the meeting of Cistercian abbots and novice masters in October
1964.[36] Still, with all of this going on, "[m]ost of his day was spent
saying the offices and teaching his novices."[37]

Yet during his interaction with the *Zhuangzi* between 1960
and 1965, he also found reasons to be at peace due to eremitical
permissions and perhaps due to the influence of Zhuangzi.[38] In
December of 1960, Merton was spending hours at his hermitage.
Years later, the abbot permitted him his first full day in his her-

34. *The Thomas Merton Encyclopedia*, vii-viii: *The Solitary Life, Spiritual
Direction and Meditation, Disputed Questions, The Wisdom of the Desert, God is
My Life, The Ox Mountain Parable of Meng Tzu, The Behavior of Titans, The New
Man, New Seeds of Contemplation, Original Child Bomb, Hagia Sophia, Clement
of Alexandria, Loretto and Gethsemani, A Thomas Merton Reader, Breathrough
to Peace, What Think You of Carmel?, Life and Holiness, Emblems of a Season
of Fury, The Solitary Life: A Letter of Guigo, Seeds of Destruction, Come to the
Mountain, La Révolution Noire, Gandhi on Nonviolence, Seasons of Celebration,
Monastic Life at Gethsemani, The Way of Chuang Tzu.*
35. Merton as quoted in *The Seven Mountains of Thomas Merton* (Boston:
Houghton Mifflin Co., 1986), 354.
36. *Seven Mountains*, 337-468.
37. *Seven Mountains*, 371.
38. See *Christian Contemplation*.

mitage on December 16, 1964.[39] By the spring of 1965, it looked as if Merton would be able to pursue full-time eremitical life. At last, he began to accept himself and find a sense of contentment and happiness.[40]

Having reviewed Thomas Merton's liabilities in *The Way of Chuang Tzu,* the reader should note that Merton's work on Zhuangzi has received professional recognition. The sinologist, John C. H. Wu, his "chief abettor and accomplice" to whom Merton dedicates *The Way of Chuang Tzu,* responded to Merton upon reading the work:

> I have come to the conclusion that you and Chuang Tzu are one. It is Chuang Tzu himself who writes his thoughts in the English of Thomas Merton. You are a true man of the Tao, just as he is.[41]

As Merton's mentor on the book, John Wu had a stake in the book's success, so his word of affirmation on the quality of the book is not enough to assume that Merton made a significant accomplishment.[42] For a second opinion, one need look no further than Burton Watson, whose 1968 complete translation of the *Zhuangzi* is still an authoritative rendering of the *Zhuangzi* tradition. He writes:

> Readers interested in the literary quality of the text should also look at the 'imitations' of passages in the *Chuang Tzu* prepared by Thomas Merton. . . . They give a fine sense of the liveliness and poetry of Chuang Tzu's style, and are actually almost as close to the original as the translations upon which they are based.[43]

In addition, it is simply incredible that decades after its publication, *The Way of Chuang Tzu* appears in bibliographies of scholarly works on the text.[44]

---

39. *Seven Mountains,* 352 and 408.

40. *Seven Mountains,* 410-411.

41. *Hidden Ground,* 631.

42. In addition, Wu admired Merton nearly to the point of adoration, so his judgment is hardly unbiased; Lucien Miller, "The Thomas Merton—John C. H. Wu Letters: The Lord as Postman," The Merton Annual 19 (2006): 148.

43. Burton Watson, *The Complete Works of Chuang Tzu* (New York: Columbia University Press, 1968), 28.

44. For example, Wu Kuang-ming, *The Butterfly as Companion: Meditations on the First Three Chapters of the Chuang Tzu* (Albany: State University of New

What Merton did in this little book was not only of literary interest, but also of a broader, spiritual interest. He made a difficult thinker like Zhuangzi available and relevant to primarily lay, Christian audiences. In Merton, readers found a dependable interpreter of Eastern thought in the 1960s, when the American spiritual landscape was being flooded by pop-wisdom from China, Japan, and India. Authors presenting many of these religions suggested that readers replace the traditional religions of the West, and embrace Eastern alternatives. Merton showed readers that they need not be overly critical of their own tradition and abandon it for greener religious pastures. A person could read someone like Zhuangzi deeply and not have the need to jump ship to become a Daoist. Merton, by example, demonstrated the spiritual stability that allows one to be a Christian and at the same time have an enriching experience of Daoism that, in turn, makes one a better Christian.

THE CRAFTSMAN, COOK DING

Though the *Zhuangzi* is divided into sections and chapters and has undergone redaction, taken as a whole, it is a coherent work expressing several themes. One of the major themes is *ziran* (spontaneity or, literally, "self-ly" or "self-so"). It means being or operating out of that aspect of oneself that is the true imprint of the Dao. *Ziran* allows one to be in harmony with all things, like the Dao itself, which then brings to one's life a sense of strength and ease. Other themes include the use of language to point to the Dao, without exactly signifying it, the nature of knowing, non-action (*wu-wei*), the man of Dao, and the way of Dao. Merton and others have written on these themes.[45]

I would like to examine another theme in *The Way of Chuang Tzu*, not fully explored in Merton—Zhuangzi's value of skillfulness. Merton selected several paragons of skillfulness from Zhuangzi in the following chapters: "Cutting up an Ox," "Duke Hwan and the

York Press, 1990); *Essays on Skepticism, Relativism, and Ethics in the Zhuangzi*, edited by Paul Kjellberg and Philip J. Ivanhoe (Albany: SUNY Press, 1996); *Zhuangzi*, translated and introduced by Hyun Höchsmann and Yang Guorong (New York: Pearson/Longman, 2007) over forty years after the publication of *The Way of Chuang Tzu*!

45. See Cyrus Lee, "Thomas Merton and His Translation of Chuang Tzu," in *Chinese Culture* 25 (3, September 1984): 31-42; Ekman P. C. Tam, *Christian Contemplation and Chinese Zen-Taoism: A Study of Thomas Merton's Writings* (Hong Kong: Tao Fong Shan Christian Centre, 2002).

Wheelwright," "The Woodcarver," and "When the Shoe Fits." It is not enough to see sagehood in the craftsmen, but one must go further to take seriously the craftsman image presented in the *Zhuangzi.* Skill itself is something worth cultivating for Zhuangzi.[46]

Skill is a broad term that can be applied to a great number of activities. Skill is reflected in actions that:

> reflect the mastering of techniques that overcome diffi-
> culties inherent in the activity. Moreover, they reflect the
> particular standards of excellence the activity exemplifies.
> Finally, they can be evaluated accurately only by people
> who have considerable experience with the activity.[47]

Skill reflects a certain kind of knowing, much different from doc-trinal knowledge promulgated by language. Knowledge communi-cated by language is too provisional, too static, and too difficult to adapt to the variety of situations one experiences in life. Language can only indicate reality, but not tell exactly what is there.[48] Skill on the other hand is "an adaptive responsiveness to change" and "a unification of the physical and mental."[49] It is a knowing that is intuitive, not intellectual.

Furthermore, the *Zhuangzi* prefers types of skills that are aes-thetically pleasing, significant, bodily, and benign.[50] For example, while Merton is a skilled writer and poet, his skill is not the type showcased by Zhuangzi. Merton's work is aesthetically pleasing, but it does not involve the body. More specifically, in the case of Cook Ding in "Cutting Up An Ox"—from the Inner Chapters—what is pleasing and revealing of the Dao is his performance of the skill.[51] The result, pieces of meat cut from a whole ox, can only indicate the earlier presence of the skill. In Merton's case, the skill is concealed. Our only evidence of the skill is what we read. Skill is present but it is of a different kind than that demonstrated by Cook Ding. It is to Cook Ding we now turn.

---

46. "Zhuangzi's Understanding of Skillfulness," 154-182.
47. "Zhuangzi's Understanding of Skillfulness," 164.
48. Philip J. Ivanhoe, "Zhuangzi on Skepticism, Skill, and the Ineffable Dao," in the *Journal of the American Academy of Religion* 61 (1993): 639-654.
49. "Zhuangzi's Understanding of Skillfulness," 165.
50. Philip J. Ivanhoe, "Was Zhuangzi a Relativist?" in *Essays on Relativism, Skepticism, and Ethics in the Zhuangzi,* edited by Paul Kjellberg and Philip J. Ivanhoe (Albany, NY: State University of New York Press).
51. "Zhuangzi's Understanding of Skillfulness," 167-171.

Cook Ding

Cook Ding is the affectionate name given to the butcher in Zhuang-zi's chapter entitled by Merton, "Cutting up an Ox:"[52]

Prince Wen Hui's cook
Was cutting up an ox.
Out went a hand,
Down went a shoulder,
He planted a foot,
He pressed with a knee,
The ox fell apart
With a whisper,
The bright cleaver murmured
Like a gentle wind.
Rhythm! Timing!
Like a sacred dance,
Like "The Mulberry Grove,"
Like ancient harmonies!

"Good work!" the Prince exclaimed,
"Your method is faultless!"
"Method?" said the cook
Laying aside his cleaver,
"What I follow is Tao
Beyond all methods!"

"When I first began
To cut up oxen
I would see before me
The whole ox
All in one mass.

"After three years
I no longer saw this mass.
I saw the distinctions.

"But now, I see nothing

---

52. Some scholars do not consider the character *ding* (丁) to be the name of the cook, but a rank. Philip J. Ivanhoe, "Was Zhuangzi a Relativist?" in *Essays on Relativism, Skepticism, and Ethics in the Zhuangzi*, edited by Paul Kjellberg and Philip J. Ivanhoe (Albany, NY: State University of New York Press), note 3, 211.

With my eye. My whole being
Apprehends.
My senses are idle. The spirit
Free to work without plan
Follows its own instinct
Guided by natural line,
By the secret opening, the hidden space,
My cleaver finds its own way.
I cut through no joint, chop no bone.

"A good cook needs a new chopper
Once a year—he cuts.
A poor cook needs a new one
Every month—he hacks!

"I have used this same cleaver
Nineteen years.
It has cut up
A thousand oxen.
Its edge is as keen
As if newly sharpened.

"There are spaces in the joints;
The blade is thin and keen:
When this thinness finds that space
There is all the room you need!
It goes like a breeze!
Hence I have this cleaver nineteen years
As if newly sharpened!

"True, there are sometimes
Tough joints. I feel them coming,
I slow down, I watch closely,
Hold back, barely move the blade,
And whump! The part falls away
Landing like a clod of earth.

"Then I withdraw the blade,
I stand still
And let the joy of the work
Sink in.
I clean the blade

And put it away."

Prince Wen Hui said,
"This is it! My cook has shown me
How I ought to live
My own life."[53]

Cook Ding's movements are aesthetically pleasing: "Like a gentle wind./ Rhythm! Timing!/ Like a Sacred dance/ . . . . Like ancient harmonies!" The beauty of the movements reveals something of the beauty of the Dao. Words cannot communicate this or how to do it. There is a "knack" to it that one has to feel for oneself in order to really get it. The feeling is in the body, not in perception from the eyes: "But now, I see nothing/ With my eye. My whole being/ Apprehends./ My senses are idle." The body serves, then, as a medium for knowing. In the case of Daoism, it is a means of knowing the Dao, the "Way," that is, the way to live: "This is it!/ My cook has shown me/ How I ought to live/ My own life." Simple intellection of moral codes is not enough for Zhuangzi. Life changes too quickly and situations are too numerous to think much about responding to it. Paragons like Cook Ding reveal that the knowledge of how to live a good life can be discovered in the body through a skill.

Once the skill is attained, there is no method to it: "What I follow is Tao/ Beyond all methods!" Skills themselves, however, are not attained spontaneously, but require training and a specific method. Cutting up an ox is not like cutting up a piece of wood.[54] Furthermore, attaining a skill requires time and assiduous labor: "I have used this same cleaver/ Nineteen years./ It has cut up/ A thousand oxen." One should note that Cook Ding and his high level of skill have been his for nineteen years, but the training to get him there took at least as long, probably longer.[55]

One should cultivate skill, but doing something skillfully is only penultimate to Zhuangzi's ultimate spiritual state. The fruit of perfected skill is the possession of ability beyond what is normally

53. *The Way*, 45-47.
54. But learning how to carve wood can also be a means towards following the Dao. See "The Woodcarver" in *The Way*, 110-111.
55. Robert Eno, "Cook Ding's Dao and The Limits of Philosophy." In *Essays on Relativism, Skepticism, and Ethics in the Zhuangzi*, edited by Paul Kjellberg and Philip J. Ivanhoe (Albany, NY: State University of New York Press, 1996), 127-151.

attained by humans. It allows for the realization of cosmic power and the expression of spiritual activity.[56] The realization and expression is accompanied by a certain detachment from the fruits of one's work. Instead, the pleasure is found in the work itself. This describes the ultimate spiritual state found through skill: "tranquility, easy movement; power without effort; attentive adaptation to changing externals; unification of the mental and physical; pleasurable fulfillment that is present at any moment; and harmonious joyful accommodation to the rhythms of a larger whole."[57] Philip J. Ivanhoe writes:

> People who grasp the Way and embody it are able to move through life with profoundly enhanced power and ease; like the edge of Cook Ding's chopper, they remain keen and unscathed while the rest of us become blunted and dulled in the course of life.[58]

What attracted Merton to the kind of skill presented in passages like "Cutting Up An Ox"? One may be tempted to look to Merton's life as a contemplative writer or his interest in photography, drawing, or calligraphy, but in these Merton always struggled with the risk of self-expression. He wanted to transcend himself in his work. Self-expression most often falls under the auspices of art, rather than craftsmanship. For example, concerning his writing, Michael Mott notes:

> Writing in the manner he did may have made him vulnerable; it also intensified the struggle with self-consciousness. Where he felt the gains were concern, commitment, even fear, his work had brought him nothing of the self-forgetfulness that Gabriel Marcel, Victor Hammer, and others described in a craftsman's application to his labor.[59]

Or in the case of his calligraphy:

---

56. *De* (德 "virtue or power") and *shen* (神 "spirit") respectively.
57. "Zhuangzi's Understanding of Skillfulness," 176.
58. "Zhuangzi on Skepticism," 644.
59. *Seven Mountains,* 366. Victor Hammer was an Austrian born artist and a friend to Merton. His picture of a woman and child, Merton called *Hagia Sophia* and composed a poem about it by the same name. William H. Shannon, Christine M. Bochen, and Patrick O'Connell, *The Thomas Merton Encyclopedia* (Maryknoll, NY: Orbis Books, 2002), 193.

In the summer of 1964 there was talk of an exhibition of
Merton's calligraphies. His excitement was only a little
spoiled by the anxiety of wondering what Victor Hammer would think, the fear that Hammer would see this as
pretension and an example of self-expression, not serious
craftsmanship.[60]

Furthermore, these activities involve the body less than the crafts
portrayed in the *Zhuangzi*. A writer or calligrapher sits at his or
her desk with only a nominal use of the body. Cook Ding uses his
whole body: "Out went a hand,/ Down went a shoulder,/ He planted
a foot,/ He pressed with a knee."

The type of craftsman in the *Zhuangzi* present in Merton's life is
the Shaker. Merton's interest in Zhuangzi is contemporaneous with
his interest in the Shakers.[61] When Merton visited the abandoned
Shaker colony known as Shakertown, Pleasantville, or Shawnee
in Kentucky in 1959, he was struck by what the craftsmanship
revealed:

> Merton walked in the large bare, rooms, the sunlight filter-
> ing in, feeling exhilarated. Everything stressed plainness—
> a more than Cistercian plainness, which should have been
> cold, which should have left him chill with a sense of 'the
> cold and cerebral,' and which had the opposite effect.
> Some quality of the hand-worked wood and the propor-
> tions created an atmosphere that was, at the same time,
> warm, human—and yet visionary, clear, sane, supernatural.
> Merton found himself thinking of [William] Blake, then of
> what Victor Hammer had said about the craftsman losing
> himself and finding himself in a sense of work—a sense few
> who talked so much of 'creativity' and 'self-expression'
> ever came to know.[62]

Merton sensed a self-transcendence in the Shaker work that sparked
a desire to leave himself behind, to go to that place where the self
is abandoned in favor of an identification with God.

On another trip to Shakertown in 1962, he remarked: "How

60. *Seven Mountains*, 400.

61. For a fuller treatment of Merton's attraction to the Shakers, see Thomas
Merton, *Seeking Paradise: The Spirit of the Shakers*, introduced and edited by
Paul M. Pearson (Maryknoll, NY: Orbis Books, 2003).

62. *Seven Mountains*, 343.

the blank side of a frame house can be so completely beautiful I cannot imagine. A completely miraculous achievement of forms."[63] The truth and beauty revealed in the craftsmanship escaped words, which for Merton was quite something:

> their consummate perfection, their extraordinary unselfcon- scious beauty and simplicity. There is, in the work of the Shakers, a beauty that is unrivaled because of its genuine spiritual purity—a quality for which there is no adequate explanation.[64]

The Shakers affirmed Merton's interest in the skill found in the *Zhuangzi,* but the Shakers were closer to him than the tradition of ancient China. As Christians, the Shakers were spiritually proxi- mate, and with Shakertown only about sixty miles away, they were geographically proximate. Presenting Zhuangzi to his novices may have raised some eyebrows with his superiors, but the value of skill was clearly present and more accessible in the Shakers, who he felt were the kin of the early Cistercians:

> To me the Shakers are of a very great significance, besides being something of a mystery, by their wonderful integra- tion of the spiritual and the physical in their work. There is no question in my mind that one of the finest and most genuine religious expressions of the nineteenth century is in the silent eloquence of Shaker craftsmanship. I am deeply interested in the thought that a hundred years ago our two communities were so close together, so similar, somehow, in ideals, and yet evidently had no contact with one another.[65]

And:

> The Shakers, like the first Cistercians, while giving no conscious thought to the *beauty* of their work, sought to build only honest buildings and to make honest and sturdy pieces of furniture. In doing so, they produced buildings and furniture of extraordinary, unforgettable beauty.[66]

---

63. Merton as quoted in *Seven Mountains*, 372.
64. Thomas Merton, *Mystics and Zen Masters* (New York: Farrar, Straus, Giroux, 1967), 196.
65. *Hidden Ground*, 32.
66. *Mystics*, 197-198.

Note that Merton refers to the "Cistercians of a hundred years ago" and the "first Cistercians" in reference to Shaker craftsmanship. He felt that the Cistercians of his day lost "it," that is, the cosmic dimension of work that connects one physically to the Spirit of God: "The Shakers saw . . . that their work was a cooperation in the same will that framed and governs the cosmos . . . ."[67]

Perhaps this sentence is the single insight that connects Merton to Zhuangzi with regards to the skill stories. Merton saw in the Shakers and in Zhuangzi that through the body and through honest, skillful work one can find tranquil insight into God or the Way that, in turn, shapes one's very being. Merton felt that this way was missing in the Cistercians and in his life, yet he could recognize it. He saw it in the flashing blade of Cook Ding and he saw it in the walls and furniture of the Shakers. Ironically, he could not see it in himself. Yet it had to be there for him to recognize it. Only a spiritual master can discern mastery.

67. *Hidden Ground*, 37-38. Also, "The simplicity and austerity demanded by their way of life enabled an unconscious spiritual purity to manifest itself in full clarity. Shaker handicrafts are then a real *epiphany of logoi*." Thomas Merton, *Ascetical and Mystical Theology: An Introduction to Christian Mysticism From the Apostolic Father to the Council of Trent*, 64: Mimeographed copy of lectures given at the Abbey of Gethsemani in the archives of the Thomas Merton Center, Bellarmine University, Louisville, KY, as quoted in Paul M. Pearson, "Seeking Paradise: Thomas Merton and the Shakers," in Thomas Merton, *Seeking Paradise: The Spirit of the Shakers*, introduced and edited by Paul M. Pearson (Maryknoll, NY: Orbis Books, 2003), 40.

ECOLOGICAL WISDOM
IN MERTON'S *CHUANG TZU*[1]

Donald P. St. John

INTRODUCTION

If one word captures Merton's estimate of the Taoist/Daoist philosopher Chuang Tzu, it is "wisdom." Writing to John C. Wu,
Merton confesses that he has become "more and more struck by
the profundity of his thought." The monk considers him "one of the
great wise men." His wisdom "has a marvelous wholeness" which
is simple but also "utterly profound."[2] It is this "marvelous wholeness," that links this Taoist philosopher to Merton's own thought
and to ecological philosophy. Furthermore, Merton believed that
God had "manifested His wisdom so simply and so strikingly in
the early Chinese sages." Christians must have the humility "to
learn and learn much, perhaps to acquire a whole new orientation
of thought . . . from the ancient wisdoms which were fulfilled in
Christ." Encountering and learning from these wisdoms can lead
Christians to strive earnestly for "spiritual wisdom" and a "higher
and deeper fulfillment" demanded by Christ.[3]

Merton certainly found a deep resonance between his beloved
Sophia and Tao. In his now famous letter to artist Victor Hammer,
Merton notes that Sophia as the Wisdom of God "is also the Tao, the
nameless pivot of all being and nature, the center and meaning of all."
Like Tao, Sophia is the "feminine principle in the universe . . . the
inexhaustible source of creative realization of the Father's glory in
the world and is in fact the manifestation of that glory." Personified

---

1. This is a substantially altered version of an earlier article, "Merton's
Chuang Tzu: An Ecological Reading," *Teilhard Studies* No. 37 (Winter/Spring
1999), 21-36. Not only does ecosophy play a more important role in this paper,
but it hopefully benefits from a decade of research on Merton, Chuang Tzu and
environmental philosophy.

2. Thomas Merton, *The Hidden Ground of Love*, William H. Shannon, editor (1985), 613.

3. *Ibid.,* 613.

she is a "feminine child" who plays in the world.[4]

Chuang Tzu himself displays the cosmic humility and playfulness of one who is aware of his place within the great mystery of the Way. (Chinese landscape paintings capture something of this spirit.) His wisdom "manifests itself everywhere by a Franciscan simplicity and connaturality with all living creatures." In fact, "Half of the 'characters' who are brought before us to speak the mind of Chuang Tzu are animals—birds, fishes, frogs, and so on."[5] This signifies, for Merton, Chuang Tzu's nostalgia for "the primordial climate of paradise."[6] Paradise, under the gentle guiding presence of Tao/Dao, is characterized by a state of peace and harmony that is at once individual, social, and ecological.

This paradise "is still ours, but we do not know it," says Merton, "since the effect of life in society is to complicate and confuse our existence, making us forget who we really are by causing us to be obsessed with what we are not."[7] Both Merton and Chuang Tzu were very critical of those social forces that work against the full flourishing of and harmony between humans and the natural world. However, they both felt that we are capable, when freed from alienating social conventions, of acting "in perfect harmony with the whole."[8] The fundamental and first task, therefore, towards regaining a spiritual sanity is to shake off the pathologies that distort our view of reality. Philip Ivanhoe notes that Chuang Tzu's "mind-bending, unsettling, exhilarating, and always amusing stories are designed as cognitive therapy, a means of freeing the mind and self."[9]

This paper takes seriously Merton's invitation to learn from Chuang Tzu's wisdom—which it approaches as an ecological

4. Thomas Merton, *Witness to Freedom: The Letters of Thomas Merton in Times of Crises,* William H. Shannon, editor (New York: Farrar, Straus, Giroux, 1994), 4. A solid study of Tao and Te especially with relation to its feminine imagery is Ellen Marie Chen, *The Tao Te Ching: A New Translation With Commentary.* St. Paul: Paragon House Publishers, 1989. For Sophia in Merton see the splendid study by Christopher Pramuk, *Sophia: The Hidden Christ of Thomas Merton.* Collegeville, MN: Liturgical Press, 2009.

5. Thomas Merton, *The Way of Chuang Tzu* (New York: New Directions Press, 1965), 27.

6. *Ibid.,* 27.

7. *Ibid.,* 27.

8. *Ibid.,* 28.

9. Karen L. Carr and Philip J. Ivanhoe, *The Sense of Antirationalism:The Religious Thought of Zhuangzi and Kierkegaard* (Lexington, KY: Carr & Ivanhoe, 2010), 103.

wisdom, an eco-sophy. In 1973, Arne Naess, a Norwegian ecophilosopher and father of the "deep ecology" movement, coined the term *Ecosophy* to describe "a philosophy of ecological harmony or equilibrium . . . philosophy as a kind of *sofia* [wisdom]."[10] We use the term Ecosophy to refer to both the Wisdom (*sophia*) of the Earth Home (*oikos*) and the human wisdom that seeks to know and live harmoniously with Earth Wisdom.[11] This provides a bridge to Christian theology's *Sophia* and *Logos* and Taoist philosophy's *Dao/Tao* and *Tian/T'ien* (Nature, Heaven). Wisdom is manifest in and inseparable from the Earth's ecological functioning. In this context, one might say that the vocation of humankind as a self-conscious and technologically enhanced part of the whole is to blend wisdom and action, *theoria* and *praxis*, into a way (*dao/tao*) that is attuned to and accords with the Great Harmony that is also the Great Transformation.

My five ecosophical meditations/reflections on Merton's "readings" of the *Chuang Tzu* must of necessity be brief and the texts selective. They share Merton's conviction that the message and wisdom of Chuang Tzu is as relevant today as it was 2,300 years ago—in some ways, even more relevant.[12] It is certainly relevant to those who believe that the root (*radix*) of our current situation goes much deeper than technological or economic "fixes" alone can reach. The ecological crisis forces us to ask once again radical (*radix*) questions: who are we and what is our place as a species, what should our relationship be with other members of the earth community, the earth, and the cosmos; where lies the source of the creativity, energy, and wisdom needed to turn ourselves around; what are the obstacles that stand in the way of such a liberating and transforming experience? As we move back and forth between the sage's musings and our own questions we will hear a third voice in the background. It is a tribute to his reading of Chuang Tzu from the

---

10. Cited in Hwa Yol Jung, *The Way of Ecopiey: Essays in Transversal Geophilosophy* (New York: Global Scholarly Publications, 2009), 99.

11. Ecology, on the other hand, refers to the scientific study (*logos*) of organisms and their relations to one another (*oikos*) and their environment. As important as it is, ecology and scientific findings cannot substitute for an ecological wisdom or ethics. Nor can environmentalism as long as it is wedded to an anthropocentric outlook whose primary concern is the sustainability of humans without radically questioning the assumptions that created the problem.

12. "How modern he is! It has taken centuries to rediscover a little of what has been forgotten since Chuang Tzu." *Witness*, 616

depths of his own spirituality that it is hard at times to know where Chuang Tzu's thought stops and Thomas Merton's begins.

MEDITATION ONE

Merton captures something of Chuang Tzu's therapeutic approach in the selection he calls, "Great and Small." Merton's selection picks up on a lecture in-progress by the Overlord of the Northern Sea to the Earl of the Yellow River at the beginning of "Autumn Floods" (Chapter 17). The Earl was full of arrogance. His self-importance was as swollen as his river until he reached its mouth and looked out upon the Northern Sea. Awestruck, he admits to feeling like a narrow Confucianist who suddenly sees the true Way (*Dao/Tao*). The Overlord agrees, noting that trying to tell a scholar who is "bound by his doctrine" about the Way is like telling a frog at the bottom of a well about the sea ("he's stuck in his little space") or describing ice to an insect of the summer ("confined by its season").[13]

Wisdom, then, begins with an expansion of one's mental horizons, a realization of the limited nature of one's knowledge and a humble acceptance of one's place in the universe—as an individual or species. Puncturing the anthropocentric balloon, the Overlord states, "When we designate the number of things there are in existence, we refer to them in terms of myriads, but man occupies only one place among them. . . . In comparison with the myriad things, would he not resemble the tip of a downy hair on a horse's body?"[14]

The Overlord continues his speech in Merton's section, "Great and Small":

When we look at things in the light of Tao,
Nothing is best, nothing is worst.
Each thing, seen in its own light,
Stands out in its own way.
It can seem "better"
Than what is compared with it
On its own terms.
But seen in the light of the whole,

13. Victor H. Mair, *Wandering on the Way: Early Taoist Tales and Parables of Chuang Tzu* (Honolulu: U. of Hawaii Press, 1997), 153.
14. *Ibid.*, 153-154.

No one thing stands out as "better" (87).[15]

In the complex world of nature or "the ten thousand things," all beings are bound to all other beings in an incredibly complex web of relationships, interconnected on various levels and in a variety of contexts. A predator is not better than its prey or microbes worse than eagles. Diversity is essential but all are equal in that Tao is their source and their unity.

If, however, you *measure* differences in order to draw comparisons, problems arise. If you measure size and label one thing "great" because it is bigger or more important than something else, then "there is nothing that is not 'great,'" claims Chuang Tzu. If you label "small" what is smaller than something else, then "there is nothing that is not 'small.'" Thus, since beings in the visible universe vary so dramatically in size, what is "small" in one comparison (bush to an oak) is large in another (bush to a blade of grass). Furthermore, whether something is deemed "small" or "great" depends on who or what is doing the judging. An elephant might judge a hyena "small" whereas a termite might consider it "large." "So the whole cosmos is a grain of rice,/And the tip of a hair/Is as big as a mountain —/Such is the relative view" (87).

Instead of comparing beings or ranking them according to some arbitrary standard, Chuang Tzu suggests that humans ought to see each "in its own light" and appreciate its uniqueness. As part of the whole, each being has its individual talents, uses, gifts, and capacities. Each niche and positive role comes, of course, with limitations.

> You can break down walls with battering rams,
> But you cannot stop holes with them.
> All things have different uses.
> Fine horses can travel a hundred miles a day,
> But they cannot catch mice
> Like terriers or weasels:
> All creatures have gifts of their own.
> The white horned owl can catch fleas at midnight

---

15. Subsequent quotations from Merton's "readings" themselves will be referenced simply by page number in the text. For further readings on equality in nature and relativity in knowledge, see "The Breath of Nature" (38-39), "Great Knowledge" (40-41), and "The Pivot" (42-43), all from the important second chapter of the *Chuang Tzu*.

And distinguish the tip of a hair,
But in bright day it stares, helpless,
And cannot even see a mountain.
All things have varying capacities (87-88).

On the other hand, the anthropocentric approach selects one or
two characteristics allegedly unique to or abundant in the human
species, declares them superior to all other qualities, uses them to
rank other creatures and thereby justifies their oppression. Thus,
the unique gifts and capacities that each species or being possesses
are either ignored or trivialized. This is not science but a justification for a bias akin to racism or sexism.[16] Humans select language
or reason then declare themselves superior to chimpanzees who
are superior to dogs who are superior to birds, and so on. But, of
course, any species can win at that game—but they don't play it
(which might be a mark of *their* superior wisdom). Chuang Tzu
might want to point out that if bats were constructing a hierarchy
of abilities by which to rank species, we would end up near the
bottom. We cannot fly at night, have no inbuilt radar and cannot
catch our food on the wing.

The last section of "Great and Small" could well be addressing the question: "What would happen to this complex natural
world filled with beings of various abilities if they adopted human
attitudes?" Typical of Chuang Tzu, he answers our hypothetical
question by creating a series of short exchanges among some
colorful creatures. We meet a "one-legged dragon" who is "jealous of the centipede." The dragon exhibits a humanlike desire to
compare abilities when he asks the centipede: "'I manage my one
leg with difficulty:/ How can you manage a hundred?'" The dragon
implies that the ability to "manage" something is worthwhile and
a legitimate power, reflecting his own experience. However, "The
centipede replied:/ 'I do not manage them/They land all over the
place/Like drops of spit'" (89-90).

At this point one would expect Chuang Tzu to praise such notions
as *ziran* (spontaneous, natural actions) or *wu-wei* (non-action). But, of
course, these are creatures plagued by human traits. And so instead,
he has the centipede become jealous of a snake who effortlessly glides

16. The eco-feminist philosopher Karen Warren exposes the sequence of
stages leading to a justification for the domination of women and other species as
a Logic of Domination, in "The Power and the Promise of Ecological Feminism,"
Environmental Ethics, Vol. 12, No. 2 (Summer, 1990), 125-146.

along without even one leg who is himself jealous, etc.

Part of the humor of this story centers on creatures exhibiting jealousy and other traits of an ego, such as the need to favorably compare oneself with the "other" as a way to alleviate a basic insecurity rooted in the self's dependence on the other for its identity.[17] Animals and plants, on the other hand, are naturally, "spontaneously" (*ziran*) who they are. They accord with Tao and engage in effortless non-action (*wu-wei*).

MEDITATION TWO

An anthropocentric view that sees and values all in the "light of the human," so to speak, neither respects the other as Other, nor values it as an equal member of the earth community. One of the problems with this commonly accepted "truth" ("everyone knows humans are superior") is that it easily translates into action. And these actions can cause pain and death. The brief tale, "Symphony for a Seabird," illustrates what can happen when humans—even for the best of intentions—use themselves as the standard by which to judge others while ignoring the different good (*telos*) of another creature. Once upon a time, a sea bird was blown ashore and landed in a sacred precinct. "The Prince ordered a solemn reception. / Offered the sea bird wine in the sacred precinct, / Called for musicians / To play the compositions of Shun, / Slaughtered cattle to nourish it: / Dazed with symphonies, the unhappy sea bird / Died of despair" (103). What is the moral? "Water is for fish/And air for men./Natures differ, and needs with them" (104). And so, out of respect for this principle, "the wise men of old/Did not lay down/ One measure for all" (104).

Each creature, including the individual human, has its own "capacity" (*de/te*) by means of which the Way (*Dao/Tao*) stimulates individual growth and guides its harmony with others. The imposition of an external, arbitrary standard or "measure" easily distorts

---

17. This is reminiscent of Merton's lovely passage in *New Seeds of Contemplation* (New York: New Directions, 1961) that reads: "A tree gives glory to God by being a tree. . . . The more a tree is like itself, the more it is like Him. . . . No two created beings are exactly alike. And their individuality is no imperfection" (29). Then Merton goes on to contrast the illusory, private self that stands "outside" of God compared to my true self which is hidden in God (35). While Chuang Tzu does not use "self" language as we do in the west, there is a similarity between his contrasting of the social identity which takes us away from our identity as rooted in *de/te* and *Dao/Tao*.

or terminates growth, bringing suffering and even death, as in this case. Not coincidentally, given Taoism's critique of Confucianism, the sea bird in the story lands in a "sacred" precinct and becomes a victim of ritual courtesy (*li*).

Li in its more explicitly religious form is evident in the selection Merton calls, "The Sacrificial Swine." In this tale, pigs who are destined for ritual sacrifice are told by the Grand Augur (Priest and Government Official) that they should feel privileged because their special status and destiny entitles them to the best in food, drink, and living conditions. They have been blessed with a far nobler existence than other swine. However, in an unguarded moment, the Grand Augur looks at this situation through the eyes of the swine. "Of course, I suppose you would prefer to be fed with ordinary coarse feed and be left alone in your pen" (108). He wonders if they would prefer fewer honors and longer lives.

Quickly, however, he dismisses such a radical thought, perhaps frightened by this heady escape from his own epistemological confines. And so he reiterates that the swine have been chosen for a higher, nobler type of existence. But the philosophical "damage" remains. The Augur recognizes something of his own situation in that of the swine. Indeed, while he too is honored with title and position, fed well at state expense, it is likely that his own career, if not his very life, will be shortened given the volatile nature of politics. This realization only reinforces in his mind the correctness of his decision not to let the swine off the same hook. "So he decided against the pigs' point of view, and adopted his own point of view, both for himself and for the pigs also" (108). "How fortunate those swine," says Merton, "whose existence was thus ennobled by one who was at once an officer of the state and a minister of religion" (108).

Interestingly, once having taken the pig's perspective, he can't escape the fact that they share at least some common destiny. What is the significance of his quick recourse to the language of honor and sacrifice? Does he glimpse, perhaps, a common logic and rhetoric behind the "sacrifice" of humans for the good of the State and the sacrifice of animals for the good of humans? Every year tens of billions of "lower" animals are sacrificed to please the palate and allegedly advance scientific knowledge meant to increase the health and welfare of "higher," more "noble" animals. The irony, Chuang Tzu might point out, is that, in the light of our behavior towards one another (war, genocide, torture), human claims to superiority based on rational and moral superiority sound more like the self-justifying rhetoric of the Augur than the conclusions of men and women of wisdom (*sophia*). Perhaps if we start with the understanding that we are all members of one Earth Home (*oikos*), then the ritual actions (*li*) by which we celebrate and enact our kinship relations would be less exploitive, coercive, and destructive.[18] Perhaps, given the fate of the seabird and the swine, Chuang Tzu would suggest that we first use our mind-heart (*xin/hsin*) to see the world through the eyes of other creatures and bracket our discourse on human exceptionalism. Then maybe, as with the Augur, when we return to our own view point, we will ask afresh why we call farms "factories" and humans "resources"? Could looking at ourselves through the eyes of other creatures shed light on the social and personal causes behind our destructive treatment of the natural world?

MEDITATION THREE

For Chuang Tzu, we are cosmic beings first, children of Tao, siblings of the ten thousand things, equipped with the potential to both flourish as ourselves and find our place in the midst of an incredible universe. The energies (*qi*) that flow through and link together all beings are available to us for internal renewal and external movement and action in the world. Human communities that take shape under the guidance of Tao benefit from the spontaneous "virtues" of self-realized members while at the same time nurture, guide and support this unfolding in new members. They help infants and children to actualize their capacities, shape and discover their own identities both as individuals and as members of a human and earth community.[19] For Chuang Tzu, civilization was interfering with

18. One is reminded of Merton's insights into Native American religions and into the cave paintings of Paleolithic peoples. He felt that ancient Taoist thinkers were "fighting to preserve" these "immemorial modes of vision." Paleolithic art (*wen*) and ritual (*li*) were "a celebration of this awareness and of the *wholeness* of [this] communion with nature and with life." *Conjectures,* 307.

19. Although we catch brief glimpses of an utopian communalism or anarchic primitivism in the *Tao Te Ching* (chs.17, 80) and the *Chuang Tzu*, the latter leaves the details to the spontaneous workings of Tao, appropriate to the variables of time and place. Merton includes one selection reflecting this tradition in, "When Life Was Full There was No History" (76). There is a glimpse of ruling by non-ruling in "Leaving Things Alone" (70-71). Michael LaFargue uses the term "organic harmony" to capture the "good" of the working of Tao on the individual, social, and cosmic levels. *The Tao of the Tao Te Ching.* Albany: SUNY Press, 1992.

the moving in the opposite direction; it was interfering with *de/ te* and its natural unfolding while restructuring and redirecting the energies of mind and body so as to serve the external demands of political hierarchies and the needs of the growing division of labor. A system of rules and laws with rewards and punishments were aided by a new socio-cultural class represented by the Confucianists dedicated to the task of intentionally replacing the "natural" virtues and moral sentiments with ones geared to support the web of social relations. (See "When Life Was Full There Was No History," 76 and Chapters 18, 38, 51 of the *Daodejing/Tao te Ching*.)

The fate of an old tree provides Chuang Tzu with a metaphor for the fate of humans at the hands of social carpenters—or managers of human "resources." This is captured in a section that is edited and creatively re-presented by Merton as "The Five Enemies."

> With wood from a hundred-year-old tree
> They made sacrificial vessels,
> Covered with green and yellow designs.
> The wood that was cut away
> Lies unused in the ditch.
> If we compare the sacrificial vessels with the wood in the ditch
> We find them to differ in appearance:
> One is more beautiful than the other
> Yet they are equal in this: both have lost their original nature (78).

The irony of this is not lost to Merton, as his wording indicates. Here, again, we have the natural being destroyed by representatives of the cultural. Ironically, those most highly trained in the virtue of reverence prove insensitive to and irreverent towards the sacredness of the old tree that stands in front of them.[20] The Taoists criticized a strictly humanistic concept of "virtue" contrasting it with a spontaneous (*ziran*) virtue (*te/de*) springing naturally from the cosmic Tao and hence sensitive also to the "ten thousand things."

Not only will the vessels be set aside from natural objects and defined as "holy" but also as "beautiful," bearing "green and yel-

---

20. Early Taoists would say that when, due to civilization, humankind lost spontaneous virtue (*de/te*) (see "When Life Was Full . . ." Merton (76)), then the Confucianists came along teaching a self-conscious virtue very narrow in vision and application. Hence, we also get "sacrificial" vessels that will hold the blood of animals (perhaps from a few of the swine from the last story). Chuang Tzu might protest that the real Power (*de/te*) and beauty is in the living tree.

low designs" on the finely carved contours. According to cultural conventions (*wen*), there is a great difference between the painted, shaped vessels which had human labor added to them and the chips and chunks in the ditch. But, Chuang Tzu will have none of this. Drawing attention to the appearances of different pieces of wood ignores their tragic similarity. That both vessels and chips lost their inner vital impulse and capacity for growth does not register in a world where instrumental value reigns—regarding *both* natural and human beings. This is made clear when Chuang Tzu shifts to the carving of humans by the socialization process. The latter, from ecosophical and social ecology perspectives, then conditions people for carving up trees and the earth itself.

> So if you compare the robber and the respectable citizen
> You find that one is, indeed, more respectable than the other:
> Yet they agree in this: they have both lost
> The original simplicity of man (78).

Society praises the "respectable citizen" (sacred vessel) and condemns "the robber" (profane waste). But, Chuang Tzu wants to point out, the same destructive process that created the one, created the other. True, society uses different value-laden labels to carve up and thus differentiate one from the other. The citizen has value as part of a smooth running social machine. (See "Active Life" 141-142.) He or she was successfully ornamented and finished off while the robber "mysteriously" ended up as socially deviant. The unfolding from within of their original simplicity and the subsequent wholeness had been rendered impossible along with possible social realizations in continuity with their integrity (*de/te*).

How do we lose touch with that original simplicity, the uncarved block (*pu/p'u*)? Society, according to Chuang Tzu, creates a new set of desires for both tangible and intangible goods external to the person and promises fulfillment. There is no emphasis upon the exploration and development of unique inner capacities but upon the chase after economically produced externals. "Desires unsettle the heart" and are increased "Until the original nature runs amok," renders Merton (79). And, running amok, running becomes an end in itself. We even lose touch with our own body and control over our senses.[21]

---

21. In A. C. Graham's translation, Chuang Tzu wants us literally to reclaim control over and contact with our own senses so that we "trust in the essentials of

If that was a problem in ancient China, what would Chuang Tzu say about a modern consumer society where the senses are bombarded with advertising and images of the "good life" encourage people to increase their quantitative resources, personal and financial, in the hopes of increase their happiness. Addicted to the "rush" that social and economic rewards provide, we must get our fix, either legally or illegally. Yet, as Chuang Tzu concludes, "If this is life, then pigeons in a cage/Have found happiness!"(79).[22] Note again that the philosopher chooses the condition of an animal in an unnatural state imposed by humans as an analogy for what happens to the Natural or Heavenly capacities of humans at the hands of social machinery. Since true freedom is lost, the legal division of people into "free" and "imprisoned" masks the spiritual non-freedom of most people.

> In short, before we can regain contact with Tao and its guiding force, we must abandon the misguided and harmful distinctions society has inculcated in us from birth . . . we must work to eliminate the various artificial categories and unnatural orientations that warp our perceptions and judgments and lead us to pursue fruitless and destructive ends. We must *undo* our socialization . . . . [23]

Ecologically, we come full circle. The human products of social carving return to the natural world to carve up more trees and destroy other earth beings. Those who have had their own unique potentials deadened and have become dependent on the new identity given by society, also accept the primacy of a growing economy

---

our nature and destiny." We are to hear with our own ears and see with our own eyes, not as others have trained us to see or hear. *Chuang Tzu: The Inner Chapters and Other Writings from the Book of Chuang Tzu* (Indianapolis/Cambridge: Hackett Publishing Company, 2001), 203.

22. In Graham's fuller translation of this passage Chuang Tzu uses strong images of constriction, colorfully commenting on this internal caging and external binding: "And to have inclinations and aversions . . . blocking up the inside of you, and . . . memorandum tablet in belt and trailing sash, constricting the outside of you . . . to be inwardly squeezed inside the bars of your pen, outwardly lashed by coil on coil of rope, and complacently in the middle . . . suppos[ing] that you have got somewhere" is like a wild animal in a cage supposing he "has got somewhere too." Our living potentials that would flow out and nourish our lives on all levels are stifled, "squeezed" inside by "inclinations and aversions" we develop to deal with the social reality. Ibid., 202.

23. Carr and Ivanhoe, *Ibid.,* 99.

and rising "lifestyle" when moral questions are raised concerning nature. The "essentials of their nature and destiny" have become identified with the well-being of the system that has tried to prohibit them access to their true nature.

The fate of the old tree represents the fate of the earth: consumer products on the one hand, waste on the other—and in both cases, a loss of self-renewing energies. The fate of nature may depend upon whether consumers redefine "the good life" to include both the life and the good (*de/te*) of all beings, whether they can rediscover and recover their natural capacities, return to the Source of the earth's and their own original goodness and thereby contentment. For Chuang Tzu, this means first freeing ourselves from our mental and emotional cages so as to see clearly (*ming*) and live "naturally" (*ziran/tzu-jan*) with full integrity (*de/te*). The domination of our Heavenly/Natural capacities has led to our cooperation with the same forces and interests in their and our domination of Nature. The loss of "paradise" where humans serve and are renewed by their being a part of the "marvelous wholeness" of Tao/Sophia means a self-defeating attempt to build "the City of Man" on anthropocentric illusions and non-sustainable cannibalizing of the source of life.

Meditation Four

Since one of the problems that both trees and people share is being "useful," a possible tactic for survival is becoming "useless."[24] Significantly, the very first selection in Merton's book is called "The Useless Tree." Hui Tzu (Huizi), Chuang Tzu's friend and debating partner, complains about a large useless tree that he has, which he says is useless. Its trunk is "distorted" and "full of knots" and its branches are extremely "crooked." As a result, "No carpenter will even look at it." In fact, Hui Tzu sarcastically remarks to Chuang Tzu, "Such is you teaching—/Big and Useless" (35). Chuang Tzu then notes how a wildcat (and a weasel) has very useful skills for tracking prey but the same display of skills lands them easily into

---

24. We know from Merton's lovely meditation on the "useless" rain pouring down on his cabin during a December 1964 evening, that he (like Ionesco and Chuang Tzu) delighted in and saw the profound levels of meaning in the usefulness of the useless. Keeping people and the rain free from the clutches of social, political, and economic opportunists might provide the space necessary to regain a sense of the intrinsic value both of humans and earth others. "Rain and the Rhinoceros," *Raids on the Unspeakable* (New York: New Directions Press, 1966), 9-26.

a trap or net. Some other seeming advantages such as size make catching a mouse impossible for a yak. Usefulness is limited and can be dangerous whether as a criterion, a category, or a personal characteristic. In the selection "Monkey Mountain" (143) it is the flaunting of its useful skills by a monkey that brings it death. Meanwhile Yen Pu'I "learned to hide every 'distinction.'" He in effect made himself useless so that society didn't know "what to make of him." Unable to make anything of him (like the useless tree), "they held him in awe" (143).

So, while from the carpenter's point of view, the tree is "useless," from the tree's perspective, uselessness is its salvation. One need only remember the "useful" old tree that ended up as wood chips and sacred vessels. Chuang Tzu implies then that being *cursed* as "useless" might paradoxically be a singular *blessing*. Uselessness can provide a "freedom from" those who want to use us and twist us to serve their purposes, a "freedom for" nurturing and developing one's capacities (*de/te*) so as to have a "freedom to" mirror and move with the energies and patterns of Dao/Tao. In being crooked, twisted, and full of knots, the tree not only is itself but also protects its original simplicity which allows it to live out its full life. "No axe or bill will ever cut it down" (36). There is an intrinsic value and cosmic integrity, a wholeness that transcends narrow categories of useful and useless, being attractive or unattractive to a carpenter's or anyone else's gaze.

Hui Tzu's obsession with usefulness displays both his narrow utilitarian mentality and his distinct lack of imagination. Chuang Tzu tells him to loosen up his logical categories, to "chill" as we might say. A more contemplative mode will allow him to see alternatives for trees than making planks for coffins or making a profit from sacrificial vessels.

> So for your big tree. No use?
> Then plant it in the wasteland
> In emptiness.
> Walk idly around,
> Rest under its shadow;
> No axe or bill prepares its end.
> No one will ever cut it down.
> Useless? You should worry? (36)

Chuang Tzu encourages Hui Tzu himself to be useless, to walk idly and roam easily underneath the shade of the tree. In the text, this selection by Merton comes at the end of a section that begins with Hui Tzu complaining that the seeds he had been given produced a gourd "of huge capacity" (like a mind?). However, it proved useless for making ladles when cut up or holding liquid when hollowed out. So he smashed it to pieces. Chuang Tzu tells Hui Tzu that the problem was not with the bigness of the gourd but the littleness of his mind, locked into certain ways of seeing things. "Why didn't you think of tying it on your waist as a big buoy so that you could go floating on the lakes and rivers instead of worrying that it couldn't hold anything because of its shallow curvature? This shows, sir, that you still have brambles for brains!"[25]

"Walking idly around" and "floating on the lakes and rivers" symbolize useless activities and a contemplative state of "wandering" outside of conventional thinking. It is a return to a "paradise" state, a "child mind" that too often gets ignored and "unused" in a society obsessed with justifying everything in terms of some goal determined by an organization. Just as the tree was spared (and the gourd could have been) when humans find imaginative, spiritually enriching alternatives, so the earth needs minds and spirits able to wander freely among possibilities not entertained by specialized minds focused on conventional instrumental ways of thinking.

The concept of uselessness sheds light on our abuse of nature in another way. In Merton's selection, "The Useless Tree," Hui Tzu is again criticizing Chuang Tzu's teachings as "centered on what has no use." Chuang Tzu responds this time, "If you have no appreciation for what has no use/You cannot begin to talk about what can be used." He points out that, of the whole broad expanse of the earth, a person uses only what is immediately underfoot. What would happen, Chuang Tzu asks, if you were to cut away all of the earth from around the feet leaving "nowhere solid except right under each foot:/How long will he be able to use what he is using?" Hui Tzu acknowledges that it would lose its usefulness relatively soon. Chuang Tzu drives home his point: "This shows/ The absolute necessity/Of what has 'no use'" (153). Likewise, the madman of Chu after turning Confucius on his head, says, "Everyman knows how useful it is to be useful./No one seems to know/ How useful it is to be useless" (59).

There is ecological wisdom to this madness. Modernity is hope-

---

25. Mair, Ibid., 8.

lessly utilitarian, dangerously focused on exploiting "the useful" in nature (and humans), ignoring or cutting away the useless. Having lost the wisdom of seeing things "in the light of the whole," we are blind to the fact that each thing we label as "useful" is attached to and supported by millions (myriads) of diverse others that we label "useless." Judged useless, we decide they need not be preserved. The words of Henry David Thoreau leap into mind: "In wildness is the preservation of the world."[26] The process of evolution with the self-renewing and creative energies of the biosphere are in danger of being shut down due to our exploitation of the "useful." Indeed, we know the usefulness of the useful but we have not yet learned the usefulness of the useless.

Supposedly the *realistic* view—in the tradition of logician Hui Tzu—is that an ever-expanding, self-enclosed human world powered by an ever-increasing extraction of "resources," fed by animals and monoculture crops raised on the destruction of grasslands and forests, about to drown in its byproducts and wastes—is sustainable. Chuang Tzu, however, might note that today's hypothetical "feet," standing on "useful" ground, are themselves expanding even as increased technological power cuts away the "useless" earth at an alarming rate.

MEDITATION FIVE

Liberating ourselves from confining self-and earth-destructive mindsets and behaviors, for Chuang Tzu, does not leave us in a nihilistic, meaningless, and absurd world. There is the Cosmic Way (*Dao/Tao*) and there are human ways (*daos/taos*), and when they fit together, individual life is nourished, creative possibilities unleashed, and the Great Harmony restored. Chuang Tzu was confident that once we open our minds and free our spirits we can find ways of living and acting that are personally enriching and

---

26. Merton read Thoreau in his own cabin in the woods near a pond. Merton wrote that "Thoreau's idleness (as 'inspector of snowstorms') was an incomparable gift and its fruits were blessings that America has never really learned to appreciate." *Conjectures,* 249. Euro-Americans considered wilderness a roadblock in the way of the advance of Lady Liberty just as were the wild, "primitive" indigenous peoples who inhabited nature's wildness. The Plains were filled with useless native grasses that needed to be burnt up, plowed under and grazed over (and so came the dustbowl). Tropical rainforests are useless until cut down and grazed on by cattle destined for North American and European markets. And so go the lungs of the earth.

ecologically wise and rediscover our embodied harmony with the energies and patterns of Nature. Yet modern technology presents an immense challenge to it realization at a societal level.

Eco-philosopher Hwa Yol Jung has pointed out that "Technology, which is the vehicle of material progress . . . offends and violates the Sinitic [Chinese] conception of nature as *ziran*" [spontaneous, self-so]. Jung notes that for Chuang Tzu "when man works like a machine his heart grows like a machine and he will lose his simplicity as well as his communion with 'ten thousand things.'" Jung adds that modern technology "is inherently anthropocentric."[27] This implies that a change in one requires a change in the other. And such a change will also necessitate a transformation on all levels so that technology serves both ecological and human well-being.[28] Might there be an alternative?

Perhaps cook/butcher Ding in "Cutting Up An Ox," offers some clues to an alternative relationship of humankind to both nature and technology.[29] In this case, a Prince stands awestruck at the graceful rhythm and timing of his butcher's movements: "Out went a hand, / Down went a shoulder, / He planted a foot, / He pressed with a knee, / The ox fell apart / With a whisper, / The bright cleaver murmured / Like a gentle wind. / Rhythm! Timing! / Like a sacred dance, / Like 'The Mulberry Grove,' / Like ancient harmonies!" (45). Thinking to praise his cook, the Prince expresses admiration for his "method." Laying his cleaver aside, the cook replies: "What I follow is Tao / Beyond all methods!" (45).

A method or technique is a formulaic, standardized way of doing things, and thus easily mastered by most people through practice and repetition. Ideally, it can be applied uniformly in a variety of situations, thus having certain characteristics in common with a machine. The cook rejects that whole mentality and methodology.

27. Jung, *Ecopiety,* 105.

28. Merton insists that technology, once an instrument or means by which rational goals were achieved has become an end in itself and has subjected both creation, and its own human creator, to "its own irrational demands." We are told that technological progress has led to an independence from nature. But the truth is that we have become dependent on the "pseudonature of technology, which has replaced nature by a closed system of mechanisms with no purpose but that of keeping themselves going." *Conjectures,* 76-77.

29. Elsewhere in Chuang Tzu, a cicada catcher, wheelmaker, ferryman, swimmer, bellstand carver, and other "commoners" teach similar lessons to the elite. See "Duke Hwan and the Wheelwright," (82-3) and "The Woodcarver" (110-111).

This does not mean that the cook had not trained in or mastered a set of skills. If, as a pianist, you lack technique, you will not play Mozart, no matter how sensitive you are to the composer's music. On the other hand, good finger dexterity and correct execution do not guarantee great music. If Mozart is to play through you, as Tao played through the butcher, both excellent technique and spiritual sensitivity are needed. The former, however, must move with and be completely subservient to the latter as the description of Ding's craft as dance and music indicates. Following Tao changes everything, from how one perceives the ox to how one experiences the swishing of the blade. It is the art of harmony and harmonizing, *theoria* as well as *praxis*: a wisdom born of and nurtured by lived experience, by a relationship with Life. A *dao* that follows *Dao* is a discipline involving body, mind, spirit and the flowing circulation of energy (*qi*).

The cook then chronicles this transformational process over the years in terms of his perception of the ox. When he began, he saw the whole ox as "one mass"; three years later there was no mass but a myriad of "distinctions"; now it is not simply what he sees that has changed but the nature of "seeing" itself. Seeing is now apprehending the ox with his "whole being." In this mode,

> My senses are idle. The spirit
> Free to work without plan
> Follows its own instinct
> Guided by natural line,
> By the secret opening, the hidden space,
> My cleaver finds its own way.
> I cut through no joint, chop no bone (46).

While there are differences in translation and interpretation of this explanation among scholars, there is a general consensus that in ancient Chinese thought there is no dualism here between spirit and body or spirit and mind. In fact, the Chinese notion of "body" differs from the Greek and subsequent western concept. Francois Jillian's study emphasizes that body-mind-spirit is an increasingly subtle modulation of a single actualization (*xing/hsing*) of a cosmic energetic (*qi/ch'i*) process or Tao. When aligned and coordinated in a concentrated fashion, it opens up a mode of spontaneous, effortless action (*wu-wei*). Spirit is not a separate reality but a exquisitely subtle mode of perception and awareness that can direct the (*qi/ch'i*) energies throughout the body in accord with a "seeing" or "holistic contact" with the patterns of Nature—in an ox, for example.[30] So to follow Dao is to follow subtle, spiritualized sensitivities which are in accord with Heavenly patterns (*tian li/t'ien li*) which in this situation means to effortlessly, flawlessly follow the lines of the ox, finding the openings and spaces.[31] The cook goes on to explain that the level of a butcher's art can be inferred from the keenness of his blade. A good cook changes cleavers once a year ("he cuts"); a poor cook needs a new cleaver every month ("he hacks"). But Ding's cleaver has cut up thousands of oxen over a nineteen year period and "Its edge is as keen /As if newly sharpened" (46).

But why should this matter? And what light might it shed on our technological problem? Cook Ding does not think of the cleaver as a tool separate from himself or as an efficient instrument with which to accomplish the goal of preparing meat for dinner. Technology changes when placed within this context of this aesthetic-spiritual performance. It is the polar opposite of modern "autonomous" technology that is an end in itself and that reshapes humans in its image and wields its own powerful impact. The blade is an extension of the moving energy (*qi/ch'i*) of the cook and not alien to the integrated movement of the whole person. The keenness of the edge reflects the cook's *dao* and not merely metallurgical strength. Thus, when the butcher pauses, senses an opening, and swish! the blade follows the pattern and finds its way; it fits and unites the cook's art and the ox's body. Hackers and cutters not only have no *dao*, they leave waste and a bloody, mutilated body behind. "Small" is not only a more appropriate technology, its use can be "Beautiful."[32] The butcher's movements are like a ballet flowing to hidden music. As *wu-wei*, the performance proceeds effortlessly with a minimum of wasted energy or a mutilated carcass. The perfectly channeled energy of the cook's body extends through the blade and enters

---

30. For a fascinating and careful analysis of Chuang Tzu's perspective and that of the classical Chinese world in general concerning body, soul, spirit, breath-energy, etc and their difference from the western tradition's view, see *Vital Nourishment: Departing from Happiness*, by Francois Jillian, transl. by Arthur Goldhammer, New York: Zone Books, 2007.

31. Michael Puett, "The Notion of Spirit in the *Zhuangzi*," in *Hiding the World in the World* Edited by Scott Cook (Albany: SUNY Press, 2003), 256.

32. See E. F. Schumacher, *Small is Beautiful: Economics as if People Mattered*. Originally published in 1973 by Blond & Briggs, Ltd (London), it has been republished and reprinted several times by Harper & Row (Perennial Library).

into the body of the ox.

Moreover, if humankind and its activity becomes more integrated with the earth, its perception of the earth will become more subtle and nuanced. The body of the earth, like the body of the ox, is a network of geological, biological and atmospheric patterns. As Francois Jullien notes, "the ox's body, which had initially been at the stage of a perceived object or a banal presence, enters into a partnership with the butcher's internal perception, with which it evolves in concert." The ox has been "relieved of its opacity" and "has been opened up for him."[33] The human changes its view of and relationship to the earth from one of a dualistic subject-object structure where the earth is an object for technological manipulation to a more coordinated *pas de deux*. Like Cook Ding, we will need an expansion and refinement of human faculties to make them "sharper and more alert" thus permitting a greater degree of flexibility and a more finely tuned way (*dao*) to deal with a diverse, complex and dynamic planet.[34]

Perhaps a new contemplative ecology is needed, aware of the marvelous wholeness, yet attuned to the diverse nuances of the earth. Human wisdom joined with Earth wisdom. This type of wisdom incorporates science into it, opening it up to its wider cosmic meaning and ecological relevance and away from service to dominating ideologies and destructive technologies. Something of this is hinted at when Merton says that the world, including the world of nature,

> . . . though "external" and "objective," is not something totally independent from us, which dominates us inexorably from without through the medium of certain fixed laws which science alone can discover and use. It is an extension of our lives, and if we attend to it respectfully, while attending also to our own freedom and our own integrity, we can learn to obey its ways and coordinate our lives with its mysterious movements. The way to find the real "world" is not merely to measure and observe what is outside us, but to discover our own inner ground.[35]

---

33. Jullien, *Vital Nourishment*, 90.
34. Ibid.
35, Thomas Merton, *Contemplation in a World of Action* (Garden City, NY: Doubleday, 1971), 170.

Note that Merton suggests that we follow not the "laws" but the "ways" (*daos/taos*) of nature and "coordinate our lives" "with its mysterious movements," like a dance. Centered and free yet flowing and responsive, we "discover our own inner ground" which opens to the common ground where we move to a common beat. Like a tango, the dance with nature must be about "attend[ing] to it respectfully" and responding sensitively to where it wants to go, coordinating our now more agile (less obese) body with cosmic music and earth rhythms. Cook Ding dances with a live ox!

PART III
THE SPIRITUAL FRIENDSHIP
BETWEEN THOMAS MERTON
AND JOHN WU

GOD-INEBRIATED:
AN INTRODUCTION TO THE
JOHN C. H. WU—THOMAS MERTON
CORRESPONDENCE

John Wu, Jr.

Ever since my childhood, I have always been haunted by the
desert within me, "mysteriously designated by the finger of
God." It is in the desert that I meet you, Father. It is in this
desert that I find the living waters and learn the lessons of
true love. Every word of yours finds an echo in me.

Wu to Merton, 12/26/62

To encounter living in you the spirit of Chuang Tzu with
such liveliness and force is, I must say, an experience. I
am glad there is still such a dragon hiding around corners
and behind clouds in our rather stuffy world.

Merton to Wu, 6/9/65

Should this introduction seem less than cricket, if I appear to sing
for my father more than propriety would warrant, let me blame biol-
ogy more than lack of love and affection that I have for that other
equally lovable fellow about whom most readers of these letters
will already have some or even a good deal of knowledge. After
all I am the ninth son and the thirteenth and last child of John C. H.
Wu (1899-1986). If I may at all claim any relationship to Thomas
Merton (1915-1968), then I simply wish to stand quietly alongside
the innumerable spiritual sons and daughters the monk has sired
during his lifetime and since he unexpectedly exited this world on
December 10, 1968.[1]

---

1. A significant date, exactly twenty-seven years to the day (December 10,
1941) after he entered the Abbey of Our Lady of Gethsemani, a Trappist monastery
in the then solitary Kentucky wood. From his classic, best-selling autobiography,
The Seven Storey Mountain published in 1948, we know he went there famously
to "get lost." But his legion of readers were not fooled and knew in his efforts to

Since his death in Bangkok in 1968, there has developed deservedly, especially in the United States, an astonishing Merton industry that has grown from mere passing fancy to very extensive research into nearly every aspect of this extraordinary monk's life and writings, which included an intense and beautiful romantic interlude. Further, it is common that no monk in human history possibly has been as widely read as Thomas Merton, at least not in such short a time.

In the summer of 1991, on a most pleasant and educational visit to the Norfolk, Connecticut, home of New Directions publisher and poet, James Laughlin, Christine Choy, my wife Terry's former schoolmate and our dear friend, the fine documentary movie maker who had originally suggested the visit, blurted out to the tall Connecticut guru that I was someone "crazy about Thomas Merton!" Without skipping a beat, Laughlin, the person most instrumental for putting the likes of Ezra Pound, Thomas Merton, William Carlos Williams, Henry Miller, Tennessee Williams and a host of other poets and writers on the literary map in the 20th century, rejoined with childlike zest, "Good for him! The more you read Tom, the more you'll want to read him. You can never get enough of him!" The incorrigible octogenarian sounded as if he were recommending the Hardy boys or Ben and Jerry ice cream.

There were so many Mertons circling around this extraordinary being that touched us in countless ways. Merton the writer, for one. His writings are the direct, unadulterated cables sent to inform the soul that force us to draw aside our self-made curtains for a more naked look at ourselves. Few writers used language in quite the same way he did. At twenty-six, Merton had entered the monas-

---

speak to God alone and be forgotten by his fellow humans, he not only chanced upon himself in altogether surprising ways but taught others to do the same by "getting lost" too.

Merton was born in Prades in the French Pyrenees on January 31, my birthday too, again twenty-seven years to the very day he was born, hence making him no more than a few years older than my eldest sibling, also a Thomas, who was born in 1918. Now, if I suddenly decided to become very Chinese and regard dates, numbers, and names not as pure coincidences but destiny itself, I suppose I could, pleading uncommon indulgence, claim generational equality and exact little sibling status from the monk. And, to assure our familial legitimacy on any future Mertonian pantheon, my wife and I named our first offspring Thomas Merton Wu, who we think very possibly was conceived on the occasion of our honeymoon in summer, 1968 while we, unsuspecting newly weds, were encamped on the very grounds the original Thomas Merton was then traipsing upon.

tery ostensibly to give up writing, a totally failed intention that his various soul brothers, such as the Zen adepts and ancient sages like Chuang Tzu, have cackled merrily over surely at his expense.

Then there is the Merton who identified with the suffering masses—from the victims of the Holocaust to the napalmed innocents of Vietnam—that got him into a heap of trouble with authorities within and without the monastery. One is hardly likely to find in a contemplative monk someone more fiercely committed and compassionate. He took the world as a desert, stripping it of excessive baggage, and proceeded to go beyond conventional limits and to see the whole of creation in its universal and original plenitude. And though the connection might not be obvious, in sharing the desert experience, he shared intimately the *little way* of both the Taoist Lao Tzu and the Carmelite saint, Thérèse of Lisieux, prodigals in the practice of a way in which the self shrinks or even disappears to the degree that the True Way may have its way. As Merton put it in an early letter to my father, by practicing the *little way*, "we return to the root by having no answers to questions" (*Merton*, 5/29/61). This simple but profound insight would seem to anticipate the now famous "incident at Polonnaruwa" during the Asian journey that claimed his life.

A key in trying to understand the *activist* Merton is to view him through the lens of the *contemplative* Merton, his true vocation, for rarely did he fail to acknowledge the salient fact that he drew constant strength from the Contemplator Himself. This flame burned constantly in him. By the same token, my father's life was nurtured by a similar intense but perhaps lower-burning flame that the Gift-Bearer never allowed to be extinguished. It would seem that at different stages of their lives, as soon as each stopped searching for answers in rationalistic ways and were no longer obsessed over the self, they were jerked into an altogether more subtle and sublime consciousness that led naturally into the True Way. Mystery informed everything they felt, thought, and wrote, and neither was shy in acknowledging this life-long debt.

John Wu, Sr. came into the world on March 28, 1899 on the opposite end of the earth in Ningpo, China in the coastal province of Zhejiang just south of Shanghai. His life came full circle at age 87 on February 6, 1986 in Taipei, Taiwan after having lived an extraordinarily rich life as judge, lawyer, diplomat, educator, legislator, and the initial drafter of modern China's first constitution. On his life's way, he wrote books dealing with such diverse disciplines as jurisprudence, literature, Eastern and Western philosophy and religion, and comparative mysticism. He rendered the Taoist classic, the *Tao Teh Ching* into English as well as *The Psalms* and *The New Testament* into updated versions of classical Chinese. Yet, despite an active and eventful life which he seemed to have fulfilled more out of duty than joy, the later, spiritually transformed Wu would regard the world as a *cloister*. Those who knew him well and, in fact, he himself as he confesses to Merton in a missive, even went so far as to see him as a *hermit* in the world. Here, again, we are able to see another link to the monk, an obvious sharing and understanding of the necessity of the solitary life.

My father loved the whimsical. As a teacher of law in the 1920s in Shanghai, some students referred to him affectionately as Professor of Juris*im*prudence, a name for which I now suspect he was at least partially responsible in having bestowed on himself given the nature of his large aptitude for playfulness even when dealing with the serious business of the Law. In retrospect he would have felt far more at home sitting on a park bench with ragamuffin Zen practitioners than on the official Bench in Shanghai in the late 20's. Author, publisher, my father's friend, Frank Sheed in the introduction to *Beyond East and West*, my father's autobiography chronicling his conversion to Catholicism and published by Sheed and Ward in 1950, said of him, "He is totally Catholic, totally Chinese, and totally himself." Which says it all, I suppose.

John Wu was an anomaly (not only in his own family which did not have a tradition of scholarship but also in an age principally dominated by such prevailing philosophical winds of positivism, utilitarianism, pragmatism, and relativism) in that his mental constitution simply refused to be drawn into what he almost from the very beginning of his intellectual and professional life considered invidious claws that expanded the possibilities for factual knowledge but diminished human wisdom. Instead, he was naturally attracted to their very opposite, towards ever greater harmony and synthesis in nearly everything he chanced upon. He could not talk of the old without airing the new, or the East without the West, or justice without love. Nor could he, following his conversion, explicate on China's three main religions and philosophies (Confucianism, Taoism and Buddhism) without seeing each as ideal harbingers of Christ.

Later still, his life and writings reflected without apology the relationship between faith and reason, of contemplation and action, of mysticism and the everyday, and most *nonpareil* of all, of a keen and unfailing intelligence with a childlike simplicity. These polarities, seemingly contradictory, might have made him appear to be intellectually repulsive had he been a lesser person and writer, a veritable mental disconcertion. But the fact was that he experienced and creatively resourced these polarities with much grace and equanimity. In him, thought and the person came together seamlessly.

As a child of nine or ten, I somehow knew something quite grand yet simple was at work behind it all, then later, that his particular kind of authenticity was marked by the intellectual and the simple, self-effacing man co-existing as one, a rare phenomenon anywhere. In time, it also dawned on me that he saw all the polarities as necessary fuel in the dramatic and joyous unfolding of truth.

A shocking range of interests possessed both Wu and Merton, and had they not been caught by the Hound of Heaven, both possibly would have gone further in a professional and worldly sense, my father in the fields of juridical and philosophical studies and even politics, and Merton as poet and novelist and social and political critic. James Laughlin expressed his conviction that Merton, with his abundant gifts, would have attained star status as a writer *out in the world* had he stayed put there. By the time he was accepted as a monk of Gethsemani, he had already written five novels, none yet published and three or four he had already foolishly put to the fire. Well, maybe not so foolish after all.

Merton may not have made it in the world in the conventional sense, and yet at the time he met his untimely death by a freak accidental electrocution in Bangkok while on his first extended journey away from his beloved monastery, he had become the most famous monk/writer of the 20th century. One can only speculate as to what might have become of him had he lived beyond his 53 years. By then he had begun to venture into some untapped areas of experience with which monks are not ordinarily identified.

But Merton was neither ordinary monk nor person. A close examination of his intellectual activities and commitments would indicate that the last decade of his life, rather than reflecting some queer ventures was very much a coming to fruition of those areas of his life that he had commenced upon decades ago. More specifically, he had embarked upon a projected long poem—*The Geography of Lograire*, published posthumously as so many of his books have been—which promised to be his *Cantos* and has proven to be more readable than Pound's grand opus.

On the only occasion I had in meeting Merton, in June, 1968—a few days short of six months before his passing, during that same honeymoon trip with Teresa Wong, my new bride—the monk told us matter-of-factly there were then—he thought—more non-Catholics reading him than Catholics since many of the latter original Merton fans brought into his camp through his autobiography had become disenchanted with his so-called "non-Catholic" or "secular concerns." These included his support for the American civil rights movement, and his anti-war and anti-Vietnam writings, as well as his growing enchantment for the humanistic and mystical traditions of Asia, an interest that threw many readers into a state of incomprehension. Not to mention that Merton was writing about his delight with Herbert Marcuse and the New Left.

Yet, as far as my wife and I could judge during our visit with him in 1968, he did not appear at all nonplussed at the way many of the more pious Catholics and now former and disenchanted fans were thinking of him. He certainly did not speak as a writer who felt abandoned by his audience or who mourned a loss of popularity which he communicated to us as onerous and more an albatross. The Merton who stood before us was not a pious-looking or pious-speaking monk—what we had expected to find—but an ordinary, plain-speaking bald man in a blue farmer's overall looking sometimes like Pablo Picasso, sometimes like Jean Genet and even like Teilhard de Chardin, when tired and austere-looking.

In reviewing his life and writings, what stands out in relief is the overwhelming fact that he never lost sight of the hard demands of his ever-evolving vocation, which came to include roles as a cultural critic and socially- and politically-committed writer. He was leaving mostly everyone behind and simply following the clear promptings of the Spirit within him. He knew he had no choice but to get on with it, like chores that had to be done whether he liked it or not.

In engaging the world, Merton's method appeared wholly consistent with what he perceived as the one true vocation of any monk, Christian or otherwise: the monk as *the one person who must quest for the truth wherever he met it* and in whatever tradition the truth lay. His writings were noble and eloquent for they brought to acknowledged dark and confused times a prodigious light and hope. Like all authentic words, they do us the great service of hurling back to us echoes of what is most treasured and deepest in us. In answer to Merton's self-doubts, as to whether his excursions into Chinese ways of thinking were superficial, my father gave his friend these reassuring words:

> When the natural gift is reinforced and uplifted by the gifts of the Holy Spirit, as it is in your case, your mind becomes transparent like a fire burning white-hot, and all bits of knowledge become welcome fuel for the fire.
>
> *Wu to Merton*, 3/20/61

Upon reading Merton's seminal essay "A Philosophy of Solitude," my father rhapsodized "Your mind is like a crystal not only in its transparent clarity, but in the wonderful fact that every unit of it possesses the characteristic features of the whole" (*Wu*, 12/16/62). Was there any other correspondent of Merton's who wrote to him with such openness, sincerity, and purity of insight.

Whatever the future verdict on Thomas Merton, it is safe to say the world is unlikely soon to meet up again with a Christian monk who wrote as voluminously and as perceptively on as many social, political, and spiritual matters and who, with the exception of the great Christian saints and holy men and women of other hallowed traditions, has influenced the lives of such diverse people in so many different ways. And, as the many fine biographies and critical writings through the years have documented, once he entered the Abbey, rather than allowing the cloistered life to shrink his sensibilities as man and artist, Merton, remaining true to himself, never stopped growing, and in the end, fulfilling his roles as monk and writer in ways hardly hinted at even among those who knew him at close range.

Merton stayed engaged by reading everything that came into his hands and through a vast correspondence. One estimate has it that he wrote to over a thousand persons and this in addition to the nearly sixty official full-length books that are now credited to him. In his correspondence, he often sought out people during times when he had become interested in some particular area of knowledge or tradition. He was especially attracted to men and women of the East whom he felt were able to give him a perspective whose shadings and hues were different from those found in his own tradition. Considered retrospectively, he became closely involved with the thoughts and lives of such people as Mahanambrata Brahmachari (whom he first met when he was a student at Columbia University in the 1930s), the Zen master, D. T. Suzuki, His Holiness, the XIV Dalai Lama, the Pakistani Sufi psychologist, Reza Arasteh, and others not so much for love of their deep and far-ranging teachings but more out of confirmation for his own insights. For Merton, always doing his homework well, never did anything in half measures. And as these letters so well testify, he was quite capable of holding up his end in any cross-cultural dialogue. These qualities of intense involvement, absorption, and abiding interest, rooted I believe in deep piety and unconditional respect for the other, was clearly indicative of Merton's compassionate universal heart as the Dalai Lama has often pointed out during his public lectures.

It was Merton's longstanding interest in Chinese philosophy and specifically in the Taoist master Chuang Tzu that initially gave him the idea of contacting my father. While it is true that many of the ninety-one extant letters covering a seven-year period from March 1961 until the monk's passing concerned his pet "Chuang Tzu project," all the credit for the work in the end, including the published book, *The Way of Chuang Tzu,* belongs wholly to Merton, as my father rightfully acknowledged. The irrepressible monk had somehow not only gotten deep under the old Taoist's skin, but also through the often, impenetrable medium of language effected his very incarnation in 20th century America. Or, as my father proclaims joyfully upon reading the finished product, Chuang Tzu would have written in a similar vein had he been writing in English!

In the early goings when Merton insisted that my father first give a literal translation of some of the selected texts from the *Book of Chuang Tzu,* my father casually reassured the anxious Merton that no mystical writing can truly be translated but only "paraphrased," adding, "all genuine mystics feel and see the same things which are no-things. Chuang Tzu is one, and you, Father, are one" (*Wu to Merton,* 10/21/61). Playful yet wise, it would seem. Later, when he was indeed proven right and became ecstatic over his younger friend's astonishing achievement, he said of the book: "It is infinitely more valuable than a mere translation. . . . Like the silkworm you have devoured the leaves of the mulberry trees of the Garden of Chuang Tzu, and emitted pure silk. . . . This nosegay is bound to be immortal" (*Wu to Merton*, 6/13/65). To this day, few would argue with this assessment.

Four years before in an earlier letter, Merton may already have hit upon a valuable insight for his future work on Chuang Tzu when he wrote enthusiastically,

> I am more and more struck by the profundity of his thought. He is one of the *great* wise men: I will not say "philosopher" in the speculative sense, for his wisdom has a marvelous wholeness, and that is what makes it "simple."
>
> *Merton*, 4/1/61

On the other hand, in describing the Taoist's "marvelous wholeness" and simplicity, was not the monk unintentionally pointing to his own self and to all persons of true wisdom? And was it not these shared qualities that gave Merton such a deep feeling of affinity with Chuang Tzu and made his "imitations" so close to the spirit of the Taoist master and such a joy to write? In fact, to his friend, W. H. Ferry and many others he declared it his favorite among all the many books he had given birth to (see *Letters from Tom*, to W. H. Ferry, Fort Hill Press, Scarsdale, 1984, 48-9).

While these letters of Merton to my father provide insight as to how the monk brings about this transformation, like a true Taoist, he kept his deepest gifts a well-concealed secret. He neither gave us the slightest hint of how he entered into the old Taoist's mind nor, thankfully, did he put us through some beaten and officious discursive mill. Everything of value in Merton has its roots in a hidden wholeness, which is wholly unknown, hence, inimitable.

In my father's case, fame and reputation and, later, a large dosage of notoriety resulting from frequenting the houses of the so-called "sing-song girls" in Shanghai, which he unabashedly recounted in *Beyond East and West*, had come to him almost too easily. In fact, by his late twenties he was by many accounts one of the most famous judges and important legal thinkers and writers in China. When he left the bench and became a practicing attorney, he regularly commanded the highest legal fees. He confesses, however, that his most professionally successful years were also years of great spiritual and moral impoverishment, even degradation. Later, in his early thirties, he was assigned the task of drafting the first constitution ever for pre-Communist, Republican China.

Further, we may speculate that had China not gone the way

of Communism in 1949, he might very well have become either a Minister of Justice or of Education. But such was not to be his portion and, in his heart of hearts because of the way he had developed as man and thinker, and particularly in having lost much of his taste for worldly ambitions as he matured spiritually, he now preferred more than ever to remain out of the political limelight for which he never had the stomach in any case.

The pivotal event in my father's life, as it was in Merton's, was his conversion to Catholicism. He was baptized in Hong Kong on December 18, 1937, one year before the future monk's own conversion. His religious conversion was all the more surprising in that being an intellectual, he was not at first attracted to the giant learned edifice that had grown around Catholicism but rather by the *simplicity* of her message, the inscrutability of God's love and child-like faith awakened in him through a chance reading of a short piece of writing in French on St. Thérèse of Lisieux (1873-97), an obscure Carmelite nun. "The Little Flower," as she was later known, had been a victim of consumption, dying at age twenty-four. We are told also in Merton's autobiography that the monk attributed his own vocation to the Lisieux saint, so the connection with Thérèse of both men is not merely one of passing fancy. It can likewise be said of my father that, like Merton, the sort of literary output that ensued would certainly have been unthinkable outside the context of that one momentous event that had opened the way to becoming the basis of a life-long adventure of the soul.

My father's first writing following his conversion, not surprisingly, was *The Science of Love*, an adoring tribute to the saint for showing him the now famous Theresian *little way*. His translations of The *Psalms* and *New Testament*, the former he regarded as "paraphrases" rather than translations, were projects commissioned by Chiang Kai-shek, the then President of the Republic of China, in the very dark years of the early 1940s when Chiang's armies were in the midst of a life and death struggle to save China from the invading Japanese armies. My father whose love of and loyalty to friends was one of his strong cards, never forgot this debt to his President, and in his later writings revealed a deeply-seated spiritual side in Chiang that biographers seemed to have either overlooked or rarely bothered to investigate or regard as significant. In fact, it was this sense of debt that made him scurry back to Taiwan in the mid-60s to begin the writing of the biography of Dr. Sun Yat-sen on Chiang's behest.

His translations—now regarded as modern Chinese classics—and later his rendering of the *Tao Teh Ching* into English, and his writings on Christian mysticism and Zen Buddhism, are all the more astonishing to those who did not know the extent of his scholarship, given that he was known as a legal expert and not primarily a man of letters. His literary output, including translations of Chinese love poems, often came to light under pseudonyms, a good many of them under my mother's name, "Teresa Li."

While my father was often judged an intellectual maverick by many of his compatriots, who often did not know what to make of him, he most certainly broke new ground in such cross-cultural studies as, for instance, his intimating the deeply spiritual link between Lao Tzu and the Little Flower. Yet, always remaining faithful to the highest standards of both classical Chinese and Western scholarship, his natural bent for knowledge on a renaissance scale seemed traditional to the core. He was only concerned that his knowledge and love of subject would ultimately do justice to what he was interested in at the moment, an attitude strikingly similar to Merton's. Both men abidingly believed that penetration to the roots and understanding of life through the heart should always take precedence over academic or political correctness.

The diversity of my father's intellectual interests was already apparent at the time he went abroad to study law at the University of Michigan in 1920. His readings at the time indicate a broadness rarely seen among any students, let alone in a foreigner preparing for a career in law in a foreign land. Justice Oliver Wendell Holmes, with whom my father had begun a correspondence in 1921, seeing the genius the young impressionable Wu had for the Law and fearing that he would soon dissipate his intellectual energies in the more abstract fields of philosophy and psychology, used his persuasive powers to convince his young friend to accept as his life work the establishment of a firm legal system in a China, which was regarded by nearly everyone as hopelessly mired in feudalistic habits. What Holmes could not quite comprehend was that the young man's intellectual restlessness was rooted in his seeking after a broader basis for the law, broader than the one Holmes the positivist himself represented. Hence, though smitten with an avaricious appetite for all sorts of learning, the young Wu in fact knew well the duties his country called him to undertake.

Law became his profession, and he pursued its development in China with a seriousness that marked all his other later endeavors. Even at this early stage of his professional and intellectual life, he would never allow his legal work to detract from his other loves, and with the passing of years his other loves gained an increasingly stronger foothold on his life. One could very well make the case that his juridical writings benefited considerably from those so-called sidelines. For his approach to the Law was, indeed, compared to contemporary trends, *organic* in its thrust, particularly during an era when narrow positivistic tendencies had become the fashion of the day. Through nature and nurture, my father in contrast fell hopelessly in love with the entire Natural Law tradition in the West.

In fact, it was this solid grounding in the Natural Law that later served as a guide for all his philosophical and spiritual preoccupations. He had first broached its rich incipient tendencies in native Asian philosophical and ethical traditions, first as a child in his study of the *Four Books*, which formed the very foundation of the Confucian canon, then in the metaphysical and mystical writings of the philosophical Taoists. Hence the first strong impulses he felt for the tradition had come fresh to him initially in his own soil. What he later encountered in the West helped reinforce this love and filling up that original intuition and making it grow ever stronger, adding fuel to an already strong fire.

As a university teacher, first in Hawaii, then at Seton Hall in New Jersey, he had little patience for anything slavishly academic. His writings, in clear expository style—the fruits of his legal training—are nonetheless nearly always personal, spiced with insights culled either from his rich life or from the writings of others whose experiences he thought spiritually edifying and bountiful. They resonate with the conviction that words, too precious to be relegated to mere verbal exercises, must instead closely reflect the very struggles of a person's soul. And it was clear that legal writings, being for him organic and whole, should also naturally form part of what he liked to call "the living tissues of life."

My father's letters to Merton introduce the reader to a simple, self-effacing man convinced he had been granted the outrageous boon of having chanced upon a spiritual universe—after a long bitter search his true natural habitat—where he was already living in the midst of untrammeled joy. This rapturous delight, surely a heavenly glimpse of things to come, granted him the understanding that no man, including himself, has any claims over his own soul; and, in such a heady atmosphere only the delectable and ever-refreshing dialogue of one's soul with its ever-gracious Maker truly matters. Here again in his natural playfulness he expresses that playful joy:

> Look at me, Father, I am supposed to be a lawyer, and a lawyer is supposed to be as sober as a Scotchman, (yet) even I have not been able to resist the overwhelming hospitality of our Divine Host. In your case, Father, the resistance is almost nil.
>
> *Wu*, 12/26/62

His direct, unabashed style is borne out even in his 12-year correspondence with Justice Homes, which he had initiated at age 22 while the 80-year-old Great Dissenter was still active in the Supreme Court. In his letters to his children, particularly to my brother Peter, there is an exposure of soul and disarming humor rarely found in letters from parents to offspring. There seems in him always the great wish to bring others into his personal universe, to be warmly embraced.

The following by William Goddard in the Prologue to my father's *The Four Seasons of T'ang Poetry* in which the writer suggests the idea of John Wu being a "mystic" may help us grasp better the tenor of my father's complex psychological makeup. Goddard indicates the significant role that both Buddhism and Taoism played prior to his embracing Christianity:

> Perhaps this is the result of his earlier Buddhist training before he embraced Christianity. John C. H. Wu would have been a most inviting study for Sigmund Freud, who would, doubtless, have found the Wu mysticism a Christo-Buddhist mood. There is, however, a definite Taoist strain in all his thinking and writing.
>
> Whether he writes of law or literature, his manuscript is a palimpsest, with the Taoist or Buddhist reflection showing through.
>
> *The Four Seasons of T'ang Poetry,* John C. H. Wu,
> Charles E. Tuttle, Rutland, VT, 1972, 15

Goddard goes on to summarize a picture of a man his students may have had trouble understanding fully. Who could have blamed them otherwise?

> I do not know of any other outstanding lawyer in any
> country, who combines in himself such apparent opposites,
> for we do not associate the legal mind to either poetry or
> mysticism. Legal rationalism and poetic sensitivity seem to
> belong to different personalities. Yet in the author's case,
> these are blended into a perfect unison.
>
> *Ibid*

To illustrate what Goddard may have meant, let us listen as my
father sings of man's common law as a poet would. He adroitly
melds lovely images, nature, consciousness, and mystery into a
seamless continuum:

> In the enchanted garden of common law, there are many
> shady groves which cheer the heart and refresh your spirit
> at the same time that they lure you to new vistas. It is not
> a closed garden, but one which is continuous with the wild
> fields, hills and rivers on one side, and leads to the streets
> and marketplaces on the other.
>   At first, you feel all but lost in the labyrinthine ways
> and paths; you want to discover some design, but you find
> none. But daily saunterings in the garden familiarize you
> gradually with the genie of the place, the atmosphere, the
> ever-changing moods of the garden, with the inevitable
> result that you are more and more fascinated by it.
>   You begin to divine a certain vague design. You do not
> find a general design, except perhaps the design of nature
> or of a mysterious Providence. What you find is not logical
> consistency arrived at once for all, but an endless series of
> organic adaptations which must be renewed every day.
>
> *Fountain of Justice*, John C. H. Wu,
> Sheed and Ward, New York, 1955, 96-7

The Law was indeed for him far more than an utilitarian tool. In
time, his own legal philosophy went beyond the pragmatic Holm-
esian philosophy of law, which he initially seemed to have mastered
only to be used as a vehicle to transcend it.

In an early Merton letter we find the following with its delightfully limpid images that neatly complement the above. One need not
take a giant leap to speak of "Nameless *Tao*" in the same breath as

the *Word* in the beginning of the Gospel of St. John, nor see Jesus as the personification of Natural Law. In fact, in his Chinese translation, my father had rendered it, "In the beginning was the *Tao*":

> Now I enjoy the quiet of the woods and the song of birds
> and the presence of the Lord in silence. Here is Nameless
> *Tao*, revealed as Jesus, the brightness of the Hidden Father,
> our joy and our life.
>
> *Merton, 5/19/61*

One could rightfully ask here: which of the two is the more mystical, the lawyer or the monk?

In *The Springs of Contemplation*, two retreats by Merton for a group of contemplative nuns, the monk's words dealing with the relationship between Christianity and Buddhism could very well also be applied to his older friend. Nurtured from his earliest years in the comforting arms of Buddhism, my father never forgot its lofty spiritual *milieu* that prepared him for his fateful meeting with Christ. Merton's remarks during these retreats provide insight as to the way the Catholic monk was to view his own tradition in relation to Buddhism and other religions:

> If the Buddhist is really united with God, he is united with
> God in Christ, but *he doesn't know it*. It seems to me, from
> what I know of Buddhist converts, that their conversion
> consists in the realization that Christ is the real fulfillment
> to which Buddhism has been tending. . . . When they real-
> ize that Christ is the fulfillment, they realize it *in depth*.
> (Emphasis added)

The monk then speculates a possible link between the Buddhist *void* and the Trinity:

> . . . there's room for a personal understanding of what (the
> Buddhists) call the "void." . . . Suzuki talks about the void
> in a kind of Trinitarian way, about intelligence coming forth
> from the void and about love and wisdom in the void. It gets
> to be startlingly close to the doctrine of the Trinity.

For both Merton and Wu, one profound flowering in religious experience was the personal revelation of God, the startling awareness of the relationship of the creature before a loving, personal God. Below, the monk expresses sentiments that illustrate the kind of

awakening through grace that might very well have preceded my
father's own conversion; at the same time, because he sees clearly
the depth to which Buddhism strives in terms of coming to pure
consciousness, he indirectly gives the intriguing suggestion that
one's path to Christ may very well be through the Buddha:

> These converts often have a deeper appreciation for what
> this relationship to God means, because they go into it more
> deeply than most of us. We just go halfway. . . . When Bud-
> dhists become Christian, they're not just caught up into a
> rudimentary idea of the soul being saved by Christ. They find
> the church an elaboration of Buddhism. It's not a deepening
> of their own Buddhism they come to, but a rethinking of it in
> personal terms. They retain their pure kind of consciousness;
> they don't develop an ego to be saved. They remain stripped
> of this. And it's within this deep emptiness that they see a
> personal relationship with God.
>
> *The Springs of Contemplation,* Thomas Merton,
> edited by Jane Marie Richardson, Farrar, Straus, Giroux,
> New York, 1992, see 222-4

* * *

These letters, a variegated tapestry, constitute a part of each man's
literary history. They reveal a good deal of Merton and Wu during years very crucial to both. As mentioned above, Merton had
written to my father proposing a joint project to translate some
selections from the Taoist *Book of Chuang Tzu.* But the letters soon
became something beyond that, for as Michael Mott, Merton's official biographer, notes in his very fine and extensively researched
The Seven Mountains of Thomas Merton, "From this beginning,
modest in every sense, their correspondence developed into one
of the warmest friendships by letter, as well as one of the most
beneficial" (382).

In my father's case, the younger man's letters were surely an
essential impetus that kept his life afloat spiritually during a very
difficult and painful period. For with the death of my mother in
November 1959, the ballast and keel that had kept him before the
wind over four rich decades had suddenly been jerked rudely from
under him. To Father Louis—what we deferentially called him at
home—he hints of his sufferings by beginning in humor but end-

ing in undisguised domestic tribulation, at least as much as he was able to muster up:

> I am sure that Our Father has something of the Grandma in Him. This I have discovered since my dear wife passed on. When she was living, all that I needed to be was to be a father to my children; but now I have to be both father and mother, and I found that what they really want is a grandmother. During these three years, I am nailed to the Cross with Christ.
>
> *Wu*, 12/26/62, 2nd letter

It was providential then that Merton should have sent off an initial missive in March 1961 during some dark days in my father's life. For the monk too the decade would also prove to be one of emotional and spiritual turbulence. With the exception of a telltale post card sent in August 1966, and a missing letter, lines of which my father quotes in his reply, Merton's letters to my father in 1966 give no indication of difficulties and anxieties. When my father showed me the card, he said calmly but with concern, "It looks like our Father Louis is in need of prayers. He's in trouble." Upon hearing this I immediately thought of the possibility of his leaving the monastery and perhaps the priesthood. My father gave me the original postcard which he promptly pasted on the inside of the back page of his paperback copy of Merton's *Conjectures of a Guilty Bystander*. Neither of us suspected—at least I did not think my father suspected nor had knowledge—of his having fallen in love with a student nurse.

As for the general tone of Merton's letters to my father, perhaps the young man's sense of deference towards an older Asian friend would not allow him to go beyond a certain self-imposed propriety; in contrast, my father's letters were an unstudied and spontaneous gushing forth of what lay deepest in him. This depth of feeling seemed perfectly balanced by a playfulness and joy springing from the heart of a child. They warmed up to each other immediately, as Merton's second letter in response to my father's initial reply bears solid witness:

> Your wonderful letter was a joy and an encouragement. I have no more doubts about the (Chuang Tzu) project being by God. It has the marks of the Holy Spirit's action upon it everywhere, doesn't it?

The older man was not apprehensive in baring his soul for he regarded the monk not only as a friend but as a spiritual father and master as well. His attitude of piety, quaint to this secular, non-pietistic age perhaps, was fully consistent with the way he deferentially approached all priests, as *other* Christs. The strong fraternal love he held for Merton strongly indicates the unmistakable relish he took in the friendship itself, which he thought an undeserved bounty.

Among priests gifted in intellect he regarded their basic holiness with far more interest than he would their keen minds. On occasion, he showed an ill-concealed impatience with religious who harbored intellectual pride, an attitude he thought incompatible with genuine spiritual life. If, as a layman, he had found untoward pride a vice harmful even to himself, he knew how it could play havoc with those living the religious life.

In his seemingly naïve simplicity redeemed by a profound faith, few things gave him greater joy save the company of simple religious who understood, as Thomas Merton did, that joy shows its authentic face only when one is convinced that "nothing worse can happen to you" and that we deserve absolutely "no merit" for our so-called accomplishments (see *Conjectures*, 261). He was rather uncompromising on this point and, if he regarded his own achievements to be of any significance, they were so only as far as they gave glory to God. Had my father not been a basically simple person, perhaps his penchants for being proud and excessively scrupulous might very well have gotten the better of him.

One supposes too that because he understood the necessity of standing empty-handed before God, he was able to write perceptively about Zen; and once Zen confirmed in him the reality of a true self beyond the ego, it doubly convinced him that Christ, rather than contradicting, instead, fulfilled and brought to perfection, all the natural truths he found in other traditions. It was natural then that he saw in the hidden, cosmic Christ both the seed and genuine fruits of the self.

In finding Christ or, what he most certainly would prefer, in *Christ finding him*, he felt he had lost nothing from his own native traditions but understood them in a far more profound way, as mirrors of a reality holding the potential seeds of eternal life. Zen taught him the futility of looking at reality in a dualistic and broken way; at the same time, it also taught him that life experienced as it is, in its original state of innocence, is at least a glimpse of Paradise itself. And this was made possible in the loving and suffering Christ—the New Man.

For in Christ, God the Father's *Gift* to the world, Paradise had been irreversibly regained and, along with it, the recovery of what Emerson had once called the *aboriginal self*. My father found in the miraculous mending of human brokenness a *wholly free gift* generating from the mercy of divine love. And what was critical to him was the difference that marked the unbridgeable gap between man's unceasing assertiveness—the belief that whatever we accomplish, even spiritually, is *ours*—and genuine piety and gratefulness, the deep human conviction that our smallest personal achievements spring from the secret workings of grace, not from our accumulated merits or action. Thus it came naturally for him to see—and to say with genuine joy—that no achievement of his had any merits whatsoever and that joy, therefore, if it be lasting, could not be based on any fleeting accomplishments, or on actions for which we desire acknowledgment.

The knowledge that one can claim absolutely no merit in one's thoughts and works—in effect resulting in a total freeing up of one's meddlesome ego—was the one great insight, indeed, spiritual treasure, that my father carried with him throughout his adult life, supporting his mature spirituality and accounting largely for his mystical flights and *carefreeness*. He knew that all true expressions of the heart were informed and fueled by divine grace, and the joy that results from this comes from the realization that one will never be abandoned, even as Christ was not abandoned by His Father.

The central, controlling image I have of my parents—the one, a scholar, and the other, a woman of no formal education—is that of two wholly different, yet astonishingly similarly simple souls kneeling humbly and empty before the altar of God at Mass each morning and offering their coming day's physical and mental toils completely to Christ. Every morning they could be found, in a phrase's of Merton's to his novices, "casting your cares to the Lord" and, in the words of Dilsey, the black maid who was a favorite character in William Faulkner's novel *The Sound and the Fury*, calls the "unburdening" of oneself to Jesus.

For my parents, concerns over the question of success and

failure, a question that most people think makes the world go round but which dissipates our precious energies, had somehow been transcended in their daily habit of offering their joys and sorrows to the Creator. Their only abiding concern was that Christ would condescend to accept what little they could give as a token of gratitude for the enormous gifts they felt they had already *superabundantly* been rewarded in life.

Being steeped in his own traditions, particularly in the practice of filial piety in which sons and daughters are taught that they owe their very physical existences to their parents, he was able after his conversion to sublimate this naturally-conceived filiality and fully apply it to the transformed state of gratefulness in all its ramifications to a Divine Father and Mother—which is what he considered God to be. He saw this sublimation as a fulfillment of a native tendency intrinsic to each person. Perhaps that is why he gave himself generously in both word and deed for he believed a generous heart was never rooted in one's self but in the love, mercy, and wisdom of God working its way imperceptibly in and through the deepest recesses of our soul.

My father's estimation of Thomas Merton in a letter dated September 6, 1966 reflects such pregnant thoughts in which he sees in his friend a perfect blending of what is most profound in East and West:

> Your way (of compassion) . . . is (to) let the Lord beat your heart into a pulp, so that it is no longer your heart but the Heart of God with its all-embracing Compassion. This is the Way of Tao in which you are so steeped, the way of knowing the masculine and sticking to the Feminine. The beautiful thing about you, Father, is that your heart is as great as your mind. Thus, in you love and knowledge are united organically. Herein lies your profound significance for this great age of synthesis of East and West.

Different as their lives and constitutions were, the two friends seemed to have met effortlessly in the Center, sharing a profound love of the desert experience in which one learns to cultivate a deep thirst for God and, in that thirst, come face-to-face with the naked self awakened to the liberating and joyous truth that all human schemes are but straw in the wind. And with the emergence of the self—a self that cannot be made known to us through the

obsessive and neurotic seeking of it as an object of knowledge—
in solitude one paradoxically identifies with all humankind. For
solitude in the Christian is identification with the Mystical Body
of Christ which embodies not only Christians, but the whole of
humanity the Father had mercifully sent His Son to redeem. One
can only marvel at how a person living actively in the world could
share so intimately the experience of a great contemplative monk.
The following, which only a fellow mystic and poet could have
conceived, was written after the monk had been given permission
to live as a hermit:

> You are more mine in your present hermitage than ever
> before. For I am by nature a hermit. There is no greater
> delight, O Father, than for friends to enjoy the solitude of
> each other. *Nor can there be a greater togetherness.*
>
> Wu, 11/16/65—emphasis added

In *Silent Lamp*, William H. Shannon's very personal biography of
Merton, the author makes the salient point that Merton had begun
"running to the East" as early as November 16, 1938, the day of
his baptism. He contends that the East was the "place of Christ, the
Rising Sun in the East that never sets,"

> For the risen Christ, whom the liturgy is fond of calling
> the Oriens, the East, is not just the Christ of the Christian
> West. He is, as Paul puts it so strikingly in Colossians, the
> cosmic Christ through whom and for whom God made all
> things and in whom God reconciles all peoples to God's
> very self, breaking down all barriers of separation.

Shannon concludes that the true significance and final fulfillment of
Merton's Eastern journey lay in the meeting of the "known Christ
of the Christian tradition" with the "unknown Christ of Asia," for

> (Merton) began to understand that the Logos of God is
> not a Western Word but a divine-human Word speaking
> in diverse ways and in varied cultures to all women and
> men of good will.
>
> The search for the God of Mystery, symbolized for
> Christians by the journey to the Oriens, was not—as Merton
> came to see—solely a Christian venture; it was a human
> endeavor as old as humanity itself. (272-3)

In my father's reply to Merton's first letter he had made the following suggestive comments concerning a marriage of East and West
and what was demanded from those involved in this sacred task:

> ... only a man like yourself, ... steeped in works of great
> Christian mystics, can know what Lao Tzu and Chuang Tzu
> were pointing at. . . . The Logos of God who enlightens
> everyone coming into this world illuminated their minds
> in a very special way for reasons of His own. One of the
> reasons surely is that He meant to prepare the Chinese
> mind (and the "post-Christian" mind) for the recognition
> of the True Light.
>
> *Wu, 3/20/61*

To which Merton takes up the theme and runs with it:

> It is all important for us to *be* in Christ what the great sages
> cried out to God for . . . may we be able to bring to the orient
> hope and light, which by right is theirs: for Christ rose up
> in the East, and we sing to Him *"O Oriens"* in Advent. His
> is what William of St. Thierry called the *orientate lumen.*
> To that great light let us be humbly devoted and let us seek
> its tranquil purity in which all lights are fulfilled.
>
> *Merton, 4/1/61*

In the very next letter, convinced of the significant role the East
will play in the future development of Christianity, my father
makes quite clear his own position and ends almost with an audible
sigh:

> The way to the re-Christianization of this post-Christian
> West lies through the East. Not that the East has anything
> really new to give to the Gospel of Christ; but its natural
> wisdoms are meant by God to remind the Christians of
> their own infinitely richer heritage, which, *unfortunately,
> they are not aware of.*
>
> *Wu, 4/7/61*—emphasis added

In retrospect and, I think, ironically, their true vocations were not
ones with which they can facilely be identified; rather, their true
vocations were in their steady and joyous coming to awareness
of the Incarnation, beyond the many cultures and traditions out

of which they were nurtured. What they shared essentially was a magnificent and daring Christology in which, because Christ had come to redeem all humanity and, therefore, the Incarnation being an irrevocable universal phenomenon, they steadily sought the prefiguring of this overwhelming truth in all traditions, sacred and secular, East and West, in all the works that reflect and manifest human truth. Particularly, as it can be seen in the many 1960s writings of Thomas Merton, this truth lay in the often obscure margins of humanity, among forgotten strangers, where he believed Christ lived and could be seen more commensurately in relief than elsewhere.

By opting to live along the desert of their own hallowed traditions, they *aimed without aiming*, not with overly-conscious design, to perceive the truth from the very heart of the Great Contemplator where palpable emanations of love and mercy mysteriously hidden from us support and make whole the brokenness of the human spirit. And, in so doing, the two proclaim through their respective God-inebriated existences the delightful truth that in the severed and discontinuous heart and incoherent and broken chords of the human voice ultimately lie the convivial gift from which any genuine hope and constancy might spring. Did their greatness not lie in their unfazed willingness to defer to that Hounding Word wherever it wished to lead them? From the way of the mind, with a sublime hand from the Divine *Logos*, they had traveled millenniums and begun to master the universal Way of the Heart. They had indeed like blind lions gropingly sought and finally tasted the Eternal Spring in the desert.

THE THOMAS MERTON— JOHN C. H. WU LETTERS: THE LORD AS POSTMAN

Lucien Miller

Working together on *The Way of Chuang Tzu*, Thomas Merton and John C. H. Wu discovered a project and a friendship willed by God. Prior to their relationship, both published autobiographies that were simultaneously on the Catholic best-sellers book list,[1] and both were writing works on Asian philosophies and religions.[2] Opposites in politics, brothers in the spirit of hermit and extrovert, and mourners over the loss of a woman, they inspired, taught and consoled each other through a correspondence of six and one-half years.

INTRODUCTION

The hitherto unpublished manuscript of the letters between Thomas Merton and John C. H. Wu (Ching-hsiung Wu, 1899-1986) marks a hidden yet seminal movement among the religious encounters between East and West in the twentieth century. Writing to Thomas Merton at the midway point of their six and a half year correspondence, March 14, 1961—August 18, 1968, John C. H. Wu observes: "Between true friends the Lord Himself serves as the postman."[3] Wu's comment epitomizes the consciousness that he and Merton come to share regarding the true nature of the ninety letters they exchange:[4] theirs is a threefold encounter between self and other,

1. Thomas Merton, *The Seven Storey Mountain*. New York: Harcourt, Brace and Company, 1948. John C. H. Wu, *Beyond East and West*. New York: Sheed and Ward, 1950.

2. Thomas Merton, *Mystics and Zen Masters*. New York: Farrar, Strauss and Giroux, 1967. *Zen and the Birds of Appetite*. New York: New Directions, 1968. John C. H. Wu, *The Golden Age of* Zen. New York: Image Books Doubleday, 1996. Orig. 1967.

3. Letter dated 11/16/65.Thomas Merton, John C. H. Wu, "The Thomas Merton—John C. H. Wu Correspondence," unpublished manuscript. I wish to thank Jonathan Montaldo for generously providing access to this manuscript and for encouraging research and writing on this project.

4. Merton wrote thirty-seven letters, Wu fifty-three.

Christianity and Asia, the human and the divine.

PART I: RELATIONSHIPS

As we begin to read the letters, it is interesting to observe that it is
Thomas Merton who initiates a correspondence for which John Wu
has been silently waiting. Writing to Wu, Merton requested his help
with a translation of the Chinese philosopher, Chuang Tzu [Zhuangzi].[5]
Merton asks for Wu's guidance in the study of the Chinese Confucian
Classics and Taoist mysticism. Merton is familiar with Wu's books
and feels Wu is "exactly the kind of person who would be of immense
help."[6] John Wu is ecstatic. He receives Merton's letter on the feast
of St. Joseph, opening it after Mass while still on his knees before
the Blessed Sacrament. He tells Merton that he has been waiting for
Merton to take the initiative, believing their friendship is fated, and he
is quite happy to serve Merton as his "altar boy."[7]

As their correspondence unfolds, direct address and signatures
indicate the two men are soon on familiar terms, with Merton
signing off as "Tom"[8] and Wu jokingly calling himself "your old
good-for-nothing in Christ."[9] Before long Merton and Wu are fast
friends, locked in their mutual translation enterprise and sharing
the revelations of the Asian Holy Spirit.

Merton's initial need for Wu is professional—he wants a
specialist in ancient Chinese literature and culture.[10] Wu solicits a
preface by Merton for a book Wu is doing on St. Thérèse of Lisieux
and Lao Tzu.[11] Soon, the two men discover through their mutual
professional interests an admiration and need for one another. There
are minor differences, quirks in personality and contrasting passions that appear along the way. Wu meets Merton's Abbot, James

---

5. Zhuangzi. 莊 子. Merton and Wu's collaborative translation project cul-
minated in Merton's *The Way of Chuang Tzu*. New York: New Directions, 1965.
For a study of the project and Merton's book, see Lucien Miller, "Merton's *Chuang Tzu,*" available through the Thomas Merton Center, Bellarmine University,
Louisville, Kentucky.

6. 3/14/61.

7. 3/20/61.

8. 3/14/61; 12/12/61.

9. 12/27/62.

10. 3/14/61.

11. 4/15/61. Wu's study was published as an essay, "St. Thérèse and Lao
Tzu: a Study in Comparative Mysticism," in *Chinese Humanism and Christian
Spirituality: Essays of John C. H. Wu*. Ed. Paul K. T. Sih. Jamaica, New York:
St. John's University Press, 1965.

Fox, and writes Merton: "Ever since I came to know him, I have been in love with him. (He is your Joseph, Father.)"[12] This type of comment must have galled Merton, who struggled mightily with his Abbot. Merton informs Wu about issues of peace and war he writes about in *The Catholic Worker* which cry out for attention,[13] but Wu reads them not as personal calls to action for peace and justice, but as the reflections of a true mystic. Merton tries to draw out Wu on the Vietnam War, but Wu does not respond.[14]

From the start, Wu is candid and open regarding himself. Merton may admire his writing on St. Thérèse and Lao Tzu, but Wu laments "the yawning gulf" between his writing and his sinful self.[15] Wu agrees when Merton discerns that Wu's spirit is akin to the "playful samadhi" of the Chinese Zen (Chan) Master, Hui Neng, combining light-heartedness and deep seriousness.[16] But in fact, as Wu tells Merton,[17] for several years he has been depressed over the death of his wife, Teresa Teh-lan Li (1899-1959), and feels he has been "nailed to the Cross with Christ."[18] He is deeply consoled by Merton, who is "indescribably moved" upon reading Wu's later published description of Teresa's "death in Christ,"[19] and calls it an Asian epiphany of Christ the Savior.[20] From time to time Wu deals with another mysterious depression that seems unrelated to the loss of his wife. There are moments of calm and peace writing calligraphy[21] followed by days of ashes,[22] and "the darkest tunnel so far" when he discovers compassion for those who are suicidal.[23] In Wu's Preface to his *The Golden Age of Zen* he writes: "There is no telling how much the friendship of this *true man* has meant to me during all these lonely years of my life."[24]

For his part, Merton empathizes with Wu's suffering, deeply

---

12. 12/7/65.
13. 12/12/61.
14. 6/9/65.
15. 8/4/61.
16. 1/31/65; 2/5/65.
17. 5/25/61; 3/9/62.
18. 12/27/62.
19. See John C. H. Wu, *The Golden Age of* Zen. New York: Doubleday, 1996. Orig. 1967. 214-15.
20. 12/28/65.
21. 1/1/66.
22. 1/10/66.
23. 3/26/66.
24. John C. H. Wu, Preface, *The Golden Age of* Zen.

admires him, and comes to need his support when faced with a personal crisis of his own. In the first year of their correspondence, Merton remembers Wu in his Easter Masses, asking the Lord "to give you every blessing and joy and keep ever fresh and young your 'child's mind' which is the only one worth having. May He grant us, as you so well say, to be both inebriated and sober in Christ, Confucians and Taoists."[25] A year later, Merton offers Mass for Wu's intentions, for China and all Wu loves.[26] Wu's visit to Gethsemani the same year is a grace for Merton and the monastic community.[27] In Wu, Merton encounters the spirit of Chuang Tzu, and it is to Wu that Merton insists on dedicating *The Way of Chuang Tzu*.[28] Merton misses Wu deeply when the latter moves to Taiwan and writes that he keeps trying to get over his consternation that Wu is gone.[29] When Wu returns to New Jersey, Merton rejoices, eagerly looking forward to having Wu revisit Gethsemani.[30]

A poignant moment of personal want surfaces when Merton writes Wu, "As to me, I need your prayers, life is not always easy!!! I am in trouble, so please pray and get the saints at it too."[31] Although we cannot be certain, in all probability Merton is hinting about his affair with "M," the student-nurse with whom he fell in love in March 1966, when he was hospitalized while recovering from back surgery. The relationship unfolds over the spring and summer of 1966, and Merton last sees "M" October 27 of that year.[32] In Wu's September 6, 1966 letter to Merton, he mentions receiving Merton's August 27, 1966 letter, but the latter is missing from the Merton-Wu manuscript. In his Footnotes to the Merton-Wu letters, John Wu Jr. suggests his father may have destroyed Merton's August 27 letter to forestall a scandal.[33] There is no extant correspondence between Wu and Merton after Wu's September 6, 1966 letter until Wu writes again, January 2, 1967.

25. 4/1/61.
26. 6/7/62.
27. 7/10/62.
28. 6/9/65.
29. 7/11/66.
30. 9/12/67.
31. 8/5/66.
32. See *Learning to Love: Exploring Solitude and Freedom*. Ed. Christine M. Bochen. The Journals of Thomas Merton. Volume 6 (1966-1967). San Francisco: HarperCollins, 1997. 150-151.
33. John Wu, Jr., "Footnotes to Merton-Wu Letters," unpublished manuscript. Footnote dated 9/6/66.

Merton's appeal for Wu's support and Wu's September 6, 1966 letter reflect the deep trust and intimacy Merton and Wu share. In his letter, Wu comforts and encourages Merton, echoing the role Merton often plays as Wu's friend. If we read Wu's letter as referring to "M," its meaning is clear.

Quoting Merton's missing August 27, 1966 letter (which I assume refers to "M"), Wu assuages Merton's agony by assuring Tom he is experiencing the way of the Cross and following the way of Tao: "It is so characteristic of you to write: 'It is a little hard to laugh off the heartbreak of another person.' Indeed, Father *Misericordieux* (I mean Compassionate), this is the worst cross to a man of boundless generosity like yourself. The simplest way out would be to turn the heart into steel. But this is the coward's or the cynic's way. Your way, I am sure, is let the Lord beat your heart into pulp, so that it is no longer your heart but the Heart of God with its all-embracing Compassion. This is the Way of Tao in which you are so steeped, the Way of knowing the masculine but sticking to the Feminine."[34]

In a posthumously published private journal entry which Wu would not have seen, Merton reviews his affair with "M" and says most of the pain of loneliness he felt for "M" on Holy Thursday and Good Friday of 1966 came out, "but very obliquely," in the poem he wrote describing his hospital stay, "With the World in My Bloodstream."[35] Merton's reference to his suffering over "M" in the poem may have been oblique to Merton, but it seems that it was transparent to Wu. When Wu reads a copy of the poem sent by his son, Francis, he writes Merton that the poem is "a poetic version of 'beating the heart into pulp.'" "Even your hospitalization is fruitful," Wu assures Merton, citing the prophet, Isaiah (*Isaiah* 32:15): "Together with oxygen *the Spirit is poured upon you from on high, and the wilderness becomes a fruitful field.*" Quoting the closing lines of "With the World in My Bloodstream":

> While the frail body of Christ
> Sweats in a technical bed
> I am Christ's lost cell
> His childhood and desert age
> His descent into hell.[36]

34. 9/6/66.

35. *Learning to Love*, 122.

36. Thomas Merton, "With the World in my Bloodstream," in *Follow the Ecstasy: Thomas Merton, The Hermitage Years 1965-1968.* John Howard Griffin,

Wu marvels "at the God who is working in you" and concludes that in becoming a fruitful field and descending into hell, "The poet has become a Divine Poem."[37]

We are left wondering what Merton may have said about "M" and her anguish in his missing letter. It is hard to imagine that she found her heartache redemptive, as Wu found Merton's. Wu's attention however, is on his friend, Merton, not on the woman he leaves behind. What is significant is the way he responds to Merton's plea with a firm but timely sense of Asian grace. Here Wu reveals his instinctive awareness of the mutual flowering of Eastern and Judeao-Christian spiritualities when planted in a shared garden of Gethsemani. Compassion is self-bruising, Wu affirms. Merton's descent into hell and beaten heart are intimations of the Heart of God and the Way of Tao. Such inter-religious insights move Merton throughout the course of his correspondence.

Reviewing his first year of contact with Thomas Merton, Wu is deeply grateful for a divine gift of friendship.[38] Gradually, he comes to view Merton as his spiritual father, and himself as Merton's son.[39] For his part, Merton finds it is Wu who, like a spiritual father, spurs him forward with "my own vocation to see things Asian in their simplicity and truth." When Wu honors Merton's move to the hermitage with the Chinese pseudonym "Mei Teng" or "Silent Lamp,"[40] Merton feels he has been "'baptized' Chinese" by Wu with a Chinese name he must live up to, for "a name indicates a divine demand."[41] In the very last letter Wu wrote to Merton the year Merton died, Wu asks: "But need I tell you that your friendship has sunk so deep into my psyche that it has become a part of me?"[42]

Merton and Wu share an affinity for one another and similar personality characteristics. In certain respects they are soul mates. In reading the letters, we find Wu often identifies with Merton. He tells Merton that the whole time he was reading an article Merton sent him on "Mystics and Zen"[43] he felt "as though every word came from

Ed. Fort Worth, Texas: JHG Editions/Latitudes Press, 1983. 73-76.

37. 9/6/66.

38. 12/19/61.

39. Undated card, December 1964.

40. Mei Teng 昧 燈. 12/17/65.

41. 12/28/65. Later on, Merton mocks himself with the epithet "Old cracked Mei-Teng." 2/7/66.

42. 1/26/68.

43. Published as "Mystics and Zen Masters" in Merton's *Mystics and Zen*

my real self."[44] Sometimes Merton triggers in Wu an awareness of
something latent within himself. Merton's comment in an introduction to Christian mysticism linking the spiritualities of St. Thérèse of
Lisieux and the German Rhineland mystics such as Meister Eckhart,
John Tauler, and Henry Suso strikes Wu with a sudden illumination. The Rhineland mystics "are really Chinese," says Wu, in that
their spirituality is Chinese. And now that Merton has likened their
spirituality to St.Thérèse's "little way," Wu understands "the secret
of the magical power the divine witch of Lisieux has exercised on
me."[45] "Every word of yours finds an echo in me," he tells Merton,
who he says is "in a conspiracy with the Holy Spirit to enlighten
me."[46] Reading Merton makes him realize that, like Merton, he has
been haunted all his life by the desert within, and that it is the Lord
who had led them both into this desert where they "meet and take
delight in each other." "The Lord has whispered to me," adds Wu,
"'Seek first the desert, and everything else, including the friendship
of my modern Prophet Thomas Merton will be added unto you.'"[47]
When Merton moves into his hermitage, Wu writes that he himself
is by nature a hermit and that in solitude they are now closer than
ever and "[y]ou are more mine."[48]

At the close of their second year of correspondence, December
1962, Merton and Wu exchange two letters on the paradox of sanity
and madness. Both are attracted, on the one hand, to the "madness"
of the poet and the recluse. Merton especially is drawn to persons
who are marginal, social misfits, or radical critics. They rejoice
together in the "insanity" of the Gospels and Chuang Tzu which
is really the deepest sanity. In his Christmas letter, Merton tells
Wu that the world cannot silence the Christ-child or Chuang Tzu
for "[t]hey will be heard in the middle of the night saying nothing
and everybody will come to their senses." As for himself, Merton
claims that "the very name of Chuang Tzu restores me to sanity."

Masters. New York: Noonday Press, Farrar, Straus and Giroux, 1967. 3-44.
    44. 3/31/63.
    45. 3/9/62. [Unidentified Merton work: Wu's reference to Merton's *Intro-duction to Christian Mysticism.*] For Wu's writing on St. Thérèse of Lisieux see
"St. Thérèse & Lao Tzu," in Wu's *Chinese Humanism and Christian Spirituality.*
St. John's U Press, 1965, and his book, *The Interior Carmel.* New York: Sheed
& Ward, 1952.
    46. 12/26/62.
    47. 12/27/62.
    48. 11/16/65.

"Anything but his quiet debunking view is plain insanity." Merton delights in his discovery of the "mad" Nicaraguan poet, Alfonso Cortés, who writes "the most amazingly sane poetry" and who reminds Merton of Chuang Tzu, for "in his madness he accuses all the right things for the right reasons." Allying himself with Chuang Tzu and Cortés, Merton encloses in his Christmas letter to Wu "another poem of a madman you know well [Merton]: he beats out his poems on the back of a saucepan, on top of a little hill, while the snakes dance in the woodshed."[49]

Merton's "Chineseness" in his Christmas letter amazes Wu. He muses that he will not know why Merton is so Chinese in the way he thinks until they both get to heaven. Even Merton's use of "madman" is typically Chinese, reminding Wu of the Tang poets. He simultaneously views Merton's "madness" in both Asian and Christian terms. Wu claims St. Paul was also very oriental, like Merton, when St. Paul affirmed the sanity-madness paradox, saying "If we were out of our mind, it was for God; if we are sane, it is for you. . . ." He links Paul's "madness" with a traditional Chinese notion of intoxication, translating St. Paul's phrase as, "if we are *drunk* . . . if we are sober." Expanding on his drinking metaphor, Wu tells Merton that no one can be a saint who has not been filled "by the intoxicating Spirit of Love. And, Father, you have drunk like a whale." With his "overwhelming hospitality," "our Divine Host" and "mad Lord" has urged Merton to "bottoms up"[50] over and over again, and Merton's resistance, even worse than Wu's, has been "almost nil." Only a "dead-drunk man" like Merton can understand Wu's own "timeless moment of void."[51] Three years later, Wu wraps up the theme of madness, concluding that: "Only a contemplative like you can burn with such Christ-Love as you have radiated in all your letters. You are mad with the very madness of Christ; yet this madness is a mysterious blend of the Fire of Love and the Water of Wisdom."[52]

There is one feature of the relationship that we find peculiar to Wu, and that is an admiration for Merton that sometimes borders on adoration. That extreme degree of respect partly stems from the intensity and flamboyance of Wu's personality, but mainly results

---

49. 12/20/62.
50. "Bottoms up." *gan bei* 乾杯.
51. 12/27/62.
52. 2/5/65.

from Wu's appreciation for Merton's interest in Asian thought and culture.

There are many examples of Wu's awe for Merton the person coupled with Wu's esteem for Merton the student of the East. At one point in his collaborative project with Wu translating the *Chuang Tzu* text, Merton tries to learn a little Chinese. Knowing Merton's intellectual prowess, Wu imagines Merton making great strides studying Chinese and comments: "the fire of your spiritual wisdom turns every bit [every Chinese written character] into *light*, informing all information."[53] The truth is Merton had no time to study Chinese and got practically nowhere learning Chinese characters. What is noteworthy is Wu's utter confidence in Merton's light-transforming wisdom. For Wu, meeting Merton face to face the first time at Gethsemani, and walking and talking with him and sharing silence are blissful experiences.[54] He wants Merton's "holy hands" to touch up his translations of Chinese Buddhist texts.[55] Praising what he calls Merton's "Integral Humanism," Wu remarks that since the apex of Merton's pyramid is in heaven, "you [Merton] could not be otherwise than universal."[56] Indeed, Merton is a masterpiece, created by the Divine Artist using nature and grace, a "sublime" landscape of "towering peaks hidden in clouds and mists," of flowing streams merging "with the infinite Void," and an "ineffable" blend of Confucianism and Taoism.[57] "All things you do and write, Father, are poetry; and you are His great Haiku," writes Wu.[58] "Every time I receive a letter from you, I feel as though I had a new satori!" he exclaims. "A subtle and indefinable peace begins to seep into my soul and fills it with a deep and inexplicable satisfaction."[59] "If this is attachment, let there be more attachment!" Wu chortles.[60] Reading Merton's *New Seeds of Contemplation*, Wu feels like he is "strolling on a mountain, breathing the pine-scented air."[61] Sending Merton a newspaper clipping where a photograph of Merton and another of Pope Paul VI appear side by side, Wu

53. 3/9/62.
54. 6/30/62.
55. 7/17/62.
56. 12/26/62.
57. 11/16/65.
58. 11/16/65.
59. 12/7/65.
60. 1/1/66.
61. 1/21/66.

tells Merton he likes to see the two famous figures together, as they represent "the two aspects of Christ—the inner and the outer. You are supporting his diplomatic efforts ontologically."[62]

PART II: CHRISTIANITY AND THE EAST

Poor Merton! How his ears must have burned! And how he must have loved it! How did Wu get this way, an altar boy idolizing his priest? We might also ask, what is it that Merton discovers in Wu? While never effusive, Merton clearly needs and respects Wu, loves him and learns from him.

As noted previously, Wu, like so many readers, identifies with Merton spiritually and emotionally. Prior to letter writing, Wu is deeply touched by Merton as monk and spiritual writer. But why does Wu say that he has been waiting for Merton to write? There is in Wu an intuitive sense that their encounter is providentially ordained. Before their correspondence begins, Wu has made a significant discovery: Merton understands the East. Through subsequent letters, while at the same time reading unpublished or recently published Merton writing on Asia, Wu awakens more and more profoundly to the awareness that Merton grasps the spirituality of Chinese Taoism, Confucianism, Buddhism and Chinese poetry in a contemplative Christian sense that is uniquely his own. Equally momentous for Merton is the fact that Wu approaches the Gospel through Asian spirituality. Wu's findings, and his revealing and teaching his own understanding must have thrilled Merton, as Wu brings out a latent awareness in Merton. Equally momentous for Wu is his waiting has come to an end.

Let us turn to the practical evidence of Wu's and Merton's grasp of things Chinese, and then move to Wu's theory of the mind of Thomas Merton through which he makes sense of Merton's and his vision of the Christian need for the East.

At one point barely two months after they have initiated correspondence, Merton comments to Wu: "Now I enjoy the quiet of the woods and the song of the birds and the presence of the Lord in silence. Here is Nameless Tao, revealed as Jesus, the brightness of the hidden Father, our joy and our life. All blessing to you, joy and grace in Him."[63] We do not know Wu's reaction, but we can surmise that he is deeply moved with the awareness that Merton

62. 1/24/66.
63. 5/19/61.

has penetrated the mystery of Tao through the visible Christ who reveals the invisible Source. "To have seen me is to have seen the Father" as Christ says to Philip in the Gospel of John.[64] Wu is ardent about the *Logos*, the Word-Event that is Christ in the Judeo-Christian scriptures and which he sees in classical Chinese texts.[65] Both Merton and Wu respond to this Word-Event, Christ, with the whole of their beings. In his very first letter to Merton, Wu speaks of Lao Tzu and Chuang Tzu, the forefathers of Taoism, and tells Merton that "the Logos of God who enlightens everyone coming into this world illuminated their minds." Through Lao Tzu and Chuang Tzu, God prepared both the Chinese mind and the modern "post-Christian" mind to recognize the True Light. Conversely, says Wu, we cannot fully understand the Taoists nor the Confucianists unless we are one with the Word incarnate."[66] In his second letter to Merton, dated Good Friday, 1961, Wu reiterates his conviction about the *Logos* and the *Tao*. While reading Merton's *The Wisdom of the Desert*, Wu is constantly reminded of the moral intuitions and spiritual insights found in sayings and anecdotes by Chinese sages such as Lao Tzu, Chuang Tzu, Confucius, Mencius and Buddha. This experience reveals to Wu a thrilling truth: "*The Tao Incarnate* is absolutely the *Same Tao* who was from the beginning with God and is God. Before Lao Tzu was, He *is*" (Wu italics).

Assuming this close identification between *Logos* and *Tao*, Wu readily points out to Merton his awareness that the post-Christian West needs the spirituality of the East to re-discover Christ and be re-Christianized. The natural wisdoms of the East are meant by God to remind Christians of a richer heritage that either they are unaware of or have forgotten.[67] Indeed, Wu surmises, the ancient Zen masters would be better Christians than many today, because had they heard Christ's teachings they would have understood them, while Christians have lost their ear for the words of the Gospel and the " 'impractical' living counsels of the Living LOGOS" [Wu capitals]. Were Christ's sermons or Paul's letters to be submitted to chancery offices today, says Wu, many passages would be considered

64. *John* 14:9.

65. "Word-Event" is a term coined by the late Japanese Dominican and master of Christian-Buddhist encounter, Shigeto Oshida, OP, of the Takamori Community, Japan, for an experiential reading of Scriptures. "The Mystery of the Word and Reality," 1981. Unpublished essay.

66. 3/21/61.

67. Dated "First Friday," 4/61.

heretical.[68] Merton concurs with Wu in his belief that Christians need the East and that a whole new orientation is required. An erroneous sort of "supernaturalism" and blind adherence to legalistic formulas, gestures and rites have impaired living and understanding the Gospels. Allowing that many of his fellow priests would not understand his perspective, Merton speaks of a need at present for the "wonderful natural wisdoms that came before Christ" and that are fulfilled in Christ and the Gospel, so that Christians may themselves achieve the fulfillment Christ requires of them.[69]

One concrete example of Merton's East-West integrative approach that impresses Wu is Merton's teaching on self-nature or the person as void. According to Merton, in the West the person is commonly viewed as a divided self—an individual empirical ego and an inner real self. The truth, says Merton, is:

> What is most ourselves is what is least ourself [sic], or better the other way around. It is the void [emptiness] that is our personality, and not our individuality that seems to be concrete and defined and present, etc. It is what is seemingly not present, the void, that is really I. And the "I" that seems to be I is really a void. . . . It is the No-I [not I] that is most of all I in each one of us. But we are completely enslaved by the illusory I that is not I and never can be I except in a purely fictional and social sense.
>
> And of course there is yet one more convolution in this strange dialectic: there remains to suppress the apparent division between empirical self and real or inner self. There is no such division. There is only the Void which is I, covered over by an apparent I. And when the apparent I is seen to be void it no longer needs to be rejected, *for it is I.* How wonderful it is to be alive in such a world of craziness and simplicity.

Merton adds, poking fun at his analysis: "I get this way from sleeping nights in the hermitage and watching the stars."[70]

Wu, in contrast, terms Merton's analysis as a "transparent perception" penned by the "Not I." Merton is "Father Void," a wizard, pointing to the moon. "With this fundamental insight"

---

68. 12/17/64.
69. 4/1/61.
70. 1/31/65.

about the nature of self as void, says Wu, "we can spin the Buddhist scriptures" like boys playing tops. As he signs off, Wu extends Merton's East-West insight as to human self-nature to the divine nature of Ultimate Self: "With filial love in the Word Who is the Void."[71] Here Wu links Christ the Word with Buddhist emptiness (Void), intimating but not explaining a mysterious and provocative analogy.[72]

Wu's study of Tang Chinese Buddhism, *The Golden Age of Zen*, and Merton's role in its formation reflect the shared vision of East-West encounter we find throughout the Merton-Wu correspondence. In terms of their production, *The Golden Age of Zen* and Merton's *The Way of Chuang Tzu* mirror one another, as Wu longs for Merton's assistance with his work, while Merton absolutely requires Wu's for his.[73] Wu very much wants Merton's input and criticism as he writes,[74] and he sends manuscripts of chapters, asking for "a sound beating" from Merton the Master.[75] Merton begs off the editing job, claiming incompetence as well as being too busy.[76] He gently finds fault, saying Wu's statements sometimes miss his target, his choice of words may be inappropriate, or more explanations are needed for the general reader. Later he compliments Wu on the readability of his revisions, especially in one section where he is charmingly informal and spontaneous.[77] Wu feels Christ himself has praised him.[78] Merton believes in the worthiness of Wu's book project, and he revels in reading material he considers magnificent. "It is a wonderful book," Merton concludes, "and certainly one of the best things on Zen that has come out. It provides a very welcome change of pace and perspective

---

71. 2/5/65.

72. A further East-West insight Merton and Wu share is an understanding of Zen and Tao. Both detest Western popular Buddhism's tendency to reduce Zen to *zazen* or sitting meditation and the solving of *koans*. Merton terms such simplifications a "stinking skeleton." 6/23/63 Wu and Merton find a fundamental likeness between Tao and Zen and a oneness in modality that, says Wu, traditional devout Buddhists do not acknowledge. 12/2/65.

73. See my "Merton's *Chuang Tzu*" for Wu's role in the creation of *The Way of Chuang Tzu*. Merton's *The Way of Chuang Tzu* is published in 1965. Wu's *The Golden Age of Zen* is published in 1967.

74. 6/13/65; 8/6/65.

75. 8/14/65.

76. 7/11/65.

77. 12/28/65.

78. 12/31/65.

from Suzuki, and throws such abundant light on Chinese Zen, it is going to be invaluable."[79] In a subsequent letter to Wu, Merton says students of Zen will find the book indispensable.[80]

What Wu really wants from Merton is an Introduction to his book that is similar to the one Merton writes for *The Way of Chuang Tzu*.[81] "Am I asking too much?" he asks, pleadingly, adding with emphasis, "*O Father, hermit or no hermit, I need your help.*"[82] Again and again he begs and cajoles Merton for the Introduction. When at last Merton sends the Introduction to Wu in Taiwan, and its arrival is delayed in the mail, Wu comments: "Our friend the Devil is trying to hinder the publication of this book, whose aim is to open the door of Our Church."[83] Upon reading the Introduction when it does arrive, Wu is elated. He finds Merton's comparative study of Christianity and Zen "a living bridge between East and West," and "a masterful summing up of the spirit of Zen."[84] In his own Preface to the book, Wu generously suggests *The Golden Age of Zen* may be regarded as a long footnote to "the profound insights embodied in his [Merton's] introduction."[85] We have here

---

79. A review of the 1996 reissue of *The Golden Age of Zen* (originally published in 1967) praises Wu's book for its detailed characterizations of Tang dynasty era Zen, wealth of background information, and contextualizations of famous sayings of ancestral teachers. See Frank J. Hoffman, "*Zen Keys; The Golden Age of Zen,*" *Philosophy East and West*. Vol. 48, No. 1 (Jan., 1998), 165-167. Another finds it prophetic. See John A. Lindblom, "John C. H. Wu and the Evangelization of China," in *Logos* Volume 8, Number 2 (Spring 2005), 130-164. Wu's decidedly Christian perspective links Buddhism, Taoism, and Christian contemplative or mystical traditions. Wu and Merton, both pioneers in Christian-Asian religious encounter, offer alternative visions largely ignored in scholarly secular studies. For Buddhist scholarship illuminating the field Wu introduces, see Stanley Weinstein, *Buddhism Under the T'ang*, Cambridge: Cambridge University Press, 1987; Steven Heine, *The Koan: Text and Contexts in Zen Buddhism*, Oxford: Oxford University Press, 2000; Heinrich Dumoulin, *Zen Buddhism: A History*, New York: Macmillan, 1988.

80. 9/12/65. The book was rejected several times by various publishers before eventually being published by the College of Chinese Culture Press and the National War College in Taiwan, in co-operation with the Committee on the Compilation of the Chinese Library, Yang Ming Shan, 1967.

81. 8/12/65; 12/2/65.

82. 11/19/65.

83. 9/6/66.

84. 9/19/67. Merton's Introduction in *The Golden Age of Zen* is re-published as "A Christian Looks at Zen" in Merton's *Zen and the Birds of Appetite*. New York: New Directions, 1968. 33-58.

85. John C. H. Wu, Preface. *The Golden Age of Zen.*

an indication of Wu's high hopes and expectations. *The Golden Age of Zen*, like *The Way of Chuang Tzu*, may unbolt closed doors and provide access to Asian spiritualities helpful for the reawakening of Christian contemplation.

PART III: WU'S THEORY OF MERTON'S MIND

We glean from various remarks Wu makes during the first two years of their correspondence the emergence of a general theory of Merton's intellect. As he dialogues with Merton or reads his letters and writing, Wu observes Merton's mind in action and comments on its qualities and the way it works. Perusing Merton's *Disputed Questions* as well as *The Thomas Merton Reader*, Wu remarks: "Your mind is like a crystal not only in its transparent clarity, but in the wonderful fact that every unit of it possesses the characteristic features of the whole. And is this not how the Creator Himself works? There is no atom which does not reproduce more or less faithfully the structure of the solar system!"[86] Because of this transparent clarity, Merton's vision is genuine. He exemplifies Goethe's ideal thinker: "one who can divide so deeply that he can unite, and [who is] united so deeply that he can divide."[87] There is a mystical quality about Merton's mental processing, which Wu terms "catholicity." He likens Merton's intelligence to a dancer who somehow dances while suspended over a cliff and dances on flat ground at one and the same moment. Like St. Thomas Aquinas, Merton stretches the Mystical Body of Christ in his writing to the ultimate limit, yet does no more "than register the necessary growth toward the full stature of Christ." Merton's mind and writing have "the beauty of the Golden Mean [Confucian], and "the spontaneity of the inevitable [Taoist]."[88]

Wu's general theory reflects and illuminates his specific perceptions of Merton as a perfect blend of East and West, and his concrete encounters with a mind that is simultaneously Asian yet centrally Christian in spirituality. In his first letter to Merton,[89] Wu immediately cites particular examples which reveal that Merton is "Asian" in disposition or background, or that he is a gifted interpreter of Asian matter, particularly Chinese. The monk-writer has a natural gift for "seeing the essential in everything," a capacity which

86. 12/16/62.
87. 3/31/63.
88. 8/14/65.
89. 3/20/61.

is complemented by the gifts of the Holy Spirit. Studying Chinese material, Merton's mind becomes transparent "like a fire burning white-hot," and he grasps Chinese ways of thinking with penetrating insight. In certain ways Merton is both Confucian and Taoist. The practice of monastic obedience enables Merton, says Wu, to recognize that Confucian rites are an external expression of what is internal. Faithfully carrying out daily tasks in the monastery means that Merton has "*lived* Confucianism" [Wu emphasis], and knows rites not as something imposed externally, but rising from within.[90] Certain works by Merton on Western subjects sound Asian to Wu. A book like *Seeds of Contemplation* reveals a similarity between Merton's mode of thinking and the Taoist patriarchs, Lao Tzu and Chuang Tzu. When Merton writes in *Seeds*, "The Holy Spirit is sent from moment to moment into my soul," Wu proclaims the sentiment is exactly what Chuang Tzu would have written were he a Christian. Merton's phrase, "selflessness is my true self," declares Wu, "sums up Lao Tzu and Buddha and the best of Hinduism." *Seeds of Contemplation* is a remarkable book from an Asian perspective, and "may be called a bridge between East and West."[91]

In yet higher praise, Wu terms Merton's *The New Man* a "perfect synthesis of East and West," which echoes the non-dualistic thinking of the Chinese sages. He believes this parallel is due to Merton's habit of reading contemplatively, absorbing whatever he reads in terms of personal experience and understanding. Reading *The New Man* Wu finds echoes of the "Oriental sages" and gains a new understanding of their insights. "You are so deeply Christian that you can't help touching the vital springs of the other religions— Hinduism or Buddhism." Calling Merton a major prophet of the age, he tells him, "You need not bother about improving your knowledge of Chinese. You *are* Chinese, because you are universal."[92] When Merton remarks in his "Mystics and Zen" article that for Hui Neng (638-713), the Sixth Patriarch of the Chinese Zen sect of Buddhism, "*all life was Zen*,"[93] Wu writes, "It couldn't be better put. Did I not say that my Father Louis was a Chinese?"[94] Merton's

---

90. 3/20/61.

91. "First Friday," April 1961.

92. 11/28/61.

93. See "Mystics and Zen Masters" in *Mystics and Zen Masters*, 21 [Merton emphasis].

94. 3/31/63.

remarks in that article so move Wu that he experiences non-duality in a union of minds. He ticks off Merton's achievement as follows: Merton's "explanation of 'Mind' as 'Spirit' and of Prajna as *Light*, the Light that illumines all," his "discernment of the empirical self from the *Real Man* in the Chuangtzean sense," his concept of "pure affirmation," his differentiation "between *is* and *has*," his "awareness of full spiritual reality," his "speaking of the 'true face' as 'a discovery of *genuine identity* in and with the One,'" his . . . "repeated insistence on all-embracing Catholicity as the earmark of a true Catholic," and his reservations on a Buddhist metaphor for enlightenment, "The mirror has no stand." The cumulative effect of encountering Merton's acuity of vision, says Wu, is [it] "wrought in me the transcending of the subject-object relationship. There is no longer Father Louis or John Wu, but the Vagabond Spirit, the Divine Rascal Who comes and goes like the Wind."[95]

Merton's Buddhism, or rather, his understanding of Buddhism, is something which particularly strikes Wu, sometimes leaving him "speechless," as when he re-reads "Mystics and Zen Masters" years after he read it the first time, and finds Merton's interpretation of "Zen enlightenment" as "an insight into pure being in all its actual presence and immediacy." Wu exclaims that Merton's perception is the very point of his own work on Buddhism that he is currently writing and now he no longer cares if it gets published.[96] Wu's discovery of what might be termed "Merton's Buddhism" is important, because what is striking is not Merton's contribution to knowledge of Buddhism *per* se, nor the question of his being a Buddhist scholar or Buddhologist—which he most decidedly is not. What is significant is Merton's existential grasp of Buddhism as a Christian contemplative. In effect, Wu, the Buddhist scholar, is saying that Merton, monk and poet, understands Buddhism better than he does. Equally important today is the fact that Buddhologists and Asian specialists who are not steeped in the Gospels of Jesus and the Christian contemplative traditions like Merton, could miss Merton's contribution entirely.

Wu's reasoning is partly playful. Early in their correspondence, while commenting on Merton's *Seeds of Contemplation* as a text Buddhists of the Rinzai school would prefer, Wu jokes that he suspects Merton must have been a Zen master in a previous life,

95. 3/31/63.
96. 3/26/66.

and that in the present one he will attain Buddhahood.[97] Merton
knocks the Buddhahood ball back to Wu's court, saying: "If I once
reached Buddhahood and redescended to my present state, all I can
say is that I made a really heroic sacrifice." Continuing the joke
and admitting his attraction to the hermit life and things Chinese,
Merton adds: "Whatever I may have been in previous lives, I think
more than half of them were Chinese and eremitical."[98] Furthering
the banter about identity in later letters, Wu refers to some sketch
Merton makes of himself and declares: "The 'Old Rice Bag' [Mer-
ton's nickname for himself] looks very much like Hui Neng."[99]

While Wu loves to tease Merton, there is no doubt he profoundly esteems Merton's Buddhism. Merton's "fundamental
insights" are likened to rivulets forming a sea of understanding.[100]
Indeed, notes Wu, as other Asian specialists such as Father William Johnston, have observed, many of Merton's works are "full
of Zen," even those not dealing directly with Zen,[101] including ones
such as *Seeds of Contemplation* written when Merton was young
and may not have heard of Zen.[102]

Speaking only partly in jest, Wu says whether Merton is among
his Gethsemani monks or goes one day to visit Zen monks in Japan,
he might "serve as the occasion for their awakening to the Logos."
Merton is the answer to the famous Zen *koan*, "What is your Original
Face before you were born." "For you, Father, you are already *yourself*, the 'Original Face;' who is everywhere, including Japan, and
nowhere, not even in Gethsemani."[103] Sometimes Merton's observations serve to confirm Wu's views—e.g. the Zen masters are the heirs
of Lao Tzu and Chuang Tzu,[104] or clarify passages that were formerly
obscure,[105] or make connections between Buddha's teachings and Zen
that Chinese masters overlook.[106] While collaborating with Merton
on his project translating Chuang Tzu, Wu is also writing chapters
on various Zen masters for his *The Golden Age of Zen*. Merton's *The*

---

97. 5/25/61.
98. 5/29/61.
99. 12/27/64.
100. 8/14/65.
101. 8/3/65.
102. 12/7/65.
103. 12/27/64.
104. 2/5/65.
105. 5/11/65.
106. 8/14/65.

168 • Lucien Miller

Way of Chuang Tzu "opened my eyes to many things," says Wu, and "helped me to understand these monks of towering stature."[107] He believes *The Way of Chuang Tzu* reveals "the original affinities between Zen and Chuang Tzu."[108] After reading Merton's "The Zen Koan" in *Mystics and Zen Masters*, Wu concludes: "it can no longer be doubted that you have a clearer understanding of the whole damned thing than any of the modern Zennists, so far as I know."[109]

CONCLUSION

After exploring the unpublished letters between Thomas Merton and John C. H. Wu, we can readily agree with Wu's statement with which we began this essay: "Between true friends the Lord Himself serves as the postman." The encounter is providential for both. They need one another professionally for writing *The Way of Chuang Tzu* and *The Golden Age of Zen*, and each relies on the friendship, trust and encouragement of the other. They share a spiritual affinity for solitude and an attraction to that which is offbeat or original in poetic temperaments and spiritual masters East-West. Merton understands Asian spiritualities as contemplative monk and poet. Wu finds Christ in ancient Chinese Taoism and Buddhism. Both agree that Western Christianity needs the East, and that a reawakening to the Gospel can occur through an encounter with Asian traditions. In Merton, Wu discovers a mind of transparent clarity, a mystical intelligence able to hold both ends of a paradox in one hand. The monk is a synthesis of East and West, who like Wu sees the West in the East and the East in the West. Wu discovers Merton's Buddhism, his "Asian" or "Chinese" self, and helps him to see Asia more clearly. Merton names Wu's playfully profound *samadhi* and conspires with the Holy Spirit to bring Wu to enlightenment. In the last analysis, the encounter and interaction between Thomas Merton and John C. H. Wu uncovers what is latent in each. Merton becomes Father Void and Wu discovers the *Logos* in the East.

WORKS CITED

Frank J. Hoffman. Review: "*Zen Keys; The Golden Age of Zen,*" in *Philosophy East and West*. Vol. 48, No. 1 (Jan., 1998), pp. 165-167.

---

107. 2/2/65.
108. 11/16/65.
109. 1/19/66.

Thomas Merton. *The Seven Storey Mountain*. New York: Harcourt, Brace and Company, 1948.

———. *The Way of Chuang Tzu*. New York: New Directions, 1965.

———. *Mystics and Zen Masters*. New York: Noonday Press, Farrar, Strauss and Giroux, 1967.

———. "Mystics and Zen Masters" in Merton's *Mystics and Zen Masters*, New York: Noonday Press, Farrar, Straus and Giroux, 1967, pp. 3-44.

———. *Zen and the Birds of Appetite*. New York: New Directions, 1968.

———. "A Christian Looks at Zen." In *Zen and the Birds of Appetite*. New York: New Directions, 1968. pp. 33-58.

———. Introduction to John C. H. Wu. *The Golden Age of Zen*. New York: Doubleday, 1996. Orig. published by the National War College in cooperation with the Committee on the Compilation of the Chinese Library, Yang-ming-shan, Taiwan 1967.

———. *Follow the Ecstasy: Thomas Merton, The Hermitage Years 1965-1968*. Ed. John Howard Griffin. Fort Worth, Texas: JHG Editions/Latitudes Press, 1983.

———. "With the World in my Bloodstream." In *Follow the Ecstasy: Thomas Merton, The Hermitage Years 1965-1968*. Ed. John Howard Griffin. Fort Worth, Texas: JHG Editions/ Latitudes Press, 1983. pp. 73-76.

———. *Learning to Love: Exploring Solitude and Freedom*. The Journals of Thomas Merton. Volume 6 (1966-1967). Ed. Christine M. Bochen. San Francisco: HarperCollins, 1997.

Thomas Merton, John C. H. Wu, "The Thomas Merton-John C. H. Wu Correspondence," unpublished manuscript.

Lucien Miller. "Merton's *Chuang Tzu*." Thomas Merton Center, Bellarmine University, Louisville, Kentucky.

Shigeto Oshida, OP. "The Mystery of the Word and Reality," 1981. Unpublished.

John C. H. Wu. *Beyond East and West*. New York: Sheed and Ward, 1951.

———. *The Interior Carmel*. New York: Sheed & Ward, 1952.

———. "St. Thérèse and Lao Tzu: a Study in Comparative Mysticism," in *Chinese Humanism and Christian Spirituality: Essays of John C. H. Wu*. Ed. Paul K. T. Sih. Jamaica, New

York: St. John's University Press, 1965.

———. *The Golden Age of* Zen. With an Introduction by Thomas Merton. New York: Image Books Doubleday, 1996. Orig. published by the National War College in cooperation with the Committee on the Compilation of the Chinese Library, Yang-ming-shan, Taiwan 1967.

———. John Wu, Jr. "Footnotes to Merton-Wu Letters," unpublished manuscript.

PART IV
THE COLLECTED LETTERS OF
THOMAS MERTON AND JOHN WU
(1961–1968)

TM TO JW

March 14, 1961

My Dear Dr Wu:

Father Paul Chan[1] wrote to me some time ago saying that he had kindly spoken to you about a project of mine which came to his attention, through a letter I had written to Archbishop Yu Pin.[2] So you are already acquainted with the fact that I have been for some time persuaded of the immense importance of a prudent study of Oriental philosophy by some of us in the West, particularly in the kind of perspective that guided some of the early Church Fathers in their use of Platonism, and St. Thomas in his use of Aristotle.

Naturally, there is a great deal of irresponsible and rather absurd dabbling in things Oriental among certain western types, and I don't want to make myself sillier than I already am by joining their number. Besides, I am very much lacking in background, and do not even have the most elementary knowledge of the languages that might be involved.

It is very important that one in such a position should have guidance and advice from someone who is an expert in the field. I am very glad Father Chan suggested you, as I am familiar with your books and realize that you are exactly the kind of person who would be of immense help. Since Father Chan says that you have expressed a willingness to do something of the kind, I therefore write to you without too many apologies, and indeed with great gratitude for your kindness.

Where shall I begin? The one concrete thing that Father Chain seized upon in my letter to Archbishop Yu Pin was the tentative project of a selection from Chuang Tzu[3] which New Directions

1. Father Paul Chan: secretary to Archbishop Paul Yu Pin (later Cardinal) who headed the Sino American Amity, a center for overseas Chinese students on Riverside Drive in NYC. Fr. Chan was the one who recommended Dr. John Wu as a potential Chinese translator to Merton in their collaborative effort to study the Chuang Tzu text.

2. Archbishop Yu Pin (1901-1978): later Paul Cardinal Yu Pin. Yu Pin visited the monastery on June 1, 1949 for the centenary of Gethsemani Abbey and spoke of Buddhist contemplation. In his *Journal* entry, Merton says of Yu Pin that he "by no means dismisses the Buddhist monks as hypocrites or 'dreamers,'" and notes that the Buddhists reproached the Christians for "building hospitals" and having "no contemplatives" (see *Entering the Silence: Journals of Thomas Merton*, Vol. II, p. 321).

3. Chuang Tzu: the greatest of the Taoists after Lao Tzu, its founder. He

would like to publish. But this is perhaps premature. I don't know if you saw a raw attempt of mine to say something about Chinese thought in *Jubilee*. It may have seemed articulate but I am sure you would have realized that I have only the most superficial grasp of the Confucian Classics,[4] which is what I was mainly talking about. I do think it would be important perhaps for me to read some more and if possible discuss the Four Classics with you on the most elementary level, like any Chinese schoolboy of the old days.[5] I would like to really get impregnated with the spirit of the Four Classics, which to my mind is perfectly compatible with Christian ethics, and then go on to what really attracts me even more, the mysticism of the early Taoists.[6] Then after that I might be able to talk more sense about Chuang Tzu, and if you are still interested, we could perhaps work together on a selection, and you could do an original translation of the things we selected. I have the Legge[7] translation here which looks suspiciously doctored to me.

I would be interested in your reaction, and would welcome any suggestions as to how to proceed and what to read now. And then, when you are free, I would like to invite you down to Gethsemani

flourished towards the end of the classic period of Chinese philosophy (550-250 B.C.E.) and died around 275 B.C.E.. Merton wrote *The Way of Chuang Tzu* to contemporary readers especially in the West who might be interested in the ancient wisdom of Taoism.

4. Confucian Classics: the 13 classics whose compilation has been attributed to Confucius. They cover, among others, the *Four Books* (*The Analects*, the *Book of Mencius*, the *Great Learning* and the *Golden Mean*) as well as the *I Ching* (*Book of Changes*); *Book of Poetry*; *Book of History*; the *Spring And Autumn*; the *Record of Rites*; and the *Book of Filial Piety*, appearing as canonical books during the early days of the T'ang Dynasty in the 7th century.

5. "like any schoolboy of the old days": Merton is making reference to the tradition in the past (practiced as late as the early part of the 20th century) of schoolboys memorizing, if not the entire classical canon, at least the *Four Books* for purposes of passing the state civil service examinations or for one's own edification. This is significant as Wu and his contemporaries were the last generation raised on this time-honored tradition.

6. Taoists/Taoism: the names conventionally associated with this school of thought are the ancients, Lao Tzu, its founder, and Chuang Tzu whose writings, though unquestionably mystical and full of allusions to nature, were, like writings typically of the classical period, presented as political treatises. This is certainly true of Lao Tzu's *Tao Teh Ching*, the veritable bible of Taoism.

7. James Legge (1815-1897): for a good part of the 20th century, Legge's translation of the *Chinese Classics* (he rendered 10 of the 13 into English) was regarded by scholars as definitive. Among his other translated works included the *Texts of Taoism* (the *Tao Teh Ching* and *The Book of Chuang Tzu*).

for a few days or a week. This could be made worthwhile materially speaking by lectures which could be arranged at neighboring colleges and Father Abbot would certainly want you to talk here. You could perhaps address my class of mystical theology on Chinese spirituality and mysticism. In a word there would be ways of covering expenses, and no doubt you might enjoy the change. We would certainly enjoy having you here as our guest. Can we discuss this further?

Meanwhile, as a token of esteem, I am sending a privately printed thing on Meng Tzu.[8] I keep you in my prayers and beg that this project may be fruitful in the sense in which it seems to be suggested by the will of God.

Very cordially yours in Christ,

[No Signature]

---

8. Meng Tzu: aka Mencius (372-289? B.C.E.): regarded as the greatest Confucian after the great teacher himself. The writing referred to is an English rendition of the famous "Parable of Ox-Mountain" (Mencius 6A:8) which analogically and unequivocally sets down Mencius's conviction that human beings are basically good by nature. For text (Merton's own rendition) and commentary, see Merton's *Mystics and Zen Masters*, pp. 65-8; hereafter known as *MZM*.

JW to TM

3 Reynolds Place
Newark 6, New Jersey

March 20, 1961

My dear dear Father Thomas:

The Feast of St. Joseph happens to be celebrated today this year. As I usually drop in at the mail room of the university,[9] I got your letter this morning and brought it with me into the chapel. After the Mass, I opened the letter, still on my knees, and read it right before Our Lord in the Blessed Sacrament. It is a memorable day for me, Father.

Let me tell you first what I felt when I read your article in *Jubilee*. I thought you are a wizard, Father! You have such a penetrating insight into the Chinese ways of thinking, and your judgment of the relative merits of the different schools shows such a sureness of touch, that more knowledge of the original materials will only serve to confirm the insights and fill up the outline. There is absolutely nothing "superficial" about your grasp of the Confucian classics. Your God-given gift for *seeing the essential* in everything you study prevents you from being in any way superficial. When the natural gift is reinforced and uplifted by the Gifts of the Holy Spirit, as it is in your case, your mind becomes transparent like a fire burning white-hot, and all bits of knowledge become welcome fuel to the fire.

In one sense, it is easier to appreciate Taoism than Confucianism, because it is easier to see the originality of the former than to realize the *genuineness* of the latter. It is because you, Father, have *lived* Confucianism—that is, you have striven with all your might to perform the ordinary duties of the monastery as loving bidding from Our Father—that you can consider the Confucian system of rites as something not imposed from without but springing "*from within men themselves*." Nor are you blind to the danger of such a system degenerating into a squeezed lemon, "an outward façade of

---

9. university: Seton Hall University, South Orange, New Jersey where Wu first taught in its School of Law, later in its Far Eastern Studies, from 1951 until his retirement in 1968. Thereafter, Wu went to Taiwan to live and teach at the College of Chinese Culture (later Chinese Culture University) until his passing in February 1986, just before his 87th birthday.

Ju."[10] I used to say that Confucius was the greatest Taoist, because he realized the extraordinary in the ordinary. But the tragedy is that so many "Confucianists" became, as you so keenly observe, legalistic formalists. They were so narrow and mundanely provincial as to condemn Taoism sweepingly. You are right in saying that Confucianism is natural ethics or natural law in a very refined and traditional form. Thus, its kernel is sound and immutable; but the trouble with many Confucian scholars of old took the traditional forms as an inseparable part of the natural law, thus confusing human traditions with the laws of God.

When such ossification happens, there is a call for the revival of the spirit of spontaneity and freedom as found in Lao Tzu and Chuang Tzu. But the unfortunate thing is that none of the later Taoists seem to have attained the depth and the height of the two founders. In fact, Taoism as a *religion* became a cult of *Yin* and *Yang* more than a cult of the Tao. At first it attempted to find the Elixir of Life, hoping to achieve immortality of the body. Ironically, many an emperor shortened his life by taking a purported Elixir. Only later did the more philosophically minded Taoists expound the doctrine that the real Elixir of Life is to be found in our own being. It has become Yoga for purifying the spirit as well strengthening the body. This Yoga is centered on attaining the harmony of the *Yin* and *Yang* elements in the person. The *anima* (*P'o*) belong to the *Yin* pole, while the *animus* belongs to the *Yang* pole (*Hun*). At death it is the *Hun* that achieves immortality, while the *P'o* returns to earth. The strange thing is that this doctrine has been taken by Dr. C. G. Jung as an independent confirmation of his own psychological discoveries.

Now to return to Chuang Tzu. I am more than willing to cooperate with you, Father, on compiling an anthology of *Chuang Tzu*. I say "More than willing" because I clearly see in your request an operation of Providence. For the last few days I had been rereading the works of Chuang Tzu in preparation for an article on his philosophy, which the International Philosophical Quarterly has asked me to do.[11] I have come to see, for the first time, that Chuang

10. Ju: (770-221 B.C.E.): traditionally the school of Confucian scholars who interpreted Confucius's teachings.

11. "the International Philosophical Quarterly has asked me to do": the article, "The Wisdom of Chuang Tzu: a New Appraisal," appeared in *IPQ*, Vol. III, No. 1, Feb. 1963; hereafter known as "Wisdom."

Tzu is neither a Pantheist pure and simple nor a Theist pure and simple, but a mixture of the two, a *prototype* of what von Hügel[12] calls "Panentheism." Chuang Tzu is the wizard of ancient China. His humor and apparent frivolities cover abysmal profundities. My friend Lin Yutang[13] seems to be mainly attracted by his humor and wit, but I don't know if he has seen the depth of his spiritual insight and metaphysical vision. In fact, it seems to me that only a man like yourself, who are steeped in works of great Christian mystics, can know what Lao Tzu and Chuang Tzu were pointing at, and how utterly honest and earnest they were. The *Logos* of God who enlightens everyone coming into this world illuminated their minds a very special way for reasons of His own. One of the reasons surely is that He meant to prepare the Chinese mind (and the modern "post-Christian" mind) for the recognition of the True Light. "In Thy light shall we see Light!"

I agree with you perfectly that the Legge translation looks "doctored." Have you seen the translation by Herbert Giles?[14] I have two copies of it; and if your Abbey does not have a copy, I should regard it as a great privilege to present one to it, so that you may use it. Neither translation is satisfactory. If Legge is too academic, Giles writes rather glibly. In not a few places, both seem to me to be inaccurate. In the case of Giles, they seem to be mere conjectures. In the case of Legge, he follows some of the Chinese commentaries too slavishly. I still prefer Legge to Giles. Although

---

12. von Hügel: Baron Friedrich von Hügel (1852-1925), born in Florence of Austrian and Scottish parents, was a Roman Catholic theologian who influenced, among others, Evelyn Underhill, a female Anglican writer and a foremost exponent of mystical writings in the 20th century. Von Hügel welcomed the tension between scientific development and religious faith as a positive challenge to the believer. His pan-en-theistic view holds that God is in everything and everything is in God.

13. Lin Yutang (1895-1976): author of numerous scholarly and popular books including *My Country and My People, The Art of Living, The Wisdom of China and India: an Anthology, The Wisdom of Laotse* and *The Wisdom of Confucius*. He is credited with popularizing Chinese studies in the West, especially in the US. Lin and Wu were on the staff of the *T'ien Hsia Monthly*, an influential literary and scholarly journal published in English in Shanghai and Hong Kong that had a run from 1935 to 1940. Many of Wu's writings that were later published in the West first appeared in this journal.

14. Herbert Giles (1845-1935): a distinguished English sinologist and translator, Giles, along with Legge, Arthur Waley and Richard Wilhelm were four of the most prominent students of sinology in the latter part of the 19th and first part of the 20th centuries.

misguided sometimes, Legge seems to have a better mastery of the language. Giles has literary intuitions, but philosophical insights he has none.

So, Father, we have to produce a new translation of all the passages we may see fit to select. Please go ahead to make your selection, and I shall attempt to render it as literally as I can and you will turn it into literature. For the purpose of making the selection, Legge may well be used as a working basis.

I don't know if your edition of Legge is the same as mine. Mine was first published in 1891, second impression in 1927. It is entitled *The Texts of Taoism*, containing both *Tao Teh King* (a very poor translation) and *The Writings of Chuang Tzu*. The volume has 323 pages. If yours is a different edition, then tell me yours that I may get one from the bookstores here. When we are using the same edition, you need only tell me the page numbers of all the passages you intent to select.

In Lin Yutang's compilation of *The Wisdom of China and India* are included thirteen chapters from Chuang Tzu, based upon Giles' version. I suppose you have seen this. It is a Random House publication.

The more I read your *Jubilee* article the more I admire it. Your comments on Hsun Tzu,[15] on the legalists, and on the ossification of classic thought since the Han confirm my own conclusions. But what I like most is your comments on Taoism. There not only the gifts of knowledge and understanding, but the Gift of Wisdom, are unconsciously revealed. Being fundamentally a Taoist, I too feel the need of the counter-ballast of Confucianism. You are of the mind of St. Paul, who says to the Corinthians, "If we are out of our mind, it is for God; if we are sane, it is for you." In my Chinese version of the New Testament,[16] I render it as: "When

---

15. Hsun Tzu (312-230 B.C.E.): represents the so-called "right-wing" of Confucianism. Contrary to Mencius's innate theory, Hsun Tzu believed human nature to be evil or depraved and goodness therefore only the result of education and artificial training. Note however that both Confucian wings emphasized the importance of education and cultivation of the true self (also known by Chinese philosophers as "the superior man").

16. "Chinese version of the New Testament": originally published in Hong Kong in 1948, the work was commissioned by President Chiang Kai-shek of the Republic of China. Wu had rendered *The Psalms* into classical Chinese in October 1946, also at the behest of his president. The story of how these works materialized is intriguingly told in Wu's autobiography, *Beyond East and West*.

we are inebriated, it is for God; when we are sober, it is for you."
It seems to me, Father, that only Christ has made it possible for
us to be honestly drunk and sincerely sober at the same time, for
our sobriety itself springs from Love. Only when we are united
with the Word incarnate can we be full-fledged Confucianists and
thoroughgoing Taoists at the same time.

Our friendship, Father, is predetermined. I have waited for you
to take the initiative, because you are "another Christ," while I am
only a member of His (Church). Let it be part of my vocation to
serve you as an altar boy and to cooperate with you in your Chinese
studies. I am going to be sixty-two on the 28th of this month. It is
Lao Tzu and St. Thérèse[17] who have helped me to remain a little
child, so that my heart always thrills whenever I respond "Ad Deum
qui laetificiat juventutem meam."[18] As I recall, St. Thérèse also
played a significant part in your vocation.

Perhaps, latter part of July or early August will find me, the
Lord willing, in Gethsemani. In June, my son Peter,[19] a seminarian
in Maryknoll, will be ordained. His old father will be his altar-boy
and serve him as a son serves his Father. What a Romance Our Lord
has made of our life! By the way, Father, last time I saw Peter, he
mentioned your *Jubilee* article with great admiration. Please keep
him in your prayers.

In the latter part of June I shall have to take charge of a Seminar
in the Catholic University in Washington on Natural Law, and to
deliver a paper on "The Natural Law with a Growing Content."[20] I
think so far the writers on the natural law have neglected the idea of
St. Thomas that the natural law can be *changed* by way of addition.
Please pray for me, Father, for this paper and other intentions too

17. St. Thérèse of Lisieux: (1873-1897) aka "The Little Flower of Jesus":
French Carmelite saint who was declared by Pope John Paul II a Doctor of the
Church in 1997. She was famous for her autobiography, *L'histoire d'une âme*
(*The Story of a Soul*), which chronicles her spiritual journey. She was influential
to both men, Wu attributing his own conversion to her and Merton dedicating to
her his priestly vocation.

18. "Ad deum qui laetificat juventutem meum": (Latin): "To God Who gives
joy to my youth" (opening response to the Latin Mass).

19. "my son Peter": Rev. Peter Augustine Wu (b. 1932), ordained a Maryknoll
priest in June 1961 and a missionary in Taiwan since 1962.

20. "The Natural Law with a Growing Content": published as "The Natural
Law and Christian Civilization" in *Philosophy and the Integration of Contemporary Catholic Education*, ed. George F. McLean, Catholic University Press,
Washington D. C., 1962.

long to put on paper.

Convey my humblest filial respects to Father Abbot.

Filially yours in J.M.J.,

John C. H. Wu

JW to TM

Jhs

3 Reynolds Place
Newark 6, New Jersey

Good Friday, 1961

My dear Father Thomas,

The Wisdom of the Desert came yesterday. By this time I have read through the whole volume. To have spent the Holy Thursday and the Good Friday in reading and meditating on such a feast of spiritual wisdom has made me realize more than ever our infinite debt to the Crucified Christ. Just imagine if any of the old monks could have attained such heights in *The Verbum* or *The Tao* of God had God had not become flesh and bones and redeemed mankind?

Your introduction is a jewel of Christian spirituality—so simple and yet so rich in content. It brings into focus the universal teaching of sages and saints that whoever uplifts himself uplifts the world. *Qui s'élève élève le monde*, as Madame Leseur puts it.

The true significance of the moral intuitions and spiritual insights of Sages such as Lao Tzu, Confucius, Buddha, Chuang Tzu, and Mencius in the framework of Christianity has been brought home to my mind. In reading through your book, I am constantly reminded of sayings and anecdotes in Chinese books. This reveals to my mind the thrilling truth that *The Tao Incarnate* is absolutely the *Same Tao* who was from the beginning with God and is God. Before Lao Tzu was, He *is*.

As I do not think it likely that you have a copy of Giles' version of *Chuang Tzu*, I have mailed it to the Father Abbot in trust for you, Father. (By the way, the English law of trusts arose from the fact that the Franciscans positively refused to own anything in law, not even a penny, so that people had to resort to the ingenious device of "*ad opus*.")[21]

Now, Father, please make your selections of Chuang Tzu, whether from Giles or from Legge, and from both. I shall gladly

---

21. "ad opus": (Latin) "to the use of." See Wu's *Fountain of Justice* (Sheed and Ward, 1955), p. 154, footnote 65: ". . . the idea of trust, which plays such a vital role in the Common Law, originated in the 13th century in England when the Franciscan friars positively refused to own any property so that their benefactors had to resort to the ingenious devise of conveying their property to some borough 'to the use of' the friars."

re-render them for your final revision. A labor of love is *repese* or *quies* enough.

I must confess before I conclude that your book has made me anticipate somewhat the coming of Easter, for, Father, I laughed (immoderately) last night at least twice—at XXXIII and at LXXI. Confucius himself would have laughed, and Chuang Tzu would have risen from the dead.

Happy Easter, Father!

Your son in Christ,

John C. H. Wu

TM to JW

April 1, 1961

Dear Dr Wu:

Your wonderful letter was a joy and an encouragement.[22] I have no more doubts about the project being willed by God. It has the marks of the Holy Spirit's action upon it everywhere, doesn't it? The way you received the suggestion and your wonderful response is all the evidence one needs. I am sure we will go on to work together very happily and very fruitfully, and I know I myself will surely benefit in every way.

So let us then proceed with love for the God Who manifested His Wisdom so simply and so strikingly in the early Chinese sages, and let us give Him glory by bringing out the inner heart of that wisdom once again. One of the defects of a wrong kind of supernaturalism is that by rejecting those wonderful natural wisdoms that came before Christ and cried out for fulfillment in the Gospel, they set aside the challenging demands which would make us Christians strive for the highest purity of our own spiritual wisdom. And then, while claiming to be supernatural, we live on a level that is in some ways *below* nature; the supernatural becomes the unnatural "sanctified" by legalistic formulas and appeals to gestures and rites whose inner meaning is not understood. And the whole thing is kept going by the magic formula *ex opere operato*. Certainly God in His mercy deigns to give grace to woefully unprepared souls, but this should not be an excuse for the complacency and obscurantism one meets everywhere.

I would not be able to explain this to many of my fellow priests, but I can say it to you with all confidence: it seems to me that this act of humility is demanded of us by God, that we condescend to *learn* and learn much, perhaps to acquire a whole new orientation of thought (which is simply the recovery of our own Christian orientation) from the Ancient wisdoms which were fulfilled in Christ, so that we ourselves may reach a higher and deeper fulfillment which He demands of us. It is a question of a renewed perspective for

---

22. "... a joy and an encouragement": (possible *Appendix* in *Turning Toward the World: The Journals of Thomas Merton*, Vol. 4, p. 102): "When I got back there was a superb letter from Dr. John Wu in answer to one I had written to him about collaborating on some selections from Chuang Tzu. A letter of great humility and nobility . . . ." (to the end of paragraph).

Christian wisdom itself.

What you say of the later Taoists taken up by Jung is very interesting and fits very well into some thinking I myself have been doing about personalism. One of the defects of popular personalism among us, including Christian personalism in some thinkers, is that the person is equated with the *anima* (P'o) and this is thought to be what survives, what is to be "cultivated" and "developed" so that actually a different kind of practical anti-personalism is the result.

I am so happy you are doing a study of Chuang Tzu and I look forward to reading it, avidly. I am more and more struck by the profundity of his thought. He is one of the *great* wise men: I will not say "philosophers" in the speculative sense, for his wisdom has a marvelous wholeness, and that is what makes it seem "simple." Indeed it is simple, but at the same time utterly profound. I think he has in him an element which is essential to all true contemplation, and which is often lacking in Western "contemplatives." His grasp of the fact that most of what is done in the name of "perfection" is actually perversion. His respect for the wholeness of reality which cannot be seized in a definition. The real meaning of *nature*. One must respect nature before one can rise out of it to be a person. Certainly he is well prepared for the "true Light" which shines out in the resurrection of Christ. The wisdom of Chuang Tzu demands the resurrection, for the resurrection goes beyond all moralities and moral theories, it is a totally new life in the Spirit.

Now as to the practical details. I have not seen the Giles translation and would be very glad to have it at hand while going through Legge. We do not have anything but Legge here. My edition of Legge may well be a reprint of the one you have. It too is very big, called the *Texts of Taoism* but it was printed quite recently by the Julian Press with a preface by Suzuki. Hence the pagination may be different, that is the only problem. It looks as if they photographed the old pages and did them up again in offset. What I can do is tentatively send you a list of passages that interest me in the first four books, and see if you can located them without difficulty. I will do this in a couple of days when I can get to it. Then you will let me know how it comes out. If I have the Giles book here I can give further references which will help you to locate the texts, but anyway with the subdivisions in Legge it would not be at all hard to give precise indications.

I have Lin Yutang's *Wisdom of India and China*, but have not yet done much with it. I agree with your mode of procedure, and we will go ahead that way.

God bless you, belatedly, on your birthday this Holy Week. I will be keeping you in my Easter Masses and ask the Lord to give you every blessing and joy and keep ever fresh and young your "child's mind" which is the only one worth having. May He grant us as you so well say to be both inebriated and sober in Christ, Confucians and Taoists. It is all important for us to *be* in Christ, what the great sages cried out to God for. May our studies help us to live what they hoped for, and may we be able to bring to the Orient hope and light, which by right is theirs: for Christ rose up in the East, and we sing to Him "*O Oriens*" in Advent. His is what William of St. Thierry called the *orientale lumen*. To that great light let us be humbly devoted and let us seek its tranquil purity in which all lights are fulfilled.

I look forward then to your coming later in the summer. If you think Lin Yutang would like to come, and can, then by all means bring him. Or perhaps you would prefer to come alone this first time and bring him some other time. In any case you will be most welcome. And finally do let me know the date of Peter's ordination and we will all be praying for him. I am so happy for you and for him and share with you the joy that is to be yours. God bless all of you. I will send you in a few days a list of selections from Chuang. Do please indicate any more books that would help me in my understanding and will broaden my background. Thanks again for your very wise letter, and let us go on united in prayer and in the joy of Christ.

Cordially yours in Christ our Lord,

Tom Merton

(in TM's hand) *Your thesis on the natural law is vitally important—you have all my good wishes for success, + my prayers. Do let me read your talk after you have given it.*

TM TO JW

April 4, 1961

Dear Dr Wu,

I am having a really wonderful time with Chuang Tzu and today I am sending you a first tentative list of selections from the first three books of the Legge translation in the edition that I have. I am only sending the selections from the first books so that you can see if my indications fit your edition. I am giving the numbers of the *Book* + the numbers of the *sections* as given by Legge + and the page number according to the edition I have here.

Please let me know soon if those indications are sufficient for you. If they are not, then I will make a complete list and send you the book I have here along with it. That ought to settle the difficulty.

The wisdom of Chuang Tzu delights + shames me. There's so much in him that we ought to be knowing + practicing in the monastery. Alas, we are all trying to be "superior men" + we are "standing on tiptoe," "limping about" with our virtuousness.

There are some metaphysical sections in Bk II which might be too complex to explain. I would not want to do so unless I could say something intelligent about the Tao of "pantheism" with which we absolve ourselves from giving any further thought to oriental metaphysics. This is something we could discuss.

Books IX, X, XI are simply superb. I love his paragraphs about horses. He is as consummate an artist as the T'ang painters—or whenever the great painters were. We ought to try and illustrate the book with some pertinent examples from Chinese art. What a splendid book this might be!

This is just a hasty note but it brings you my best wishes, blessings + prayers. Yesterday I said mass for you and for our project.

Very cordially yours in Christ,

Tom Merton

(M Louis)

JW to TM

3 Reynolds Place
Newark 6, New Jersey

April First Friday, 1961

My dear Father Louis:

Your gracious letters of April 1 and 4 have come. I like your selections very much. They not only represent the essential thoughts of the first three books, but also are of such a nature as would interest readers.

Although the pages of the two editions of Legge are different (about 50 pages apart), it has been easy for me to locate them, thanks to your careful notations of the books and sections. So please go ahead with the work of selecting.

I have already attempted to render one passage (Bk. II, #7), which seems to me to stand in special need of re-translation:

Great Tao is beyond names.
Great eloquence is silent. (lit. "without words")
Great humanity is not merely human.
Great integrity is not angular.
Great courage is not ruthless.

When the Tao is articulated, it is no longer the Tao.
When speech is eloquent, it falls short of its aim.
When humanity takes on fixed forms, it does not come to
    fruition.
When integrity shines bright, it is wanting in sincerity.
When courage is ruthless, it accomplishes nothing.
These five are like roundness aspiring to be square.

Therefore, to know how to rest in what one does not know is the summit of knowledge. Whoever knows the eloquence of silence and the inexpressibility of the Tao may be called "Heaven's treasure-house." Pour into it, and it is never filled. Draw from it, and it is never exhausted, nobody knowing whence comes all this. Such a one may be said to contain the Light within him.

The same passage is found in Giles, pp. 25-26. My language, of course, needs a great deal of brushing up; but I have tried to give the real meaning, after having consulted the Chinese commentaries.

I have been rereading your *Seeds of Contemplation*. I am struck by the similarity between your mode of thinking and that of Lao Tzu and Chuang Tzu. For instance, on p. 96, you write: "The Holy Spirit is sent from moment to moment into my soul, etc." This seems to me exactly what Chuang Tzu would have written, had he been a Christian. "Selflessness is my true self" (p. 46). This sums up Lao Tzu and Buddha and the best of Hinduism. There are so many remarkable things in the book that I think that it may be called a bridge between East and West.

Everything that you say in your letter of the 1st finds an echo in me Father. The way to the re-Christianization of this post-Christian West lies through the East. Not that the East has anything really new to give to the Gospel of Christ; but its natural wisdoms are meant by God to remind the Christians of their own infinitely richer heritage, which, unfortunately, they are not aware of.

I just had a phone talk with Yutang. I have extended your kind invitation to him. He appreciates it very warmly, for he knows of your works. It is, however, not likely that he could free himself from constant work of writing to make a special trip to Kentucky. He is the only one of my friends who lives exclusively by writing. His mentality is more akin to Hui Tzu than to Chuang Tzu.

Let me stop here now, for I have to file the income tax returns.

Who pays his taxes as for Thy laws
Upon Thy boundless coffer draws.

O Father Louis, how happy we are! The Lord has enabled us to live unconditionally in this very much conditioned world.

Your humble child in Christ,

John C. H. Wu

TM to JW

April 11, 1961

Dear John,

Thank you for your very good letter, for the Giles translation which I have now received + which is clear, idiomatic English, throwing light on Legge's more cautious + careful translation. Thanks above all for the first sample of your own translation. I like the almost poetic form + think we ought to use that often. I will discuss the details later—whether for instance it is better to use "benevolence" or "humanity," etc. I will send you my ideas of a literary revision.

Here is another list. I have given the sections according to Legge + where it might be useful to do so I have also added the page numbers in Giles. I think it will be all clear. More will follow soon.

Do you know what? We are reading *Beyond East and West*[23] in the refectory now. It was Father Abbot's idea, highly encouraged by me, + everyone is enjoying it. You are so right in your great love for China + in your realization that Christianity transcends all racial and national limitations—a fact that has been too often forgotten.

I enjoy Chuang Tzu more + more. The liberty of spirit he seeks is found truly in St. Paul's Epistles + in St. John. We underestimate St. Paul. We do not realize what a liberation he went through + how carefree + undetermined a Christian really should be, with no care save to listen to the Holy Spirit + follow wherever He beckons! Let us seek more + more to do this in the gaiety + childlike joy of Chuang Tzu. I think spiritual childhood must be a characteristically Chinese grace, I mean one which the Chinese temperament was prepared for. Bearing in mind what you said about Lin Yutang resembling Hui Tzu, I laughed very much at the story of the minnows, Bk XVII, #13 (Giles p. 218). I know something is certainly missing in Lin Yutang's edition of Lao Tse.

God bless you again + always

All joy in Christ our Lord,

Tom Merton

---

23. *Beyond East and West*: autobiography published by Shed and Ward, 1950, while Wu was in Honolulu teaching at the University of Hawaii. Coincidentally, Merton's *The Seven Storey Mountain* and *Beyond East and West* were one and two for a time on the best-seller lists of Catholic books.

JW TO TM

3 Reynolds Place
Newark 6, New Jersey

15 April 1961

Dear Father Louis:

Only today did the lovely thing on Meng Tzu come! It has taken a month *in travelling*.

Your interpretation of the term "*yeh chi*"[24] as "the merciful, pervasive and mysterious influence of unconscious nature" is truly illuminating. The whole piece reproduces the very spirit and meaning of the original. It gives me the same aesthetic delight as the chanting of the original used to give me.

This is the way to translate the Chinese classics. Instead of slavishly sticking to the letter, you have achieved an equivalence of values and ideas in another language.

I am glad to note that you use "love" to render what Legge renders as "benevolence and righteousness." This reminds me of Chuang Tzu's "Ta jen pu jen,"[25] which I have tentatively rendered as "Great humanity is not merely human." I think it would be better to say, "True love is not sentimental."

Your good letter of the 11th came yesterday. I am tickled to learn that *Beyond East and West* is being read in the refectory.

Your selections are invariably good, Father. I have not begun the work of translating; but I am reading the original and the commentaries more carefully in order to get a firmer grasp of the ideas. I shall begin as soon as I have all the selections in. I think that most of the work has to be done in the summer. I shall dedicate the whole month of July to it. I shall come to Gethsemani in August.

Father Abbot has graciously written me, assuring me of a warm welcome. He has sent a copy of the beautiful "God Is My Life."

---

24. "yeh chi" (aka "the merciful, pervasive and mysterious influence of unconscious nature"): found in the "Parable Ox-Mountain" of *Mencius* (see VI, pt. 1, chap. 8).

25. "ta jen pu jen" (aka "Great humanity is not merely human"): this is comparable to "shang teh pu teh" in the *Tao Teh Ching* which Wu renders, "High virtue is non-virtuous (therefore, it has virtue)." In *New Seeds of Contemplation*, Merton writes: "Sometimes virtuous men are also bitter and unhappy because they have unconsciously come to believe that all happiness depends on their being more virtuous than others" (Chapter 8, p. 58). In Wu's writings, he humorously calls such people the "goody-goodies," who are more moralistic than authentically moral.

What you say about St. Paul is so true. I remember when I was translating the New Testament, I felt most at home with his Epistles. I felt as though Chuang Tzu was writing, especially in the two Corinthians and Philippians. In the Pastoral Epistles, he was more Confucian. But whenever he let himself go, he was Taoistic to the bones.

I am going to mail you some unpublished papers on St. Thérèse. The one on "St. Thérèse and Lao Tzu"[26] I want you, Father, to scrutinize carefully, because I am not quite sure whether the comparisons are valid. Anyway, Father, I beg you to tell me without any reservations what you think of the paper, as well as the other one on "Thérèse and Celine." Last year I submitted these papers, together with a former study of the teachings of the Little Flower, "The Science of Love,"[27] to Mr. Frank Sheed. He turned it down, because he thinks that there is little market for such things, there being already too many books on her.

If, Father, you should think that the papers are not beyond mending, then I would want to have a lift from you. I want you to write a substantial introduction to the booklet. This will help me to find a publisher.

I am inclosing here Mr. Sheed's letter for your reference. He and I are very good friends, and I have respect for his judgment. But he can be wrong. In fact, I suspect that his mind has been somewhat prejudiced against Therese's writings by some of the recent books about her, including Father Robo's. Anyway, Father, I want your views. If you should agree with his judgment, then I will mend.

Your son in Jesus—thru Mary—with a smile,

John

---

26. *"St. Thérèse and Lao Tzu"* and *"Thérèse and Celine"*: which appeared as "St. Thérèse and Lao Tzu: a Study in Comparative Mysticism" and "Thérèse and Celine" in Wu's collection of essays *Chinese Humanism and Christian Spirituality*, St. John's University Press, 1965. In a talk to his fellow monks, Merton raved about the first essay, calling it "seminal"; hereafter, known as *CHCS*.

27. *"The Science of Love"*: Wu's first ostensible Catholic writing following his conversion in 1936, first published in Hong Kong in June 1947, later appearing as Appendix in *CHCS*. It had fairly extensive circulation and was translated into numerous European and Asian languages.

TM TO JW

April 21, 1961

Feast of St. Anselm

Dear John,

Thanks for your good letter. I am very glad the Mencius finally arrived + I knew you would like it. I am glad you approved of the "night spirit"—it seems to me that Chinese is full of wonderful things that the West does not support—like your observations on the lunar month which deeply touched me in *Beyond East and West*. There are so many fine things in your book—I especially enjoy the notations from your diary that are being read now. The community was in a state of near-riot when you described your marriage.[28] I am in love with your parents. The book is most enjoyable and moving.

I have just finished reading the first paragraph (sections) of Bk XXIV of Chuang Tzu + really I believe it is one of the most superb passages in all literature. He is not only a wonderful thinker (he would repudiate the term, but in our poor English we have no alternative) but a fine poet. How modern he is! It has taken centuries to rediscover a little of what has been forgotten since Chuang Tzu. Legge's translation of this section seems quite good.

What are the ideograms for *True Man, Heaven like Man,*[29] etc? What is their root meaning? What is their relationship to the ideogram for "Superior man" in Confucius. I would like to *see* these pictures if I can.

The Mencius will be in the *Commonweal* one of these days. Of course, I did not translate it, just took the literal translation from the back of I. A. Richard's book[30] and gave it form.

I am glad you like *Seeds of Contemplation*—I have just com-

---

28. "... when you described your marriage": in the first chapter, "The Gift of Life."

29. True Man, Heaven-like Man: in Confucius, the "superior man" is the "gentleman" which, at least on the surface is the ethical man but, in essence, *the complete person* whose cultivation enables him to carry out both private and public duties equally.

30. Ivor Armstrong Richards (1893-1979): an English literary critic who is revered as one of the fathers of modern English literature. He is the author of *Mencius on the Mind: Experiments in Multiple Definition* (Kegan Paul, Trench, Trubner & Co.: London; Harcourt, Brace: New York, 1932). See Thomas Merton's *Mystics and Zen Masters*, p. 66; hereafter known as *MZM*.

pletely rewritten it, leaving all that was there essentially + adding more with a new perspective. It is the only book of mine that has been translated into Chinese. Would you like a copy?

Your MS. on St. Thérèse will be read with interest when it arrives. I am sure I can help you with other publishers. Frank Sheed is not endowed with infallibility. I am sure you will have a very special insight into the little way.[31]

All blessings + cordial good wishes,

Tom Merton

I am happy with your plan to proceed with the translation in July. I will send *all* the selections together next time. About the preface— I will tell you if I think your book needs it + we can discuss the matter when you come down. It depends on Fr. Abbot. I will be glad to write one if it will be of use.

---

31. "the little way": see *CHCS*, p. 96: "(The Little Flower's) teaching is of one piece with her life; it consists in an endless series of paradoxes. To be empty is to be filled. To be poor is to be truly rich. Suffering is a blessing. To come down is to rise. To be little is to be great. Weakness is strength. Life is exile. To die is to live. To be deprived of joy is true joy. To be homeless is to furnish a home to the Lord. To forget yourself is to be remembered by God. The more you drink the more you thirst; yet this very thirst has that which can satisfy it. To love the unlovable is true love. Do your duty with all your might, but set no store by it. To give all is to give nothing. To choose nothing is to choose all. To cling to the One is to embrace the whole universe. Indeed, her way comprehends all ways, yet she calls it the 'little way.'" To understand the "little way" of Thérèse is to understand Wu's spirituality for there was nothing closer to his heart than the Sermon on the Mount upon which these paradoxes are based.

JW TO TM

3 Reynolds Place
Newark 6, New Jersey

April 25, 1961

Dear Father Louis:

I should be most delighted to receive a copy of the Chinese translation of the *Seeds of Wisdom*.

The ideogram for True Man is:

(ideogram is drawn in Wu's hand)
    Chen   *Jen*

Of course, (ideogram for *Jen*) symbolizes a man. As to (ideogram
for *Chen*), according to an etymological dictionary, it is supposed
to be a picture of an immortal with a transformed body ascending
Heaven. It is significant that this word is not found in the Six
Classics. It is found for the first time in the Taoist Classics. Its
current meaning is *true, real*. If you, Father, have not raised the
questions, I should not have imagined that such a popular word had
a Taoistic origin. In a later Taoistic book it is said, "A *Chen Jen*
is one in union with Tao."

The ideogram for Heaven-like man is:

(ideograms are drawn in Wu's hand)
    T'ien   *Jen*

The word (symbol for *T'ien*) is composed of (symbol) (one) and
(symbol) (great). Thus, it signifies the only One Great or the Great
One.

The Superior Man is

(ideograms are drawn in Wu's hand)
    Chün   *Tzu*

(Symbol for *Chün*) is composed of (radical for *Chün*), which is
supposed to picture someone sitting on a seat of authority; and
(symbol) which is a picture of the mouth, signifying issuing orders.
(Symbol for *Tzu*) means a son. Thus, *Chün Tzu* signifies one of
royal blood, belonging, that is, to the ruling class, or the nobility.
This is a typically Confucian term, not frequently used in Taoistic
literature. In the hands of Confucius and Mencius, it comes to sig-

nify a man of noble character rather than a nobleman. Confucius' idea is that a nobleman should be noble in reality, to be worthy of his name. This illustrates the Confucian revolution under the innocent cover of "rectifying the names."

I am happy to read what you say regarding the MS on St. Thérèse. I am only afraid that you will be disappointed on seeing it. But one thing is certain: your introduction is sorely needed. I will write to Father Abbot about this matter.

Indeed, Father, Bk XXIV of Chuang Tzu is a pearl. Some commentators (Buddhists) have seen in the whole essay seeds of Mahayana Buddhism.

This is a hurried note, Father. I have to attend to my classes. Let this do for the moment.

Filially + smilingly yours in Christ,

John [Chinese Chacters Follow]

TM to JW

May 19, 1961

Dear John,

Forgive me for the delay in writing to you. I have been busy finishing up my course in *Mystical Theology* and various other tasks and now I have a little time to "return to the roots" and let the things that are more important come to the surface. Your manuscript on St. Thérèse I consider one of these "more important" things. I think the three items you sent me will go together to form a very fine little book and I do not understand Frank Sheed's criticism of it, unless he is allergic to some aspects of St. Therese, as most people are.

Actually I think your essay on St. Thérèse and Lao Tzu is very profound and interesting, and the one of Celine, which is Confucian, admirably balances it. I think the earlier pamphlet is less profound, more popular, and perhaps it ought to be re-done to fit the tone and manner of the other two—that is to say, there ought to be more explicit references to Chinese classical texts. Then all three would be on the same level. If you can think of a fourth essay, it would nicely round out the book which is still a little short. I will gladly write a preface, if Fr. Abbot permits. We can see about that.

As to a publisher, I have several ideas, and I think we might start with Doubleday when you have brushed up the *Science of Love*. I am sure someone will be eager to publish it, although there have been many books on St. Thérèse. This one, however, is most unusual.

I have finished making the selections from Chuang, but will type out the whole list in a few days to make sure you can read it.

Paul Sih[32] sent me your translation of Lao Tzu and this I like very much. I am hoping to write an article on this and the Hsiao Ching,[33] which is a beautiful little book. Your translation of Tao Te Ching[34] seems to me to be the best I know. I have two questions

---

32. Paul Sih (1909-1978): Wu's student in China and godson, Dr. Sih was Director of Asian Studies first at Seton Hall University, then at St. John's, and later one of its vice presidents. Wu regarded Sih his most faithful student, following his teacher from juridical to religious to Asian studies.

33. ". . . hoping to write an article on this and the Hsiao Ching": see "Love and Tao" in *MZM*.

34. *Tao Teh Ching*: the Taoist classic attributed to Lao Tzu. Wu's version was first published in the US by St. John's University Press in 1961, and then

about it. In #23 the word "Loss" [Chinese Character]—is it loss in a good sense or in a bad sense? Would you enlighten me? And in #12—"The sage takes care of the Belly not the eye." What is meant by "belly?" Does it by any chance correspond to the "bowels" in Scripture, i.e., the inmost heart?

I enjoyed very much your last etymologies. It is very important to me to get the wonderful differences of nuance and meaning which have tremendous importance. It is so easy for the English reader to slur over "Superior Man" and "Heavenly Man" as if they were synonymous—especially in Taoism!!

Now I enjoy the quiet of the woods and the song of the birds and the presence of the Lord in silence. Here is Nameless Tao, revealed as Jesus, the brightness of the hidden Father, our joy and our life. All blessing to you, joy and grace in Him.

Fraternally in the Holy Spirit,

Tom Merton

redistributed by Shambhala Press in 1989.

JW TO TM

3 Reynolds Place
Newark 6, New Jersey
May 25, 1961

My dear Father Louis:

Your good letter is a tremendous spiritual uplift to me. I am so happy to know that you like the two later pieces of St. Therese, because they were done last year when I was suffering keenly from my wife's death the year before, as in fact I am still suffering. We were forty-four Springs together, and the fact that I was not a model husband only adds to my nostalgia.[35] In my present period of dark night, although I may still produce writings, I am absolutely incapable of judging their qualities. So, Father, you can imagine how wonderfully you have reassured my spirit. I am so grateful to God for giving me your friendship, for you are not only kind but *candid*. I will certainly rewrite the first part in conformity to your advice, and add a fourth part to the whole thing. When time comes, I shall make bold to ask our good Abbot to favor me with your Introduction. The book will be dedicated to my wife, with whom the Abbot must have become familiar through the reading of my *Beyond*. I will therefore ask that favor in *her* name. When I come to see you, Father, I will tell you how divinely beautiful her deathbed scene was.

I have remained silent all these days because I have been absorbed in reading books on Zen. I have come to know two German books. One is Father Lassalle's *Zen: Weg zur Erleuchtung*. The other is Father Dumoulin's *Zen: Geschichte und Gestalt*. Both draw upon your *Ascent to Truth*. Both are rather solid works on the subject. They belong to the Soto school.[36] I shouldn't be surprised

---

35. "... only adds to my nostalgia": Wu and his beloved wife, Teresa Teh-lan Li (1899-1959) were betrothed in childhood at age 6, then united in wedlock as teenagers in 1916. Still in mourning at the time of the correspondence, Merton's letters and friendship was, as Wu so candidly states in the letters, the one great consolation during this very lonely period of his life.

36. Soto school: one of two major schools of Japanese Zen, the Soto school (Chinese: Ts'ao-tung) was founded by Dogen Kigen (1200-53) who, at age 23, went to China where he attained enlightenment. He then introduced Zen to his native country. The primary text of the Soto school is Dogen's *Manual of Zen Buddhism*. Soto believes that "practice and enlightenment are one" and on the necessity for "sustained exertion" (see glossary in Philip Kapleau's *Zen: Merging*

if your *Seeds of Contemplation* would be preferred by the Rinzai school.[37] I almost suspect, Father, that you were a Zen Master in your previous existence, attaining Buddhahood in this life.

The word "Loss" in the 23rd chapter of the *Tao Te Ching* is used in the bad sense. Your interpretation of the "belly" as the "inmost heart" is wonderfully fit, especially as it is reached by way of the "bowels" in Scripture. I only thought of the outer (the eye) and the inner (the belly).

I have been called to a meeting in Formosa in July; but I shall return in August and come to you. This may affect somewhat, though not entirely my work of translating the Chuang Tzu. Now, Father, suppose you do half of the selections first, and I shall do the checking. In one way, this is a better procedure, because it will preserve your style better. Think of that marvelous piece on Mencius.

Your humble child in Christ,

John C. H. Wu

of East and West); hereafter known as *ZMEW*.

37. Rinzai school: together with the Soto school, forms the two major branches of Japanese Zen. In China, it was named after the monk Lin-chi (?-866) who, though he did not initiate the practice, made famous the so-called shouting method as a means to bring the Zen aspirant to enlightenment. "The one thing necessary," from what Wu understands of Rinzai (Lin-chi), "is the perception or awareness of the *true man of no position, degree or title* as one's real self. All expedient methods or discursive formulas are of secondary importance and temporary utility" (see *The Golden Age of Zen* [Doubleday, 1996], p. 157; hereafter known as *GAZ*).

JW TO TM

3 Reynolds Place
Newark 6, New Jersey
May 27, 1961
My dear Father Louis:

On June 4 I shall be at the Rockhurst College in Kansas City, delivering a commencement address. Can you imagine I had never heard of the College before its President Father Maurice Van Ackeren, S.J., wrote to inform me that its board of trustees had resolved to confer on me the honorary degree of "Doctor of Letters."

I am inclosing here a copy of my address. It is hastily done, as you will note. But I am happy to be able to weave some of your thoughts with Father Van Ackeren's definition of liberal education as "that pursuit of Truth which makes men free." (See the conclusion, pg. 9).

As I look at the map, Missouri is next neighbor to Kentucky. Were it not for my son Peter's ordination on the 10th, I should surely be making plans to come over to Trappist monastery. Even as it is, there is a possibility of stealing a day from my schedule in order to make a flying visit. But do not expect me, Father. My duties at the Law School are likely to interfere. I have one hundred and fifty blue books to look over and to grade.

Filially yours in Christ,

John

TM to JW

May 27, 1961

Dear John,

I want to finish my list of passages in *Chuang Tzu* and my type-writer has gone wrong, so I will have to write it out. I forgot where I left off, but this time I will begin with Book XV, following the paragraph numbers as given by Legge.

Bk. XV. Use the <u>entire book</u>

Bk. XVI. Use #2,4

Bk. XVII #1,2

> #3—Second 1/2, beginning with "what can be discoursed about in words is the _____ of things—to end of #—_____ pg. 204
> #6—second 1/2. "there is no end of beginning to the Tao" to the end
> #7—begin about 9 lines from the start "Fire cannot burn him who is perfect . . ."
> #8 whole section
> #11 whole section
> #12 whole section
> #13 whole section

Bk. XVIII

> #1 _____ second and third paragraphs (see Giles 220-221)
> #5 Begin about half way through—story of the sea bird (Giles 226-227)

Bk. XIX #2 Begin 1/2 way through. "Take the case of a drunken man falling from his carriage . . . ." to end of section

> #4 whole section

Bk. XX #1 whole section

> #2 whole section
> #4 whole section
> #5 about 2/3. End at "The union that originated without cause will end in separation without cause"
> #7 whole section
> #9 whole section

Bk. XXI #4 last part, "Look at the spring the water of which rises and overflows" (Giles 268)

#5 whole section
#7,8,9 whole section
#10 last paragraph, "The King of Kim(?) and the ruler of Fau"

Bk. XXII. #1 whole section

#3,4,6 whole section
#7 Begin 1/2 way through. "Grand purity asked infinitude . . . ." (Giles 288).
#8 whole section

Bk. XXIII. #4, 5, 6 whole section

#8 Begin about 12 lines from beginning "that tower has its guardian" (Giles 302)
#9 whole section
#11 Finish 2/3, down to "the state of inaction in which it accomplishes everything" (q. Giles 307-308)
#12 whole section

Bk. XXIV. #1,2,3 whole sections

#4 First paragraph only, down to "they are hampered by external restrictions?"
#7 whole section
#8 whole section
#10 Last paragraph. "A dog is not reckoned good because he barks well."
#11 whole section
#12, 13 whole section

Bk. XXV. #2,5,6,7,8 whole sections

#11 Last 18 or 20 lines. "Infinite, unceasing, there is no room for words about the Tao."
down to end of book XXV

Bk. XXVI. #1 Only second ½. When wood is rubbed against wood to end of section

#2 whole section
#6,7,8 whole section

#10 whole section
#11 Last 7 lines. "Fishing stakes are used to catch fish, etc."

Bk. XXVII. #1 (I leave you to decide if any of this ought to be taken-to me it is difficult but seems interesting).

Bk. XXVIII. #3,4 whole section

#6,8,10 whole section

Bk. XXIX. #2 (?) Do you think some of this would be worthwhile?

Bk. XXX. whole book

BK. XXXI. We could use this, but I leave you to edit it a little for your convenience.

Bk. XXXII. #1,3,4,5,6,7,8,9,11,12,13 (whole sections)

Bk. XXXIII. #1,4,5 We could end with Lao Tzu "A true man indeed."

Here is my list. I hope it is comprehensible to you. I will try to clarify if you do not understand, but if you are in doubt I leave it to your discretion to edit the section suitably. I know these general indications are sufficient, you will be able to add what is better in the Chinese and subtract what is useless. Please do not feel confined by my suggestions. Anything I have missed that is really good should not be omitted.

I look forward to seeing you and the translation and hope we will have weather as perfect as we have here now. It is delightful.

All best wishes and blessings, as ever
in the Holy Spirit

Thomas Merton

TM TO JW

May 29, 1961

Dear John:

I had written out my list Saturday and I received your fine letter this morning. There is certainly no hurry and if a trip to Formosa holds up your work a little, it is no matter. I do not know if I grasped your suggestion about how you believed I ought to proceed. If I work on some of the selections, it will really only be a manipulation of what has already been said in English by Giles and Legge, so of course it will be really nothing. The Mencius I was able to do because I had a literal, word for word English translation with the Chinese characters above each word, and that plus natural ingenuity enabled me to bluff my way through. If I had the Chinese characters of *Chuang Tzu* paralleled with English, I might possibly be able to begin. Do you have any such text?

Really though I think that your insights into the meaning would be so much more real and profound that it is a question of you getting the real substance and my merely polishing up the English expression.

However, I might take a fling at a few passages I like just for the joy of doing it.

I am so happy that you want to complete the little book on *St. Thérèse and Chinese Philosophy*, and that this will be an offering of piety in memory of your dear wife. We all love her here, since the book was read in the refectory. I will be glad to add my own tribute, if Father Abbot permits, and I don't see how he could have the heart to refuse.

I have carefully gone through your fine translation of *the Tao Te Ching*, and it is all superb. I really mean to get down to the article. I loved the Hsiao Ching too. It is so completely in tune with reality. The Zen books you speak of interest me, but my German is slow. I shall be eager to see if they appear in English translation. If I once reached Buddhahood and redescended to my present state, all I can say is that I made a really heroic sacrifice. But I don't regret it, as the other Buddhas seem to have done the same. Yourself for instance. Thus we go along gaily with littleness for our Mother and our Nurse, and we return to the root by having no answers to questions. Whatever I may have been in previous lives, I think more than half of them were Chinese and eremitical.

I hope soon to send you my dialogue with Suzuki, about which I think I told you. It is being printed. I like Zen, and from what I know of it, which is not much, I think the Rinzai school is probably more my line at the present stage, but I must say I don't like the looks of some of their masters and I would take good care to keep out of the way of their hossu.[38]

All blessings for the forthcoming ordination, I will be there in spirit. Don't forget to tell me the day, so that I can remember you all at Mass.

May God prosper all your goings and comings. Every blessing and best wish, and all cordial affection in Christ,

Tom Merton

This is a borrowed typewriter with different idiosyncracies from my own. Please forgive the errors.

---

38. hossu: a whipping stick to keep the Zen aspirant awake during meditation.

TM to JW

July 31, 1961

Dear John:

All this time I have refrained from writing to you because I sup-posed that you were in Formosa and I did not know when you would return. Now I am putting in the mail your manuscripts, which I had been holding here for the same reason. By the way during this time I gave it (them) to a couple of the novices to read and they enjoyed your work and were enlightened by it. I think it did them much good and also this is a further indication that their publication is most desirable.

So these manuscripts are on their way to you.

Meanwhile, I suppose you are still considering coming down here. August is probably the best time and August is already here. One week is going to be a little busy for me, and that is the week from the 13th to the 20th. Also the 10th is a bad day, but the rest of the month is open. September is not so good, because we have the priests of the Louisville diocese filling up the guesthouse. So now that you see the situation, I hope you will be able to make your plans and I look forward to hearing when we may expect you.

Have you been doing anything with *Chuang Tzu*? I have been rereading some of the wonderful chapters and coming to the conclu-sion that I do not know anything about him yet, but want to more and more. Really one would like to put everything else aside and simply spend a good part of the day on this, but of course there are many other things to be done, and I have a few other studies on hand also: which is perhaps itself not in accordance with Chuang Tzu and accounts for my obtuseness.

I think much of you and of China. Dr. Sih is sending me a couple of his books, and he too plans to come down later on in the fall. If you did not come in August and wanted to come with Dr. Sih in October that would be all right too. I leave you to decide.

By the way, when you come you might like to go over and give a talk to the nuns at Loretto, which would help you to cover some of the expenses. Let me know if you would like this and I can arrange for it, and even for other talks, for instance at Bellarmine College, Louisville. But I do not want you to come here and just run around the country exhausting yourself. On the contrary you must have a nice quiet time and we can sit under the trees and talk of Chuang Tzu and many other things. You will also have time for thought and reading yourself as I will have to devote my usual time to my novices etc.

The picture of the ordination was on our bulletin board and the *Interior Carmel*[39] is being read in the evening chapter, to the satisfaction of all.

Now I must close, but I will say at least this: I am glad you are not in Formosa and that we can hope to see you here soon.

Very cordially yours in Christ, with all blessings,

Tom Merton

---

39. *The Interior Carmel*: Sheed and Ward, 1952. Wu's book-length exposition of what he calls "The Threefold Way of Love" is based on the Beatitudes and it draws heavily on the Carmelite mystics, St. John of the Cross and St. Teresa of Avila. The chapters were based on class lectures he gave on courses on Christian Mysticism at the University of Hawaii between 1949 and 1951.

JW TO TM

3 Reynolds Place
Newark 6, New Jersey

August 4, 1961

Dear Father Louis:

It is always an uplifting and thrilling experience to receive a letter from you. So powerful is the influence radiating from your secret rendezvous with the Nameless whose name is Jesus!

But can you imagine, Father, that since I wrote you last I have been held in suspense all the time until yesterday when I was definitely informed that the meeting I promised to attend in Formosa, which was supposed to have taken place around the end of last month, will be held on the 20th of this month! Yesterday I received a round-trip flight ticket, and just now I am beginning to prepare for the journey.

I have not been able to do anything with the *Chuang Tzu*, except reading more of the Chinese commentaries about it. I did a part of Book XV, which you have selected. (This is also one of my own predilections.) But I was interrupted.

I have discussed the matter with Paul. He is entrusted with with [sic] the prospect of publishing the projected translation together with the Chinese original, especially as something coming from your hands. We think that the best way of proceeding with the work is this: That you, Father, should make the first draft, after having compared the translations of Giles and Legge (together with Richard Wilhelm's[40] German version, which I have just ordered from Paragon Book Gallery to be sent directly to you as my humble present) [Wu's note in margin: On the whole I have more confidence in Wilhelm than in any other Sinologist]. I will also send a French translation of *Chuang Tzu*, by Rev. Leon Wieger, S.J. This book contains also the Chinese text. Paul and I think that if you compare these four versions, it is likely that you will be able to have an intuition of your own into the real meaning. As a profound Christian mystic, you are able to catch the overtones and undertones and half tones of the musings of Chuang Tzu. All this may

---

40. Richard Wilhelm (1873-1930): early 20th century German sinologist who translated many ancient Chinese texts but who is best known for the *I Ching* (*Book of Changes*) which he rendered into German in 1924 and later made available in English by Cary F. Baynes. Wilhelm's original translation had a strong influence on C. G. Jung who wrote a long foreword to it. Wilhelm was Wu's preferred English translator.

sound awfully adventurous; but, Father, after you have done the first draft, I will check it word by word, and I guarantee the accuracy of our translation. Not that I know the real meaning of all the passages any more than any of his commentators. There are obscure passages, and there are passages susceptible of two or more renderings. But whatever rendering we may finally decide upon will be supported not only by reason but also by some of the competent commentators throughout the ages. We also think that from the point of view of style, it is desirable that you, Father, make the first draft.

I expect to start for Formosa around the middle of this month, and return around the middle of September. I want you to pray for my safe journey and also for speaking the right words at the right time. The meeting is for the reexamination of the cultural directions and educational policies of Free China.

From the coming Semester, Seton Hall has asked me to offer a course on "Oriental Philosophies and Religions." I am taking a leave of Jurisprudence, which I have taught for the last ten years.

The manuscripts on St. Thérèse have arrived. I shall rewrite "The Science of Love,"[41] and revise the others, in accordance with your suggestions.

My son, Father Peter, is here with me for a few weeks. He has been assigned to Hongkong, but he will have to spend a year at Georgetown for the study of linguistics for future missionary work. He is very proud of the friendship which you have so generously shown to me.

I am very grateful to the Father Abbot for introducing my humble book *The Interior Carmel* even into the evening chapter. But Father Louis, one of the greatest pains in life is to see the yawning gulf between what one writes and what one has attained. May the Lord turn this stone into a living Child of His. What a consolation it is that what is impossible with man is yet possible with God!

Filially yours in Christ and Mary,

John C. H. Wu

---

41. *"The Science of Love"*: as far as it is known, Wu never rewrote it. It was not his will to rewrite anything that had already been published with the exception of the *Tao Teh Ching*, first published in the *Tien Hsia Monthly* in the late 30s, which underwent extensive revision before its US publication. Though he seemed willing enough to revise the essay according to Merton's advice, he probably refrained from doing so for fear that he would be interfering with the original spirit that inspired him in the first place.

TM TO JW

Aug. 12, 1961

F. of St Clare

Dear John:

Many thanks for the letter. It is too bad we cannot look forward to receiving you at the end of the month, but it is good that your uncertainty is now over and that you know when the meeting is to be. My prayers certainly go with you on this important trip. You have all my sympathy and best wishes in this critical time. I hope that the Holy Spirit will guide you and all your associates.

I am reading Paul Sih's book about China at the moment. It is very clear and informative, and tells me a lot of things about which I knew nothing. When we are up against a monster propaganda machine, the task is discouraging, but we must nevertheless stick to the truth. The trouble is that there is also a monster ambiguity to deal with at the same time as though the propaganda machine had not only changed the "truths" but even changed the "truth" itself. As if it had somehow created a new kind of truth, in the face of which all former truths, however true, become irrelevant. This is the problem.

Personally I think China is going through the same kind of crisis as in the time of the Legalists when the Middle Kingdom was first unified. The old Confucian wisdom (adapted of course and not in any formal dress) will find its way back. And I hope it will also be Christian. The Legalists cannot hold all the power for long, because human nature is stronger than any willfulness of man. The trouble is, though, there are such mighty new means and weapons involved . . . .

Before I can attempt to do anything myself with *Chuang Tzu* I am going to have to learn about two hundred fundamental ideograms. I don't think I can honestly approach the task otherwise. I need to orient myself somewhat in Chinese text which I am so glad to have. I have to make at least some kind of gesture at thinking through the ideograms and not just through sentences in western language. Can you suggest the best collection of ideograms for a beginner? I will get it from the Paragon Book Gallery. Does this seem practical? Or is there some other approach?

The Wieger is good to have. He is breezy and to some extent

helpful, but above all it is fine to have the Chinese text. Wilhelm has also arrived and I agree with you, he strikes one as very very solid and trustworthy. I like his work, and am glad to have this. With these translations I ought to be able to do something eventually. It will necessarily be slow and awkward, however.

Can we count on you coming down this fall with Paul Sih?

I am delighted to hear about your coming course in Oriental Philosophies. I wish I could take it.

Best wishes to you and all the family, including Father Peter. And again, may God bless your journey. Perhaps you could convey my humble respect to Archbishop Yu Pin and ask his blessing for me.

With all cordial good wishes and blessings in Our Lord,

Tom Merton

JW TO TM

3 Reynolds Place
Newark 6, New Jersey

Assumption of Our Lady, 1961

Dear Father Louis,

This is my last letter before my flying to Formosa. Yours arrived yesterday. Paul (Sih) is travelling with me. We expect to come back in September before the opening of school.

For the learning of Chinese ideograms, I suggest that you write to Paragon (Mr. Farber—I am not sure of the spelling of the name—but I know that he has on stock some textbooks on the Chinese language). I have found Mathew's *Chinese English Dictionary* useful.

Yes, Father, I shall convey your message to Archbishop Yu Pin. Thank you for your prayers. I need them more than ever.

Filially yours in Christ + Mary,

John

(on another piece of paper)

In case you wish to communicate with me during the month, my address will be

c/o Mr. Edward Wu[42]
Foreign Ministry
Taipei, Taiwan (Formosa)

---

42. Edward Wu (1920-2006): Wu's second son out of thirteen children, a career diplomat who later became ambassador to Bolivia and the Holy See (Vatican). Wu himself was Minister Plenipotentiary to the Holy See from 1946 to 1949, at the time a controversial choice of President Chiang Kai-shek as Wu was the first Roman Catholic from a non-Christian nation to represent his country at the Roman Catholic center of the world.

TM TO JW

Oct 11, 1961

Dear John:

Are you back from Formosa? I presume you must be. And you are probably very busy at Seton Hall. As for me, I have tried my hand at one or two little sections of *Chuang Tzu* and have enjoyed working on them in the way suggested, using the various translations. The German version is particularly helpful. But I find it takes an enormous amount of time to do it this way. Anyone translating from the original would move much faster. Consequently very little has been done. I have hopes of getting back to it, after I have cleared the way. I still have a couple of small writing jobs that have been hanging fire for many months.

And now the question arises: what about you and Paul Sih coming down here? If you come now it will be a pleasant visit, but we will have nothing definite in *Chuang Tzu* to talk over. Perhaps we should wait until we have some texts to discuss between us.

On the other hand the most important consideration is the time that will be convenient for you both. During the school term I presume you will both be pretty busy. The Christmas holidays are not convenient for us, here. Thanksgiving you will probably want to spend with your families . . . .

Why don't you let me know what would be the convenient times for you to come down, if not this fall, then early in 1962. Then we could plan on something definite.

When you do come down I will be able to arrange for you to give talks at the Jesuit scholasticate, West Baden, Indiana, and other colleges around here.

Looking forward to hearing from you,

With all blessings and cordial regards,

Devotedly yours in Christ,

Tom Merton

JW TO TM

3 Reynolds Place
Newark 6, New Jersey
October 21, 1961

My dear Father Louis:

Early part of 1962 will suit me perfectly. I will write you further about the date.

My long silence may have caused you some concern, Father. Let me tell you briefly what has happened.

I went to Taipei around the middle of August. On the very day of flight your letter of Aug. 12 came. So I flew with that letter in my pocket together with some reliques of St. Joseph and Saint Thérèse. The trip could not be happier. The cordialities and hospitalities that I received during the one month in Taipei and one week in Hongkong surpassed all that I had received my whole life. But all this was way too much for my health. I did not feel it so much then; but after my return in the latter part of September I felt exhausted, and I am still suffering from the effects of it, although I am on the way to complete recovery.

I am happy to learn that you have already started on the translation, and that you find the German version particularly helpful. I beg you to let me see the two little sections that you have done. You say, Father, that anyone translating from the original would move much faster. Here, Father, you may be wrong, that is, so far as the mystical writings are concerned. The words he used are capable of so many interpretations that one is easily confused. My theory is that all genuine mystics feel and see the same things which are no-things. Chuang Tzu is one, and you, Father, are one. The same Living Tao that taught him (rather vaguely) is revealing Himself to you everyday afresh. In *His* light you see the lights.

Did I tell you that from the present semester I am teaching (at the request of the university) two graduate courses: *Chinese Poetry* and *Oriental Philosophy and Religion!*[43] They cover well-nigh the whole field of Oriental culture. And my interest in these subjects

---

43. Oriental Philosophy and Religion: a relief for Wu as he was now released from his courses in law and jurisprudence to which he never returned and was able to pursue areas of research now closer to his heart. He taught in the Far Eastern Studies until his retirement in 1968. Later in Taiwan he continued teaching Chinese philosophy and literature, particularly Zen and Taoism into his early 80s.

is simply absorbing. This perhaps explains partly why I have been so slow in recovering from the fatigue.

I am inclosing here some specimens of my attempts to render Chinese poems into English. I desire your opinion, and revisions from your hands. You must be as frank with me as if I were confessing. I did these for my class on *Chinese Poetry*, in order to bring out one of its qualities, namely, its pregnantness, or power of evocation. The Chinese poets generally do not invoke or provoke, they evoke. Probably, the Zen has its origin in this.

Filially yours in Christ,

John C. H. Wu

JW TO TM

3 Reynolds Place
Newark 6, New Jersey

Nov. 28, 1961

My dear Father Louis:

Some days ago I received *The New Man.* Although I have not yet
finished it, I have read enough of it to say that this is the *living
synthesis* of East and West. It seems to me, Father, that you read
contemplatively. I mean, you absorb everything you read because
it serves to confirm your own experience and insight. That is why
much learning has not made you a pedant.

For my part, reading through the pages constantly reminds
me of—or rather opens my eyes to the new meanings—of certain
insights of the Oriental Sages. For instance, on pg. 123, you write:
". . . our whole life of faith is a life of attentiveness, of 'listening'
in order to receive the word of God into our hearts." I wrote two
words on the margin: [Chinese Characters Follow]. "The ears
docile or attuned." That, as you know, is from *The Analects of
Confucius*—where he says at sixty his ears became docile.

On p. 122, you write: "We truly realize ourselves when all our
awareness is of another—of Him who is utterly 'Other' than all
beings because He is infinitely above them." I write on the margin: "Truly non-dual!" You are so deeply Christian that you can't
help touching the vital springs of the other religions—Hinduism
or Buddhism.

I am thrilled with many other piercing insights, such as: "The
path lies through the center of our own soul." This again confirms
my own conviction about Chu Hsi and Wang Yang-ming.[44] Chu
Hsi is theoretically more transcendent. Wang Yang Ming, more
immanentist. But I feel that Wang is more spiritual than Chu. My
conclusion was that if one is thorough-goingly immanentist, one is
bound to arrive at a transcendence more authentic than a rationalist
could conceive of.

"The spiritual anguish of man has no cure but mysticism." I

---

44. Chu Hsi and Wang Yang-ming: Chu Hsi (1130-1200) and Wang Yang-
ming (1474-1529) represent two branches of the neo-Confucianist Movement,
the former the so-called "orthodox school" faithful to the dominant Confucian
philosophical schools of his day, and the latter the "idealist school" oriented
towards the pursuit of wisdom and the inner life.

too have but recently realized the significance of Existentialism. I think that Existentialism is a bridge from the materialistic, utilitarian, pragmatic tendencies to a more spiritual philosophy of life.

"The vocation to charity is a call not only to love but to *be loved*" (pg. 91). This speaks volumes!

Father, I honestly think that you are (a) major prophet of this age. You need not bother about improving your knowledge of Chinese. You *are* Chinese, because you are universal.

Just now I have to go to make an appointment, I will continue to write to you.

The book is beautifully printed, although I see some misprints—showing how careless the proof-reader is.

Filially yours in Christ,

John

TM to JW

Dec 12, 1961

Dear John:

Today is the Feast of Our Lady of Guadalupe, significant to us all in a very special way I am sure. At any event, Our Lady has brought me a moment of time in which to reply to your two good letters. I have got myself involved in a lot of thinking about peace and war, since it seems to be necessary for someone to speak out forthrightly on this awful problem. But it has taken up a great deal of my time, and the question gets so terribly involved when one listens to the opinions of men about it. And one has to. It is a great mystery most of which is pure delusion and self deception. It gets to be more and more subtle and more and more self important, this thinking of experts, and yet in the long run the answer should be quite simple and quite plain: we should be Christians, and we should be prepared to follow Christ even if the consequences do not seem to us to be immediately profitable or expedient. It is the fact that we have unfortunately become so involved in expediency and in commitment to temporal interest above all, that we have had to follow the complications of military minds and of statesmen. And of course one cannot afford to be too impatient with the actual situation, either, unpleasant though it may be.

I think my time would probably have been spent better with *Chuang Tzu*, except that I cannot see my way to doing this at the moment. Perhaps after a couple of months, when I have settled my mind as to exactly what line I ought to take and how to clarify that position.

As to your illness, I am sorry to hear of it but I hope you are now perfectly rested and reestablished. These fast air trips half way around the world are not exactly restful, as far as I can see. I have never made one, however. I have made short flights like from here to Minnesota and that is the extent of my flying. It is more profitable and more comfortable to rise on the wings of the wind with the old Taoists and sport about among the clouds, but this is not possible until one renounces the idea of getting anywhere.

Your courses in *Chinese Poetry* and *Oriental Philosophy* sound marvelous. Are you mimeographing any notes? I am so grateful for the poems you sent, I enjoyed them very much. I cannot put my hand on the copy at the moment, and I would not attempt to emend them as I still worry about not knowing Chinese! Someone has recently sent me a marvelous book, *Poems of Solitude*, a collection including Juan Chi, Pao Chao, Wang Wei, Li Ho, and Li Yu. Maybe you are right about my being Chinese, because this kind of thing is just what makes me feel most happy and most at home. I do not know whether or not I am always happy with mystical writings that are completely out of touch with ordinary life. On the contrary, it seems to me that mysticism flourishes most purely right in the middle of the ordinary. And such mysticism, in order to flourish, must be quite prompt to renounce all apparent claim to be mystical at all: after all what difference do labels make? I know you agree, for this is what St. Thérèse so well saw. And by the way, how are you coming along with that book?

Your remarks on the *New Man* obviously made me very happy. What nicer compliments could any man have, than to be told he has approached something which is the object of his greatest admiration and respect? To have been told that the book has a really Oriental quality is all the reward I ask for having written it, because I know that there is in the fact of having written it a value that cannot be taken away. I hope you will like the *New Seeds of Contemplation* which I hope will reach you soon.

I enclose a tentative draft of an article on peace. I have not been able to go through the copies to correct all the errors left by the typist, so I hope you will excuse them.

And now: when would it be convenient for you to come down this next spring? Would you like to come mid year, for example, at the end of January, or whenever the break in your school year comes? Or would you prefer to come later? The weather here is sometimes mild in winter and sometimes just as cold as it is in the east, we never know quite what to expect. It would be wonderful if you could meet my old friend Victor Hammer, an Austrian artist and printer who lives in Lexington. If he could not come here then, I could possibly arrange for you to give a talk at the University of Kentucky there if you so desired, and you could meet Mr. and Mrs. Hammer. You would like them. He is printing a thing of mine on Wisdom at the moment. He does very limited and rare editions which are quite beautiful. I think you received the Meng Tzu parable, which he printed last year. In fact I know you did, for you mentioned the printing.

All best Christmas wishes and warm blessings for the new

year. May Our Lord come to us in peace and in simplicity, and increase our faith and love for Him. And may this poor world have peace, somehow, in spite of the madness and absurdity of men and weapons. For now it is the weapons themselves that make all the decisions: men humbly obey the creations of their own technology. I wonder if a few of us may persuade our fellows to retain at least enough freedom to use machines instead of being used by them.

With all affection and blessings,

Cordially yours in Christ,

Tom

JW to TM

3 Reynolds Place
Newark 6, New Jersey

Dec 19, 1961

My dear Father Louis:

This Christmas, as I look back upon the whole year, I have a special reason for thanking Our Lord. The gift of your friendship, Father, is a tremendous gift.

I *have* been following your very wonderful utterances on the Christian ethics and Nuclear War in *The Catholic Worker*. I enjoyed every word of it. As to whether it was an excuse, it reminds me of what once happened to Blessed Henri Suso.[45] Like you, Father, Suso was a mystic and a poet. Once, you remember, he refused to be interrupted in his contemplation and sent away a penitent. Our Lord gave him a lesson *à la* Zen. He lost all taste for contemplation. How can a true mystic like you refuse to enter into discussion on a subject that concerns the fate of mankind. I often thought that even if a man is really united with Our Lord, his spirituality is bound to be *incarnational*. He is bound to return to the *ordinary*.

Some pedants have said that Christ is not a Mystic. But He is infinitely more than a Mystic, for He is *Mystery*, the Supreme Mystic teaching plain truths. In this sense, The Little Flower, the Chinese poets, and yourself, Father, are past-Mystics. Like a clear sky in Autumn, the past-Mystics are *crystally fathomless* [Chinese Characters Follow].

To imitate Lao Tzu, I would say

High mysticism is not mystical
Low mysticism has more smoke than fire.

I have written this to amuse you, Father. Instead of sending a Christmas card, I prattle like a baby.

Filially yours in JMJ,

John
_____

45. Blessed Henry Suso (1290-1365): Catholic mystic and poet who belongs to the German mystical school begun by Meister Eckhart and continued through the Flemish mystics. In *The Interior Carmel*, Wu quotes Suso: "The interiority that reaches the exterior is an interiority more interior than the interiority that remains in the interior only" (p. 83). As a contemplative and man of the world, Wu seems to have patterned his own life on these very paradoxical words.

JW TO TM

3 Reynolds Place
Newark 6, New Jersey

March 9, 1962

My dear Father Louis:

Your *Introduction to Christian Mysticism* is simply an inexhaustible treasure house of spiritual Wisdom!

I have not read it continuously. From time to time I came back to it and feasted myself with some snatches of it. My experience has reminded me of what Our Lord—the Supreme Poet—has related about the lover of the Kingdom of God—who finding a pearl in a field covers it in order to come back to it again. In my case, the pearl has given birth to numberless tiny pearls. Whenever I come back to it, I find new pearls. I take these with me, and cover up the field, then come back again . . . and the process is endless.

The other night, I was thrilled to this pearl: the *little way* of St. Thérèse "has many elements in common with the 'true poverty of spirit' of the Rhenish mystics."[46] As the Rhenish mystics are really Chinese, I suddenly realized the secret of the magical power the divine witch of Lisieux has exercised on me.

I must leave my inheritance, and on the highroads
Walk alone, wherever free love bids me go.

But, Father, I *did* leave my inheritance, but free love has unexpectedly led me back to it, and I am thrilled to find that the inheritance is really from God, not from my ancestors!

Your treatment of St. Augustine is marvelous. I have come to know him more intimately now. "By following the leads of a certain delight, and inward mysterious and hidden pleasures, as if from the house of God there sounded sweetly some instrument . . . ." Father, I confess to you that for a number of years I felt exactly the same ineffable experience. At present the sweet music is still discernable; but since the death of my wife, I am hearing discords torturing that sweet note. *However*, deep down in my heart, Father, there is an intimate conviction that these discords are but the

---

46. Rhenish mystics: or, Rhineland mystics living west of the Rhine River, the most prominent being Meister Eckhart (1260-1337). Others, some contemporaries of Eckhart, included John Tauler, Henry Suso, John Ruysbroeck, Gerhard Groote, Nicholas of Cusa, and Peter Canisius.

beginnings of counterpoints. The Lord is tempering the wind for me by shutting my interior ear to these noises. "Let them rage, let them rage!" says the Lord, "for it is I!"

By this time, Paul (Sih) must have seen you, Father. I imagine that you are making strides with your Chinese. I do not mind seeing you become more and more learned, for the fire of your spiritual wisdom turns every bit into *light*, informing all information.

The other day—a few weeks ago, I and some of my children enjoyed "The Soul's Landscape" in which you figured through Father Davis. For a brief moment, we say Eternity.

With all my filial love in Mary,

[No Signature]

POSTCARD FROM TM TO JW

April 18, 1962

+

A Holy + Happy Easter

Dear John,

I have been a very bad correspondent + have not been a good student of Chinese either—reason: I am trying to finish a book. But I want to thank you for your last letter, and say how much I enjoyed Paul Sih's visit. If you see Miss Brenda Hsu and she urges you to come here, take it as the message of an angel + come! Seriously, I hope we can see you this summer. June is bad. In Xti—

Tom

JW TO TM

3 Reynolds Place
Newark 6, New Jersey

May 1, 1962

My dear Father Tom:

Your postcard delights me and also Brenda (Hsu), although the joke was on me when I phoned her up and asked her sister (who came to the phone): "Is this my angel?" Her grim answer made me realize that I was not talking to Brenda. You can imagine, Father, how embarrassed I was. To save the situation I told her that I had an important message from Father Merton for Brenda. Her sister, who knows nothing about angels, had heard of Thomas Merton; and it was only the mention of your name, Father, that quieted her down. Later Brenda phoned me up to inquire what was Father's message, and I told her the whole story and we had a good laugh over it.

I am happy to learn that you are now absorbed in another book. As to writing to me, while I treasure every letter from you, the thought of your friendship is enough to make me happy without expression.

You will be interested to learn that my Korean friend, Francis Kim, secretary to the Archbishop of Taegu, is translating your article "The General Dance" into Korean. He wishes to know whether he can render "active intelligence" as [Chinese Characters Follow], which is literally "self-dependent intelligence." I have answered in the affirmative, since "self-dependent intelligence" seems to constitute an exact counterpart of "God-dependent" insight. I suggested, however, that a note should be added to the effect that [Chinese Characters Follow] is rational, analytical and conceptual, in contradistinction to the intuitive, simple and contemplative insight infused by God. Is my answer correct, Father? Or do you wish to add something?

I am enclosing herewith a letter from Father Charles Meeus, my dearest friend among the missionaries. As you will see, he has stated the question very clearly.

With my filial love in Christ,

John

* please give me a reply—a few lines will do.

TM TO JW

June 7, 1962

Dear John:

I had better get this letter written before any more time flows under the bridge (what bridge? What time? This is our illusion.) But in any case time has something to do with the fact that I am going to say Mass for your intentions on June 15th, a week from tomorrow, which will be Friday in Whitsun week, and I shall be praying that you obtain not only that gift of the Holy Ghost which is assigned by the St. Andrew's missal for that day, (whatever ideas the St. Andrews missal may have on the subject, and I don't especially care) but for you to receive all the gifts in all abundance and all the fruits and beatitudes and the Holy Spirit Himself in incomprehensible fullness. This mass is being said for you at the request of Mrs. O'Brian[47] and I promised her a long time ago I would let you know. We don't have, or seem not to have, those little mass cards around here, so I am sending you a letter. In fact it finally occurs to me that in this matter of saying Masses and getting notices out to people about it I am at the topmost peak of inefficiency and I do not know how I survive in the American Church with such slapdash methods: I just say Mass for people when I get a chance. Primitive, almost heretical.

But it will be a joy to stand in the presence of the Heavenly Father, in Christ, and speak of you and all whom you love and of China.

Paul Sih has obtained for me a wonderful reprint of the Legge translation of the Chinese Classics, and has also sent the Wang Yang Ming. I am awed and delighted with the great volumes of the Classics. I do not intent to read them lightly however, and they are waiting until other things can be cleared away. But I must admit I have done absolutely no work at all on Chinese, because I find that I simply waste too much time fumbling around in the dictionary and so little is done that it does not make sense to continue until some time in the future when I can get some instruction. So it will all have to wait a bit. I am working on the Latin Fathers, with whom I can make enough headway to know what is happening. Perhaps

---

47. Mrs. O'Brian: "Dez" O'Brian who shared an interest in Theresian (Thérèse of Lisieux) spirituality, visited often and was generous in supplying Wu with books on spirituality.

I shall do a translation of an excerpt from Cassiodorus. I think you would like them. He is very much the Confucian scholar, Latin style. A great librarian and student and copyist of books but also a polished writer and an engaging thinker, besides a man of prayer. His monastery of Vivarium is most attractive: it was a monastery of scholars.

And now to turn suddenly from scholarship to less pleasant subjects. I hesitate to send you the enclosed angry and bitter poem. It is savage, and its savagery hits everything in sight, so that it is not kind to anyone, even to the poor sad desperate Chinese girl whose picture broke my heart and suggested the poem.[48] I wish I could have said something full of mercy and love that would have been worthy of the situation, but I have only used her plight to attach the hypocrisy of those who find no room for the Chinese refugees, and who always have a very good reason. And the sad plight of a whole society which nods approval, while pronouncing a few formulas of regret. I suppose I should not get angry, and that it represents a weakness in myself to get excited still about the awful tragedies that are everywhere in the world. They are too awful for human protest to be meaningful, so people seem to think. I protest anyway, I am still primitive enough, I have not caught up with this century.

If I can find a copy of the Ladies Jail poem, which I think I never sent you, it may make up a little in compassion for what the other lacks. But anyway this all comes with my blessing and my unending joy and amusement at the story of your telephone call with the sister of your angel. All blessing and friendship in the Holy Spirit,

Tom Merton

---

48. ". . . suggested the poem": "A Picture of Lee Ying" tackles the abuse of language through Merton's anti-poetry. His satirical poem uses newspaper accounts of Lee Ying's deportation after being refused asylum and turned back into communist China by the colonial British authorities in Hong Kong.

JW to TM

3 Reynolds Place
Newark 6, New Jersey

June 19, 1962

My dear Father Louis:

How wonderful the Providence of Our Father! When you wrote your gracious letter of the 7th, you did not know that I was going to see you before the end of the month. Nor did I. Nor did Mrs. O'Brian.

I was asked to participate in a "Conference on Oriental-Western Literacy and Cultural Relations" June 20-24 in Bloomington (Indiana U.), and to read a paper. I picked up the subject: "Justice Holmes: Interpenetration of East and West."[49] My paper is scheduled on the 22nd Friday. The Conference will end on Saturday morning, and I shall be free in the afternoon of that day, when I shall make a bee-line to my Spiritual Father to the Abbey of Gethsemani. You will hear from me when I am in Bloomington. In the meantime, please tell the Abbot about it. I would like to stay 2 or 3 days.

You may be surprised to know that I like "A Picture of Lee Ying" even more than "There Has to be a Jail for the ladies." The compassion is, if anything, more intense in this new poem. Like Christ driving the merchants from the temple, you are simply pent up with compassion. The rage is *material*. This poem is what Holmes would call "first-intentioned."

I am now at the point of starting for Bloomington. So I am writing in haste.

Filially yours in the bosom of Christ,

John

---

49. Justice Holmes: Oliver Wendell Holmes, Jr. (1841-1935), associate justice of the US Supreme Court (1902-32). Wu and Holmes corresponded between 1921 and 1933 (109 extant letters). Wu, a student of law at the University of Michigan, was a mere 22 and Holmes a venerable 80 at the time the young Wu first wrote to him. Some of Holmes letters to Wu have been published but not the entire two-way correspondence.

JW TO TM

3 Reynolds Place
Newark 6, New Jersey

June 30, 1962

My dear Father Louis:

Your *Dharmakaya (Fa Sheng)* is with me, although physically you are far far away. Not so far, after all. It took me only one hour and fifteen minutes to fly from Louisville to New York, although at Idlewild I had to wait two hours for my son's car to fetch me home.

I cannot begin to tell you what a blissful experience it was for me to see you face to face, and to talk and walk with you. Let silence do where speech fails.

Let me then dwell upon the incidentals. I am happy that you were initiated into the mysteries of the Chinese dictionary. Counting the strokes is full of pitfalls. So I will give some concrete examples here:

[Chinese Character] (*Fa*) counts as 8 strokes, because [Character] is counted as one stroke.

[Chinese Character] (*Sheng*) 6 strokes. [Character] counts as one stroke.

[Chinese Character] (*Tao*) 13 strokes. [Character] as one.

[Chinese Character] (*Ti* earth) 6 strokes. [Character] [Character] both one.

[Chinese Character] (T'ing Court) Seven strokes. [Character] is counted as two strokes, although it seems to be continuous.

Let me give you some tests: Suppose you take up the first chapter of the *Tao Teh Ching:* How many strokes do you find in the following words:

1. [Character] (*K'o*) (5)   (5)
    [Character] (*Kuan*) (25)

2. [Character] (*Ming*) (6)   (6)
    [Character] (*Wei*) (16)

   3. [Character] (*Miao*) (6)   (7)
       [Character] (*Chiao*) (15)

   4. [Character] (*Wu*) (12)   (8)
       [Character] (*Chung*) (11)

for the first time in my life I have learned that the 8th word should be written [Character] without a [Character] on the top. So it consists of only 11 strokes.

So far, I have ignored the *roots*, which will be the subject of my next letter. By way of introduction you will find to your great surprise that the root of [Character] is not [Character], but [Character] (*mu*), the eye!! There are quite a few surprises like this even to a well-read Chinese.

I had a good drive with Bernard Fox the other day. The impression he had given me at the very beginning was just an accident.

I have already written to the good Abbot.[50] His charity is most resourceful. You see, Father, at the point of my departure, he came to my room, and during our conversation he handed over to me an envelope, saying that it was some spiritual souvenir for me to keep. Opening it I found a check! Of course I refused to accept. He said graciously, "You see we have made you work." I said, "Abbot, it is an *honor* for me to speak to the holy monks." The Abbot yielded. But what was my surprise, when Bernard and I went to the office of the American Airlines, I was told that they could not accept my money, for it was all taken care of by the Abbot. There is no beating the Abbot in his game.

Now I am going to prepare my lectures on Chinese history and culture to a group of high school and elementary school teachers who teach Chinese. This summer program entails my lecturing five days a week for seven weeks. I think it is good for me to have to look into the history of Chinese culture in a matter-of-fact way, and present it in such a simple manner that everyone can understand. This may be the start of a book.

Do not forget, Father, that I need your prayers very badly.

---

50. Abbot: Dom James Fox (1896-1987), a former U. S. Navy officer who later became a hermit at Gethsemani in 1968. Fox was a graduate of Harvard Business School prior to joining the Abbey of Gethsemani. He introduced the mechanization of the farm and other products in the monastery surroundings. The contemplative spirit of Merton got irritated and often criticized Abbot Fox for running the Abbey as a business.

When you meet Father Andrew, tell him what a delight it was to meet and talk with him. I did not say goodbye to him, because he was "retreating" some priests, and I did not like to interrupt. Also, I wish I had seen Father Raymond.[51]

Your spiritual child,

John

[Character] [Character]

How many strokes in each?

---

51. Father Raymond (1903-1990): Raymond Flanagan, often referred to ironically as "the other writer" since he predated Merton at Gethsemani. Wu was familiar with his writings too. Author of *The Man Who Got Even With God*, *God Goes to Murderers Row*, and *Burnt-Out Incense*.

JW TO TM

3 Reynolds Place
Newark 6, New Jersey

July 3, 1962

My dear Father Louis:

I have started with my summer schedule since yesterday—a course of *Chinese History and Culture* for secondary and elementary school teachers who are teaching Chinese or about to teach. The field of history being new to me, the interest is simply engrossing. Thanks to archaeological excavations, the modern historical scholars actually know more about the early China than Confucius himself! This does not mean that they are wiser.

Everyday I must be prepared for one lecture, five days a week, for seven weeks. Even now I am in the midst of preparation. But I can't help writing to you, because today is the Feast of your friend St. Irenaeus.[52] I salute you, Father, in his name.

In my first lecture I quoted a saying of Confucius:

[A Whole Line of Chinese Characters Follows]
Wen Ku Erh Chih Hsiu K'o I Wei Shih I.

Literally, it reads:

Warming up the old, you come to know the new. In this way, you can be a teacher.

How would you translate it, Father?

You are warming up St. Irenaeus. I am warming up Lao Tzu and K'ung Tzu (363, in Wu's hand). We meet in the new.

Filially yours in Christ,

John

---

52. St. Irenaeus (142?-202?): flourished in second century in Asia Minor, was Bishop of Lyons, and may have been martyred. Famous for the treatise "Against Heresies" and wrote that in the Eucharist we see the world as God sees it. Irenaeus refuted Valentinian Gnostic teachings by stressing the unity of the Old and the New Testament. He opposed the Gnostic view that matter is evil and also rejected the accidental creation of an evil demiurge. Gnostics like Valentinus thought that one can only be saved through a loving encounter with divine wisdom ("gnosis" or "hagia sophia"), not through faith alone ("pistis").

TM to JW

July 10, 1962

Dear John:

Many thanks for your two letters, and above all, thanks for coming. It was certainly a grace to have you here, a grace for me and a grace for us all.[53] Therefore we hope you will return soon. And I am sure you will do that, now that you know what to expect: our disappearances and appearances, the long silences, the informality, and everything else down to Father Abbot's coy jokes about picture cards in the envelopes. This is just the way we are.

I have counted the strokes, but I will write a special letter about that, when I can take time to make sense and draw out some of the ideograms and ask questions. At the moment I am at the typewriter down in the monastery with a jackhammer going in the reservoir site below the wall and a tractor ploughing up a nearby field. I cannot think of ideograms.

Then I am preoccupied because one of my novices tells me that I have a neighbor: a snake has taken up residence in the woodshed up the hill. I don't want to disturb him. I knew he was there since he left his skin on the woodpile. I did not know he was a permanent resident. He appears to be harmless. Yet I don't like to be pulling apart the woodpile and suddenly have a family of snakes fall out all around me. So I will have to get together with Tao and wait for something to work itself out. Maybe I will just talk to him reasonably, or maybe we will just settle down and be neighbors. I hate to kill even a snake, and anyway there seems to be no real reason for killing this one.

I thought I would finally type out one of the "versions" I did after *Chuang Tzu*. Very much "after" I fear. But anyway, it no longer even pretends to be a serious rendering. I might insert it in a collection of poems I am getting together, as an experiment.

Your course in Chinese history sounds fascinating. You should really write a small book about the Chinese Heritage, or something of the sort. It is needed, and would be very welcome.

I will go into the poems more in detail later, suffice it for the moment to say that I enjoy them very much (your translations, I mean).

Then we will get to the preface. Is there any special hurry?

53. "... grace for us all": (see *Conjectures of a Guilty Bystander*, p. 231).

I also enclose a poem, landscape, especially with a quail in it. The quail, as I seem to remember, is also a bird loved by Chuang Tzu. The quail is called, popularly, "bobwhite" around here. I thought you might like this.

Thank you for remembering me on the feast of St. Irenaeus, I did not know it would be around so soon. Of course I prayed for you at Mass on that day.

Finally, I sent the prayer of Cassiodorus, and my translation, about which I spoke to you. It is a beautiful prayer, I think.

More later. I must now close, but with every blessing and good wish,

Most cordially and fraternally in Christ,

Tom Merton

JW TO TM

3 Reynolds Place
Newark 6, New Jersey

July 17, 1962

My dear Father Louis:

I got yours of the 10th some days ago. I need not tell you how delighted I was with Abbot's coyness and the snake's innocence. But don't talk to the snake yet. First make a friend of him by feeding him what *he* wants. (Please study his habits.) Before you can "Merton" it, you must "snake" it.

After Chuang Tzu is a misnomer. You have taken him by the forelocks not by the tail. I swear that I am not flattering when I say that this is exactly what Chuang Tzu would write had he learned English. I may be flattering myself, but so long as I cannot get out of my own skin, I cannot help perceiving that you are the true Chuang Tzu whom the BUTTERFLY dreamed of.[54]

Even the tone "You should worry!" is revealing.

Confucius spoke of *The Odes* (*Shih Ching*)[55] in these terms: "*The Odes* can stimulate your mind, can be used for the purposes of contemplation and observation, can promote sociability and conviviality, and can vent your feelings of resentment. . . . Incidentally, you will learn the names of birds, beasts and plants." This I feel about your poems, Father. *Bobwhite*, for instance.

My course in Chinese history is going stronger than ever. I realize now that it is impossible to appreciate Confucius at his full value without looking at him against his background. When he

---

54. ". . . whom the BUTTERFLY dreamed of": famous passage of Chuang Tzu and the butterfly respectively dreaming each other, see last paragraph, chapter 2 of any works on Chuang Tzu. Wu's comments follow:

Chuang Tzu was not a dreamy man. It was rather because he was more awake than most others that he perceived a higher Reality than the reality of this life. To say that life is a dream is a very different thing from saying that life is an illusion. To Chuang Tzu, even dreams have a certain degree of reality, only not quite as real as waking life. But compared with the "Great Awakening" (life's passing), our waking life becomes a Big Dream, which, while belonging to a higher level of reality than our dreams, is infinitely lower than Reality itself. Chuang Tzu's is a thorough-going realism, with heaven and its Tao as Supreme Reality, the Cosmos as the most real of existing things, and all other things as more or less real (p. 21 in "Wisdom").

55. *The Odes*: aka *The Book of Poetry*, one of the 13 Classics.

says, "Pay due respect to the spirits and demons, but keep them at a distance," he has the superstitions of the preceding dynasty, Shang-Yin,[56] in mind. He is really more religious, and less superstitious than the Shangs.

Yes, Father, I will produce a little book on the Chinese Heritage, with your blessings.

The preface to the translation must not be written until I have given you the whole anthology which is still in the making. Those which I have submitted to you are only half of it. Some pieces will have to be omitted, the others touched up by your holy hands.

Now let me return to my preparations for today's lecture. I am now at the period of Spring and Autumn, 722-481 B.C. Tomorrow I shall come to *Chuang Tzu*, and I want, without your permission, to use "After Chuang Tzu." Anyway, I too have a share in it, seeing that I have discovered a typographical error in the seventh line from the bottom. For "The" read "Then."

I have not yet read the prayer of Cassiodorus. Usually I don't read prayers. It feels like reading other people's love letters. You peeping Tom! No wonder that even the snake is falling in love with you.

Filially yours in J.M.J.,

John

Is the Abbot still laughing?

---

56. Shang-Yin: Chinese dynasty (1766 B. C.-1000 B. C.).

JW to TM

3 Reynolds Place
Newark 6, New Jersey
December 16, 1962

My dear Father Louis:

The books—*Disputed Questions* and *Reader*—arrived some time ago. It is only today that I am beginning to look into them. They are reserved for this holy Season of His Birthday, which is beginning today. I have begun with "The Philosophy of Solitude." To put it moderately, it has whetted my appetite for further feasting. Your mind is like a crystal not only in its transparent clarity, but in the wonderful fact that every unit of it possesses the characteristic features of the whole. And is this not how the Creator Himself works? There is no atom which does not reproduce more or less faithfully the structure of the solar system! This essay on solitude is exactly what Chuang Tzu in his mature years was trying to say.

For the past month or so, I have been absorbed in writing an article on "The Philosophy of Chuang Tzu: A New Appraisal" at the request of Father Norris Clarke for his *International Philosophical Quarterly*. Only two days ago was I able to present the whole thing to him. In my hurry to beat the "deadline"—which was extended three times—I did not ask your permission to reproduce "After Chuang Tzu." The fact is, I had used it in my classes and my students, including those who knew Chinese, have been deeply impressed by your version. Why, even the tone is that of Chuang Tzu. "You should worry!"

Will you, O Father Louis, ratify my theft so that I may again feel respectable?

I am sending under another cover a mimeographic copy of my article. I want you Father to read it carefully and give me the benefit of your insights. Although it is too late for the book which I have in mind—a book on the main currents of Chinese Thought, which naturally will incorporate the article with its necessary revisions. As you know, Father, Chuang Tzu is the least understood of all Chinese philosophers, but he is the most representative of the Chinese mentality. The understanding of Chuang Tzu is the key to the "inscrutable" Chinese mind.

This season must be very busy for you. Please tell Father

Abbot, Father Andrew and Father John of the Cross how dearly I cherish them in my filial memory. As for you, O Father, you are always in mind, in season and out of season.

Your little son in Christ and Mary,

John

TM to JW

Dec 20, 1962

Dear John:

I was so happy to get your letter this morning. I am putting aside all others to answer you immediately: such is the power of Chuang Tzu and Tao to get action out of one buried in the inertia of too much activity. The very name of Chuang Tzu restores me to sanity, at least momentarily. You deserve the fruits of the lucid moment.

How I wish I could devote months to quietly working on versions of *Chuang Tzu*. I suppose the chief reason why I do not is that I still don't dare translate from one of the most difficult languages in the world, when I don't know the language and am even baffled by the first steps. But then too there are other things I have to do, or seem to have to do. How real are most of our seeming obligations?

Anyway, I am sure I will get back to *Chuang Tzu* in the spring and if you send me your article (you say you have sent it, good.) then that will get me back where I belong, even before spring. It will be my Christmas reading.

Insanity. Anything but his quiet debunking view is plain insanity. Even within the framework of the Gospel message there is too much temptation to forget what Jesus Himself warned at every step. One thing is necessary. Christianity as it has developed in the West, including monasteries of the West, has become a complex and multifarious thing. It takes Chuang Tzu to remind us of an essential element in the Gospel which we have simply "tuned out" with all our wretched concerns. The whole Sermon on the Mount, for instance. And the Discourse at the Last Supper. Even the central message of the Cross and the Resurrection. And the crib full of straw, in which the Lord of the world laughs and says, "You should worry!"

I am proud that you should want to use my "version." By all means do so. You know, by the way, one of my distractions and I think it is legitimate, is that I have "discovered" a Nicaraguan poet who is something like Chuang Tzu, but with of course many great differences. First of all he is mad. He is locked up. But he writes some of the most amazingly sane poetry. I will send you a few. He is called Alfonso Cortés.[57] Nobody in this country has ever heard

57. Alfonso Cortés (1893-1969): A Nicaraguan poet who was given the title

of him. Of course, he *is* mad, but in his madness he accuses all the right things for the right reasons.

I also enclose another poem of a madman you know well: he beats out his poems on the back of a saucepan, on top of a little hill, while the snakes dance in the woodshed.

Now I must go back to my nonsense. But I promise to stay with Chuang nevertheless. I will certainly read your article with pleasure and share with you my joy.

I am glad you like "Philosophy of Solitude." It is one of the things I have most wanted to say, perhaps the only thing I have said that needed to be said.

All best wishes always, and every blessing in this holy season when the animals and the shepherds show us the way back to our child-mind and to Him in Whom is hidden our original face before we are born. Be of good cheer. They cannot silence either Chuang Tzu or this Child, in China or anywhere. They will be heard in the middle of the night saying nothing and everybody will come to their senses.

Ever yours in Christ Our Savior,

Tom

---

of "el Poeta Loco" because he suffered mental problems in his later years, but in his moments of lucidity wrote anti-poetry. *Song of Space* remains one of his most famous poems. He was buried next to the other famous Nicaraguan poet, Ruben Darío. See Merton's comments on Cortés in *CFT*, pp. 176-178.

JW TO TM

3 Reynolds Place
Newark 6, New Jersey

December 26, 1962

My dear Father Louis:

It is indeed a blessing to have you by bedside during this glorious Season of His Birthday. *Disputed Questions* have fascinated me. To begin, I have come to know Pasternak[58] much more intimately after reading your moving account. And as to *Love* and *Solitude*, who knows their secrets better than you, Father? That Solitude is nothing but *"Cum Christo Vivere,"*[59] which is the acme of Love, seems to me to sum up Christian Wisdom of all ages. Your warning against *legalistic* tendencies in spiritual life is on a par with Christ's struggles against the Pharisees. Some years ago, I published a book called *Fountain of Justice*,[60] making a study of Christ's own philosophy of law and art of judging. Our subjects are different, but our mode of thinking is exactly the same. I shall ask my publisher to send you a copy of it, for I think you will enjoy it.

At the midnight Mass my thoughts were of you, Father. After my return home I opened the New Testament rather casually, and you cannot imagine the thrill I experienced when my eyes fell upon St. Luke, 5.14-16: "And he charged him to tell no man. . . . But so much the more the tidings spread concerning Him, and great crowds gathered together to hear Him and to be cured of their sicknesses. *But He Himself was in retirement in the desert, and in prayer.*" I immediately thought that this was the meaning of your philosophy and solitude. St. Luke did not say that in the daytime. He was curing and preaching, but He retired into the desert at night. Even when engaged in curing and preaching to the crowds, He was always in the desert and in prayer. The strange thing is that when I was translating the New Testament, these same verses

---

58. Pasternak: Boris Pasternak (1890-1960): Nobel Laureate, poet and author of *Doctor Zhivago*, banned for decades in the Soviet Union and one of Wu's favorite novels. Merton's correspondence with Pasternak lasted two years from 1958 to 1960. For letters between Merton and Pasternak, see *The Courage for Truth: The Letters of Thomas Merton to Writers*, pp. 87-93; hereafter known as *CFT*.

59. "Cum Christo Vivere": "To live with Christ."

60. *Fountain of Justice*: subtitled *A Study in the Natural Law* and published by Sheed and Ward, 1955.

did not convey to me this new meaning at all. You, Father, are in a conspiracy with the Holy Spirit to enlighten me. I am a willing victim of your conspiracy.

I confess to you, Father, ever since my childhood, I have always been haunted by the desert within me, "mysteriously designated by the finger of God." It is in this desert that I meet you, Father. It is in this desert that I find the living waters and learn the lessons of true Love. Every word of yours finds an echo in me.

In the *Reader*, I chanced upon your mention of my version of the *Tao Teh Ching*. I am very grateful, in a human way.

Yours is an *Integral Humanism*, with Humanity of the Divine *Logos* for its scope and depth. Since the apex of your Pyramid is in Heaven, you could not be otherwise than universal. O Father, how I love you!

I trust that my "Philosophy of Chuang Tzu" has arrived by this time. Please give it some time. It may be the beginning of a book.

Filially yours in Christ,

John

JW TO TM

3 Reynolds Place
Newark 6, New Jersey

[no date . . . in pencil, in upper right hand corner Dec. 26, 1962]

My dear Father Louis:

This morning I mailed out a letter to you. This noon your letter
came. This evening I am writing to you again. I don't want to let the
Feast of my Patron Saint[61] go by without writing to you, Father.

If the Lord had not led each of us into this wonderful *desert,*
how could we meet and take delight in each other? The Lord has
whispered to me, "Seek first the desert, and everything else, including the friendship of my modern Prophet Thomas Merton will be
added unto you."

We shall know it in Heaven why you are so Chinese in your
ways of thinking. Even your use of words, such as "madman"
is so typically Chinese. The T'ang poets like to call themselves
madmen. Li Po sings: "I am originally a madman of Ch'u." His
friend, Ho Chih-chang, a Ningponese[62] like myself, signed himself
as "The Mad Guest from Szu-ming Mountain."

St. Paul was also very Oriental when he said, "If we were out
of our mind, it was for God; if we are sane, it is for you . . . ." In
my Chinese translation, this is rendered as: "If we are *drunk* . . . if
we are sober . . . ."

Whether we call it madness, drunkenness, or living beyond
reason, one thing is certain: no one can be a Saint of God who
has not been filled to the throat by the intoxicating Spirit of Love.
And, Father, you have drunk like a whale. The fault is not yours;
the "mad Lord"—you remember that his folks used to think Him
mad—in His unreasonable hospitality has urged you "Bottom up"
too many times. [In margin, Chinese Character="dry the cup"].
Look at me, Father, I am supposed to be a lawyer, and a lawyer is
supposed to be as sober as a Scotchman, even I have not been able

---

61. Patron Saint: St. John the Evangelist (1-100), author of the 4th Gospel,
Epistles and the Apocalypse. With Peter, the closest and most constant companion of Christ who called him "Sun of Thunder." Popularized the notion, "God
is Love."

62. Ningponese: designating both a native and the language spoken in Ningpo,
a major seaport in Chekiang Province on the eastern coast of China and a stone's
throw south of Shanghai. Wu was born in Ningpo on March 28th, 1899.

to resist the overwhelming hospitality of our Divine Host. In your case, Father, the resistance is almost nil.

But who but a dead-drunk man like you can "know my timeless moment of void?" Who else could embody "the extreme purity of virginal thirst?" O, that stanza which begins with:

> When I come I lift my sudden Eucharist
> Out of the earth's unfathomable joy—

What a drunken hymn to the Mystery of Incarnation!

You are so filled with wine that even your exhalation has an intoxicating effect.

As to Alfonso Cortes' "The Truth," he too is Chuangtzuish:

> The only law that centers you in virtue
> Prophet, wise man, artist, proletarian,
> Is *mystery* . . . .

It is exactly the same insight which made Chuang Tzu and Lao Tzu so mad against the dry moralistic scholars of their times (later scholars are drier still). And this:

> Stronger than destiny is pain.

How true! Did Christ not overcome the destiny of mankind by his Pain?

Many things I do not understand; but I am impressed by the question:

> Time, you and I
> Where are we,
> I who live in you
> And you who do not exist?

And I like the "bees of death" and "roses of life." The whole poem "When You Point Your Finger" is enchanting.

It may well be that your reading of his poetry lifts it to your own interior landscape. Perhaps, there are two darknesses: the higher and the lower, as Violet Clifton[63] suggested. Perhaps, to you who are enveloped in the higher Darkness, even the lower darkness is Dark. At least, it has the merit of not pretending to be Light. Like Our Lord, you rate the harlots far above the Pharisees. So do I.

63. Violet Clifton (1883-1961): Author of *The Book of Peru*, *Talbot Vision*, and *Islands of Indonesia*.

But Father, by this time, I have gone ever farther than Our Lord, by His own way. I regard the Pharisees as Harlots, prostituting their religion, and therefore they too deserve our compassion, they *need* it more than the harlots.

But when it comes to the question of association, I would much sooner associate with the harlots than with the Pharisees.

"Now I must go back to my nonsense." It is perfectly this kind of nonsense, Father, that serves as the necessary manure for the flowers of our spirituality. True, sometimes the manure is a bit too concentrated; but so much the better for the fragrance of the flower. However, if I persist in this line of thinking, I may land ultimately in cynicism under the delusion that I was being holy.

Why should my neighbor serve as my manure? Should I not treat them as myself? If, as I have maintained, the use of the cloister is to evoke the interior cloister, and if the monks are only living in the external cloister, can I help weeping with Our Lord and suffering with Him the agony in the Garden of Gethsemani? On the other hand, the times and hours are different for each individual. The hard thing, as you say, is discretion, and good humor. I am sure that Our Father has something of the Grandma in Him. This I have discovered since my dear wife passed on. When she was living, all that I needed to be was to be a father to my children; but now I have to be both father and mother, and I have found that what they really want is a grandmother. During these three years, I am nailed to the Cross with Christ, and I have come to see why some mystics, like Lady Julian of Norwich,[64] call Christ "Mother."

One of the greatest consolations that the Lord has deigned to give me during this period is to know you, Father, and to know that you are the Master of Novices. What a vocation! O the fruitfulness of *virgin thirst!*

Your old good-for-nothing son in Christ,

John

---

64. Lady Julian of Norwich (1342-1416): 14th century English recluse and author of *Revelations of Divine Love*, a mystical classic in line with the writings of John of the Cross and Teresa of Avila. There is very little biographical information available on her. Merton said of her that Julian was one of his favorite Christian mystics. In her *Sixteen Revelations of Divine Love* (1393) Julian developed a mystical theology of hope by quoting: "All shall be well, and all shall be well, and all manner of things shall be well." Also her views on Christ being the Mother distinguished her from other mystical theologians.

TM to JW

March 28, 1963

Dear John:

For a long time I have been wanting to thank you for your last letter and for the valued gift of FOUNTAIN OF JUSTICE [Merton's caps] which I have been wanting to read long before you mentioned it. I am still waiting to do so, and I think the time is getting close because I have been going through the Hannah Arendt[65] articles on Eichmann,[66] and she brings out some strange statements here and there. She seems to adopt the view that because Eichmann appealed to "conscience" and "duty" and to "moral imperatives" à la Kant, that therefore conscience is discredited and moral law does not objectively exist. This is the impression I get so far. The articles are tremendous but there is a weirdly hallucinated perspective throughout. Perhaps however she is only saying that Eichmann discredits Kant. I don't know. This gives me every reason to get in to FOUNTAIN OF JUSTICE and give it a careful, thoughtful reading. How else should I read you? Certainly not in a hurry.

Now here is something you may be interested in: an article on Zen. It is not corrected, but I am sending it along just as it is, so that you can show what I need to change and improve. I am going to do more work on it. I slipped in a few words about the *Platform Scripture*, which ought to cheer Paul Sih a bit, but I do not know when the book is supposed to appear. I think Dumoulin[67] is very interesting but that he has a very central weakness: he doesn't understand Zen. He equated it with more familiar forms of con-

65. Hannah Arendt (1906-1975): a German political philosopher raised in a secular Jewish home. Her most influential work was *The Human Condition* (1958). Merton read with interest her reports of the Eichmann trial found in her book, *Eichmann in Jerusalem: A Report on the Banality of Evil* (1963).

66. Adolf Eichmann (1906-1962): A Nazi German born in a Lutheran family. Eichmann was in charge of the logistics of mass deportation of Jews to concentration camps. He faced trial in Israel and was executed in 1962. Merton wrote on Arendt's report that Israeli psychiatrists found that Eichmann was "normal." During the trial Eichmann said that he just followed orders. Merton wrote about the meaning of sanity in a world that excludes love. He concluded that Eichmann's sanity is totally "disturbing." See Merton's *Raids on the Unspeakable* (New Directions, 1966), pp. 45-47.

67. Heinrich Dumoulin (1905-1995): A German Jesuit theologian known for his writings on Zen Buddhism. Ironically Merton said of him in a letter to Dr. Wu that Fr. Dumoulin "doesn't understand Zen."

templation. However, I may be too severe with him on this point. He certainly has a mass of wonderful material in his book.

The birds are singing and the sun is out at last. The love of God fills everything and the spring is pure joy. Soon it will be Easter and we will know that all along our joy has been sacramental, even when it seemed not to be, or even when it seemed not to be joy.

All blessing to you, and you are more than ever in my prayers and Masses as Lent draws to a close. When will we see you again?

With the most cordial friendship in Christ,

Tom

JW TO TM

3 Reynolds Place
Newark 6, New Jersey

March 31, 1963

Dear Father Louis:

Your letter came yesterday with your article on "Mystics and Zen."
I have read it today; and I did it in two hours lying down in bed,
and all the time I was feeling as though every word came from my
real self.

I too have read Dumoulin, and I too have felt that he did not
understand Hui Neng.[68] My impression is that if possible Father
Dumoulin would have preferred Shen Hsiu[69] to Hui Neng. This
seems to me true even of Dogen,[70] who goes to the extent of equat-
ing zazen[71] with Zen. I wonder what Hui Neng would have said
to Dogen.

> While living one sits up,
> When dead one lies flat.
> In both cases a set of stinking skeleton,
> What has it to do with the task of enlightenment?

---

68. Hui Neng: (638-713): the Sixth Patriarch in the Zen sect. In *The Golden
Age of Zen*, Wu says Hui Neng belongs "to the company of Lao Tzu, Confucius,
Mencius and Chuang Tzu," and regards his masterpiece, *The Platform Scripture*
(aka *The Altar Sutra*), as "the work of a true sage who speaks from the fullness
of his heart and mind" (p. 43). In contrast to Shen Hsiu's idea of "gradual enlightenment," Hui Neng was famous for his "instantaneous enlightenment," or the
recognition of one's "self-nature" (p. 51; hereafter known as *GAZ*).
69. Shen Hsiu (605?-706): a contemporary of Hui Neng, known for his idea
of "gradual enlightenment" which consists of his doctrine of *sila* (moral discipline
leading to abstention of all evil), *prajna* (wisdom through pursuing of all good),
and *dhyana* (recollection and peace leading to purification of one's mind). See
GAZ, p. 51.
70. Dogen: Dogen Kigan (Chinese name, Tao Yen, 1200-1253): founder
of the Soto School of Japanese Zen. Attained enlightenment in China and introduced Zen to his native Japan. His basic method was called *shikan-taza* ("just
sitting") and he emphasized the principles, "practice and enlightenment are one"
and "sustained exertion." (See Kapleau's *Zen: Merging of East and West,* p. 291;
hereafter known as *ZMEW*.)
71. *Zazen*: Chinese *tso-ch'an*, literally "sitting in meditation" or "sitting Zen."
Kapleau writes: "During true zazen the mind is one-pointed, stabilized, and emp-
tied of random, extraneous thoughts. Zazen is not limited to sitting but continuous
throughout every activity" (*ZMEW*, p. 298).

As you know so well, Hui Neng is not against Sazen as such any more than any other activities; but to identify Zen with *zazen*! "For Hui Neng *all life was Zen*." It couldn't be better put. Did I not say that my Father Louis was a Chinese? Now I have discovered that the Chinese in question was Hui Neng!

I know your vision is genuine, because it is transparent. It was Goethe who said that the ideal thinker is one who can divide so deeply that he can unite, and united so deeply that he can divide. That's you. I would also agree with you that Dumoulin's book is *useful*. It has profited me, by way of historical information. But he cannot aspire to the *uselessness* of Chuang Tzu.

Your explanation of "Mind" as "Spirit" and of *Prajna*[72] as *Light*, the Light that illumines all, and your discernment of the empirical self from the *Real Man* in the Chuangtzean sense, your "pure affirmation," your distinction between *is* and *has*, your "awareness of full spiritual reality," your speaking of the "true face" as "a discovery of *genuine identity* in and with the One," your "elementary rule" on page 3, your *old-womanish*[73] repeated insistence on all-embracing Catholicity as the earmark of a true Catholic (on p. 1), and your reserves on "The mirror has no stand" and so forth, have wrought in me the transcending of the subject-object relationship. There is no longer Father Louis or John Wu, but the Vagabond Spirit, the Divine Rascal Who comes and goes like the Wind.

Speaking of *genuine identity*, Jesus, making the best of human language, pointed to the Vine-and-its-branches.[74] And yet theologians insist upon a *forced duality*! Beatific Vision is nothing but *entry into the joy of the Lord*; yet how many Christians still think of it as if it were like watching an eternal Television! God is both One and Three, therefore neither One nor Three. He is both Personal and Impersonal, and therefore neither. Yet Chuang Tzu has been called an "atheist" simply because He calls God by a different name.

---

72. Prajna: (Sanskrit): in Buddhism, supreme knowledge or wisdom; spiritual awakening; wisdom which brings liberation. (See *The Asian Journal of Thomas Merton*, p. 393; hereafter known as *AJTM*.)

73. "old-womanish": Wu's footnote: "a Chinese compliment "as merciful as the old woman's heart."

74. Vine-and-its-branches: see John 15:1-2: "I am the true vine, and my Father is the vinedresser. Every branch of vine that bears no fruit, he takes away, and every branch that does bear fruit he prunes, that it may bear more fruit" (*Revised Standard Version*).

The word "Unconscious" needs some reconsideration. The Chinese original is "No-Mind." My understanding is that it is equivalent to "no-reflection" or "no discursive reasoning" therefore it means a direct awareness.

Some days ago I mailed a reprint of my article on Chuang Tzu. Have you received it?

———————

The Bohdi is in reality no tree,
Nor is the bright mirror a stand.
Originally there is not a thing:
Where can dust arise?

This is as literal as I can make it. It seems that "pen lai" refers to "before Adam was." The word "je" [Chinese Character Underneath "je"] in the last line means "be provoked or stirred to rise."

———————

It is definite that I shall have to go to Formosa before September of 1964. The Jesuits who have undertaken to run the Law College for the Catholic U. of China[75] have pressed me to take up the dean-ship. They even want me to go this year; but I have to perform my promise to Seton Hall to write a book on the Main Currents of Chinese Thought. In the meantime they have appointed a Jesuit Father to be the acting dean.

Of course, Buddhism, especially Ch'an, is one of the main currents. So I am just beginning to write on this. It is therefore Providential that both Dumoulin's work and your comment have come into my hands. Of course, I draw mostly upon the Chinese texts. But your comment gives me a welcome guide.

———————

I wish and pray that someday you will be asked to organize a Trappist monastery in Formosa.

Your old affectionate son in Christ,

John [Chinese Characters Follow]

———————

75. Catholic U. of China: Fu Jen Catholic University, Hsinchuang, Taiwan.

TM TO JW

June 23, 1963

Dear John:

Your two fine letters have been waiting long for a reply. I was especially happy that you agreed with me both on Dumoulin and on Dom Graham's book.[76] I too was surprised that he came out with such an unusual amount of insight. He must really be going through quite a development. That is encouraging, because it is so easy for people in that kind of position to simply stay put and be ensconced in their stuffed shirts. There are signs of life, then, everywhere. But there could be more.

Your remarks on Zen in the first letter are very helpful. Yes, the real point is this fact that Zen is NOT *zazen*. And everybody wants to reduce it to that, even with their *koans*[77] and all the rest. In both cases a set of stinking skeletons. Let's throw out the skeleton for good and all and take off for nowhere with that Vagabond, (that notorious illuminist, the Holy Spirit).

I have had a very amusing Chuang Tsuean experience. With deliberate intention to wreak mischief and with tongue deeply in cheek, I wrote a long fiery article defending Fénelon[78] against Bossuet. (Of course I like Fénelon, but the idea was to puncture the Bossuet-image and the French national collective ego, which is anti-Fénelon.) Then I sent it to the censors of the Order in Eng-

76. Dom Graham: Dom Aelred Graham (1907-1984), Benedictine Prior at Portsmouth Priory, now Portsmouth Abbey, Rhode Island and writer on spiritual subjects. The book mentioned is *Zen Catholicism*. Back in 1953, Graham had written a scathing indictment of Merton's "otherworldliness" in *The Atlantic Monthly* ("Thomas Merton: a Modern Man in Reverse") in which he said Merton's "message was marred by a strident ascetic tone" (see Graham's *The End of Religion*, Harcourt Brace Jovanovich, 1971, p. 63). Later, according to Graham, after a visit to Gethsemani, they became "firm friends."

77. *Koan*: A Zen Buddhist riddle which transcends rational thinking and its meaning must be found in intuitive understanding. *Koans* are viewed as shock therapy tools by the Zen practitioner so that he or she may have a spiritual breakthrough and thus attain *satori*, or enlightenment.

78. François Fénelon (1651-1715) vs. Jacques-Bénigne Bossuet (1627-1704): Bossuet's controversy with Fénelon was based on Mme. Guyon's (1648-1717) quietistic doctrine, a heretical position condemned by the Church for advocating inner passivity and total annihilation of the human will. Ironically, Merton favored Fénelon's spiritual theology over Bossuet because the type of quietism that Fénelon embraced in his teachings was more in line with the monastic idea that God alone suffices and that inner passivity must be understood as mystical receptivity.

land, who obviously rushed to approve it, and sent their approval to the Abbot General, probably letting him know the contents of the article (he can't read English). Report came back from our patriotic French General, a staunch Gaulliste and a most humorless chauvinist when it comes to things like this. He granted the *nihil obstat*, I can almost hear the muttered recriminations with which he did so, and then added in a special note that he did not want his name associated in any way with such a piece of effrontery. It was magnanimous of him not to put me on bread and water for a year and stop me writing altogether.

But talking of Chuang Tzu: I am really hoping to get down to some work on him, and in fact I am well on the way to finishing a small book of selections. I thought I would send one piece along to you now, to see how you like it. It contains a few minor liberties with what must be the original meaning. You will tell me if I am too wild and wide of the mark, and what to change. But anyway, Chuang Tzu is my delight.

Thank you for the note on No Mind. Yes, the term Unconscious is misleading, and very much so. The thing is to get a real equivalent to the direct awareness *in depth*, the pure and complete immediacy implied by it. The problem of English terms like "no reflection" is that they seem to imply a kind of sensible quietism, a *surface* intuitiveness, more or less a rest in the immediacy of *sense* experience. That is of course only the least part of it. On the other hand we are bedeviled with the Platonist prejudice against senses, so that when it becomes an interior quietism of the *zazen* type, then some are satisfied with that. The old forced duality. And how they like to force it.

Yes, I did receive your article on Chuang Tzu, a long time ago, and it is very fine. I will be able to guide myself by it in writing the preface to my little pieces. I am looking forward, too, to receiving your chapter on Zen. The whole book on Chinese Culture interests me immensely. Have you a publisher ready and waiting? I have a friend at Doubleday who might be interested, though she is not very Zennish.

I am sorry we are going to lose you to Formosa in 1964. That is a long way off. With the mail it doesn't make much difference, but still there will not be much hope of seeing you if you are that far off. Still, I am sure they need you there.

Meanwhile, keep in touch with us. I hope we will see you

before you go, perhaps sometime next spring or summer. Let us keep it in mind, anyway.

Paul Sih has sent me the *Platform Scripture*[79] and it is handsomely done. He wants me to write a review of it, and I will earnestly try, but it is hard to fit in right now. But with a book like this an immediate reaction is not essential. Eventually, I hope to come through with something.

Best wishes to you, John. I will be remembering you tomorrow on the Feast of St. John the Baptist, though I seem to remember your patron is the Evangelist. No matter, any day is a good day for prayers and blessings.

Most cordially yours in Christ Jesus,

Tom Merton

---

79. *Platform Scripture*: aka *Altar Sutra*, sayings of Hui Neng, Sixth Patriarch of the Zen sect.

JW TO TM

2D, 43 Cottage St
South Orange, NJ

Aug 9, 1963

My dear Father Louis:

Yours of the 6th gave me a shock and a relief. I am happy that you were getting out of the hospital on the day you sent the letter. I hope that you are better than ever before.

Don't think that I am as impatient as I appear in my letters. Take your time, Father. I can wait. Now that I have heard of your hospitalization, I am more interested in your health than in Zen.

I suspect that you were so intensely absorbed in *The Way of Chuang Tzu* that you used more energy than you were aware. Such a work could only have been produced in white heat.

The news I am expecting now is your complete recovery. Let Soto and Rinzai and Unmon[80] wait.

Your affectionate boy in Christ,

John

---

80. Unmon Bun'en (862?-949): A Chinese Zen master who founded the "Yunmen School" and had a major influence on the *koan* tradition.

JW to TM

Undated card, sometime December 1964.

My dear Father Louis:

You have been on my mind every day, and yet I have not written you. I was in Honolulu this last summer, where I had the pleasure of a reunion with Dr. Suzuki.[81] Needless to say, he has the highest respect for you. His secretary told me that their only regret was that your dialogue with him was all too short. She said that he would have asked you a question if time had allowed. "If God created the world, who had created the Creator?" (This was the tenor of the masked question, though I have forgotten the exact wording.) This suddenly opened my eyes to one fact (not a *satori*): *Suzuki has the mind of a child!* For I have heard this question from the lips of many a child. I did not answer it; for she was only relating something not asking me. But it is important to remember that Suzuki has, besides, the *heart of a child*. There's a saving grace for everybody!

I also met Dr. John McKeon,[82] who told me that you had mentioned him in your *Seven Storey M.* I like him, but he showed some signs of senility. He was so long-winded that it almost spoiled the conference!

I am working on a history of Zen.[83] I showed one chapter to Dr. Suzuki. The chapter (on the fundamental insights of Hui neng) will be mailed to you under another cover. My question to him was: "Have I misrepresented Hui-neng's thoughts at any point?" His answer was *no*.

---

81. Dr. Daisetsu Teitaro Suzuki (1870-1966): reunion at the International Philosophical Conference held at the University of Hawaii where Wu and Suzuki were participants. The two of them had first met as faculty members at U of H in 1949. For an intimate portrayal of their relationship, see Appendix: "My Reminiscences of Dr. Daisetz T. Suzuki," pp. 216-22 in *GAZ*. It is ironic that Merton too had had a short clandestine meeting with Suzuki in New York City at Columbia University in mid-June shortly before Suzuki attended the IPC in July and August. See *Encounter: Thomas Merton and D. T. Suzuki* (Larkspur Press, 1988, edited by Robert Daggy), pp. 75-90, and *Dancing in the Water of Life: the Journals of Thomas Merton*, Vol. Five (HarperCollins, 1997, ed. Robert Daggy), "The Suzuki Visit," pp. 111-17, detailing their meeting.

82. Dr. John McKeon: not John, but Richard McKeon, the renowned Aristotelian scholar from the University of Chicago.

83. history of Zen: *The Golden Age of Zen*, first published in Taiwan, 1967; later, brought out by Doubleday Image Books, 1996.

Suzuki was happy that you did *not* like Dumoulin's history. On the other hand, he was glad that you approved of Dom Aelred Graham's *Zen Catholicism*, which he also liked.

Pray for me, Father, that the Lord will *renew* my (indecipherable word) life every day during 1965. Remember that you are my father in the Lord, and I am your son.

Please convey my filial homage to the good Abbot James.

John

TM ᴛᴏ JW

Dec. 23, 1964

Dear John:

It was a great joy to get your card and note. What happened to our correspondence? The last letter I wrote was sent when I thought you were soon to go to Taiwan and when I did not get a reply I thought I had missed you. And I did not know where to write next. Now I find you are still in New Jersey, and maybe that is better in the long run. But now I heard you met Suzuki in Honolulu and the deep secret of my mysterious voyage is out. It had to be a total secret and I saw no one in NY except Suzuki, none of my other friends yet know that I was there, I was under strict orders to slink around with false moustaches and dark glasses and foreign names. But I am glad you met him. I think you are perfectly right about his having a child's mind and heart. It is perfectly true, and that is his greatness.

I am very anxious to see your history of Zen, and anything else you have been working on. I still have not given up the idea of various versions of *Chuang Tzu*, but have not been able to do anything about it lately. As a matter of fact in my last letter I sent a version which may have been so bad that I attributed to it, also, your silence!

In my new book I printed some letters, my own, and included one I wrote to you.[84] I forget if I mentioned this to you, but there is nothing personal in it so I assume you would not have objected. A copy of the book will be on its way to you and will I hope find its way to you by New Year.

Next year I expect to have a great deal more time at the hermitage, and that will be most welcome. Though I will still have the novices to take care of.

This fall, Fr. Dumoulin wrote from Japan and urged very strongly that I ask permission to make a trip there and meet some of the Zen monks in their monasteries. He wrote quite a strong letter to the Abbot General about this, which ought to have meant something since he is a member of the Secretariate for Non-Christian religions. However all my superiors managed to gather from this request was that I was half out of my mind. They are completely

84. ". . . included one I wrote to you": see *Seeds of Destruction*, pp. 277-79 for letter to Wu dated June 7, 1962 and later "Cold War Letter #82."

unprepared to understand any such thing. They told me my request was completely incredible and that was that. I think I might have learned very much from it, but there are other ways of learning the same things and I must admit that I am not keen on travelling.

There is much Christmas mail to be attended to so I must stop now, but do not cross me off your list! I will certainly remember you in my Christmas masses and at all the feasts of the holy season, most especially Epiphany which is coming to mean more to me somehow than Christmas itself. There is not so much tinsel and the air is clearer so to speak. Even in the monastery I am afraid that the air of Christmas becomes completely surcharged with nonsense.

God be with you. Keep well. Have joy and peace. Blessings upon you and all the family. Here is a picture to scare the crows away with.

Best of friendship always in Christ Our Lord,

Tom Merton

JW to TM

3 Reynolds Place
Newark 6, New Jersey

December 27, 1964

Dear Father Louis:

I am thrilled to read yours of Dec. 23. First of all let me tell you that I am so happy to have one of your letters to me included in your new book. There can be no better gift for the New Year. But the wonder of it is that you seem to be apologetic about it! O Father, you make me laugh! As though it were not a privilege, a delight, and a blessing to be your friend! True, I am not so vain as to seek for it. Still I am not so unhuman and ungrateful as to feel sorry for it.

One reason why I remained silent so long is that I became intensely interested in the Chinese Zen literature. The dialogues of the Zen masters of the T'ang and Sung and Ming Dynasties are well nigh inexhaustible. Their irresistible charm lies in the fact that they are infinitely various in their presentation and yet always the same in their insight. I devoured one volume after another still feeling as though I had read nothing. They are so humorously serious about the "one thing necessary!" Actually, Father, they are better Christians than those professed ones who have no ear for the words of Christ. How true that "the air of Christmas becomes surcharged with nonsense." You certainly mince no words. If this is true of Christmas, it is even truer of the "Christian" life in Christendom. What is the use of being a "Christian" and still busied about many things, secretly laughing at the "impractical" counsels of the Living LOGOS? [Wu's caps] I have often thought that if the Gospel were submitted to the chancery offices for the first time, many passages among the sermons of Our Lord and of course from St. Paul would be regarded as sheer heresies! Our Lord was a Fire-Eater. So are you, Father! The secret spring of our Church's vitality lies in that in every age there are Fire-Eaters who transmit the true Spirit from generation to generation quietly but powerfully, in spite of all the nonsensical noises to the contrary. This spirit is like crocus . . . .

I am tickled by what you tell me about the decision about your going to Japan. Their reasons, I am sure, are wrong, but their decision seems to me to be right. You may be shocked by this statement of mine, but, Father, the truth is that there is more Zen in your hermitage than in any of the Zen halls. It seems to me that they too have externalized Zen as the Christians have done with Christianity.

The "Old Rice Bag" looks very much like Hui Neng. It is certainly not necessary for Hui Neng to go to Tokyo. On the other hand, to say that it is not necessary is not to say that it may not be fruitful, especially for the Zen monks. For you, Father, you are already *yourself*, the "Original Face;" who is everywhere, including Japan, and nowhere, not even in Gethsemani.[85] But for the monks who are trying to sit themselves into Buddha,[86] you can well serve as the occasion for their awakening to the *Logos*. This is something the authorities should know. They do not see the *True Man*.

I think that Seton Hall *must* be interested in the exhibit.[87] I have not yet contacted the proper authorities; but I will do so in a day or two. I am most curious to see the "Zen" calligraphy. How very Chinese is your way of thinking! But I had thought that only the Chinese characters are capable of Zen, while A B C D . . . are only crab-writing. Of course, even the crabs are nothing if not Zen.

I am enclosing herewith a chapter (one of twenty) from the history of Zen. The rest are not written out, only in notes. I beg you, Father, to scrutinize it word by word, and to be absolutely frank in pointing out the faults and defects. I would much rather receive your beatings and shouts before they are published than after. Of course, you know that all historical treatment is only Upaya,[88] just like your journeying to Japan.

You mention a version of a passage of *Chuang Tzu* in your last letter. I do not recall having received that. All your letters

---

85. ". . . not even in Gethsemani": while Wu did not discourage Merton from going to Japan, neither did he encourage the trip nor the one to Asia four years later, though as he says, he was "agog for the coming reunion" in Taiwan which, of course, never took place. (See Appendix, "Letter to Cistercian Studies.")

86. ". . . to sit themselves into Buddha . . .": a famous yet controversial story linked with Ma-tsu's (709-788) subsequent enlightenment. For two slightly dissimilar yet compatible interpretations, see *GAZ*, pp. 69-71 and Kapleau's *The Three Pillars of Zen*, pp. 23-25.

87. exhibit: of Merton's "calligraphs," abstracts done in striking black and white brushwork, a good number of which appear in Merton's *Raids on the Unspeakable*.

88. Upaya: (Sanskrit): in Zen Buddhism, the "skillful means" which the Buddha, or a Buddhist master, uses "to bring any being to a state of enlightenment and happiness" (see *AJTM*, glossary, p. 411).

are placed in a special draw as a treasure which no thiefs [Wu's spelling] can steal, yet I do not find that version.

Your old though not aging boy in Christ,

John

In Wu's hand: I am happy to learn that you are still in charge of the novices. Sometimes, the fresh insights of the young can be worth a ton of lectures. Teaching is a most creative activity.

TM TO JW

Jan. 31, 1965

Dear John:

Look how much time has passed since I received your letter and the chapter on Hui Neng. Time does not obey me, it will not stop for my convenience. This is very strange, but I must put up with it, even though time obeys everybody else. I will have to picket time for this unfairness.

Really I enjoyed your chapter of Hui Neng very much as it has much new material and I like your insight about the quiet revolution on p.10. Your pages bring out more of the real importance of Hui Neng. I like the concept of playful samadhi,[89] which comes very naturally from you.

As to suggestions and criticism: I would hardly have any since I am so little in touch with the material. But I do note in passing that there was a slip of the typewriter on p. 4 where, at the end of line 13, you surely mean "not *only* deluded etc." You have probably caught this already.

The big question is the use of the term self-nature,[90] which I think the Western reader simply cannot avoid taking as the opposite to what it really means. You are right that "mind" is a "weasel word." And when you say that self-nature is the "substance and essence of mind" you are ushering in two more weasels, so that at this point self-nature is attacked on three sides by dangerous weasels. And since essence is big enough and fat enough to be the equivalent of two or even three weasels, then I think that you have self-nature entirely surrounded and I fear that he will not escape. But on the other hand since nature is the biggest weasel of all, it turns out in the end to be a civil war, and the weasels are all fighting each other. From this kind of thing there is no resource left but to withdraw into the void

---

89. samadhi: (Sanskrit and Pali): profound meditation. In Hinduism, *samadhi* is the final stage in the practice of yoga; in Buddhism, the final step in the Noble Eight-fold Path, the Middle Way, which leads to the liberation from all evil and *dukkha* (suffering) and the achievement of *nirvana*—final enlightenment and freedom from rebirth. (See *AJTM*, glossary, p. 398.)

90. False vs. True Self: Merton understood the false self as the illusory self that is egocentric, sinful, and shortsighted. This self suffers alienation from the source of life which is no other than God, the True Self in all of us. See Merton's *New Seeds of Contemplation* (pp. 31-35 and 161), *Faith and Violence* (p. 112), *Love and Living* (p. 199), and *Conjectures of a Guilty Bystander* (pp. 95, 142, 149, 296).

and scamper about in nothingness where there cannot be a shadow of civil war. But of course this does not solve the problem of making the Western reader aware of what self nature is all about. The main thing is that it is not about 1) self, and 2) nature, as these terms are understood in the West. Is this right? I may be simply mumbling the inanities of a half frozen monk, but it seems to me that the problem lies somewhere in this area. It is a problem of communication. And if the word self nature translates the Chinese ideograms, then it is a matter of explaining that there is more in this than meets the eye, or perhaps less. Or at any rate something else.

At every turn, we get back to the big question, which is the question of the person as void and not as individual or empirical ego. I know of no one in the West who has treated of person in such a way as to make clear that what is most ourselves is what is least ourself, or better the other way round. It is the void that is our personality, and not our individuality that seems to be concrete and defined and present, etc. It is what is seemingly not present, the void, that is really I. And the "I" that seems to be I is really a void. But the West is so used to identifying the person with the individual and the deeper self with the empirical self (confusing the issue by juggling around a divided "body and soul") that the basic truth is never seen. It is the No-I that is most of all I in each one of us. But we are completely enslaved by the illusory I that is not I and never can be I except in a purely fictional and social sense.

And of course there is yet one more convolution in this strange dialectic: there remains to suppress the apparent division between empirical self and real or inner self. There is no such division. There is only the Void which is I, covered over by an apparent I. And when the apparent I is seen to be void it no longer needs to be rejected, *for it is I.* How wonderful it is to be alive in such a world of craziness and simplicity.

I get this way from sleeping nights in the hermitage and watching the stars. Things seem to be progressing in the direction of more solitude, for which I am very grateful.

I enclose a piece which will probably appear with some modifications in *Holiday* magazine. Do send more of your Zen chapters, and I hope you will translate some of the Zen texts. There is so much that is inaccessible.

Best wishes and blessings always,

Cordially yours in Christ,

[No Signature]

JW TO TM

3 Reynolds 6 N.J.

Feb. 5, 1965

My dear Father Louis:

Here is your *wonderful* letter of Jan. 31. I see eye-to-eye with you in your transparent perception of the "Self-Nature." It is the Not I himself who must have penned these words: "It is the void that is our personality, and not our individuality that seems to be concrete and defined and present etc. It is what is seemingly not present, the void, that is really I. And the 'I' that seems to be I is really a void." Now, Father Void, this is truly a pointing to the Moon. I do see eye-to-eye with you, although I cannot tell you who am I and who are you and where are the eyes and what do I mean by "with." O Father Void, you are indeed a wizard!

Your *Seeds of Destruction* came some time ago and I have read through a considerable part of it. Somehow I cannot finish this book at a single stretch, because the love you have for mankind—for the Void—is so intense as to be scathing. One conclusion is safe and cool: Only a contemplative like you can burn with such Christ-Love as you have radiated in all your letters. You are mad with the very madness of Christ; yet this madness is a mysterious blend of the Fire of Love and the Water of Wisdom. I love you, Father, although *The Advocate*, a local diocesan paper, in reviewing the book, concludes by pointing out that you send me a bitter and angry poem! Of course, the reader must understand the poem was not addressed to me, but it does sound as though my Father hated me! You see, Father, there is so much of the child in me that I can still laugh on such things—and I have laughed many times over this interesting episode. It is the Void within me who is teasing the other guy, saying, "This serves you right!!"

Father, I am so grateful to you for your discernment of spirits. Ultimately the "playful samadhi" is my native style. But just because life is a great play, we must play seriously, keeping to our roles and identifying ourselves with them, as you have done.[91]

---

91. "... we must play seriously, keeping to our roles ... as you have done": in his writings, Wu confesses Justice Holmes had a good deal to do with inculcating in him this particular attitude. There are at least two places in Holmes' letters to the young Wu where the old friend gives such advice: 1) "Life having thrown me into the law, I must try to put my feeling of the infinite into that ... to show in it

In confidence. I am in love with a Chinese lady in the forties. She sings Chinese songs and is a good calligrapher. Her character is first-rate. She has love for me, but she is somewhat afraid of the responsibility of a housewife—because she takes responsibilities seriously. The other day, I wept like a baby. . . . Well. Father, please pray for us. You see, Father, in love there is no more playful samadhi for the apparent I; if it exists at all it is in the Void. "How wonderful it is to be alive in such a world of craziness and simplicity."[92]

I entrusted the matter of exhibition of calligraphy to Father Albert Hakim.[93] He told me that it is now in the proper hands, and that they have communicated with you, or at least they are going to. Needless to say, they regard it as a treat.

O Father, what a transparent perceiver you are! (I don't mean that you are a crystal gazer). Only a wizard like you can catch the weasel mysticism of Buddhism. "There is only the Void which is I, covered over by an apparent I. And *when the apparent I is seen to be void, it no longer needs to be rejected, for it is I.*" With this fundamental insight we can spin the Buddhist scriptures as the boys toy with the tops.

Yes, I will send more chapters on Zen. Or rather write out more, now that I have been stimulated. To have your word of approval is no little matter; and the fact that you even noted such a small omission as "only" shows that the paper has received the favor of your going through it carefully. In fact, when I turn to my

---

the great line of the universal. . . . [I]t truly expresses my desire and the way I felt when called on perhaps to construe some temporary statutes, *so that untying little knots never seems drudgery*" (9/20/23); 2) "Your 'this miserable world' makes me anxious. . . . For me at least there came moments when faith wavered. But there is the great lesson and the great triumph if you keep the fire burning until, by and by, *out of the mass of sordid details there comes some result, be it some new generalization or be it a transcending spiritual repose*" (1/27/25). Emphasis added. Holmes was writing as an agnostic. Wu later saw the deeply spiritual and mystical dimension of "life as play" in the English poet George Herbert and of course in Chuang Tzu and in the Zen experience.

92. ". . . a world of craziness and simplicity": Merton himself fell in love with a nurse a little over a year later in March, 1966. For this episode, see Michael Mott's *The Seven Mountains of Thomas Merton*, pp. 435-54, and *Learning to Love: the Journals of Thomas Merton*, Vol. 6, especially the heart-wrenching "Midsummer Diary," pp. 302-48.

93. Father Albert Hakim: Dean of Academic Affairs at Seton Hall in the 1960s.

own copy, "only" is there!

Your observations on the I and the void have incidentally confirmed my surmise that the Zen masters were actually the legitimate heirs of Lao Tzu and Chuang Tzu, while the so called Neo-Taoists were bastards.

It's about time to stop, before I use worse words. Sometimes I wonder why Chuang Tzu and the Zen masters were so fond of the dirty and ugly things and words. Can you tell me, you reincarnation of Void?

With filial love in the Word Who is the Void,

John

IN WU'S HAND: P.S. I have not yet read "Rain & the Rhinoceros." But I am going to. In the meantime, I want to send this first.

JW TO TM

3 Reynolds 6, N.J.

May 11, 1965

My dear Father Louis:

It's half past one after midnight, and I have just read (in bed) your nosegay of poems called "The Way of Chuang Tzu." I am simply bewitched! As I was reading one piece after piece, I caught myself wishing that I would never come' to an end. But it did—all too soon, and as my spirit has been invigorated, I sprang out of my bed, and here I am! I have not yet checked the poems with the original passages. But I know *Chuang Tzu* intimately enough to say that in no place you have gone too far off. The only suggestion I could offer offhand is with regard to the line:

The music of the world sings through a thousand holes.

Being of the earth, earthy, I would prefer "earth" to "world." If at all possible, please change it into "earth." As you know, the typical Chinese conception of the whole cosmos is that it consists in the trinity of heaven, earth, and man. Nothing like the Holy Trinity, of course; still it is a cosmic trinity, representing the *Yang*, the *Yin*, and harmony. (Man is supposed to be harmony, but what a discord!)

Another little point: on page 12, since you have added the word *good* I think you had better add the word *wicked* as well. Otherwise, *Yang* has too much influence.

With these two stumbling blocks out of the way, I am free to tell you what I think of the nosegay. It is the work of our Friend the Holy Spirit making use of your genius in the handling of ideas and words. It has brought home to me that the Holy Spirit is not only holy but a poet to boot. In many places, you two old rogues have brought Chuang Tzu nearer to my heart. Such expressions as "No Form has no beginnings," "If there were no 'that'/There would be no 'I'"—and innumerable others—Now it's rather late, and I feel drowsy—so let me sum up my impression—If Chuang Tzu were writing in English he would certainly write like this. This is my test of a good translation, and my Father Louis has fulfilled it.

My delight is truly beyond bounds. (Don't worry. It's a serene and tranquil delight.) I have even laughed aloud several times in bed. It takes Chuang Tzu to have drawn out the rich foundation of humour in you, and I can see no end of its spurts—for you are a powerful geyser—in the time to come. I confess, Father, that I did laugh louder than as befits my grey hairs—and that at midnight. How annoying it would have been to my wife, if there is one! I laughed at page 11, where somebody is acclaimed as statesman of the year. I laughed at the inalienable rights, and at the subtle dig at the lawyers. (You seem to have forgotten I am a lawyer myself!) Besides these mortal sins of laughter, Father, I have on my conscience venial sins without number in the form of smiles. And all because of you, Father. *Mea culpa. . . .* I will write more shortly. By the way, I have written a few more chapters for my book on Ch'an—"Studies in Ch'an" rather than a regular "History." I have completed my studies in rough draft on Lin-chi,[94] on Ma Tsu, on Chao-chow, on the house of Kuei-Yang, on the immediate disciples of Hui Neng, etc. The spirit of Taoism constitutes the sinew and marrow of Ch'an. (Well, Father, I am going to sleep. Give me your absolution.)

At 11:00 A.M. Just got up and had breakfast. How wonderful that The True Man now also has got into the habit of late rising, waiting for all lazy bones at midday. You see, Father, I am one of those beginning their work at the eleventh hour, and yet I receive as much.

It is not funny that it is precisely those who have the True Man (Lin-chi's term, borrowed from your friend Chao-chow) in them as their real Self yearn to receive the True Man under the species of the Host! I already see the shadow of Chuang Tzu's whip, but I find the whip itself is but a shadow. I remember he was speaking *contre* Liturgy last night. But what if Liturgy scratches your itch of Love?

There's a radical difference between the True Man of Lin-chi and his namesake in Chuang Tzu. The latter was an ancient, who had attained his *manhood* through arduous working. The True Man of Lin-chi, on the other hand, is a present reality. For him, every one is here and now a True Man; the only trouble is that few realize the fact and therefore few realize their being. Fundamentally, Ch'an banks on the Intellect. To know is to be. In the sense that the True Man of Ch'an is a cash dealing and a present delivery, Ch'an is more realist than the dreamer of the butterfly. But in the

94. Chu Hsi (1130-1200): Neo-Confucian scholar famous for synthesizing all the major Confucian teachings and for his brilliance as a calligrapher.

sense that Trueman Chaung is historically conceived, he is more realistic than Ch'an's, I mean more existential.

Lin-chi's True Man, then, is not the same person as Trueman Chuang. But somewhere, you remember, Chuang said, "I have lost my me!" This "I" is the true True Man of Ch'an, while this "me" is the "dry toilet stick." According to Yang-shan, co-founder of the house of Kuei-yang, once I am I, even my me will be included in the bargain; and the result will be the real True Man, of whom Trueman Chuang of the ancient times is but the prototype.

I have found that all the houses of Ch'an are in one way or other permeated with the mystical insights of Chuang and Lao. Lin-chi has by temperament more the Chuang in him, while Kuei and Yang belong to the type of Lao Tzu—still waters run deep. The house of Fa-yen is the closest kith and kin of Neo-Taoism and to the Neo-Confucianism of Chu His. It is not for nothing that Chu Hsi was warm and unstinted in his praise of the traditions of Fa-yen. As soon as I have typed out a chapter it will be mailed to you. Promise me that you will read it as carefully as you did with Hui Neng.

Now to return to "The Way of Chuang Tzu." 1:00 P.M.

Before I forget, let me tell you that a few months ago I delivered a lecture on the spirit of Ch'an at the Manhattanville College for Women.[95] It was most responsively received. "No self-congratulation in success!" My trump card was a passage from you, a quotation from your introduction to THE WISDOM OF THE DESERT: "What can we gain by sailing to the moon if we are not able to cross the abyss that separates us from ourselves." That hit a fire! and set the tone for the whole lecture. And I earned a sizeable *honorarium* and in addition they—Madames of the Sacred Heart—wrote me that I had received from God the "priceless gift of communicating the inexpressible!" Am I not of the company of the true men of old, of whom you say:

They scaled the cliffs, never dizzy,
Plunged in water, never wet.
Walked through fire and were not burnt.

That piece of "The True Man" leaves nothing to be desired. I want to quote it or parts of it in my Zen book. Certain obscure passages

95. Manhattanville College for Women: Manhattanville College of the Sacred Heart in Purchase, NY, originally famous for the study of sacred music and established by the Mothers of the Sacred Heart; now a part of SUNY.

become crystal-clear to me now; for example,

> Where the fountains of passion
> Lie deep,
> The heavenly springs
> Are soon dry.

And your "Easy come, easy go" was responsible for another guffaw. What a wizard you are in manipulating words and letters! In your hands, even zinc is transmuted into pure gold. This is what the learned Germans call a "neologism." The names with which you have christened the two royal friends of No-Form sound so verisemblable. Your adding a tail to it in the form of Lao Tzu seems to fit well, like the tail of a lion. Of course, "Cracking the Safe" is delightful. Even the "Moral" is charming, because it is no moral, but the play of a moral.

"Leaving Things Alone" confirms me in my rendering of *wu-wei*[96] as non-ado. I am fascinated by the lines on page 13.

"The Kingly Man" is a pearl. He belongs to the royal family of the true men. So is the "king of life" in "How Deep is Tao."

But no pearl is so beautiful as "The Lost Pearl."

Well, Father, I have an appointment to make. Let me conclude now. I will write again.

Your naughty old boy in Christ the True Man,

John C. H. Wu

---

96. *wu-wei*: literally "not doing" or "doing nothing" but for Merton this mystical teaching was not purely quietist. It simply meant "acting without interference," like the ancient Taoist sages told us. The understanding of this notion is essential to the understanding of both Taoism and Zen. For a taste of it, see Wu's rendering of it in chapter 48 of the *Tao Teh Ching*: "No-Ado, and yet nothing is left undone"; chapter 57: "I do not make any fuss, and the people transform themselves"; chapter 64: "He who fusses over anything spoils it, etc." Other chapters the reader might consult are 38, 43, and 63.

TM to JW

June 9, 1965

Dear John:

What a wonderful letter that was! It was a pure delight, and it made me so happy that I had been insane enough to go ahead with the work on *Chuang Tzu*. To have one such reader would be enough! And to encounter living in you the spirit of Chuang Tzu himself with such liveliness and force is, I must say, an experience. I am glad there is still such a dragon hiding around corners and behind clouds in our rather stuffy world. And glad that through your encouragement I have had a glimpse of him.

Well, naturally, I have now produced practically a whole book. A great many more texts and a longish introduction. The publisher is delighted (New Directions). There is still some talk of perhaps doing a joint edition with the Asian Institute at St. John's, but the book is so long now that the complications of a Chinese text begin to look large especially since I have had the effrontery to add a little of my own here and there for good measure. I think that the kind of job I have done has become independent enough so that the Chinese text would simply upset those who read Chinese. . . . There is still time to discuss all this.

We will need illustrations, as New Directions wants to make a rather lavish book out of it. My idea is that perhaps some very fine free ancient calligraphy, perhaps something with some of the more important ideograms like Tao, *Wu Wei* and so on. I do have a little book with some Chinese drawings of trees, people and so on are found. They are adequate but not exciting. By the way I am reading Mai Mai Sze's *Tao of Painting*[97] and find the first volume very thrilling, more thrilling than any detective story or western. And while on the subject of painting, the art people at Seton Hall did contact me (many thanks) and suggested that I could send the drawings some time in the fall, but it turned out that I had already arranged for them to go to California in the fall. The business of exhibiting drawings has in any case become too extracurricular and when they get back from the coast I will stuff them all under the bed and see that they stay there and do no try to walk away by

---

97. Mai Mai-Sze's (1910-1992): Daughter of a Chinese ambassador and author of *The Tao of Painting: A Study of the Ritual Disposition of Chinese Painting* (New York: Pantheon, 1956).

their own power.

Naturally, I want to dedicate *the Chuang Tzu* book to you. So I hope you will accept, indeed I will not permit you to refuse: then your name will appear on a good blank page and we will all fly away on the back of the same dragon.

I do not know what you think about what is going on these days in Vietnam. No matter what one's view of it may be, one has to forget about Law and good sense if one is to be comfortable with the policies of Washington, as far as I can see. In the long run I think that our new President[98] is pursuing a course that will get all those he is trying to subdue both very angry and unsubdued, and also will line them up in firm solidarity with communist China. I don't see how his absurd policies can have any other effect than this. He is doing his level best to make Asia communist, and is also trying hard in Latin American. The fact that he and his helpers cannot see this is all the more unfortunate, since it means that they will not give up until it is too late. What do you think about it all?[99] In any event, the general acceptance of brute and useless terrorism as both reasonable and necessary, by many of the public here, is the most disquieting thing of all. Naturally, it is easy to find fault and a lot harder to see what positively ought to be done. Meanwhile the brutality goes on, on both sides.

That is a less pleasant subject than *Chuang Tzu*. I leave you with best wishes for a pleasant summer. Later on I hope to send you the whole manuscript, but first it must be typed, and then I suppose I will have to send my extra copies to the official censors of the Order and the Lord alone knows what they will make of it. Seriously I may need your help to get it past them, as they may very well say I ought not be attempting what I have done. We shall see.

98. our new President: Lyndon Baines Johnson (1908-73), America's 36th President.

99. "What do you think about it all?": one of the few times Merton tries to draw Wu into a political discussion. But the mere fact that Wu does not take the bait should not be construed as either indifference or evasion. Wu's "answer" to Merton's question perhaps can be found in his letter of January 24, 1966 when he comments on the monk's smile in a photo he sees in a news clipping: "I like your smile—a smile when the kettle sings. This smile gives the world more hope for real Peace than all the hectic activities in the world." He ends the same letter with a suggestive *haiku*: "I retreat further and further/Till I am involved with the destiny of /Man at his very core." Wu's words can be read as a subtle hint for Merton to remain contemplative and silent to avoid problems with certain ecclesiastical authorities and censors.

Best wishes and blessing, peace and joy in the Holy Spirit.

Ever devotedly yours in Christ,

Tom Merton

Paul sent me your new book in French[100] and I am delighted to see the essays I like so much finally between the covers of a book. I hope it will soon appear in English. And the Zen book too. I did not receive the chapter of the latter that you announced when you last wrote. Thanks for the suggested corrections—of course I made them.

---

100. new book in French: Wu's collection of essays published by Casterman, later in English, *Chinese Humanism and Christian Spirituality* (Jamaica, NY: St. John's University Press, 1965), edited by Paul K. T. Sih.

JW TO TM

3 Reynolds Place,
Newark 6, N.J.

June 13, 1965

My dear Father Louis:

I am so happy to learn that you have gone ahead with the work on *Chuang Tzu*. Rather the Holy Spirit has gone ahead with it. Was it not during the Pentecostal tide that you were inspired to complete the work?

I agree with you that it is no longer feasible to print a bilingual edition. What you have done is more than a translation: it is a *re-creation*, such as Chuang Tzu himself would have liked to see. I like the New Directions. In fact, I wish to submit my Zen book to them. What do you think? I am mailing you three chapters—on Lin-chi, [Wu's original] Tsao-tung[101] and Yun-men.[102] I want you to go into it as if it were your own work. After you have made corrections, revisions and suggestions, please send back these copies to me, so that I may have them typed out.

As to the dedication, since you do not permit me to refuse, I can only obey. Do I deserve it? Certainly not! But you, Father, have earned it for me. Why should I worry? I am only grateful to God for having given me such a spiritual father like you.

I am very anxious to receive the rest of your *re-creations*. It is infinitely more valuable than a mere translation. It is the True Man of the Tao uttering fresh insights in beautiful verse! Like the silkworm you have devoured the leaves of mulberry trees of the Garden of Chuang Chow (Tzu), and emitted pure silk. You have struck out in a new direction in the field of translation. This reminds me of my paraphrase of the *Psalms* in Chinese verse. The same Holy Spirit Who energized the writing of the Psalms in Hebrew energized your son John in rendering them into Chinese verse. In your ease, you have looked at *Chuang Tzu* in the True Light. This does not falsify his thoughts; it *transfigures* them. Essentially they are Thomas Merton's poems as suggested by the reading of the

---

101. re-creation: in his introduction to *The Way of Chuang Tzu*, Merton calls them "imitations" or "free interpretative readings."

102. Ts'ao-Tung-Tsung: A Chinese Zen Buddhist sect founded by Dongshan Liangjie in the ninth century. The sect emphasized the practice of *zazen* ("sitting in meditation").

Chuang Tzu. This nosegay is bound to be immortal; and do you think that I could help being happy in having some connection with a book which breaks down the walls of East and West? Actually there are no walls, you have only demolished illusory walls built by ignorance.

At present I am moving to an apartment. But you can still write to this address, for I will inform the post office as soon as I am settled in the new address.

In the chapters on Tsao-tung and Lin-chi I have taken some thoughts from you, which will serve to elucidate the views of Tung-shan and Lin-chi.

As soon as you return these chapters with your suggestions, I shall mail more chapters. Please handle them ruthlessly. I want you to write an introduction to the book. In the meantime, continue to pray for me.

Ever your naughty son in the *Logos*,

John C. H. Wu

JW to TM

2D, 43 Cottage Street
South Orange, N.J.

June 25, 1965

My dear Father Louis:

This is the first time I have sat at my desk since I moved into this new apartment two days ago.

I hope that you have received my three chapters on Zen, and am anxious to know your views and your suggestions. In the meantime sound out the wishes of the New Directions regarding the possibility of publishing this forthcoming book. I need a publisher to spur me to action. I am ashamed to confess this weakness. But who is strong and I am not weak?

I am waiting for your mimeographs on *The Way of Chuang Tzu.*

This note is written chiefly to inform you, Father, of my new address. I am happy to find that none of your letters were lost in the commotion of the moving.

Your affectionate child in Jesus,

John

TM to JW

July 11, 1965

Dear John:

I don't want to delay any longer in writing you at your new address, and telling you that of course I do have the three Zen chapters. But I have not been able to work over them, as I think this will require quite a bit of time and I don't know how to go about it. It is a question of making them more directly readable: your meaning will not always get across clearly. On the other hand, there is no more difficult job in the world than to try to edit another man's writing, or at least there is nothing that I find more difficult, and I warn you in advance that I may very well probably not be able to do it at all. At best I can make some suggestions. The material is terrific, and there is much that is new in the way of perspective and intuitions. Your book will be very valuable indeed and I shall certainly recommend it to the New Directions. On the other hand, they have never exactly published a book quite like this. I do not say that is a good or a bad omen, but it should be kept in mind.

Chuang Tzu is finished, but all the copies are in use, with censors and so on. I don't know what on earth the censors will make of him.

This is just a hasty note. I am trying to catch up with my mail, a frustrating task, at which I know there is no chance I will ever win. But why should one need to win? Tao will have to answer the letters.

All blessings and best wishes,

Cordially in Christ,

Tom

JW TO TM

Apt. 2D, 43 Cottage Street,
South Orange, N.J.

July 18, 1965

My dear Father Louis:

Gee! This time you have not made me laugh or even smile, but
stare! I have swum through the 22 pages of your introduction,
at every page I have wondered how in the world you could have
seen things with such an eerie *transparency.* I have changed my
theory about you. In your cycle of transmigrations, you were not
only a Chinese Buddhist monk, but also Yan Hui,[103] *Mozi,*[104] and
Chuang Chou (Tzu).[105] I have underlined Moti, because only Moti
himself could have seen his own faults so clearly and recanted so
whole-heartedly.

Your treatment of the *Ju* philosophy is the most profound and
fairest of appraisals that I have ever read. It seems to me that your
perception of its strength and weakness is more penetrating than that
of Chuang Tzu. Chuang Tzu was still too emotionally involved *vis-
à-vis* Confucianism to see its true face. He could not have written
what you have on pages 8 to 11, although I readily admit that the
elements you have woven together are to be found in the writings
of Chuang Tzu here and there. It is a truly profound insight that
the failure of Confucianism lies in the fact that it "aims at achieving
'the good' as object" (p.10). Maybe it is implicit in the second
chapter of *Chuang Tzu*; but you have articulated it.

This gem of an introduction shows clearly that you have *studied*
these things more than the world can imagine. True, "In Thy light
we shall see light," yet it takes much more than a reliance on the

---

103. Yan Hui (521-490 B.C.E.): the favorite disciple of Confucius because
of his simplicity in all things and modesty towards others. Confucius felt bereft at
his early death. The following (from Arthur Waley's *The Analects of Confucius*)
illustrates well the Master's feelings towards him: "Incomparable indeed was Hui!
A handful of rice to eat, a gourdful of water to drink, living in a mean street—others
would have found it unendurably depressing, but to Hui's cheerfulness it made no
difference at all. Incomparable indeed was Hui!" (Book VI, #9)
104. Mozi: aka Mo Tzu and best known for his idea of "universal love" which
the Confucianists found too broad and abstract a concept for it undermined the
emphasis on the Five Human Relationships.
105. Chuang-chou (369-286 B.C.E.): another name by which Chuang Tzu
was known.

Holy Spirit to be able to write these 22 pages. Solid knowledge is at the basis of every paragraph and sentence. It is only your style that makes the whole flow effortlessly like a river.

I shall write you more as I delve into the "Reading." Now I have an appointment to make.

Your starving son in the Holy Spirit,

John [Chinese Characters Follow]

JW to TM

Apt. 2D, 43 Cottage Street
South Orange, N.J.

July 19, 1965

My dear Father Louis:

I am happy to receive your first letter to my new address. I shall be quite contented if you would offer whatever suggestions may occur to your mind with regard to my chapters on Zen. This alone would constitute an invaluable help to me.

So, your "Way of Chuang Tzu" is still in the hands of the censors. Chuang Tzu is so typically Chinese that he is bound to appear inscrutable to those unfamiliar with him. So, if they do not know what to make of him, I shouldn't be surprised at all.

Now, it has occurred to my mind that in order to facilitate their understanding of Chuang Tzu's philosophy, the enclosed article of mine[106] may profitably be submitted to the censors. This paper has pleased the Jesuits, and I don't see any reason why it should not appeal to the Cistercians. You may not need this at all, but since I have felt the urge to send it along in the past two days, I am sending it all the same, even at the risk of appearing officious. At any rate, The Abbot may like to read it.

Filially yours in the Lord,

John C. H. Wu

---

106. the enclosed article: "The Way of Chuang Tzu: A New Appraisal," *International Philosophical Quarterly*, vol. III, no. 1, February, 1963, Fordham Univ. Press.

TM to JW

July 22, 1965

Dear John:

Thanks for your good letter, and for the offprint, which I will certainly send on to the censor. But you will be pleased to hear the news: the *Chuang Tzu* book was not only passed with honors by both censors, but one of them even asked to keep the ms for a good long time so that he might study it and use it more. So you must have said a good strong prayer and the Holy Spirit must have breathed over the waters of argument. In fact, though, now that I know who did the conforming, I can see they would be open to something like this. There are others who would have had seven kinds of fits.

I now have an ms available, and am sending it along. It is much more than the selection, and you are evident in the early pages. Do please let me know what corrections are needed, but there is no rush, as proofs will be long in coming.

Facing a barrage of deadlines I have no chance to work on your Zen chapters now, and will have to wait a bit. But I will do what I can by means of a general suggestion here and there. I would certainly not want to take upon myself the job of ruining your work for you: or I would have read *Chuang Tzu* in vain. I will concentrate on enjoying and profiting by the material and the way it is presented, you cannot deny me this. Then, if I go at it this way, the corrections that are really needed, if any, will arise quietly out of the truth you yourself have seen and intended. May the Holy Spirit bring it all to fruitful completion.

With all my very best wishes and blessings,

In the Holy Spirit,

Fr. Louis

JW to TM

2D, 43 Cottage Street
South Orange, N.J.

August 3, 1965

My dear Father Louis:

I have met one of your great admirers, Father William Johnston, S.J.,[107] a student of Zen. In a speech he gave here, he remarked that your writings are full of Zen—that is, including writings that do not deal with Zen. I thought it was an insight. So I made friends with him, and have come to like him. He will start for St. Louis in a couple of days, where he is to preach a retreat. But his chief desire now is to see you. He is writing a monograph on *The Cloud of Unknowing* and who can be a better advisor than the Apostle of the Lost Pearl?

I have read through the whole body of *The Way of Chuang Tzu*, and I have found no fault anywhere. You have conveyed the true spirit of Chuang Tzu. In fact, you have made him *relive* in those beautiful poems. "Only a true man can have true knowledge," as Chuang Tzu puts it.

Now, Father, when are you going to attend to my chapters on Zen? I am waiting for your suggestions before I will proceed.

I have two more chapters to send you—one on the House of Kwei-Yang, the other on the House of Fa-Yen. They are ready, but they will be mailed as soon as you have finished with the other three. You can be as severe as you like. Even if you should tear them to pieces, I should be happy, and would say, "Were it not for his love of me, Father Louis would not have taken the trouble of beating me." (This is what a disciple said after he had received a sound beating by his Zen master.)

Your ever naughty boy of the spirit,

John [Chinese Characters Follow]

---

107. William Johnston, S.J. (1925-2010): an Irish Jesuit ecumenist, university professor, and writer of Zen and spirituality who has lived and was trained for long periods in Zen monasteries in Japan. His books include: *The Still Point: Reflections on Zen and Christian Mysticism* (1970); *Christian Zen* (1971); and *The Inner Eye of Love: Mysticism and Religion* (1978). *The Still Point* was dedicated to Merton. The Trappist monk wrote an introduction to Johnston's book titled, *The Mysticism of the Cloud of Unknowing*.

TM to JW

St. Anthony Hospital
St. Anthony Place
Louisville, Kentucky

Aug 6, 1965

Dear John,

Your letter reached me here in the hospital. Nothing serious. I am getting out today. But all my work has been held up. I hope to get your Zen chapters back to you soon, but I have not been making corrections or suggestions yet. The time to think it all over has not been there, and I do not intend to say anything thoughtless. If I can, I will say *something*.

Fr. Johnston wrote a card that he might drop by the Abbey and I hope to see him. Fr. Dumoulin is going to be in this country, too soon.

All best wishes,

Cordially in Christ,

Tom

TM TO JW

Aug. 10, 1965

Dear John:

Here are two of your chapters, I do not want to make you wait any longer. This is simply magnificent material, and I revel in it. I am especially fond of Tung Shan,[108] who is rapidly becoming one of my very favorites. I can't wait to have the finished book so that I will be able to refer to it. I am also delighted with Lin Chi[109] and his shouters. This is a wonderful book and I have mentioned it to the people at New Directions.

My only problem with it is that the way it is written often deprives it of its full impact. The material is all there and your exposition of it is fine, well planned, most lively and interesting. But often the statements seem to glance off the target rather than sticking in the bull's eye: this being due to the way the statements are formulated and particularly the choice of words at times. I have attempted a couple of suggestions here and there but realize that they are totally inadequate. I am at a loss how to help out with this, because I feel myself on slippery ground. I think I know just what you mean in each case but I cannot seem to find a way to say it, or if I do, then I fear that I may be changing your meaning. It is purely a question of framing the statements in such a way that they will click with the American reader. I am not speaking at all about their content, but about getting it across. That is my only worry about the book. A publisher's reader might pick it up and fail to connect, and the whole thing would be lost on him. I don't think there would be any problem for people who have read other Zen books—there is now almost a Zen language in the book field.

108. Tung-shan (807-869): founder of the Ts'ao-tung House of Ch'an. Known for his down-to-earth approach and his identification of the noumenal and the phenomenal as indicated, for example, in the following couplet: "The noumenal and the phenomenal coming together! There is no need to avoid their crossed-swords!" Tung-shan believed both flowed from the one ultimate Source (see GAZ, p. 136).

109. Lin-chi: (d. 866): founder of the Lin-chi House of Ch'an and known for his loud shouts which he took so seriously that he even classified into four main categories. Basically, a shout was meant to cut off an aspiring monk's chain of thoughts that impeded his road to enlightenment. A most famous saying attributed to Lin-chi is the seemingly irreverent, "When you encounter a Buddha, kill the Buddha!", strongly suggesting that one essential condition for enlightenment is to remain non-attached to anything—physical or spiritual (see GAZ, p. 148).

But for the general reader and the first-time-at-Zen people I think your book would be hard to understand. I think too you probably need to give more explanations of things which are familiar to those who already know about Zen but not to others. These are only impressions I have formed, and as I say I don't know what to say that will be more constructive and helpful. It is a wonderful book, and certainly one of the best things on Zen that has come out. It provides a very welcome change of pace and perspective from Suzuki, and throws such abundant light on Chinese Zen, it is going to be invaluable. I am delighted to have had this chance to read it and look forward to the rest of it. I realize the suggestions I have made in the ms are just about useless. But as I said, this is the kind of work I am worst at.

Now I must get this in the mail. I will write more later. You may like the essay (under separate cover [in Merton's hand, annotation in the margin]) on Zen monasticism, and my book of essays including the one on *Mystics and Zen Masters*, with a lot of others, is coming out with Farrar Straus and Giroux. New Directions is coming along with *Chuang Tzu*. He is already in proof. *Wu wei* really works.

All the best and all blessings always in Our Lord,

Tom

JW TO TM

2D, 43 Cottage Street
South Orange, N.J.

August 12, 1965

My dear Father Louis:

Only yesterday I sent a letter to you, telling you that I was now more interested in your recuperation (being freshly out of the hospital) than in your reaction to my chapters on Zen.

What an unexpected joy I have experienced today on receiving yours of the day before! *Wu wei really works!* All things which are really worthwhile come unexpectedly.

Your comments on the chapters are exactly what I had hoped for. As soon as the manuscripts arrive, I shall work on them, following your clues and suggestions. You certainly have put your finger on the exact spot when you say: "Often the statements seem to glance off the target rather than sticking in the bull's eye." Yes, Father, you have pierced *my* bull's eye. This is the chief trouble with me. Even in my love letters, I too often glance off the target, by saying, for instance, that if she does not see eye-to-eye with me, I shall still be happy, seeing that it must also be the Lord's will and in the Lord's will I find true happiness. Now, Father, this expresses my true feeling; but it cuts no ice, rather furnishes the other party a temptation to slip away. Now that you have hit upon the root of my troubles, I will reform, beginning with the chapters.

Your letter is like a savory sandwich. The middle part is very meaty and full of vitamins. I will chew it carefully, so that it may be digested and turned into living tissue. Those chapters were actually no more than first drafts on the typewriter. So I already count myself lucky in being able to get away with it with so few shouts and beatings from such a severe Master.

Some of the problems can, I think, be solved by introducing a few but adequate footnotes—I mean problems vis-à-vis the general reader.

What I desire from you, Father dear, is that after my book is completed you will write an introduction comparable to that of *The Way of Chuang Tzu*. (That piece is just like the azure sky without a speck of cloud and yet of unfathomable depth. I would like to render it into Chinese someday. Through pure subjectivity you have reached pure objectivity.)

The other two chapters (on Fa-yen and Ku'ei-yang) will be mailed to you in a day or two.

Ever your infant in the Lord,

[No Signature]

JW TO TM

2D 43 Cottage Street
South Orange, N.J.

August 14, 1965

My dear Father Louis:

Now my spirit is enlivened again with the receipt of your articles and my chapters as touched up by you. They came yesterday, and I read your two pieces with avidity. I read "Contemplation and Ecumenism" first. It held my attention from the beginning to the end. Actually, Father, you were dancing over a precipice, yet, as I watch you dance, you make me feel that you are dancing on a spacious flat ground. This is what I call *catholicity*! I image that this is the way St. Thomas[110] would write if he were living in this age. The creative fire is there; yet I can see no smoke! You have stretched this Mystical Body as far as anyone can, yet this stretching, I feel, does no more than register the necessary growth toward the full stature of Christ. So it has the spontaneity of the inevitable. Oh the beauty of the Golden Mean, when it is authentic and not a cover for mediocrity!

My joy in reading "Zen Buddhist Monasticism" is just as intense, though of a different sort. It confirms my own reading of the whole movement. But you have a knack of picking out the right things from what you have read. For instance, the quotation of p. 5 of Buddha's words to Ananda[111] is so relevant to Zen that I wonder how the Chinese masters could have overlooked it. Although the tone of this passage is, as you point out, of the individualist asceticism, anyway the image of "lamp" and the idea of finding refuge in oneself have deep affinity with Hui-neng's way of thinking.

Note 6 on p. 7 is illuminating. Probably, the significance of

---

110. St. Thomas: St. Thomas Aquinas (1225-74), generally regarded the greatest of the medieval scholastics. He was called the "Angelic Doctor" and introduced Aristotle to Western Europe, thus giving impetus to the Renaissance. Merton used the scholastic language of Aquinas in his book on St. John of the Cross titled, *The Ascent to Truth* (New York: Harcourt Brace and Company, 1951), 342 pp. However, Merton was not too happy writing this book because his contemplative writings are more in tune with John's mystical theology and not so much with the dogmatic theology of Aquinas.

111. Ananda: The word means "bliss" in Pali and Sanskrit. Ananda was the first cousin of Siddharta. He became a favorite disciple of the Buddha often seen in paintings and sculptures accompanying his Master.

Teilhard de Chardin[112] is to be found here.

Note 9 on p. 9 brings something new to me. Your bringing together of fundamental insights from different fields is far from a mechanical juxtaposition. They are streamlets flowing into the same sea. [In Wu's hand in the margin: Their sources are hidden in the highest mountains.] My dear Boy, you are a Sea! I have never read Cornford; but I am ordering it.

Your subtle humor delights me, as, for instance, the action-activity-activism business. We might cap it with "Act." Certainly it has a better luck than my "tuition-intuition" muddle.

Page 15 is of capital importance. I used to consider Emerson's[113] "Self-Reliance" as the *locus classicus* of individualism. Only recently did I find that his "Self" is not the empirical ego.

Your treatment of the true nature of "koan" confirms my own surmise. It drives us to our wits' end, that we may peradventure discover a new dimension. It is only when all "human resources" are *exhausted* that one is initiated into *Religion*. This new dimension can be nothing else than "pure grace." That's why your question mark in parenthesis on p. 21 is like "adding feet to a picture of a snake." Or was it for the eyes of the censor?

To me, both parts of the essay are of absorbing interest, although I understand your recommendation to certain readers that they might read the second part first. I have found the first part enlightening and the second part gripping.

---

112. de Chardin: Pierre Teilhard de Chardin, S.J. (1881-1955), Jesuit paleontologist and writer of spirituality whose most influential works were *The Phenomenon of Man* and *The Divine Milieu*. Teilhard enjoyed widespread popularity among progressive Catholic circles in the decades of the 50s, 60s and 70s and was instrumental in helping to update the thinking of the Catholic Church in the area of evolutionary thought, though his main thrust was Lamarkian rather than Darwinian, and in furthering Christian-Marxist dialogue. See Merton's essays on "Teilhard's Gamble" and "The Universe as Epiphany: The Spirituality of Pierre Teilhard de Chardin" in *Love and Living*, eds. Naomi Burton Stone and Patrick Hart (New York: Farrar, Straus and Giroux, 1979), pp. 184-191. Also check Merton's essay, "The Plague of Camus: A Commentary and Introduction" in *The Literary Essays of Thomas Merton*, ed. Patrick Hart (New York: New Directions Publishing, 1981), pp. 214-217.

113. Ralph W. Emerson (1803-1882): A transcendentalist philosopher, mystic and poet whose major work "Self-Reliance" (1841) is considered the symbol of American individualism. But, like Merton, Emerson's notion of the Self is both transcendental and immanent. Thus the rugged individualism often seen in American culture is not the type of transcendental Self that either Emerson or Merton were fond of.

On p. 27, there is a minor mistake which must be corrected. Shih-Shuang is Sekiso, not Sesiko, in Japanese. And then, the whole quotation is from Yuan-wu, who, after quoting the words of Shih-Shuang (in the first paragraph—from "Stop" to "shrine"), proceeded to comment on the quote. You can easily find it if you check the reference once more in Suzuki's *Introduction.*

———

Let me now turn to your thoughtful suggestions and corrections in the manuscripts of my two chapters. I am surprised that there are so few of them. But I will revise them, not only according to your explicit notes, but in line with your general suggestions (in your letter). I am greatly encouraged by your response, without which I might easily have let the work stay where it was.

Let me tell you first of all that I intend to put at least twenty chapters into the book, including the following:

PART I. Bodhidharma and his immediate followers
Hui-neng: His life
Hui-neng: His Fundamental Insights (You have seen the draft)
Hui-neng's Immediate Followers (including Huai-jang, Ch'ing-yuan, Yung-chia, Hui-chung, and Shen-hui)
Ma-tsu
Nan-chuang and Chao Chow
Pai-chang and Nuang-Po
Shih-t'ou and Yueh-shan
Lung t-an and Te-shan

PART II. The Five Houses
Kuei-yang (I am mailing it)
Lin-chi (two chapters, one on the Founder, one on his descendants) (You have seen the first)
Tsao-tung (two chapters, one on Tung-shan, which you have seen, and one on Tsao-shan and others)
Yun-men (I am mailing it)
Fa-yen (I am mailing it)

Already seventeen chapters! In the Third Part, which I have not planned out, I intend to treat the tendency of the houses to merge together. This tendency already began as early as the tenth century, with men like Yung-ming (904-975) of the Fayen house and Yang-ch'i (992-1049) of the Lin-chi house. *Koan,*[114] for instance, was the joint product of the houses of Lin-chi and Yun-men. The spiritual insights of all the great masters like Ma-tsu, Chao-chou, and the founders of the five houses became the common property of all later Zennists, to whatever particular house they might nominally belong.

Last summer, in my conversations with Suzuki, we were agreed on the necessity of rising above the "houses" and going directly to the fundamental insights of the T'ang masters, and ultimately to Lao and Chuang.

The rough tactics of Huang-po will be dealt with in one of the above chapters.

All your other corrections will be incorporated. The "old windbag" is charming.

With regard to one sentence in the chapter on Tung-shan, let me explain. I was speaking of the subtle ideas embodied in his gatha to Tsao-shan, —that those ideas belong to the speculative philosophy rather than mystical realization. Then follows an awkward sentence which troubles you: "For they are mostly *desiderative* in nature, not experiential insights. . . ." You have proposed queryingly to substitute "volitional" or "affective" for "desiderative." Now, the word "desiderative" will definitely be replaced; but my real meaning, I think, can be expressed more simply by rewriting the whole sentence: *For they represent his ideals and aspirations rather than experiential insights like those embodied in the gatha on the occasion of his enlightenment.* What do you think, Father?

As to the "dry toilet stick," I wish I could use "paper" instead of "stick." It's too dirty to talk about. The T'ang used thin strips of bamboo instead of paper, which was not yet invented. Do you think "strip" will do?

---

114. koan: typically baffling sayings of the Zen masters used to instruct and test students in formal training. According to Kapleau, "the best koan is the perplexing inquiry that arises naturally out of one's own life experience and cannot be put aside until resolved" (see *ZMEW*, glossary, p. 294).

I hope that the chapter on Yun-men would not be thrown out of your windows. He is hard to deal with.

The chapters on Kuei-yang and Fa-yen, which I enclose herewith, are rather flat, I am afraid. Both of these houses are shortlived; but the seed-thoughts have been transplanted in other gardens. I feel keenly that I have not done justice to them. I am ready to receive a sound beating from your hands.

Your affectionate old boy in Christ,

John [Chinese Characters Follow]

TM to JW

Sept. 12, 1965

Dear John:

I am really very sorry to have kept your chapters on Zen so long, and I don't want to hold them up any longer. It has been a delight to read them: your book is indispensable. There has never yet been such a good, clear outline of the whole subject, and it is essential for students and for anyone who wants to enjoy Zen. My only regret is that you imposed upon me the task of reading with a pen in my hand to look for corrections to be made. This really spoiled the pleasure of just going along with your Zen masters, and I really have left nothing to show for it. I have only tried to help you, here and there, to put it more idiomatically and correctly from the point of view of English syntax and style. But I am afraid I have not been much help. I am sure though that if you go over it all very carefully and self critically, perhaps discussing it with someone there, you will iron out the wrinkles. The chief problem is that you get a lively intuition of how to say something, and I know what you are driving at, but you say it in such a way that it does not come off successfully from the point of view of English. The "twinkle" on pp. 3 and 4 of Kuei Yang is a case in point. In all such cases I think the best thing would be to make sure you are using an acceptable and familiar phrase, rather than coining a new one, unless you are absolutely sure the new one is going to come off perfectly.

That is all the severity I can muster up. For the rest I don't know which house I enjoy more. In Zen there are many mansions and my own inclination is to live in them all.

Thanks for your comments on Zen monasticism. I will see that everything is straightened out before printing.

Returning to your own book, I am delighted that it is going to be really full length and no nonsense about it. One wants more and more. I can see that the material must be rich and plenteous, and the writers on the subject in English have not even scratched the surface. So dig in and keep digging, we are all waiting for you to come up with mountains of gold, and you have begun to do so already. Give us more.

Best wishes always and all blessings. I am enclosing some pieces of mine, just to make sure that the Post Office does not go broke.

Cordial good wishes and friendship

Ever in Christ,

Tom Merton

TM to JW

Nov. 11, 1965

Dear John:

If there is one truth I have learned about the hermit life it is certainly this: that hermits are terrible letter writers. I have been meaning to get this off to you for days. I am sending off a copy of *Chuang Tzu* signed for you. I hope the publisher will by now have sent you other copies. I owe you a great debt for this. It has been a wonderful experience and something I can not repay with a few words. I will keep you always in my prayers. And may we always live more and more in that wonderful spirit of acceptance that was his. It is of course the real key to all this talk about "turning to the world."

Where are the other chapters of your Zen book? I hope you are not going to give me up because I take so long to answer. I do not promise to be more prompt but I would like to keep up with you, even though I may be incorrigible about responding, the wrong kind of *wu-wei*.

The woods are misty and quiet this morning and I have been chopping wood. It is the feast of St Martin, a saint of peace. We need his prayers.

With all cordial good wishes and blessings in Christ,

Tom

JW TO TM

2D 43 Cottage Street
So. Orange, N.J.

November 16, 1965

My dear Father Louis:

You see, Father, I persist in using "my." You are more mine in your present hermitage than ever before. For I am by nature a hermit. There is no greater delight, O Father, than for friends to enjoy the solitude of each other. Nor can there be a greater togetherness.

The more I know you, Father, the more I marvel at the Divine Artist who has created, by nature and by grace, such a masterpiece as yourself. And He is still adding creative touches to it.

But what a wonderful landscape He has produced! It is at once so sublime and so beautiful. Look at the towering peaks hidden in the clouds and mists. Look at the flowing streams merging, in the far horizons, with the infinite Void. The waterfall that hangs from the sky like the Milky Way. A village instinct with human life, in which peace and harmony have come to stay. All kinds of trees and birds each have a place in this picture. Even butterflies and dragonflies are not missing.

In you, Father, Confucianism and Taoism have blended into an ineffable unity. Only your union with Christ has made this possible. Your apostolate consists in being what you are.

"Hermits are terrible letter-writers." All the more reason why yours of Nov. 11 gives me such a tremendous stimulus. I have already produced nine chapters. In those which you have seen, your corrections have been carefully embodied. I shall mail you tomorrow these nine chapters. I still need to write three more, and the book will be complete. The title will be, perhaps, "The Golden Age of Zen," or "The Giants of Chinese Zen." You see, Father, I had intended to write a full-size history on Zen. But in the midst of my work, I have come to realize that Zen has no history. So I propose to confine my attention to the outstanding masters of the T'ang dynasty. Only two of the nine chapters you have not seen. One deals with Ma-tsu; the other with the life of Hui-neng and his immediate disciples.

The remaining three chapters have to do with (1) Bodhidharma and the four Patriarchs after him, (2) Outstanding masters in the lineage of Ch-ing-yuang Hsin-ssu, like Tao-wu, Lung-t'an, Te-shan and Hsueh-feng, (3) Outstanding masters in the lineage of Nan-yueh Huai-jang, such as Pai-ch'ang and Huang-po. The first leads to Hui-neng, the second to the houses of Yun-men and Fa-yen, and the third to the houses of Kuei-yang and Linchi. The house of Ts'ai-t'ung is descended from Yo-shan who was a joint disciple of Ma-tsu and Shih-t'ou. (This is my revision of the traditional genealogy).

Lately I have read with interest a book called "The World of Zen" compiled by Nancy W. Ross, and published by the Random House in 1960. I was delighted to find a very original thought of yours quoted on p. 254 alongside of Meister Eckhart, Chuang Tzu and Visuddhimagga, on the subject of non-attachment. The quotation is from your *Seeds of Contemplation*, in which you state: "The sense of interior peace is no less created than a bottle of wine." Belonging as it does to spiritual riches, to be attached to it is just like attachment to other created things. This is a marvelous insight, which helps me to understand why Te-shan and Lin-chi and Yun-men would use such harsh language whenever they saw any of their disciples tending to settle with anything short of the True Self. If we remember that Zen masters were really yearning for the *Uncreate*, there will be little danger of misinterpreting their words.

Your *Way of Chuang Tzu* has not arrived. Perhaps it is just as well that I have not finished my book on Zen; for I am sure there are invaluable materials to be drawn from that book which will go to reveal the original affinities between Zen and Chuang Tzu.

As to impromptitude in correspondence, which you, humorously, I should think, call "the wrong kind of *wu-wei*," I don't look at it that way. *Between true friends the Lord Himself serves as the postman* [my italics]. It is true that with me there is a tendency to give up when there is no urge from a friend. But I have often found that if it is something that He really wants done, He invariably inspires the proper friend to goad me on. Your letter has expedited the process at least six months, and I assure you that the whole thing will be ready by the end of this month.

———————

> The woods are misty and quiet
> this morning
> I have been chopping wood.

How do you like this *haiku*? All things you do and write, Father, are poetry; and you are His great *Haiku*.

With love filial and fraternal,

John

JW to TM

2D 43 Cottage Street
South Orange, N.J. 07079

November 19, 1965

My dear Father Louis:

Yesterday I mailed out my nine chapters. I am inclosing now the chapter on the outstanding masters in the lineage of Shih-t'ou. The other two chapters will be ready soon.

If at all possible, I beg you most earnestly *to do an introduction for me.* You need not speak about me. I want you only to speak about Zen referring to some of the masters treated in these chapters. Even some random thoughts and reflections of your own arising from reading these chapters will enhance incalculably the value of the book. Am I asking too much? *O Father, hermit or no hermit, I need your help.*

True, Suzuki will write a foreword to it, as he promised definitely last summer. But his will be a short one. Your introduction, on the other hand, is to be an integral part of the work.

A substantial introduction from your pen will not only profit the reader, but facilitate the finding of a publisher. If the New Directions wants it, well and good. Even if they don't, I am sure I shall be able to find one.

It seems unavoidable that I shall be travelling to the East in the coming Spring. Of all persons the leaders of the Government in Taiwan have entrusted me with the onerous task of writing a Biography of Dr. Sun Yat-sen[115] in English! This year they are celebrating the Centennial Anniversary of the "Father of the Chinese Republic." And the project for this biography is among the

---

115. Biography of Dr. Sun Yat-sen: Sun Yat-sen (1866-1925) is considered by both Chinese Nationalists and Communists as the founding father of modern China. The book, *Sun Yat-sen: the Man and His Ideas*, was published in Taiwan in 1971 by the Commercial Press. Though he expresses some enthusiasm to Merton over the project, Wu understandably did not feel his heart fully in the writing of it since it dealt with political life which conflicted with his Zen and other studies. One reason he took on the project was to pay a debt he felt he owed President Chiang Kai-shek for the help the latter rendered him and his large family—Wu, his wife and thirteen children—during and after the long Sino-Japanese conflict when Wu was commissioned, first, to translate the *Psalms*, then *The New Testament*, into Chinese. The latter works are regarded as modern Chinese classics though their readership is limited.

important items on their program. And they have announced my name in the papers!

Father, I am in the hell of a fix. I could not refuse it, you see, it is Chiang Kai-shek himself who wants me to do the work. And what makes it even harder for me to refuse is the fact that Sun Yat-sen's only son Dr. Sun Fo is a most intimate friend of mine. This is what I call "involvement." Fortunately they have not set a deadline for the work. But they have set apart a considerable amount of money for me to spend in travelling, books, and assistants.

Is it possible, Father, for me to visit you in your hermitage on my way to the East? I hear that others, including the poor Dumoulin (whom I met a few weeks ago in Columbia)[116] have been refused to see you. But tell the Abbot that I am not a Jesuit. In fact, I am a potential hermit.[117] (By the way, Father Dumoulin talked about Soto (Tsao-t'ung) Zen, as if he were treating some of the German philosophers. His approach was much too speculative and metaphysical for Zen. But I like him as a person.)

With filial love in the Lord,

John [Chinese Characters Follow]

---

116. Columbia: Columbia University: For academic year 1965-66, Wu was invited by Theodore de Bary to teach a graduate course in Taoism in its Asian Studies Department. Merton also is connected to this higher learning institution in North America. Merton entered at Columbia in January 1935 and graduated with a B.A. (1935-1938) and an M.A. (1939) in English. His thesis was entitled, "Nature and Art in William Blake: An Essay in Interpretation." While at Columbia he became friends with Mark Van Doren, Daniel Walsh, Robert Lax, Ed Rice and Ad Reinhardt. The secular Merton briefly attended communist meetings but it was short-lived. He joined the staffs of the *Columbia Review* and *Jester*. And in 1938 Fr. Joseph C. Moore received Merton into the Catholic faith. He was baptized and confirmed at the same Corpus Christi Church in New York City.

117. a potential hermit: this is said only half in jest. In fact, a short time following the passing of Wu's wife, he had indeed entertained the possibility of the priesthood, if not the monkish discipline or the hermit life itself. But these thoughts were short-lived.

JW to TM

2D 43 Cottage Street,
South Orange, N. J.

November 24, 1965

My dear Father Louis:

I received *The Way of Chuang Tzu* the day before yesterday. I have reread the whole book and I have come to the conclusion that you and Chuang Tzu are one. Therefore, I suspect that *in your former life* ———. You know what I mean. This is a truly creative work. It is Chuang Tzu himself who is writing his thoughts in the English of Thomas Merton. O Father dear! It is because you are of the same stature with Chuang Tzu that you know him so intimately. In this book you are simply exchanging your notes with him. You are a "true man of Tao" just as he is. You have met in that "eternal place which is no place," and you look at each other and laugh together. "This is perfect Tao. Wise men find here/Their resting place."[118]

The spirit of joy is written all over the pages. I can see how deeply you must have enjoyed the composing of all these poems. Joy does all things without concern, including the begetting of this lovely book. My enjoyment of it, although not deeper, is even more vibrant than your own; because almost in every poem I come across lines which are at once familiar and *new*. For instance,

That which gives things
Their thusness cannot be delimited by things.

Was it some Zen master who wrote it? I immediately referred to the original, and then I whispered to myself, "So, that's what Chuang Tzu meant!" And I am quite sure that this is the true meaning. "This is IT!" I exclaimed with Starlight.

The more I read this book, the more I am convinced that "The

---

118. ". . . their resting place": Merton dedicated the book to Wu whose gushing enthusiasm may seem exaggerated to the reader yet justified in view of what one distinguished translator and sinologist, Burton Watson, had to say later: "Readers interested in the literary qualities of the text should . . . look at the 'imitations' of passages in the Chuang Tzu prepared by Thomas Merton on the basis of existing translations in Western languages. . . . They give a fine sense of the liveliness and poetry of Chuang Tzu's style, and are actually almost as close to the original as the translations upon which they are based" (see Introduction, *The Complete Works of Chuang Tzu*, Columbia University Press, New York and London, 1970, p. 28).

true inheritors of the thought of Chuang Tzu are the Chinese Zen Buddhists of the T'ang period." Just now I am working at the chapter on Pai-ch'ang[119] and Huang-po.[120] There is an interesting story of Pai-ch'ang's conversion of a fox. The fox was, in some former life, a Zen master with many students. Once a student asked whether an enlightened man was still subject to the law of causality, his answer was: "No, an enlightened man does not fall into the realm of causal relations." For this answer he was reborn five hundred times as a fox. When Pai-ch'ang was lecturing, the fox appeared in the form of a human being. He told Pai-ch'ang how he had become a fox, and begged him to tell him the right answer. Pai-ch'ang said, "The enlightened man *does not ignore* the realm of causal relations." At this the fox was suddenly enlightened, and therefore rose above the cycle of life and death.

When I came upon

Can a man cling only to heaven
And know nothing of earth?"

I knew in my heart that this was exactly what Pai-ch'ang had in mind. The old man became a fox precisely because he clung only to heaven and ignored earth! On the other hand, even more people cling to earth and ignore heaven. "The active life! What a pity!"

Today is the feast of St. John of the Cross.[121] At the Mass, I

---

119. Pai-ch'ang: Pai-ch'ang Huai-hai (720-814) initiated the Holy Rule of the Zen monastic system which according to Wu was "comparable to the Holy Rule of St. Benedict . . . (of which) of particular interest are the rites of taking vows and the universal duty of working in the fields" (see *GAZ*, p. 82). It may be of interest to the reader that during a conversation with D. T. Suzuki in Honolulu, the Zen Master told Wu it was on a retreat at a German Benedictine monastery while working the fields that Suzuki came to a better understanding of Zen.

120. Huang-po Hsi-yün (d. 850): Chinese Zen Buddhist master, disciple of Pai-ch'ang, who stressed the importance of seeing the Buddha mind present in all things (*dharmakaya*). For Huang-po the Buddhist texts were not as relevant as direct experience.

121. St. John of the Cross: (1542-91): born in Fontiveros near Avila in Spain. A Carmelite and close associate of St. Teresa, the friar is one of the three or four greatest lyrical poets of Spanish literature. His writings, of which the best known are *The Ascent of Mount Carmel* and *The Dark Night of the Soul*, deal with the development of mystical experience in the soul. Merton's *The Ascent to Truth* (1951) is an exposition of the doctrines of St. John of the Cross, while Wu's *The Interior Carmel: The Threefold Way of Love* (1953) is based essentially on St. Thérèse of Lisieux Carmelite spirituality and insights culled from philosophical Taoism. Wu may have written a review for Harcourt Brace and Company before

thought of your book. It occurred to me that your poems stand in somewhat the same relation to Chuang Tzu's prose as St. John's *Stanzas* to his own annotations. Anyway, for me, Chuang Tzu becomes the annotator of Father Merton. And why not? You have advantages that neither he nor Confucius had.

"A Study of Chuang Tzu" covers only eighteen pages. It is a marvel. How could you enter into the souls of all these great philosophers—Lao Tzu, Confucius, Mo Ti, Tang Chu, Chuang and Hui Tzu—and get an inside view of each? Everything becomes crystal-clear; and there is not a false note anywhere. There is a sureness of touch throughout. No one has written with a greater empathy of the *Ju* philosophy with its *Jen, Yi, Li* and *Chih*. At the same time, no one has diagnosed its disease with quite the same degree of perceptiveness. It lies in the turning of the subject into an object! This criticism is perhaps implicit in Chuang Tzu; but it is you, Father, who have articulated it.[122] It opens up my eye to another link between Chuang Tzu and Zen—the primacy of the host and the subject—from there it is but a step to where there is no more subject and object.

> With one glance
> He takes in past and present,
> Without sorrow for the past
> Or impatience with the present."
> He who is wise sees near and far
> As the same,
> Does not despise the small
> Or value the great.

Is all this not true of yourself, dear Father? The very fact that you have deigned to dedicate this immortal work to your little friend shows that you do not despise the small.

I am very happy to read what you say about Zen in the West

the release of *Ascent*. See Cristóbal Serrán-Pagán's doctoral dissertation at Boston University, "Mystical Vision and Prophetic Voice in St. John of the Cross: Towards a Mystical Theology of Final Integration" where he cited Merton as a major Sanjuanist commentator.

122. ". . . who have articulated it": *Jen, Yi, Li* and *Chih*, respectively, stand for benevolence, righteousness, propriety and knowledge. For Merton's exposition (which he insightfully calls "a four-sided mandala of basic virtues"), see *The Way of Chuang Tzu*, pp. 18-19. For a clear original exposition, see *Book of Mencius*, Bk. II, pt. 1, chap. 6, 1-7.

being "identified with a sort of moral anarchy that forgets how much tough discipline and what severe traditional mores are presupposed by the Zen of China and Japan." I assure you that this thought will be stressed in the chapter on Pai-ch'ang.

The book is beautifully printed and illustrated. I want to try my luck with The New Directions—I mean the publication of the Zen book. I did not realize that they have an office in New York. Is there anyone you know personally that I may go to visit and broach the subject? They have not sent me the copies of *The Way* mentioned in your letter.

With my filial affection in the Tao,

John

JW to TM

2D, 43 Cottage Street
South Orange, N.J. 07079

December 2, 1965

My dear Father Louis:

I am inclosing here the chapter on Pai-chang and 0Huang-po. I have enjoyed writing it more than the other chapters, because your book on *The Way of Chuang Tzu* has helped me to understand these monks of towering stature. You have opened my eyes to many things.

There are people who, because they are devoted Buddhists of the traditional type, tend to minimize the fundamental similarity between Tao and Zen. I am happy to see that you and Suzuki (and a few others like Watts[123] and Aelred Graham) have pinpointed the essential oneness of the two. At least, the modality is exactly the same.

So far, I have not received any copies from the New Directions. But I have ordered several copies from Orientalia.

Two more chapters, and my book will be completed: the first chapter and the epilogue called "Little Sparks of Zen."

The other day I was invited to give a talk to the class of my godson Paul Sih. My friend Dr. Chang Chung-yuan[124] was also there. I was happy to learn that he is going to publish a book on Zen, to which you have promised to write a preface. They are very grateful and happy to have this encouragement from you.

Your Introduction to my book should be somewhat like your "A Study of Chuang Tzu."

I want to mail this letter out immediately. So let me stop here.

Your affectionate old boy in the Lord,

[No Signature]

123. Alan Watts (1915-1973): British writer of more than 25 books and articles on things Asian, notably *The Way of Zen* (1957) and *Tao: The Watercourse Way* (1975). Watts like Merton found spiritual and political inspiration in Chuang-Tzu Taoist master. Coincidentally, Monica Furlong, an English Merton biographer (see *Merton: A Biography*, New York: Harper & Row, 1980) also wrote Watts' biographies, *Zen Effects: The Life of Alan Watts* (Boston: Houghton Mifflin, 1986). In England, she published the book under the title *Genuine Fake: a Biography of Alan Watts* (London: Heinemann, 1986).

124. Dr. Chang Chung-yuan: author of *Tao: A New Way of Thinking* (New York: Harper & Row, 1975) and *Creativity and Taoism: A Study of Chinese Philosophy, Art and Poetry* (New York: The Julian Press, 1963). As far as it can be discerned, Merton never wrote a preface for him.

TM to JW

December 3, 1965

Dear John:

Well, I think there could be worse involvements, than being involved with Sun Yat Sen, especially if they will pay your ticket to the Orient and all sorts of other things. Congratulations, I hope you will do an excellent job. And I asked Fr. Abbot about your stopping off here. He said it would be all right and that he would let me see you "for a couple of hours." I suppose he will also get you to speak to the community (unless you rush through—but don't rush).

Let me know when you are likely to come this way. I am very sorry I could not see Fr. Dumoulin. That was refused to me, without my awareness. I would have enjoyed meeting him. I met one of his associates, Fr. Johnston.

Now about the Zen book (yes, I have the nine chapters and then one more) the man you must see at New Directions is Robert MacGregor. And he is probably the best person to see in the whole publishing business because he knows China and likes Buddhism, and I am sure he will be very interested in the book. Then, about the introduction: if you are not afraid that I will ruin the book and take away the reader's appetite and afflict them with permanent allergies to Zen and all things related to it, I will gladly try my hand, though I have been forbidden to write any more prefaces by my publisher who says I write too many. Since this is I hope a New Directions book, I am hoping that the (other) publisher will understand, and anyway I had promised you more or less some time ago that I would do something of the sort. So it is not so bad. But I cannot do anything now, it must wait a bit, I have been too tied up in a lot of small jobs and have other urgent things to get out of the way. So you see that though I may on occasion talk like Chuang Tzu I don't live like him. But I guess I am learning to take these things with indifference.

As to what you said about the book, well, all I can say is that if Tao did the job through me, it was done in the usual way: without my knowing a thing about it. All I know is that in the beginning especially I was doing a job for which I felt no capacity whatever, and in the end, while I still felt and had no capacity it did not make any difference, I was having a lot of fun. As to attributing it to me, well, you can do so if you like, maybe Tao is playing games and acknowledging who did the work in this particular way. Who am I to interfere with Tao? Tao does altogether very much through *you*. And having now grabbed you is about to do a book on Sun Yat Sen. What a busy writer is this unmoving Tao!

But I heartily enjoyed your letter, including the *haiku* which is yours since you *found* it. I did not have any idea that it was there and would never have known if you had not told me.

Back to the Zen books, I think this revision is much smoother and reads very well. I am very happy to browse through it again, and will continue to do so until the preface pops out sometime later. I just finished a piece which I will send you soon I hope.

Meanwhile, best Christmas wishes and blessings always; peace and joy and light in the Lord.

Most cordially always in Him, Tom

(in Merton's handwriting, on the margin)

I love the fox story. It is going to be very good to see your book as a whole—the whole world of Chinese Zen! I am now going to drink a cup of green Japanese tea in honor of you and Chuang Tzu!

JW TO TM

43 Cottage Street
South Orange, N.J. 07079

December 7, 1965

My dear Father Louis:

Every time I receive a letter from you, I feel as though I had a new *satori*! A subtle and indefinable peace begins to seep into my soul and fills it with a deep and inexplicable satisfaction. (You see, Father, only last night I was rereading your wonderful *Seeds of Contemplation* in bed. I first read it in 1948-9 when I was in Rome).

I am most grateful to the Abbot for permitting me to see you for "a couple of hours." Ever since I came to know him, I have been in love with him. (He is your Joseph, Father.)

I shall stay in the Abbey for a few days not exceeding a week. If the Abbot wishes me to speak to the community, I shall gladly obey. But the Abbot *must* promise not to repeat what he did about the ticket. Nor must he take my bag in his own hands without my permission. (Last time, before I could prevent him, he took my bag heavily laden with books to the car! Being a strong man physically, it was no use struggling with him!)

I am now writing the epilogue: *Little Sparks of Zen*. It is a cluster of little paragraphs, somewhat like the *Pensées*.[125] As I am entirely free to write what occurs to my mind, I feel in my element here.

You say that you have "finished a piece" which will be sent me soon. I am anxious to read it.

My junior, who is living with me, majors in philosophy and is your ardent admirer. He burst out laughing when he read: "I am going to drink a cup of green Japanese tea in honor of you and Chuang Tzu!" I am happy to tell you that he is better informed than I am in the current philosophical tendencies, such as Martin Buber, the phenomenologists, the Existentialists, etc. From him I learn that you are very much read and appreciated by the younger set. The copy of *Seeds of Contemplation* which I am reading now is a paperback that I borrowed from him. I have noted that he has marked out many a passage such as "The only true joy on earth is to escape the prison of our own selfhood . . ." and innumerable other places. "It was be-

---

125. The Pensées (1669): French author Blaise Pascal (1623-1662) wrote some meditations on his own religious experiences.

cause the saints were absorbed in God that they were truly capable of seeing and appreciating created things. . . ." "For me to be a saint means to be myself." And so on and so forth *ad infinitum.* Now, I realize why people say that your works are full of Zen. And what a wonder that all these things were written when you were still young and perhaps had heard nothing about Zen! You hardly can imagine, Father, what influences and power your prose and poetry have been exercising on the minds of the young!

As I am going to a party now (someone has phoned up that he is coming to fetch me) let me conclude the letter here.

With my filial affection in Christ,

John

JW to TM

Reading Father Merton's The Way of Chuang Tzu

Your pen has the magical power of portraying the spirit,—
A testimony to your Heaven-bred genius!
From the fountain of your own mind have sprung
The profound insights of Lao and Chuang!

At midnight, all alone, I am still wrapped up
In enjoying your new version, so simple and natural,
That I feel as though I were having
A *tete-à-tete* with Chuang Tzu reincarnate!

43 Cottage Street
South Orange, N.J. 07079

December 17, 1965

Dear Father Louis:

I know that you are interested in calligraphy. The sheet on onion paper is the Chinese poem. I wrote it very casually, but it turned out better than many other pieces which I had done with greater care. This one was done without any attention of success at all. In fact, when I was at the fourth and fifth lines I had already given up and wanted simply to fill up the paper before consigning it to the waste-paper basket. But when it was completed and as I was giving a last look, the whole piece appeared to be harmonious! So here you are.

The two other sheets (in hard paper) have not much Zen about them. They contain a little preface to the poem. The first two words on the right side are your name in Chinese *MEI TENG* meaning *SILENT LAMP!*[126]

My epilogue is being typed. It will be sent to you soon!

With my filial love in the Divine Baby,

John

[Four Pieces of Paper Bearing Chinese Characters Follow This Letter].

---

126. "Silent Lamp": This Chinese title was given by Wu to Merton as a spiritual master. There is a two-hour documentary on Merton with that title and William Shannon's book, *Silent Lamp: The Thomas Merton Story* (Crossroad Classic, 1992).

TM to JW

December 28, 1965

Dear John:

Your letter and poem reached me on the Feast of St. Thomas just as I was about to go to say Mass for Asia and all my Asian friends and for my own vocation to see things Asian in their simplicity and truth, if possible. So it was moving to be "baptized" Chinese with a name I must live up to. After all, a name indicates a divine demand. Hence I must be *Mei Teng*, a silent lamp, not a sputtering one. Over these quiet feast days (on which for the most part I have steered clear of everything elaborate in the community, limited myself to two concelebrations) I have been in the woods just staying quiet. And since the earth is one, I think I have plenty of Asia under my feet. The thing is to recognize it. This is the only real contribution I have to make to a tormented political situation. Instead of fighting Asia to be it. And stubbornly, too.

Your calligraphy fascinates me, and of course so does the poem, in the great tradition of Chinese occasional verse, so polished and so human. I wish I could reply in kind, calligraphy and all. In desperation, or rather no, in considerable joy, I resort again to the green tea, and in fact the kettle is whistling by the fire right at my elbow, and the sun is rising over the completely silver landscape. Instead of putting all this into a poem, I will let it be its own poem. The silent stream will rise from the teacup and make an ideogram for you. Maybe sometime I will add a poem to it as an exclamation of my own. But are such exclamation points needed?

In any event I am delighted with all you sent, and especially with the sparks of Zen. Reading that I easily saw why I had questions about your style in the other part of the book: this is what you were aiming at all the time. In the other chapters you spoke academically to some extent, yet the informality kept bursting through. Here there is no longer any sense of uneasiness about it in the reader since you are completely spontaneous and informal and it works like a charm. It is the best part of the book. And yet the other chapters had to be as they are too. I will certainly do my best to write a good essay on Zen as an introduction. I forget whether I sent you the piece on *koans*. This Christmas, as usual, has been such an avalanche that I do not know what I have sent and what I have received, consequently I have just about forgotten all of it. The sun looks in the window and the kettle sings. What else is there?

Tom *Mei Teng*!

Everything in the "sparks" hits some particular spot. I especially liked Suzuki's "living is dying" and how truly that is proved by the wonderful last pages, on the death in Christ of Teresa:[127] how truly an epiphany of the Savior, and a truly Asian epiphany. It says everything. I was indescribably moved. She simply manifested a perfect synthesis of East and West in Christ by going to Him and taking all of us with her. I will be so happy to see her when we get there. We are there but we don't know it.

---

127. ". . . on the death in Christ of Teresa": Wu's first wife, Teresa Li (née Li Yu-t'i, aka Li Teh-lan), whose moving deathbed scene is chronicled in *GAZ*, pp. 214-215.

JW TO TM

2D, 43 Cottage Street
South Orange, N.J. 07079

December 31, 1965

My dear Father *Mei-teng*:

If the old year is like this, what will the new year be? The year refuses to close without being crowned by the refreshing radiance of SILENT LAMP, whose speech is but an element of his Silence, though an essential element.

Can it be by a mere coincidence that just before I received your letter I had produced another calligraphy. This time it is a Chinese version of that *haiku* which you had generously attributed to me:

The woods are misty and quiet
    this morning
I have been chopping wood!

In the last line you will find a new title together with *Mei-teng*. I have called you *Mei-teng Tao-Jen*. *Tao-Jen* means "The Man of Tao." The poem consists of seventeen words, in four lines, 7 words—"The woods are misty and completely silent." The third line, 3 words—"Who hears me—?" The fourth line, 4 words —"Cutting wood *ting ting!*"

You see, Father, the sound brings the Silence to the fore, and the cutting and splitting reenforce the original mistiness.

I am so happy that you are delighted with the little sparks. When I remember that you are a man of Christlike yea-yea-nay-nay-ness, I feel as though Christ Himself had given me a tap on the shoulder.

You will be glad to know that Dom Aelred Graham, to whom I had sent a copy of the epilogue, says that he is "enthralled by it."

Chapter I has barely been started. *Aller Enfang ist schwer.* I have to study more closely the Lankavatara Sutra,[128] the favorite scripture of Bodhidharma. In fact, the school founded by this "Wall-contemplating Brahman" was first known as the School of Lanka.

---

128. Lankavatara Sutra: literally "Descent into Sri Lanka" Sutra, a major Mahayana ("large vehicle") sutra comprising many metaphysical and psychological insights. See Kapleau, *ZMEW*, glossary, p. 295.

O Father, I feel as though my whole being has melted into a nebula of delight and gratefulness. A delight beyond joy and sorrow, and a gratefulness unmixed with the need to thank.

Can anyone imagine a man of sixty-seven, whose mind is just beginning to open like a bud in spring?

The sun looks in the window
    The kettle sings
What else is there?

A new *haiku* that your old boy has discovered! It is the light of the Silent Lamp that opens my eyes to Poetry.

With my filial love in the Lord,

[No Signature]

JW to TM

43 Cottage Street
South Orange, N.J. 07079

New Year's Day, 1966

My dear Father Louis:

I wrote you last year. This is my first letter to you this year.

The enclosed piece of calligraphy is casually done; but it reveals a quality that I have not attained last year,—a state of calm and peace, without a trace of distracting thoughts. It is a version of your:

> The sun looks in the window
>> The kettle sings
> What else is there?

In the Chinese version, it becomes:

> The early sun penetrates the eastern window
> Green tea in living water
> The kettle sings
> Suddenly all *klesa*[129] has evaporated!

In the smaller letters, it is noted: "Depicting the internal landscape of Mei-teng Tao-jen."

"1966. New Year's Day. Ching-hsiung casual inspiration."

If this is attachment, let there be more attachment!

I have not got your essay on *koans*. Please send it along.

Your poetic child in the Holy Spirit,

[No Signature]

---

129. *klesa*: Sanskrit, literally "pain, affliction, distress, anguish." In Buddhism, "defiling forces, passion" (after Murti), and "karmic defilement, any of the hindrances to Enlightenment caused by desire, passion and delusion" (after Blofeld). See *AJTM*, glossary, p. 382.

JW to TM

2D, 43 Cottage St
South Orange, NJ 07079

January 10, 1966

My dear Father Louis:

These days it's all ashes, no inspiration. So I have not proceeded with my first chapter. I realize more than ever that every breath depends upon the movement of the Spirit.

In my utter loneliness I think of you. I have just written the enclosed *haiku* to you:

> Silent Lamp! Silent Lamp!
> I only see its radiance
> But hear not its voice!
> Spring beyond the world!

You see, Father, this poem began plaintively, but ends with a joy not from this world.

* * *

I have just called Mr. Robert McGregor on the phone. He sounds cordial, especially when I mention your name. "We are interested in what Father Merton is interested in." So I am going to mail him the "Epilogue," at the same time telling him what the book is about. Before it is published, a great deal of labor will have to be expended upon it yet. First, all the quotations must be traced to their origins in the footnotes. Second, a bibliography. Third, a glossary of names and terms. I don't expect the reproduction of the Chinese characters, but they will be romanized or latinized. Wherever necessary, the Japanese spellings like Obaku, Baso (Huang-po and Ma-tsu) will be given together with the Chinese.

Let me hear from you soon, Father.

By the way, McGregor me told that *The Way of Chuang Tzu* is doing pretty well.

Your lonely child in the world,

John [Chinese Characters Follow]

JW to TM

43 Cottage Street
South Orange, NJ 07079

January 19, 1966

My dear Father Louis:

"The Zen Koan" has just come today, and I have read it in bed. Not that I am sick, but I take a siesta when I have nothing else to do. This essay is so stimulating that it keeps me awake. So, Father, you owe me forty winks.

After reading this piece, it can no longer be doubted that you have a clearer understanding of the whole damned thing that any of the modern Zennists, so far as I know.

The demon of sleep was first driven away when I was on page 4, with the "winning ticket in the lottery of life." This is the essence of "gno" in Chuang Tzu's "*Wu shang gno.*" (Oh excuse me, the right spelling is *ngo*). Etymologically, the character *ngo* is composed of a spear and killing. This ego-centered individual is one ready to kill with a spear whether in aggression or in self-defense. He is somebody who is equipped for survival in the struggle for existence. Even the idea of "the nation *uber alles*" is egoism writ large. When I read "The individual is constituted by his ability to exist in the presence of others . . . ." I exclaimed, "What other evidence do I need to prove that *Mei Teng Tao-jen* was the inventor of the Chinese characters?"

Your interpretation of this 'ngo' as "a kind of knot of psychic energies which seeks to remain firmly tied as an autonomous 'self'" throws a flood of light upon the central doctrine of Buddhism and Taoism of Lao-Chuang. "Wu" on the other hand is identical with "Mu."

Your introduction of St. John of the Cross is the "winning ticket" in a different world, where there [Wu has left out 'is'] no need to win, the "nowhere without no."

But what cheers me most is your use of Rilke.[130] I must get

---

130. Rainer Maria Rilke (1875-1926): considered the greatest German poet of the twentieth century, he is the author of *Duino Elegies*. Merton had a great interest in Rilke's poetry. Both writers share many things in common from being poets of transcendence to their shared love for mystical paradoxes in their writings. See Merton's letters (Volume 6), *Learning to Love: Exploring Solitude and Freedom*. Ed. by Christine Bochen (San Francisco: Harper San Francisco,

his *Selected Works.*

PEACE IS NOT ENOUGH! Nor is afternoon nap! What a soul-shaking message! Now I understand the point of the fox story—"the enlightened does not ignore the karmaic world."

The conclusion—about Zen's true value for the West and about Zen's need for an *aggiornamento*[131]—has finality about it.

As to the term "philosophic monism," I beg to dissent. I prefer "non-dualism." But this is merely semantic.

Do you think, Father, I can include this superlative critique of the *koan* in my book? Say, as the second part of the Epilogue?

Is your introduction to my book proceeding?

Your very greedy child in the Holy Spirit,

[No Signature]

1997), p. 382.

131. *aggiornamento*: Italian concept associated with Pope John XXIII and in vogue during the Second Vatican (Ecumenical) Council (1962-65) generally used to convey the idea of "updating" or, more specifically, of bringing the Roman Catholic Church fully into the 20th century. This updating included inter-religious dialogue not only with other Christians but with the religious traditions of the world. Both Merton's and Wu's religious faith and writings sharply reflect deep ecumenical concerns.

JW to TM

2D, 43 Cottage Street
South Orange, NJ 07079

January 21, 1966
The Lunar New Year's Day

My dear Father Louis:

This is the New Year's Day of Old China, when you were living in the Middle Kingdom. That was long ago.

Everything is quiet here. My only companion is your *New Seeds of Contemplation*, which I have discovered only a few days ago in the library of Seton Hall. It has a healthy taste. I feel like strolling on a mountain, breathing the pine-scented air.

The enclosed piece of calligraphy contains a revised version of the *haiku* which had been sent to you some time ago. It reads:

Before the cockcrow
The woods are enshrouded in silent darkness:
A Thief! A Thief!
Hacking at wood—*ting, ting*!

This thief is the Divine Thief, breaking the dark silence for the first time. I call Him Thief because nobody had expected His creative work. In cutting wood, you are repeating His action once more.

This is the first letter I write in this Year of the Horse.

Your old boy in the Divine Thief,

[No Signature]

JW TO TM

42 Cottage St
So Orange, NJ 07079
January 24, 1966
My dear Father:

You would be tickled by the enclosed clipping. What strange bed-fellows fame makes! I don't mean the Holy Father. In fact, I rather like to see both of you together, as representing the two aspects of Christ—the inner and the outer. You are supporting his diplomatic efforts ontologically.

You look thinner than you did in the picture you sent me two years ago. But I like the smile— smile when the kettle sings. This smile gives the world more hope for real Peace than all the hectic activities in the world. As a friend of mine is sending another clipping to me, you can keep that smile.
Your filial old boy in Christ,

John [Chinese Characters Follow]

Another *haiku*:

I retreat further and further
Till I am involved with the destiny of
Man at his very core.

TM to JW

Jan. 27, 1966

Dear John:

I owe you forty winks so I will pay it back in prayers. Usually my writings are good for putting people to sleep, but you are prejudiced. Really I think you owe me the forty winks. But I know you pray for me anyway.

However, I am glad you liked the Zen *koan*. I have sent it to a magazine (and heard nothing so far). I don't know whether it would be a good idea to put it in the book or not. You don't want the book to become too much of a mixture of things. In any case I would have to discuss it with Doubleday perhaps, though if the book goes to New Directions there would be no problem and I could work it out with them. It seems to me by the way that you should have given MacGregor more than the epilogue, because the rest of the book is important and representative and without it he does not get a good idea of the whole thing. As to the introduction, I will not be able to get to that for several weeks, perhaps a couple of months. I am plagued with a lot of little jobs that have to be got out of the way first, and my publisher is after me to get down to business on a long book. After this I will certainly do no more prefaces for a long time, except of course the one I have promised to your friend at St. John's. I wonder by the way if the publishers ever sent *Chuang Tzu* to Paul Sih. They should have. If they have not, I will. Do you happen to know, off the record?

The latest *haiku* and calligraphies are most impressive. I look at the calligraphies in wonderment, wishing I could begin to read them. When you tell me where *Mei Teng* is I generally manage to pick that out, but it is no great achievement. Here then I have the privilege of being reduced to a state of complete infancy.

We have just been on retreat and so I am as usual caught with a lot of letters to answer, some of which will never get answered. But I must try, so I hasten on, leaving you for the moment. When are you planning to come down? The weather is very cold now, and the axe has plenty to do, but it will have more when the logs are out from under the deep snow. The retreat, in any case, accounts for my silence.

God bless you always. Keep warm and don't read anything that robs you of sleep: sleep is better than reading.

With warm friendship, in Christ,

Mei Teng

TM TO JW

Feb. 7, 1966

Dear John—

I am sorry that New Directions did not take the book, but as I said a long time ago I did not really think they were the right ones for it. You may better reach the readers you should reach by appearing elsewhere. However there was no harm in sending it to them. On the other hand you certainly need to send more than the epilogue— as much of the book as you can send should be sent.

A Moslem friend of mine[132] is getting interested in Chuang Tzu and asked me if I could get him an offspring of your article. Do you have one—or is the new book soon appearing (the one I read in French?) Could you please send him the offprint if you have one?

He is:

Ch. Abdul Aziz
First Floor JM 872
S.M. Sayeed Rd.
Karachi
Pakistan

He would greatly appreciate it.

Here is a French poem I suddenly wrote the other day.

All best wishes and blessings in the Lord,

Fr. Louis

Old cracked *Mei-Teng*

---

132. "A Moslem friend of mine": Merton is referring to Abdul Aziz, a Pakistani Sufi scholar who corresponded with him from 1960 to 1968. The French scholar of Islam Louis Massignon (1883-1962) encouraged Aziz to contact Merton. The three of them did share common interests in the study of Sufism and Christian mysticism. See Merton's letters in *The Hidden Ground of Love* (pp. 43-67) and in Fons Vitae volume *Merton & Sufism* (1999).

TM TO JW

Feb. 23, 66

Dear John:

Lent is upon us but I must still remember to type that Pakistan address: Ch Abdul Aziz/ First Floor J.M. 872/ S.M. Sayeed Rd.,/ Karachi. I know what you mean about my not-calligraphy but kakography. I do not have any offprints of the *Mystics and ZM* article. I threw out everything when I moved. Strange that they did not send you the magazine! The enclosed is a bit involved but you might be curious. Perhaps I will be able to get the preface done this Lent. In any event I hope to see you in April preface or no preface. All blessings always in the Lord.

Tom

TM TO JW

Mar 22 1966

Dear John—

A note to say I am just off to the hospital for a back operation—&
other problems[133]—I don't know how long I will be laid up. It will
delay the preface but only make it all the better I hope as I lie on
my back in backless Zen. Happy Easter.
In the Risen Lord,

Tom *Mei-Teng*

---

133. "I am just off to the hospital for a back operation and other problems":
These other problems are well known in Merton's circles as his affair with "M,"
a nurse that Merton met at the hospital and fell in love with. See Merton's letters
in *Learning to Love* (1997), especially his entries in sections "Being in one place"
and "A Midsummer Diary for M."

JW to TM

43 Cottage St
South Orange, NJ 07079

March 26 1966

My dear Father *Mei-Teng*:

I have received today yours of the 22th. By this time I hope that the operation is over, and that everything is going as well as can be desired. Your letter arrived early enough this morning for me to bring it with me to the 10 o'clock Mass, and naturally the whole Mass was offered for your recovery. Do not let the matter of preface weigh on your hearth. The book can wait. Its manuscript (still incomplete) is now in the hands of Mr. Philip Sharper of Sheed and Ward. The enclosed sheet is the Table to Contents. It is likely that he will accept it, although, like other publishers, they require a great deal of time to read through any manuscripts. I have told them that as soon as they express their willingness to print it, your Introduction and my first Chapter can be expedited and will be supplied.

Some weeks ago I did discover your article on "Mystics and Zen Masters" in *Chinese Culture Quarterly*.[134] Like everything you have written, it goes directly to the heart of the matter. Your interpretation of "having no mind" as *being* mind instead of *having* it, and your perception of "Zen enlightenment" as "an insight into pure being in all its actual presence and immediacy," leave me speechless. This is the point of my whole book. This gives me such a confirmation that it no longer makes any difference to me whether my book will be published or not.

As to my contemplated trip to the East, I am waiting for the travelling expenses. I hope they do not come too soon. For it is not easy to wind up my courses at the University. I hope I can finish my courses here before I am required to go there. But whether I go early or late, I shall return for the next academic year, for the university has engaged me for another year although I have reached my retirement age. (This will be the second renewal.)

For the last two months or so, I have mysteriously gone through the darkest tunnel so far. I have felt so shatteringly *lonely* that I did not feel the impulse of even writing to you! I don't know why the Lord has

---

134. *Chinese Culture Quarterly*: now defunct but which ran for a good forty years from the late 1950s to 1999, the review was published in Taiwan.

led me into this cave, except, perhaps, because He wished to open up a wholly new scope of my all-too-limited sympathies. This experience has made me think of those who are in jail and who are tempted to commit suicide. Formerly, I could never sympathize with people who kill themselves. But now I have come to understand them and therefore feel tenderness toward them. O Father, *all men without exception are our brothers.* I am sure that you had attainted this state of all-embracing, non-discriminating compassion long ago; but for me, your old boy, it is only recently granted to me. But what a suffering![135]

I feel confident, Father, that your recovery will be surprisingly quick. Still I am eager to hear the good news.

Your loving child in Christ,

John {Chinese Characters Follow}

NEXT PAGE

The Golden Age of Zen

Introduction　　　By Thomas Merton
Chapter I. The Origins of Zen
Chapter II. Hui-Neng The Sixth Patriarch: His Life and His Immediate Disciples
Chapter III: Hui-Neng's Fundamental Insights
Chapter IV. Matsu Tao-I
Chapter V. Pai-Chang And Huang-Po
Chapter VI. Chao-Chou Ts'ung-Sheng
Chapter VII. Outstanding Masters in the Lineage of Shih-T'ou
Chapter VIII. Kuei-Shan Ling-Yu: Founder of the Kuei-Yang House
Chapter IX. T'ung-Shan Liang-Chieh: Founder of the Ts'ao-Tung House
Chapter X. Lin-Chi I'Hsuan: Founder of the Lin-Chi House
Chapter XI. Yun-Men Wen-Yen: Founder of the Yun-Men House
Chapter XII. Fa-Yen Wen-I: Founder of the Fa-Yen House
Epilogue: LITTLE SPARKS OF ZEN.

---

135. What a suffering!: cf. Merton's famous "Fourth and Walnut" episode on the streets of Louisville as can be found in *CGB*, p. 156-158 in which suddenly he is struck full force by what Wu writes of here, "this state of all-embracing, non-discriminating compassion." The only difference is that Merton comes to his new awareness by way of joy, while Wu, by way of darkness, loneliness and suffering.

JW to TM

Tokyo Hilton

May 5, 1966

My dear Father Louis:

You see I am writing from Tokyo on my way to Taipei. I have been here for four days, and had a very wonderful reunion with Dr. Suzuki and his secretary Mihoko Okamura.

Dr. Suzuki is more lively and alert than in the summer of 1964 when I last saw him in Honolulu. He has received your *The Way of Chuang Tzu* and was profoundly impressed by your insights. He simply loves you. When I mentioned that you were in the hospital, he was very much concerned. I understand from his secretary that he is writing you.

My MS on Zen, which you took so much pains in touching up, delights him, and he is going to write a foreward to it as promised. I pray to the Lord that you will be in a position to produce the introduction soon. In the meantime, I have already completed the first chapter. In fact, instead of one chapter, I have written two: Chapter I, The Origins of Zen and its Modern Significance. I have described Zen as "a flower that smiles greeted by a smile that flowers." This made Suzuki laugh. Chapter II, Bodhidharma and his Immediate Successors, leading right to the Sixth Patriarch (Chapter III).

Although travelling, you are always on my mind. I hope that this letter finds you out of the hospital feeling better than ever before.

Early tomorrow morning, I am flying to Taipei. I shall write to you again when I am settled in a definite address. But if you feel like writing me in the meantime, the following address is just as sure to reach me:

C/o Professor Francis Wu[136]
College of Chinese Culture
Hwa Kang, Yang Ming Shan,
Taiwan
China

With my filial love & gratitude,

John C. H. Wu

---

136. Prof. Francis Wu: Wu's 5th son and 7th child, a student of the piano who received his degree from Rome's Santa Cecilia Conservatory of Music and taught music in Taiwan.

TM TO JW

(Undated, sometime in May, 1966: on the cover page of mimeo-graphed copy of Merton's "Love and Solitude")

Dear John:

It was very good to hear from you on your way to Taipei. Sorry to have missed you here though. Very glad above all about the good news of Suzuki. I hope he does write, I am eager to hear from him. I am sending him this piece ("Love and Solitude") today. I have not written much since getting out of the hospital. I cannot type very much yet, without trouble. And I have deadline jobs and reviews piled up to do. But I am sure I will get to the introduction in June or July. Meanwhile I am anxious to see the *two* (hurrah!) first chapters. I will write more later. This is a hasty sign of life. All blessings and joy in Christ,

Tom

TM to JW

July 11, 1966

Dear John:

For a long time I have been trying to get over my consternation at the fact that you were in Asia. And then to write to you. Back in May, about the same time, Catherine de Vinck[137] told me you had gone and your letter came from Tokyo. I was especially glad to hear of your visit with Suzuki. I have not heard from him, but I have heard from Richard De Martino[138] and have promised to write something for the *Eastern Buddhist*. Also I have written a little report on some of the articles in the first issue and some other things, which I will send separately to you.

You are probably wondering about the preface. I am still in the long stage of preparation. I simply cannot rush into a thing like this, but I think that by next week I will be ready to try getting something on paper. I want to treat the question of Christianity and Zen: in what are they alike, in what not alike and so on. A brief simple contribution to East-West understanding. But that is exactly the hardest thing to do well. It would be much easier to write about the length of Chuang Tzu's ears or something useless like that. Can I see your first two chapters some time? They never reached me.

I hope by now you must be settled in Taipei and I hope things are all right. I cannot convince myself that they are wonderful, but I am afraid we all live in strange situations these days, in which nothing quite makes perfect sense. If it did we would all drop dead from shock.

It has been slow going since the hospital. For a long time I had trouble typing and only got back to work gradually. In fact I am still not wildly producing and I don't (think?) there is any harm in that. At the moment it is very hot, anyway. I will be glad to get down to the preface. I have really given it a lot of thought, perhaps

137. Catherine de Vinck (1922-?): a poet and writer with the title of Baroness and wife of the philosopher, José de Vinck, both natives of Belgium. Her most famous mystical and devotional writings are found in *Poems of the Hidden Way* (Alleluia Press, 1994) and *Through the Gateless Gate* (Alleluia Press, 1996).

138. Richard De Martino: Wu's student at the University of Hawaii and a disciple of Suzuki's for many years. He, Suzuki (1870-1966) and Erich Fromm (1900-1980) cooperated in a collection of essays, *Zen Buddhism and Psychoanalysis* (Grove Press, 1963) that attracted considerable attention.

too much. When you get this letter, that will be the time for an extra prayer to the Holy Spirit. I really need some inspiration to fuse it all together and make sense out of it, otherwise it may just be an indefinitely long series of mumblings.

As I have other letters to catch up with, I will close this one. I hope to hear from you soon. What are you doing? Are you very busy? Are you writing? Do let us have some news. I will keep you posted and send items that might interest you and keep you in touch with your friends on this continent. We want you back among us.

All the best always, and every blessing, in union of prayer in Xt.

[No Signature]

JW to TM

No. 5, Lane 13
Chungking S. Road (Sec. 2)
Taipei, Taiwan,
The Republic of China

July 18, 1966

My dear Father Tom:

Your two letters were both received in due course of time. The second one, dated July 11, is just on hand yesterday when I went to visit my son Francis and his wife Kathy, who are living in Yang Ming Mountain.

July 11 was the eve of our friend Suzuki's death. Did you realize it? A little over two months ago he was very much alive. When I told him that you were in the hospital, he immediately asked his secretary to write you. I left with him my ms. on Zen, and he gladly promised to write a word for it. Since my arrival in Taipei, I wrote two letters to his secretary (Miss Mihoko Okamura) and so far I have had no reply. Probably, he fell sick a couple of weeks after my visit in early May. Learned about his death only through the papers.

You can imagine how grateful I am to you for remembering about the preface to my book. It will indeed be a great contribution, not only to my book, but to the world of the Spirit, if you will treat the question of Christianity and Zen. However, the Lord has his own good time, and I don't want to press you to do it when you are still in the process of recuperation.

I am inclosing here the first two chapters. After I receive your much desired Introduction (no mere preface), I shall make serious attempts to find a publisher. I really should not have approached any publishers without these necessary beginnings. So far, that ms. has been rejected three times. Even if I had submitted to a hundred, it will have been thrown out a hundred times, for the simple reason that no one could have made head or tail of it. That may still be Zen in its essence; but a book on Zen is quite a different thing.

The above typewritten address is that of a house which is being repaired and furnished for me to live in when writing the biography of Dr. Sun Yat-sen. The government here has been very considerate in not imposing any political duties on me over and above this already heavy task. In the meantime, I have read enough of the English and Chinese materials available here to realize that this formidable task is not devoid of intensely human and spiritual interest. Dr. Sun Yat-sen is a *genuine* personality. Without being a churchgoer, he is nevertheless deeply rooted in the spirit of the Cross. All people who really knew him intimately—British, American, Japanese, Filipino, German—gave him the superlative place in their estimate, not to mention the testimonies of his Chinese friends. Here goes a *man*, who has not lost the heart of a newborn child. Hence, he is greater than his writings and achievements.

Yes, Father Louis, I feel at home here. In the first place, the environment is Chinese, and I am in my element in it. Moreover, two of my sons are here in Taiwan. One is Francis, who is now professing music in the College of Chinese Culture. The other is Father Peter, who is doing his missionary work among the mountains in the middle part of the island. He is taking care of three little parishes with mountain folks as his parishioners. I have already visited one of his parishes; but he forbade me to go to the other two, for fear that I might faint in climbing the heights. An unnecessary fear, graced by his filial heart.

I am already praying to the Holy Spirit for your Preface.

Please address your next letter to the above typewritten address. I expect to move in a week.

I am happy to learn that Catherine de Vinck has already contacted you. I have also received a letter from her, telling me how grateful she feels to Our Lord for the blessing of knowing you. I trust that her husband Jose has sent you a copy of his new book, *The Virtue of Sex*, which I think is a pathfinder.

My friends in America tend to imagine that I might not feel at home so far away. But this is an illusion. In fact, the Holy Spirit stirs where He pleases, and He seems to be very active in me and around me. But I must write them more frequently.

Your old little boy in the Spirit,

John [Chinese Characters Follow]

TM to JW

August 5, 1966

Dear John:

In order to get the introduction off to you without delay, I am sending it at once without writing the long answer which I owe your
last letter. I will do that in a day or two. There have been some big
typing errors in this text but I think I have corrected them. Hope
it will be suitable. I will send uncorrected texts by sea mail and
you will have plenty. More if you ask. I do hope this will be of
some help. Any more ideas about publishers? I will give it some
thought. As to me, I need your prayers, life is not always easy!!!
I am in trouble, so please pray and get the saints at it too. Many
thanks and warm affection always in Christ,

Tom

JW TO TM

No. 5, Lane 13
Chungking S. road (Sec. 2)
Taipei, Taiwan
Republic of China

September 6, 1966

My dear Father Louis:

I have just got yours of the 27th (of August). The introduction hasn't arrived. A possible explanation of this delay is that probably in the address you had written (Sec. 3) instead of (Sec. 2). Your first letter had also (Sec. 3) on the envelope, but I noted that it was after some inquiries that it was finally delivered to this house, and I suspect that the introduction had fallen into less thoughtful hands in the postal office. Another explanation is that perhaps the introduction was pretty heavy and, there being not enough stamps, it was transformed from air mail to ocean mail. Be that as it may, I am happy to hear from you, and I am relieved that you have another copy. If however it is the only copy left, I suggest that you have some more copies made. Our friend the Devil is trying to hinder the publication of this book, whose aim is to open the doors of Our Church.

It is so characteristic of you to write: "It is a little hard to laugh off the heartbreak of another person."[139] Indeed, Father *Misericordieux* (I mean Compassionate), this is the worst cross to a man of boundless generosity like yourself. The simplest way out would

---

139. ". . . to laugh off the heartbreak of another person" (citing what Merton had written to Wu): we do not know for certain who "another person" refers to here since Merton's letter of August 27 is missing. An educated guess is that it is M., Merton's student-nurse friend he had fallen in love with beginning in spring, 1966. In a postcard dated August 5 in which Merton told Wu he had sent off to him the Introduction to the *Golden Age of Zen*, Merton had first written, "I need your prayers, life is not always easy!!! I am in trouble . . . ," words so very uncharacteristic of the monk. In the missing letter, Merton may very well have told Wu of his relationship with M. and Wu, showing discretion, might have deliberately destroyed it to prevent a foreseeable scandal. In 1967, returning to America from Taiwan, Wu gave to his son, John, Jr. a copy of *Conjectures of a Guilty Bystander* along with the August 5 postcard which he had pasted on the inner side of its back page and, in doing so, said that the monk was "in deep spiritual crisis." Wu did not elaborate on the nature of the crisis and his son assumed—only partially correctly—it involved Merton's vocation. Obviously there is no way to know for certain the "another person" is indeed M. and the words Wu quotes here may not be related to the student-nurse at all.

336 • Thomas Merton and John Wu

be to turn the heart into steel. But this is the coward's or the cynic's way. Your way, I am sure, is let the Lord beat your heart into pulp, so that it is no longer your heart but the Heart of God with its all-embracing Compassion. This is the Way of Tao in which you are so steeped, the Way of knowing the masculine but sticking to the Feminine.[140] The beautiful thing about you, father, is that your heart is as great as your mind. Thus, in you love and knowledge are united organically. Herein lies your profound significance for this great age of synthesis of East and West.

A few days ago, my son Francis forwarded to me an envelope containing your "Spiritual Fathers in the Desert Tradition," "Buddhism and the Modern World," "Is the World a Problem," and finally "With the World in My Blood Stream."

So far, I have only read two of them, the first and the last. The last is a poetic version of "beating the heart into pulp." In the first, I find this: "The conviction of one's 'self' as a static, absolute and invariable reality undergoes a profound transformation and dissolves in the burning light of an altogether new and unsuspected awareness." Perhaps, "God" himself stands in need of such a stunning transformation! I mean, our static notion of God does. Here again you furnish the key to the *Überwindung of the East and the West*. Even your hospitalization is fruitful. Together with oxygen *the Spirit is poured upon you from on high, and the wilderness becomes a fruitful field* (Isaias 32.15). The poet has become a Divine Poem:

> While the frail body of Christ
> Sweats in a technical bed

---

140. "... knowing the masculine but sticking to the feminine": see chapter 28 of the *Tao Teh Ching*:

Know the masculine,
Keep to the feminine,
And be the Brook of the World.
To be the Brook of the World is
To move constantly in the path of Virtue
Without swerving from it,
And to return again to infancy.

The Taoist classic is full of references to the feminine as well as to passivity, humility, simplicity, the lowly and, above all, *wu-wei*. Both Wu and Merton would agree the classic would be difficult to fathom outside the context of such overriding themes.

I am Christ's lost cell
His childhood and desert age
His descent into hell.

O Father, how I love you, and marvel at the God who is working in you! It is you whom I love, not your introduction, although when it comes I shall kiss it as coming from you. Even if it doesn't come, can I not kiss the air and enjoy the oxygen which is so full of the Holy Spirit? And therefore of you?

Today the typhoon (a kind of periodic tornado) is raging, and I am alone in my cell of an office. Sweet are the delights of a day of enforced contemplation.

I beg you, father, to keep me in your prayers.

Love in Christ,

John [Chinese Characters Follow]

JW TO TM

No. 5, Lane 13
Chungking S. road (Sec. 2)
Taipei, Taiwan
Republic of China

January 2, 1967

My dear Father Tom:

This is my first letter I type this year. I feel that to write to you is, in itself, a great blessing, to say nothing of receiving a letter from you. I like this *bon mot*: "The goodness and loving kindness of God our Savior has appeared." It links up the supreme goodness in the act of Incarnation with all our actions, great and little alike. Your sending me the beautiful greeting is a good instance of it.

Thank you so much for thinking of the book on Zen. At present, I am planning to have it printed here in Taiwan, at my own expense. The cost of printing is comparatively low here; and I think I can easily cover the costs by selling a part of the output in America.

Recently, Miss Mihoko Okamura, the devoted secretary of Suzuki, came to Taipei and brought to me the copy of the manuscripts which he had read over very carefully a little before he passed on. Although he did not get to write the preface, he did express his warm approval of it, according to Mihoko. Anyway your introduction is a gem. Richard De Martino likes it so much that he wants to publish it in the *Eastern Buddhist*.

Another advantage in printing the book here is that I can introduce more illustrations. I am not sure whether I can get the pictures that I want; but it is hopeful. By the way, Father, do you paint? I know that you are a noted calligrapher. But if you can also draw, would you make a sketch of some of the Zen masters whom you like especially?

I am offering a course on Zen at the College of Chinese Culture. I have nine graduate students, some of whom are pretty well-read in Zen and have proved to be of great help. One of them who is himself a professor of Chinese philosophy says that he has not read a book in Chinese or in English which gives such a comprehensive and clear presentation of the subject as *The Golden Age of Zen*, and he promises to render it into Chinese when it is published.[141] He is

---

141. "render it into Chinese when it is published": Professor Wu Yi whose

impressed greatly by your introduction. So you see, Father, I am very much encouraged and I don't feel lonely.

I intend to include an appendix to the book, which will give the original of all the important passages quoted in the text. 2,000 copies will be printed. I am making inquiries as to whether there are any difficulties in shipping them or at least a part to America and finding some distributor.

My present worry is about the biography of Dr. Sun Yat-sen. Only two chapters are written, and at every step the problems of historical accuracy arise. On the birthday alone there are three theories!

Pray for me, Father, that I may be able to concentrate on the work. I need your prayer *desperately*.

Your good-for-nothing boy,

John [Chinese Characters Follow]

translation in 1969 has sold consistently well in Taiwan. He did not, however, render the Introduction into Chinese, citing difficulty in fully deciphering Merton's style. Prof. Wu currently teaches at a Buddhist institute in California.

JW to TM

378 Valley Street, G2
South Orange, New Jersey 07079

Sept. 19, 1967

My dear Father Louis:

At last I am again in the States.

The Golden Age of Zen is being published in Taipei by the College of Chinese Culture Press. I had just done my final proof-reading before I started last Saturday. The book will be out in a week or so.

I reread your Introduction, and I like it more than ever. It is a masterful summing (up) of the spirit of Zen, and the comparative study of Christianity and Zen can serve as a living bridge between East and West. I hope you will like my preface.

The great advantage of printing it in Taipei is that I can reproduce the originals in notes.

My son, John Wu, Jr., is grateful to you, Father, for your powerful support of his stand in the matter of conscientious objection.[142] It does great credit to the American government to be so *liberal and open* to all sincere views.

You will hear more from me, as soon as I am settled after more than a year's absence. I must try to get in tune with my milieu.

Filially in Christ,

John [Chinese Characters Follow]

---

142. "in the matter of conscientious objection": Merton had sent letters of support on his and his friend, Michael Hodder's, behalf. Hodder had trekked out to Gethsemani from New Jersey but he was not allowed to visit Merton. Hodder was drafted for Vietnam and Merton wrote a letter on his behalf to the board.

TM TO JW

Sept. 24, 1967

Dear John:

Hurray! So glad to have you back. Permanently I hope! And delighted to hear that the book is so well advanced. Many thanks for the preface.[143] It is a joy and a privilege for me to be so closely associated with you in this. I must send you my own new book: you have read most of the parts that have to do with Zen or the East I believe. There may however be some little corners that are new to you.

It was also a joy to give what support I could to John Jr. and his friend.

Do please let me know if you are back permanently or at least for a long time. Will I be able to reach you at this address? Will you be able to get down here some time? There is much to talk about. Could we plan something perhaps for next spring? I might be able to work up some occasions, conferences etc in this area.

My very best wishes and blessings always,

In Christ Our Lord

[No Signature]

---

143. preface: to *The Golden Age of Zen*, in which in his typical generosity of spirit and humility he wrote, "I suggest that the reader should first study (Merton's) introduction before he proceeds to take up the body of the book. In a real sense this book may be regarded as a long footnote to the profound insights embodied in his introduction. . . . There is no telling how much the friendship of this *true man* has meant to me during all these lonely years of my life."

TM to JW

Jan. 24, 1968

Dear John:

How are you? Snowed in? I haven't heard from you in a long time. This letter is a quick one, to ask you a favor. I am starting a small mimeographed magazine[144]—an enterprise of no account, with no money involved, to be given out free, publishing mainly poetry. But I also want to devote some of it to Zen and to religious texts from Asia etc.

Therefore I would like to run a few pages of your "Golden Age" book, in the next issue, first issue: specifically the pages about Pai Chang, his philosophy of work and the bit about the old fox. Is that all right? If so, and I hope so, please also give me enough essential facts for the notes on contributors: (are you teaching at Seton Hall again, for instance? What exactly was it you were teaching there? Etc) (What is the exact name of the University in Taiwan—you were teaching there? Etc)

How is *the Golden Age* book coming along?

Is it ok I if I reprint my preface in a collection of essays[145] to be done by New Directions?

And above all, can you please send me some new and interesting texts, Chinese poems or Zen or Confucian texts that have not been done in English before or not done well?

There is at Indiana University a Richard Chi[146] who has translated Shen Hui, and I hope to meet him this week.

Remember you are always welcome here and we want to see you. We have a new Abbot now. You are invited to come and visit and give a talk to the community (which will help cover expenses)

---

144. small mimeographed magazine: *Monks Pond* which, as Merton had planned, ran a total of four issues.

145. collection of essays: published as *Zen and the Birds of Appetite* (New York: New Directions, 1968), 141 pp. This book was dedicated to Amiya Chakravarty (1901-1986), a Bengali poet, philosopher, and literary critic who was a close associate of Tagore and Gandhi. Chakravarty helped Merton with the planning of his Asian journeys in 1968 and became one of the consulting editors for Merton's *The Asian Journal* (1973).

146. Richard Chi (1918-?): Buddhist scholar and translator of Shen Hui's Ch'an. Merton invited Chi to contribute to *Monks Pond* (see fourth issue). Merton also discussed with him his upcoming trip to Asia. See letters in *The Hidden Ground of Love* (pp. 121-122).

anytime you are out in the midwest.

My very best, and all my blessings always,

In the Lord

[No Signature]

JW TO TM

378 Valley Street, G-2
South Orange, N.J. 07079

January 26, 1968

My dear Father Louis:

Yours of the 24th has just arrived this morning. I am sorry to have delayed responding to your previous letter. But need I tell you that your friendship has sunk so deep into my psyche that it has become a part of me?

Since I last wrote to you in September, my wife, whom I had married in Taipei, has come to join me. As it is her first visit to this country, she has had to be acclimatized gradually to the new environment. This has taken a great part of my time and attention. She is a nice girl of forty-four. (Her name is Agnes).[147] She had never married before. A convert in her twenties, her dominant passion was to be a Sister. She tried her luck with no less than four orders, including Sisters of the Good Shepherd, Poor Clares, Social Service, and the Carmel. But she never went beyond the stage of postulancy, because every time her doctor and spiritual director advised her against continuing because of health reasons. Last Spring, we met quite unexpectedly in Taipei, and she felt right away that finally she had found her vocation—of helping me fulfil my vocation of spreading the Gospel in the East. Truly she takes good care of me. Please give us your blessings, Father!

Just a couple of days ago, I received two copies of *The Golden Age of Zen*, in its final shape as a book. I have already ordered ten more copies, to be sent me airmail. I am using it as the main text in my course on *Oriental Philosophy and Religion*. I already gave a copy of it to the university authorities here, and in presenting it the first thing I pointed out to them was your 28-paged introduction. Of course they were impressed.

When the newly ordered copies arrive (in ten days at most), I will immediately send a copy to you. Now let me answer your queries item by item:

1. I am happy to learn that you are starting a mimeographed magazine. I should be delighted indeed to see

---

147. Agnes: née Chuk Wen-ying (January 2, 1923 on the Lunar calendar), baptized Maria Agnes, who continues to live in Taipei.

parts *of the Golden Age* appear therein.

2. I am tickled that you should have taken a particular fancy to Pai-chang's philosophy of work and the bit about the old fox. I was just last night reading that part to my wife, who was trying to dissuade me from working too hard.

3. At present I am a Research Professor in Asian Studies at Seton Hall University. Also Honorary Dean of Graduate School of the College of Chinese Culture in Taiwan. It was in this College that I was teaching Zen for a year.

4. Of course, it is ok to reprint your "A Christian Looks at Zen" in the collection of your essays. Perhaps, it is good to mention my book and its publisher (The Committee on the Compilation of the Chinese Library, Taiwan). The Chinese are not copyright-minded.

5. The courses I am teaching here at Seton Hall are *Oriental Philosophy and Religion*, *Chinese Poetry*, *Classical Chinese Literature*.

6. I will keep it in mind that you are interested in having some new and refreshing texts from the Chinese.

7. My wife likes to join me in a trip to Gethsemani. We would like to receive your blessings together. But is there any accommodations for a couple near the monastery?

Your good for nothing boy in Christ,

John [Chinese Characters Follow]

TM TO JW

March 4, 1968

Dear John:

Well, here is the magazine. I doubt if it will overturn the literary world in one bang. But I think it has good things in it, not the least your own piece.

John Jr. writes that he wants to bring Teresa and come down with you.[148] But of course. The more the merrier—up to a point. But I will be most happy to have the four of you. Would June be a good time? Let me know as there is a demand for space then.

Many thanks for *the Golden Age*, a copy of which has reached me. Would it be possible for me eventually to have a few more copies to send to people who would appreciate it? Four or five— no hurry.

At last a little smell of spring, but not much, and the nights are cold.

My very best always,

Tom

---

148. "come down with you": Wu and Merton never met again, but John Jr. and Teresa (Wong) spent two days (June 17-8) with the monk who found a spot to camp for the newly weds on the monastery grounds as part of their honeymoon excursion.

PART V
THE COLLECTED LETTERS OF
THOMAS MERTON AND JOHN WU, JR.
(1967–1968)

JWJ TO TM

25 Clifton Ave, Apt D-2008
Newark, New Jersey 07104

May 16, 1967

Dear Father Louis,

Prof. Robert Pollack[1] has made the statement often that America is like a jazz band, full of unique and spontaneous innovations. Thus, to set the proper mood for this humble letter, I have placed on my Victrola one of my favorite jazz albums which combines the God-given talents of John Coltrane[2] and Duke Ellington.[3] In a very deep, symbolic sense, they combine the old and the new and 'discover' a structure that is totally new to both of them. And it is a structure that allows the spirit to flow and speak more freely than ever before. I have opened my letter in this manner, father, because in your later works, especially on the East, you have similarly 'discovered' through genuine experimentation and intuition styles and structures that do profound justice to the subject matter with which you are involved. Needless to say, your *Way of Chuang Tzu* is a case in point. You use a style which is easily readable, using a language which is familiar to most of us, a language which, surprisingly, conveys and projects the very spirit of the Taoistic tradition. Most of all, you have taught me that even in the hustle-bustle world that is America, placidity, mysticism, naturalism (in the good sense of the word) can and *do* exist! If a certain spirit and way of life is truly genuine, spontaneous, natural and unique, it must of necessity be able to transcend all forms of artifacts, be it social, political, economic or military.

However, father, the purpose of this letter is not to engage in any petty philosophizing nor to add to the heap of flatteries and

---

1. Prof. Robert Pollak (1940-?): Professor of Biological Sciences at Columbia University and Director of the Center for the Study of Science and Religion since 1999.

2. John Coltrane (1926-1967): American jazz saxophonist and composer. He was at the forefront of Free Jazz. Coltrane studied world religions, mysticism, and philosophy and became interested in Zen Buddhism, like Merton. Coltrane had a religious experience that transformed his life and got rid of his addictions. He saw music as a healing, spiritual tool.

3. Duke Ellington (1899-1974): American composer, pianist, and band leader who elevated jazz to an art form. He like Coltrane became icons of American culture and music. And Merton as a jazz fan was fond of their music.

compliments which have already come your way. Rather, I write this letter to thank you for the large part which you played in helping me to secure my conscientious objection status. Unlike many cases with which I'm dimly familiar, mine was especially fortunate. My I-O classification came three days after I had submitted the C.O. form. With time, I am beginning to understand more deeply the commitment that one makes when he decides to become a wager against war and the military establishment. I've discovered that the card is not to be used as a shield to guard oneself against physical harm. That is too passive and negative. Rather, I find it to be an extremely positive statement, the statement being that I believe love to be the only truly active and positive force in the world, and that, in due time, love will find its rightful place amongst all the peoples. Those who are able to look in only from the outside refer to C.O.'s as blind idealists (that is the most flattering of all their labels!). But, from the inside looking outward, it is something that is very much alive, a concretized form of idealism that forms the central vision of the person, that serves as the primary driving force in both speech and actions. It is, as Robert Pollack himself might say, the 'here-already' and yet, the 'not-quite-here-yet', a situation which places a person totally in time and yet out of time in the same instance.

Again, father, a most heart-felt thanks to you for your generosity. I do hope very much you are still corresponding with my dad. He has not written me for a while now. If and when you do write him, please send him my best regards! Let us keep each other in our daily prayers, trusting that the Almighty will grant us enough energy to push forth our respective tasks. I am,

Your brother, in and thru Christ,

John Wu, Jr.

P.S. Michael Hodder, the young man who came to call for you during his Easter break, is one of my four roommates. The draft board sent him a 2-S classification which he has decided to return again. As you know, he has already applied for the C.O. form which, apparently, was overlooked by the board. He will definitely apply for it again. In any case, he is presently reading one of your books (*Raids on the Unspeakable*) and wishes to express a 'hello' to you. By the way, your calligraphy would make any professional calligrapher envious!

TM TO JW

June 9, 1967

Dear John:

The letters I really like to answer get pushed aside because I prefer to think a little before answering them and then they get lost because I have to answer so many other letters that one can answer with a minimum of thought. Yours is one I enjoy answering because it was a good one and had a lot to say. And first, I know what you mean about Coltrane because I have heard him and admire him: also I like very much Ornette Coleman[4] and especially Jackie McLean.[5] I haven't heard the Coltrane-Ellington duo. I admit though that I am still more inclined to the old jazz of my old day, not because it is better but because I hear it better.

I am very glad that the draft board was reasonable with you. Not all of them are the same, it is pretty much a matter of roulette. Of course the thing about conscientious objection, in my mind, is that simply to object to war and not to all the other things that go with it, does not make all the sense in the world. It is part of a whole attitude, and what matters is the whole attitude. There is a lot of fuss around now among progressive Catholics about objection to the unjust war but not to other wars. Well, all right, fine. But I can also well understand the military objecting to this kind of objection. One's choice narrows down to a fine little point, that one unjust war: and for the rest, one goes along with everybody else in everything, the secular city is the New Jerusalem, etc. One can drown in martinis if one wants, and make a million dollars in the bargain. It seems to me that we are asked to be a little more revolutionary than that, and one thing I do like about the world these days is that your generation is protesting louder and better and more intelligently than most of the others have so far. So good luck, and keep on going.

Naturally, I am happy to have you say all the things you say about my work. I'll send along a mimeo of part of the new poem series I am just finishing. Unfortunately it does not make much

---

4. Ornette Coleman (1930-?): American saxophonist, violinist, trumpeter and composer. Like Coltrane he was one of the pioneers of the Free Jazz movement.

5. Jackie McLean (1931-2006): American saxophonist, composer, bandleader and educator.

sense, and is especially tentative in this mimeo version. I send it as a gesture of thanks, and because you are you. Meanwhile I am busy with a commentary of Camus's *Plague*.[6] Timely, I believe.

I am worried about your father. I haven't heard from him, and I think he must be suffering a bit, perhaps in ways he himself does not understand. I must write to him, just to show a sign of life, but I am so snowed under with mail requiring that fast stupid answer. . . . Anyway, let's pray for him. I really do not envy his position at all. I think the people he is with are hopelessly wrong in many ways, and yet I can see where he would feel he had to go along with them, and I am sure he is not totally at peace with it. I admire his fidelity and understand his silence, and in the long run I know his integrity is the kind that matters, especially because it is the kind you cannot easily explain.

I hope Michael Hodder made out all right with the board. My best wishes to both of you, and all blessings, in Christ,

---

6. Camus's Plague: Albert Camus (1913-1960) author of the novel *The Plague* (1947) tells how French medical workers find solidarity while the plague hits the city of Oran. Camus as an existentialist philosopher tackles the problem of the absurd in this novel.

JWJ TO TM

96 Arsdale Terrace
Apt. 303
East Orange, New Jersey,

Feb. 13, 1968

Dearest Father Louis,

This letter is to inform you that I am still breathing and very much alive, happy and joyous at East Orange! Admittedly so, the old inner conflicts still persist within me, yet, it is also true that certain worthwhile values encased in my bosom have suddenly begun to emerge to the surface in the most dramatic ways, mainly due to these conflicts. These inner "tugs of war" which used to make my life immobile and make me scream in despair are beginning to serve a new purpose. I cannot define for you that purpose but only say that they are affecting a maturity of which I could not have dreamt when I was a bit younger. I think that the battle is between the ego and the "inner voice," and I have begun to align myself more and more with the latter, convinced that the superficial ego is nothing but a stumbling block in the search to find myself. It is not a psychological game that's played in the comfort and warmth of the living room; rather, it is a struggle that takes place every second that we are alive. And I find that every victory over the ego makes us more free, and, therefore, more alive. Putting the struggle within this context, it is, indeed, a drama, for, certainly, there is no greater drama in life than the dramatic unfolding of one's own life of which one is a constant participant. Thus, the past year has been the richest period of my life: that mysterious element of life (the "inner voice") which had gone for an over-extended sabbatical is again very much a part of all my activities and struggles. And, it is truly paradoxical that the deeper we go within ourselves, the more we become involved with the world and the more we are able to understand and to empathize with the feelings of others. Is this not a truism which defies every philosophical analysis?

Father, I hope that you will not be upset by this disclosure. I submitted the letter which you had written to me over the past summer to our literary journal at school and an excerpt of it (concerning conscientious objection) was printed. I simply hope that you will not file suit against me for not having received your permission for publication. Your short, pregnant analysis on c.o. affected me so deeply that I felt guilty keeping it for myself and wanted all the other young men to share it with me. In any case, I shall be awaiting subpoena . . . .

Following a year of absence from Seton Hall, I am again enrolled as a full-time student there. It is difficult to assume academic responsibilities after such an absence, but, the past semester found myself devouring books in the same fashion that a Zen master tears into his disciples! I am a philosophy major now, in the midst of completing my bachelor thesis on Teilhard whom I truly don't understand but whose writings thrill and mesmerize me to no end. This June, two great events will consume all my energies: one is my long-awaited graduation from the stuffy confines of SHU and the other is my marriage to a Miss Teresa Wong who has served as one of the great inspirations in my life, who has encountered numerous conflicts with her family (from Richmond, Va.) in her stubbornness to love me and who is possibly more admired by my father than by me! In September, I shall be either at the U. of Wisconsin or in Taiwan where I shall be studying Chinese. I prefer to go to Taiwan where it would be possible to get things first-hand and to study under my dad who, as you've probably heard, is planning to return there to retire. But, that is a question of economics—where to get the dough. However, things such as these no longer worry me: they belong on the periphery of life and should not affect us essentially. I daresay that it is faith that, in the last analysis, counts most, and anyone who is without it seems to me to be walking like a living skeleton. But, still, would it be too much to ask you to keep me and my family in your daily prayers and masses?

My new mother, as you know, has joined us in this country. She is a wonderfully charming, graceful and loving woman, though, perhaps, a trifle overly-concerned about the sheep (and wolves!) for whom she must serve as shepherdess. But, I don't doubt for a moment that this concern flows out of her deep and authentic love. What is of utmost importance is that she has made dad happy, having spontaneously displayed all the essential qualities for a sound companionship.

My dad has informed me of the fact that he and mom are thinking seriously of visiting Gethsemani before very long. As I am now the owner of a Chevy, I have also assumed some responsibilities for transporting my parents hither and thither. Obviously, what I am driving at is whether or not I and Terry will be allowed to tag along. I promise you that I shall not allow myself to disturb the inner solitude of the monastery, but I can make no promises nor assume any responsibilities for the behavior of my three comrades.

Concerning your article in *Commonweal* (Oct. 27, 1967): on Teilhard: it is terribly true that one finds more Teilhardian enthusiasts to be sketchy in their knowledge of their own tradition. It is also not rare to find amongst them an enthusiasm which is based solely on reactionary motives—against that particular segment of Christianity which, they feel, is out-moded and become useless. I feel that all philosophies have attempted to speak of the *noumena*, and, Teilhard, in his unique method, is no exception. However, I do think that it is one thing to condemn one's vehicle of expression and another to condemn that which lies unfathomed behind that language. And, besides, I am positive that Teilhard himself would be unhappy (were he alive) if he were to find amongst his followers monistic rather than pluralistic thinkers. I try to look at Teilhard in a symphonic manner, and believe that the Community he envisioned would be one which encompassed the most diversified elements. I would be truly grateful if you could elaborate on the theme of Teilhardian community. Impressions would more than suffice.

Thank you again for allowing me to spend these few moments with you and I look forward to meeting you in the near future.

Love in Christo Jesu,

John Wu, Jr.

TM to JWJ

Feb. 26, 1968

Dear John Jr.:

I was happy to receive your letter and to hear you are soon to be married. Also I am glad that you and Terry would want to come down with your Father and new "mother." I would be really delighted to have you all here. So let us think about concrete plans.

As things are with me now I am fairly well tied up until after May and I presume you are too. June can be very hot and July worse, but still I'd say those are the best times, being vacation months. If you go into a council with your Father and decide, then one of you let me know what would be good dates for you. I can arrange for the ladies to stay in the ladies' guest house (which takes more arranging because of limited space). Also Sundays are days off for the staff there. Hence a visit during the week for three days or so can easily be set up if I know fairly well in advance. We can all be together during the days, sit in the woods or something, and enjoy ourselves.

I am glad Terry is Chinese. American women are all right, I suppose, but . . . . Congratulations.

What you say about the inner voice is all very true and shows you are working your way through the real problems of development. You are not wasting your time. You are on the right track.

I cannot write more now.

Blessings and love to all of you,

Please tell your Father that I have received the *Golden Age* and will thank him for it as soon as I get a chance to write.

JWJ TO TM

96 Arsdale Terrace
Apt. 303
East Orange, N.J. 07018

June 10, 1968

Dear Father Tom,

Much has transpired since my last letter to you back in winter. I became a citizen of the United States in April, graduated after *eight* years of rather uninspired undergraduate studies at Seton Hall and will be married to Teresa Wong of Richmond, Va. this coming Saturday (the 15th). Right now, I feel as if I have made an excellent beginning into becoming absorbed by the Establishment. But, the primary lesson which I've learned this year is to be more concrete and practical in my outlook, to throw myself into practical affairs, yet, at the same time, cultivate a spirit of detachment. I find it necessary to involve myself in secular affairs yet knowing that I am not being motivated and driven by secular forces. Many of my so-called 'liberal' friends are convinced of my having 'sold-out' to those forces against which I have so strongly fought these past few years, yet, I think their feelings simply point to the fact that they are still apt to judge even their closest friends through external standards. They exercise a curious type of intolerance which, at bottom, may result in their own spiritual destruction. At any rate, we do pray for each other and will continue to love.

My parents will be leaving for Formosa two days after the wedding (the 17th). That is unfortunate since we had all hoped that we could get together at the Abbey sometime during the summer days. However, following some consultation with my dad, Terry and I have decided (though, in truth, we were already planning) to trek out toward Kentucky for our honeymoon. Terry has friends in Louisville where her family lived before having moved to Richmond and I'm sure that she will have some delightful meetings with her childhood buddies. But that which really clinched our decision was the prospects of meeting and talking with you and, perhaps, of drinking some beer with you in the woods. We hope to reach Trappist on the 18th, 19th, or 20th which will be during the week-days and, of course, hope like heck that you'll find some free time to share some of your solitude with us. The reason for the indefiniteness of our arrival at Trappist will be due to two factors: first, my tendency to go astray when I embark upon any journey that is more than a few miles; secondly, because we plan to camp out along the way—and who knows what kinds of creatures will be harassing us!

My relationship with Terry has not been accepted in all quarters. Her parents have (since we became rather serious three or four years ago) objected vehemently, and to this day, we are not yet certain if her father plans to make the wedding ceremonies. At first, their objections centered around the fact that I had taken so long to finish my undergraduate work. Now it seems as though my character has been brought into question because of certain rumors spread by some members of the Chinese community. What has angered (but, really saddened) us most is that one of the principal 'rumor-spreaders' is a Chinese Catholic priest who is an especially close friend of the Wong family. This priest is not particularly fond of our family. Yet, it is to be known that these crises in our relationship have strengthened rather than weakened our mutual love. Terry is a tiny woman but a tower of strength! And I thank Almighty God for that.

There is much to be written but I shall spare you of my further babblings until, hopefully, our meeting at the Abbey. God love you and keep you.

In kindred spirit and harmony,

John Jr.

P.S. Please say a special prayer on the day of our wedding.

TM TO JWJ

June 13, 1968

Dear John:

First I want to send all congratulations, blessings and love to you and Terry on your wedding day. My Mass this Saturday will be for you two, and may God bless and bring all happiness to you. My blessings and love too to your Dad and all your family. I am sorry I won't have a chance to see him and meet his new wife before his return to Taiwan. What a shame.

But it is a joy to know you are coming down this way on your honeymoon. The 17th and following days are perfectly ok here as far as I can see, and of course if you are camping there is no problem about staying on the property here somewhere as long as you like. I will look forward to spending some time with you—afternoon would probably be best. Let me know ahead—best way is to call the monastery and ask the brother at the gate to get a message to me, and I'll be on deck when you show up. The best time for me would be to meet you at the gatehouse early in the afternoon, one thirty or two or thereabouts.

I am sorry to hear of your various troubles with people. But I suppose they are all part of the preparation you must go through. It is a good sign when you meet with opposition, because this helps to deepen your own motives and to rely more trustfully on God and His Love, for we never depend on the support of His creatures, at least not entirely.

Once again, my very best wishes and blessings to all of you.

With warmest regards, in Christ,

Tom

JWJ to TM

c/o Prof. Francis Caminiti
Route 24
Chester, New Jersey
July 11, 1968

Dear Father Tom,

There are simply no adequate words for Terry and me to express our profound thankfulness for your great generosity in having received us during our honeymoon at the Abbey. To avoid pomposity, let me just say that your magnanimity of spirit is something that has affected us since we had the good fortune to meet with you and that it will continue to sustain and enrich our marital lives together. Needless to say, our two days at Gethsemani were the highlight and climax of our honeymoon expedition. And to have participated in your special Mass! That was simply too much to ask for. It was Special and not to be forgotten. Please thank also Brother Maurice (Flood) whose company we totally enjoyed. In reflection, I am rather ashamed at myself for being devoid of that youthful, enthusiastic spirit of joy and charity that is conspicuously present in each and every monk. And, to a large degree, I envy you and the rest for having attained childlikeness, a quality that is so utterly lacking in the hearts of men. To my mind, that quality is certainly the essential kernel of Christianity. One of the greatest tragedies of human beings seems to me to be the premature aging of the child in us. It seems that when the child dies in us, so does our essential nature die with it. Most people allow the child to die unconsciously—that doesn't seem to be too painful unless that person begins to realize that the event has taken place. What is painful to see and to experience is that person who *consciously* knows that he is aging but does nothing to avoid his impending doom as a human being. What I want you to do, Father, is to pray that both Terry and I shall learn to become children again. During the last two years, I find myself carrying my burdens in a heavy-hearted manner and taking myself more seriously than I would care to. My father refers to me as an *old young man* and I have often retorted by calling him a *young old man*: neither needs painstaking elaboration. They simply express unequivocal kernels of truth.

My parents have left for Formosa. I don't exactly know

what my dad is up to: I don't think he knows either. But that is not important. Dad was in good spirits when he left, and that *is* important, for, since the days of his marriage he's had to absorb much opposition from the inner family circle—his pack of wolves! We can only pity the petty. As soon as I receive their address, I shall forward it to you. As promised, we shall not reveal anything concerning your trip to the East.

Terry and I shall be spending our summer at the home of one of my former professors who has gone off with his wife and family to Germany where he will conduct a course on Nicholas of Cusa.[7] It is very pleasant here and the air is almost as fresh as in Gethsemani. The Professor is an erstwhile and favorite student of Dr. Robert Pollock and his teaching technique resembles very much that of his former teacher. He is full of life and a wonderful human being.

I have little more to add except that I am in the process of reading your *Mystics and Zen Masters* which shall be the basis of my future studies in Zen. It is a perfect reference book, but, more than that, it is flooded with extraordinary insights. I have also taken an interest in Hermann Hesse[8] and am now in the midst of his *Steppenwolf*. If you have read it, I shall like very much to know your impressions. I shall tax you no further. Please write, but only at your convenience, for I know that time is very precious to you. Stay young and cheerful and may God keep you in robust health!

Your unworthy young friend,

John Wu, Jr.

---

7. Nicholas of Cusa (1401-1464): German cardinal, philosopher, mystical theologian, jurist, and scientist. His most famous work was *De docta ignorantia* (1440).

8. Herman Hesse (1877-1962): German author who wrote *Steppenwolf* (1927). In this novel he addressed that aggressiveness and humanity are found within each human being.

TM to JWJ

July 31, 1968

Dear John:

Well, it really was a pleasure to have you and Terry here. I was happy to meet you both, talk with you, share the Eucharist with you.

My plans for the Asian trip are slowly maturing but I still cannot be completely definite. If I get to Taiwan it will probably be around the first of the year. My first stop is a meeting in India in October and a great deal will depend on the contacts I make there. If things work out I might meet the Dalai Lama[9] and if I do I hope to get into some monasteries in Nepal etc. I am still not sure when I have to come back to the US. Naturally if I can stretch it I will.

Now here is one thing that occurs to me regarding Taiwan. It may be possible for me to stay there for a while, long enough to take a course perhaps. The purpose of this would be to put off my visit to Japan until spring when it will be better weather if I visit isolated Zen monasteries. It might be a good thing to take some study in Chinese language and philosophy in Taiwan over the winter. I also thought it might be fun to get back up in the mountains with your brother and help out slightly with his aborigines while also living as a semi-hermit. These are all just vague possibilities, but I wanted to mention them in case you want to pass on the suggestions to someone in Taiwan and see what the reactions are. Would it be better to let your dad know and plan ahead? Of course, though, it would be best not to say anything until I am sure myself that I will go to Taiwan. Are you likely to be there yourself? Any definite plans yet? If you can explore some of these ideas a bit with someone in Taiwan and let me know what you think, I'd be very grateful.

So far, all I know is that from October on I expect to be in India, S.E. Asia and Indonesia and move back north in January. It all looks very promising and exciting. Hope it works out.

My very best wishes to Terry. Keep well. Peace.

Tom

Glad you are well settled for the summer. Let me have your dad's address when possible.

---

9. The Dalai Lama: aka The XIV Dalai Lama Tenzin Gyatso (1935-) who is both the political and spiritual leader of the Tibetan people. Merton met with His Holiness three times in 1968. See *The Asian Journal* (1975), p. 125.

TM TO JWJ

Monks Pond, Trappist, Kentucky

August 18, 1968

Dear John:

The other day the program etc. came in for a meeting I am to attend in Darjeeling (India) in October. Your Dad and I are both on it. So there is no point in keeping anything secret from him any longer as the kitty is well out of the sack. I will meet him there, if all goes well, and we will talk of my going to Taipei. It would still be a fine thing if I could get back into the mountains for a month or more or less retreat there. Any ideas or new leads would be appreciated. I still expect to be there in January or February. I have also been invited for a time to our monastery in Hong Kong.

Very hot here now. Take care of yourself and let me know when you are going to Asia (if). My best to you and Terry.

Blessings,

Tom

PART VI
In Memoriam OF JOHN C. H. WU

CENTENNIAL VIGNETTES: LIFE WITH FATHER

John Wu, Jr.

INTRODUCTION

These six vignettes, some lengthy and some short and embracing the serious to Zen-like jocularity, I present in loving memory of a parent whose presence in my life rather than dimming grows with the years. The stories and anecdotes include my dear mother who also played an integral part though, perhaps, in a more subtle, hidden way in my formation. She too celebrated her centennial birthday the same year my father did, on September 19. The sketches hopefully are as enjoyable to you the reader as they were to me in writing them.

My beloved father was a high-wire performer, one foot on earth, the other tilting merrily skyward. His ambiguities and contradictions and his shamanic-like ability to hold on to and to thrive by polarities evidenced the deep, inner person who understood the secrets of unbounded, rapturous flight. Scholar and man of vision to those who knew him and his writings, he was to my siblings and me all flesh and blood, so solidly grounded in both spheres that he could matter-of-factly travel from one to the other.

In his 87 years—nine rich decades in which he brought delight to others—he gave us the full scope of his humanity: deep, extensive learning, joy, and humor, wisdom, passion and not least of all childlike simplicity. He was also quite capable of sorrow and loneliness, and, on occasion, he displayed fits of Thor-like anger, which shortly after their explosions he would regret with a good deal of self-reproach and remorse before his bewildered children.

Life with him made me cognizant of the conceivability and, more importantly, the *inner demand* of fulfilling my own humanity. I came to know the necessity of living in such a way that the forces within may be brought together to help liberate this greatly anticipated fecundity that comes to those sharing and living the life of faith. That faith, in addition to the mere notion of simple belief—which, being an unfathomable mystery is in itself profound enough—lovingly adopts the life-long working out of a meaning that only the human creature and his Creator have privy to.

Father left us numerous legacies, each a clear indication of the depth and breadth of his existence. Yet, what he himself might most wish for us to bring to bear in our lives was his careful attentiveness to personal, divinely-ordained gifts, their untiring cultivation, and the faithful observance of those responsibilities that go with them. For he believed, in coming to know and love such conviviality, even as we struggle to make sense of things, we might also very well gradually come to thrill to the delicious pleasures of traipsing and concerted and syncopated singing with the Godhead, his angels and saints in the heavens, while fulfilling our most common duties on this little spot in the vast universe.

With him, the extraordinary became ordinary, the ordinary extraordinary—which he learned from both Lao Tzu and St. Thérèse of Lisieux, the Little Flower. And it was for him the Incarnation— God, *inconveniently* (for, could it be otherwise?), bursting upon earth—that made such alchemy possible. For with this inexplicable explosion that even dwarves the Big Bang, life became nonstop epiphanies of the Eternal, leaving its decisive mark everywhere.

If my father's books and writings are not in fashion today, might not this speak more perhaps of our own rather narrow preoccupations than it does about the man himself? In retrospect, the century of which we have been a part—decades of unspeakably cruel destructive political, military and technological agendas and marked by our uninterrupted infatuation with daily bursts of information that seems to usurp crassly and unthinkingly the spaces within what ought rightly to be the province of *solitude*—the twentieth century was not of great intellectual or spiritual ferment. Glitz, yes; greatness, no.

Yet, my dear father—we remembering that his long life took in *our* era as well, and therefore, one confined by similar limitations— was nonetheless able to imbibe and make use of the best of what he assimilated. A man of renaissance interests, he was somehow able to savor and live out fully the best of his Eastern traditions and those of the West as well.

If he had any personal agendas, it might have lay in his passionate endeavor to salvage and to bring illumination to what Hannah

Arendt fitfully described as "dark times" treasures we have over-looked and discarded. His uncommon foresight was that he saw angelic and godlike elements in a groveling, hapless humanity even as we, being unaware of the presence of anxious wings that would enable us to go skyward and beyond our narrow selves, choose to navigate safer grounds and paths, preferring shadows, even shadows of shadows, to the sunlight.

May we not also say he remains inaccessible—perhaps, tragically so—because we, in failing to remain attentive to our own gifts, have made it difficult for ourselves to enter into the sort of dialogue that an understanding of his life and ideas would demand? While his unstintingly deep and broad scholarship will likely remain a daunting task to quarry for any age, there is in addition an underlying hard-to-get-at quality that the scholar, no matter how intellectually astute, might still find impenetrable. That particular quality was *simplicity*, what Mencius the Confucian associated with a *childlike heart*. Simplicity—though father himself would have added, there was nothing simplistic about it—guided him in all things, including his political ideas and concept of the Law.

A first-rate biographer and scholar while gaining access into a good part of my father's mind may otherwise skirt the *whole* person, for he or she might fail to see the guilelessness that formed the man; conversely, if the writer should love his simple candor and bounteous spiritual virtues yet be blind to the role that learning and intellectual nurturing constantly played in my father's life, that person too might very well altogether miss the man. A Confucian to the core, father never tired in stressing his deeply held belief that it was only through the constant flow and interplay of ideas that the spirit could feel its freest moments to do its most natural work in us.

Hence, even as he allowed Divinity to hound and track him down, his faith was of such richness he naturally understood that each genuine idea contained at its source a beginning and an end without which the idea would be stillborn. That is the reason why in both his life and writings one finds this irresistible attention to seek the source of things, a principle he might very well have learned as a child from *The Great Learning*.

Here we come to a triad of significant realities that absorbed his life: *nature, nurture, and grace*.

Father seemed to have grasped intuitively the crucial engagement of these three indispensable realities—which make up a seamless whole—of having seen existentially the necessity of such forces working in dynamic balance and unison so that knowledge can operate in us and penetrate our being in a fully *rational* sense. Each, he believed, fueled and needed the others for its fulfillment. If he found the times disjointed, he saw the confusion the result of a tragic constriction of life, resulting in a nearly universal *ennui*, and a vanishing of interest in pursuing not so much the self—for which many of us may indeed even have an abnormal obsession— but in becoming unmindful of the *source* from which the self finds genuine expression and through which things are informed and draw sustenance, as though from a compassionate Mother.

This inability to connect life with its wellspring and therefore with the love that emanates from it he clearly delineated as directly related to loss of faith in interiority. In such a condition, we find ourselves strangers wandering aimlessly in our own interior castles, at times even as we wander, without an inkling of its priceless existence. Life, consigned to the episodic, in which exterior wares and concerns are substituted for interiority, drifts senselessly and takes on a desultory, restless quality signified by homelessness and despair.

Hence, whatever disjointedness we find in the world is reflected in our own failure to recognize the fundamental mystery of our being and the Creator, who supports its every breath. Father would not have disagreed with the contention that one's authentic being could not be evoked if there is no fundamental faith in a Totally Personal Other. He would insist that the self find authenticity in a source other than itself, in a divine Being from whence our personality is ultimately derived.

Father was of the conviction that the authentic self, or what he sometimes called the *aboriginal self*—borrowing a coinage from the American Transcendentalist, Ralph Waldo Emerson—must never be confused with the empirical ego that can be measured, talked about and, worst of all, manipulated by social engineers. Here he would be echoing the existentialists, Gabriel Marcel and Karl Jaspers. In the end, he fully supported the simple yet celestial dignity of the human person, for he could not in his daily existence help but catch sight of Christ in each of us. Moreover, he had the insight in perceiving that the lowlier we are, the more deeply and manifestly the Savior resides within us, or the closer we come to the ideal of the famous Suffering Servant, a precursor of Christ that we read of in the Book of Isaiah.

Hopefully these vignettes will do the service of at least partially reflecting my father's particular way of *seeing*, a vision conditioned by a profound desire for knowledge, natural, innate simplicity, and, most of all, absolute trust in and love of a Personal God Who would understand us *infinitely* more than we would ourselves. Finally, I hope these offerings can be seen as echoing the *Way* and vision of a contemplative who saw, tasted and cherished the myriad diversities that make up life, and who had the wonderful and holy gift of seeing things in their *primordial and undifferentiated Oneness*.

VIGNETTE #1: EDUCATING A SON

Funny how certain notions etch or edge themselves into our lives, taking up permanent residence. At first evidence, they may stand out only in vague relief, and later take on a familiar clarity such that we could not conceive when they were not a part of us. In time they may even become litanies, profound prayers resonating deep in the heart. Or, they could appear like seeds that fall randomly into our lives, a good number dying even at the moment they enter us. Yet, some, without much fuss and for the most part uninvited somehow do take root. Then the precious few that become seedlings assume some significant space, whose presence we are hardly aware of.

We could also see these notions in musical terms that might show themselves first as simple, hardly audible notes. Then, again later they assume a distinct, penetrating voice, a sound quite beyond what one thinks the self could contain and support. One might even suspect they resonate from an unearthly geography, overstepping the scope of the self, beyond an ego that craves to be merely sated materially and emotionally. The music abides in us quietly, nurtured and encouraged by other voices that long for expression, even an audience. Their vying for permanence within makes up the dramatic nature of our lives.

Soon enough, melodies appear, at first simple, then more complex and finally the polyphonic suffuses the self, the result of many voices brought together by a secret, *inexplicable* center that not only holds but imbues everything with its translucency. As we live with these melodies, they take on intelligence and meanings quite their own. In fact, by letting them alone, they enrich us in unsuspecting ways. They challenge and change us, and it seems the more unobtrusive they are and the less fuss we make of them, and the more we allow them simply *to abide*, the more they bear the mark of *timelessness* and surely the more profoundly they affect us, though darkly and in a hidden way.

Some personal experiences I had with my father touched me in ways I've described above, particularly this opening vignette.

Early July 1964. Father and I have just finished a simple lunch of chicken teriyaki at a tiny Japanese-Hawaiian cafeteria near the main campus of the University of Hawaii. A mere hole-in-the-wall, the eatery with its lazily circling ceiling fans nonetheless has a pleasant-enough ambience. I remember well the very heavy-set broadly smiling Samoan women bantering softly about as they ate with much cheer. They had come during the middle of our meal and for one woman, the kindly proprietor had to open both sides of the door to let her in. No one seemed self-conscious about it as everyone gently greeted one another.

Once out on the street in the stifling mid-day heat father and I struggle on a mild incline toward a newly built, twin-tower dormitory. To me, the prefab construction appeared a tasteless, modern monstrosity the world would have been better off without.

In a few days many philosophers, including father, will gather for an extraordinary six-week summer conference in which the campus will serve as home. In those weeks we would listen to and be in the privileged company of some of the most notable thinkers and wise men in the world. They would include Daisetz T. Suzuki, T'ang Chün-I, Thomé H. Fang, Win-tsit Chan and T. R. V. Murti from the East, and John E. Smith, Richard McKeon, Charles Moore and William Ernest Hocking from the West. Unluckily a political crisis back home in India would deprive us of her splendid philosopher and Vice-President S. Radhakrishnan.

They were halcyon days for a twenty-two year old, a time gratifyingly and delightfully spiced with unremitting intellectual and spiritual feasting. I was at a crossroads in every conceivable way and how fortuitous it was that father had suggested I attend this conference with him for, in retrospect, it would indeed be the nearest I've ever come to be in the presence of humans with what I perceived at the time as godlike qualities.

My eyes are fixed toward the direction we are plodding, and both the heat and the God-awful, rectangular boxes in the distance irritate me. I complain of how empty the whitewashed structures look against the magnificent Hawaiian blue sky. Father, huffing and puffing, but not usually a complainer, sighs audibly and answers with a favorite phrase, "Yes, *don't I know it.*"

At 65, no longer young with a head full of white hair, but still vigorous, he catches his breath, wipes sweat trickling down both cheeks onto his neck, and continues,

"*Whited sepulchers.* Yes, that's what those buildings remind me of—whited sepulchers—you know *whitewashed tombs.* How Christ in Matthew's Gospel describes the Pharisees and the hypocrites. No doubt he was suggesting they were, like the tombs, clean and white on the outside, dressed in lovely flowing robes, but within they carried dry, decaying bones. Pretty harsh words all right. You know, people adorning themselves in gorgeous garments to embellish their external selves so that they need never expose their empty inner selves.

"So, you see how very frank and direct Christ could be in his use of language when he wanted to be, when he wanted to make a point, to teach a lesson through the use of a symbol or simple parable. He would have made a poor diplomat . . . wouldn't have liked being one at all. He spoke his mind and didn't care what others thought . . . what the goodie-goodies thought. He could be tactful, but he was likely to say what he had to say, without weighing his words. But, *don't you see*, he was absolutely right about the Pharisees and people like them?"

Ordinarily, being my wont, I would have intoned something sarcastic or, at least, something like, "I see, indeed!" especially on such a sweltering noonday. But being deferential in father's company, I am even reverential, and I manage to hold my young, often slippery Asian-American tongue.

A spell of silence, then some small talk about how he has to get on with his paper ("The status of the individual in the political and legal traditions of old and new China"). It is not a paper he especially wanted to deliver for by then law was no longer a priority for him and he had since 1960 or so been doing serious work on Chinese philosophy, especially Zen. Perhaps it was more than a coincidence the change corresponded with the passing of my mother in November 1959. But onus as this academic duty was to him, he was still after four decades regarded as a legal expert and there was no way the conference committee would have allowed him to speak on Chinese philosophy, least of all Zen.

374 • John Wu, Jr.

We chitchat casually about matters of more immediate concern. Both of us are especially excited about our planned visit with the legendary 94-year-old Suzuki, the Japanese Zen master, in his hotel room off Waikiki Beach. Suzuki had nearly single-handedly brought Zen to the West. I am bemused thinking of the incongruity of a Zen master living amidst the Mecca of Hawaiian tourism. But, on the other hand, if not a Zen master, then who?

Suzuki had promised to write a preface to father's *The Golden Age of Zen*, the manuscript of which he had just completed and hand carried to Honolulu. Father was now anticipating the visit with the same relish that a child might have for a double-dip ice cream cone on a steamy summer day—like this one.

Funny thing that neither of us ever again mentioned *whited sepulchers* or *whitewashed tombs* or the Pharisees; yet, the seeds of what he said somehow take quiet root in me.

Thirty-five years later, I continue to be struck by this rather ordinary incident, a simple dialogue between father and son on a typically hot mid-summer day when the only reprieve one could wish for was to laze around doing and thinking nothing and simply allowing the trade winds to carry away the heat. Or, going for a swim and taking in the delightful sights of nubile Hawaiian lasses. Every so often, especially since his passing in 1986, particularly during unguarded moments, the singular aura and feel of that day comes back to me with striking, relief-like sharpness, more vivid than when it actually took place—if indeed that is possible.

His high-pitched voice, in clear English tinged with his quaint Ningponese accent (Ningpo, being the seaport capital of Zhejian Province in China) is, as always, strong and direct. Particularly in the words, "*whited sepulcher*," I see clearly the blinding rays of the Island sun reflecting off his glasses as he turns gently to me with his broad, toothy smile. And then there is the litany I hear, though now strangely no longer in his voice but my own: "*You're no whitewashed tomb. Be yourself—for you cannot be anyone else. You came into the world to be more than a tomb!*"

Was it a warning? He had often told me how he disliked, as he liked to say, the "goody-goodies," puritans of every ilk more moralistic than moral, those in their *external* behavior appearing as paragons of virtue, yet, *interiorly* wayward, deceitful and deceiving, unanchored and rootless. He had nearly unfailing antennae in spotting affectation in people who, he would say, become caricatures of themselves by shrinking their minds and hearts in trying to be other than their true selves. They mislay their treasures, warping their capacity for humanity and compassion and every other human quality.

Yet, his criticism of moralistic individuals was balanced by an optimism characterized by the strong belief that no genuine human treasure—truly, divine seedlings—could ever be lost, only *mislaid*. He was finally to have learned this lesson at the foot of Christ, his divine mentor but in the beginning from the Chinese ancients, his human mentors, who had prepared him so well for the divine Banquet, which, even on his earthly stay, he had long ago begun to savor.

In short, he believed that nature and grace worked together in us, yet mostly *without our knowing it.* Too wise to be entrapped by the world, he allowed himself the boon and pleasure of seeing miracles and divine seeds ceaselessly falling around him, and to live in such a way as to be always *surprised.* For that was the source of his joy. He thrilled and quickened to mystery and, living as such, nothing in life ever repeated itself.

Nor have I met another person able to spot genuineness as he could. The genuineness could be of people and things, or of books and writers in which he was expert, or ancient histories and traditions, or of what made or did not make sense in the contemporary world. Even in the service of the Roman Catholicism he converted to in his late 30s, or, perhaps, even more so *because* he was a convert, he put his natural constitution and sharp analytical mind to good use in understanding the critical difference between the baby and the dirty water.

He had an instinctive knack in drawing the line between the authentic and the inauthentic, between the merely cultural and the timeless. That is why, in the final analysis, it was the *simple heart* of the Little Flower—St. Thérèse of Lisieux—rather than the famous da Vincis and the Michelangelos and the majestic and formidable cathedrals and basilicas of Europe that finally won his heart and convinced him of the Church's truth and authenticity. His greatness was that he did not confuse the scaffolding for the authentic edifice.

Because he profoundly cherished his newly found religion and its rich traditions—though in his great piety he would always insist it was *God Who had found him*—, it was enough reason for him to feel a great responsibility in keeping a keen lookout for corrosive elements that attacked religion from both within and without. He could be radically progressive only because he was so thoroughly immersed in history and the lives of the saints the Church had nurtured. He loved all such things with a large passion. And, he loved to say, the further one looks back, the further one is able to see into the future. Such paradoxes were for him simple, commonsensical facts rooted solidly in reality and practical in the deepest sense of the word.

Father could be strongly negative with others, even with some of my siblings. On the other hand, being the youngest of thirteen, I was spoiled by both parents and even by my brothers and sisters. Or, particularly after the passing of my dear mother in my teens, seeing that conventional discipline and strong authoritative commands had little effect on me, father was forced to alter his tactics. After mother was taken away from our bereaved family, father tried his best to be our mother, too, and the playing of this impossible dual role really did help to soften his ways, especially mellowing his naturally quick temper.

In fact, he harnessed his temper to such an extent that whenever he did admonish me, especially during the years of my rather troubled young adulthood, he learned to handle me with kid gloves, very gently and cautiously. He never resorted to hell fire and damnation, and he put all preachiness aside, for he knew such ways simply had no effect on me. Instead, he would advise in soft, affectingly maternal tones:

"Johnny, accentuate the positive both in yourself and in others. While it may be true that we will never be able to rid ourselves completely of our negative qualities, however, when we stress the positive, we can at least diminish or neutralize the negative in us. In so doing, you allow basic goodness and other merits within you greater play for natural growth. This is how you practice justice towards yourself and others. And before you know it, you will feel grace working palpably in you. Then you will actually see how very much God loves you, that he wants you to be good for that is our only destiny."

In allowing the newly found gentleness to wash over him, his spirituality seemed to deepen remarkably. This softening and a deeper reflective self emerged most conspicuously after the loss of mother, during the time he and Thomas Merton corresponded

(1961-68), and when he once more immersed himself in the study of the Little Flower, philosophical Taoism and Zen. As one rereads those writings today, one is struck by the way these seemingly different traditions harmonize with one another. And they do so only because he had initially found their oneness in his own heart.

In being father and mother to me, he was also becoming an excellent psychologist. He knew well the excessive critical bent of my character and did not want to encourage either the argumentative or the disagreeable, to allow such potentially pernicious influences to paralyze or infest my yet youthful developing self. He knew well too how easily I could fall prey to casuistic ways as I was ever ready to criticize others and, in doing so, hurt them and myself.

In college, once when I brought up the subject of entering the law profession as a possible future career, he unexpectedly turned indifferent to the whole discussion. I did not know the reason for his sudden irritability towards what I thought a harmless idea until some time later. While he did not give a definitive *no*, his lack of encouragement was, for me, enough to discourage such a path. One assumed any father would have been elated over a child following him into such a potentially lucrative trade. Not father. Of course, he may have thought I lacked the intellectual equipment to be a success at it. On the other hand, he may also have so well understood my budding, small-minded combative and manipulative spirit that he feared legal practice might reinforce and in time dominate and perhaps wreck my life and character. Unlike other paterfamilias, he refused to give high place to professional success.

Later, it also dawned on me father was perhaps as fine a judge of character as a Thomas More, a lawyer himself and perhaps the one man he came close to worshipping. In fact, when I think of his lukewarm response I am reminded of the story of Sir Thomas. While Chancellor of England for Henry VIII, More reproved Richard Rich for his ambitious ways, for Rich too had studied law, in his case, mainly as a steppingstone to a future political position. Instead, Sir Thomas counseled Rich to remain simple, and, in fact, to become a teacher.

Rich did not take More's warning to heart, later indeed assuming the Chancellorship of England, and even had an important hand in bringing about More's subsequent downfall and beheading. I am of course not suggesting that I am in any way Richard Rich, but it does strike me as curious that one of the few movies father and

I saw together was "A Man for All Seasons," based on the great More's well-known struggles with his conscience over what to do with his king.

When I finally became a teacher, father was nearly beyond himself with joy. He seemed to have wished all along that I would take education as my calling. In retrospect, it is probably the only profession that I myself could have found contentment and fulfillment in. As a teacher himself, he understood the limited degree to which a teacher's cleverness could be extended before his fraudulent ways are rudely exposed, if not by students, then surely by one's own conscience. Having himself been for a short time a practicing attorney, he did not see such safeguards in the ferocious dens that govern the practices of the legal profession.

In fact, in *Beyond East and West*, we read that even before he had taken his first course at the University of Michigan's School of Law in 1919, he was already quite aware of the overly materialistic bent of young American law students of his day. Indeed, he had no illusions about the actual profession as it was conventionally practiced, though he had a lifelong love for the philosophy of law; perhaps the reason for this devotion was that he knew the *source* from whence the law is derived, as well as its potential as a civilizing tool for humanity. Had he not after all in his younger days thought of the Law as his *idol*?

W*hited sepulcher*. A warning? A mild rebuke? In reflection, I now see it as a gentle slap on a consciousness that he somehow knew was on the verge of awakening. How refreshing to have had a father who never spoke of the importance of being a professional success! He wanted nothing more from me than that I always *be* myself, that I enter paths—no matter how crooked—that would lead to true self-discovery, not a mere mirage of the self. He wanted me to come upon the self that God had, in his ineffable generosity, decided even before the dawning of time to bring into being. Perhaps his words were along the order of a Zen *koan* that helped situate a young searching soul on some path leading to possible future enlightenment and authentic engagement with life. And had not the image of a whitewashed tomb in time evolved for me into a perfect metaphor, suggesting a genuine awakening, or a rising from the dead from this fragile, passing earth?

And, is it not strange, father himself might ask in wonderment, that even on this small piece of ground inhabited by countless groveling and laughably inept human beings, where we are given the chance to work out our salvation and where we seem caught in the maelstrom of time, *eternity*—if we were only free enough to let our inmost hearts play *joyously* with time—yes, even eternity may somehow shade imperceptibly into the everyday and give us a welcomed glimpse into *whose* image we really are and for *whom* we were made? Lucky man, my sweet father. He found these answers in the midstream of his journey, unswervingly followed its Path, never looking back. He never regretted resting his will on God. With one of his favorite saints, the great Spanish mystic, St. Teresa of Avila, he could very well say without any irony, "Solo Dios basta"—"Only God suffices."

Vignette #2: Progressive Education

My brother Stephen, our parents' 10th child and 8th boy, is an inimitable storyteller who some time ago related the following that I shall do my level best to replicate, as if he himself were telling it. The reader must judge for yourself whether it is apocryphal or not:

"In Rome one day, Peter, Vincent and I (numbers 8, 9 and 10, respectively, on the hierarchical sibling ladder) received our monthly report cards. We were in our early teens. As usual, we went into daddy's study individually, one by one. Peter, being the eldest of the three, felt privileged to go in first. In fact, he was for good reason beaming from ear to ear for, you see, after having struggled academically in China where he went to over a dozen schools, he was now on his way to becoming the best student among us. When daddy saw all the A's, he said simply, not with much excitement, 'Oh, Peter, very good, keep it up.' Peter, as one might expect, walked out of the study a bit crestfallen, his lips pouting.

"Next, Vincent, with some well-founded trepidation, brought his report card in to show daddy. Unlike Peter, he was rarely an exceptional student. Now, surely this was not because he had less intelligence than us but rather he could always invent some daffy foolishness to occupy his broad imagination. His older siblings—to his face—and some younger brothers and sisters—mostly behind his back—did not call him "buffoon" for nothing. When daddy saw his grades with all the C's on it, he reacted in nearly similar fashion as he had toward Peter's A's: 'Oh, Vincent, keep it up,' even adding a cheery 'very good.' Vincent heaved a great sigh of relief, smiled handsomely and departed happily by knocking over a few classics in executing a less-than-perfect cartwheel as he left the study.

"Finally it was my turn. I walked in, not knowing exactly what to expect for, unlike my brothers', my grades were far more diverse, running the entire spectrum from A to F. Daddy, after careful examination and with much appreciative nodding, looked up and said with a grin, 'Oh, Stephen, wonderful, wonderful, how *musical* you are! Good, good, keep it up and you may yet have a future in music!' Little did he know at the time that Francis would turn out to be the real musician in the family!"

In Stephen's many tellings of the above anecdote, I must confess I have never for a second believed that such an incident took place *exactly* as he has described it. Particularly when it comes to Vincent's cartwheel. On the other hand, though Child Number 10 might have exaggerated and embellished some of the facts—as all great storytellers are wont to do—the little incident does represent perfectly for me father's true *élan*. Is it any wonder, I now ask, that he was never seriously considered for the position of his country's Minister of Education? Let us just conclude he was much too far ahead of his time.

VIGNETTE #3: WHY MEDDLE WITH THE YOUNG?

In Taipei in the mid-70s, I remember father at a private dinner in the presence of well-known educators when, towards the end of a typically sumptuous meal, the talk turned to educational reforms. One distinguished-looking, middle-aged lady, a principal at a famous girl's private high school, spoke glowingly of her school's newly-established Parents-Teachers Association, an organization that long ago in the West had become part and parcel of educational institutions. Only then had the PTA become an innovation in Taiwan. In such company, the well-coifed principal obviously expected nothing more than polite words from those around her. After listening courteously to her and other peoples' responses, father cleared his throat and gave his thoughts on the matter. What he said would leave some with gaping mouths.

"You know, I see what most of you are saying. On the surface, the PTA looks like a wonderful idea. No one can deny it is good for parents and teachers to talk, even becoming friends. Surely there is no harm in teachers finding out more clearly their students' family backgrounds, interests, hobbies, so on and so forth. *But . . .*"

I had sensed the *"But . . ."* coming, and, with it, everyone seemed to have sat up straighter and their attention more riveted on our distinguished Chinese scholar, now in his mid-70s. He was after all the Honorary President and head of the doctorate program in philosophy at what was then the College of Chinese Culture in Yangmingshan, a mountainous suburban area of Taipei still possessed of virgin forests.

"But I beg to add some words on this important question. In the principle governing the Parents-Teachers Association I think we would all naturally think how wonderful it is for parents and teachers to work together. And, at least, on the surface, I agree with its importance. However, *in the spirit of justice*, there is one significant point we all seem to overlook. We fail to give enough attention to what young students feel about such an idea and organization. In fact, as I see it, the young don't seem to have much choice in the matter, do they? After all, it wasn't they who initiated its inception.

"Don't you see, at home, our children must already contend with pressures from their parents. At school, from early morning until late afternoon, they are under the control of teachers. Now, when two such authorities and social forces come together to set up an association with the intention of comparing notes on our young people, in fact, sometimes quite *intimate* notes, don't you see the *added* pressure we are unconsciously inflicting on the young?

"I don't deny the PTA can be of enormous help in understanding our students better. But I also think sometimes the PTA, rather than being of real help, just as often makes our children feel that parents and teachers are in a *conspiracy* against them, or are even being *spied against*. The better and well-behaved students, our model students, may not feel the pressures too greatly, but surely the great majority must have some negative feelings towards it. Frankly, it's a great wonder to me that not *more* of us, young and old, suffer psychological distress because of the kind of artificial society we have created and must live in.

"Don't you think we educators have now become too concerned with organization and control and the collecting of all kinds of data on students in an effort to pry more deeply and intimately into their private lives? We become so concerned with such things that we fail to give proper attention to the deeper needs of the young, and particularly we *forget the importance of letting children grow naturally in freedom.*"

Father had certainly not intentionally meant to dampen an otherwise pleasant dinner party. By the time he finished, there were many tight-lipped, red faces around the table. No had expected an educator of his renown to make such statements about an institution that nearly everyone worldwide regarded as a positive, even sacred, educational innovation. Though I did not feel it my place to support him, as I was his son and one of the younger people there, secretly, I felt both great surprise and pride at his words, which I found sympathetic and down-to-earth.

He was, indeed, sometimes the impractical mystic many thought he was, but what most of us failed to see was that he also possessed a wonderful common sense that went so naturally along with his deep-running spirituality. Add to that the enormous faith he had for the young and people in general.

In seeing the PTA from his perspective, he was in fact suggesting that genuine educational reforms lay, first of all, in both parents and teachers recovering a basic understanding of their respective roles, and then having the courage to put them into practice. I believe his words merely reflected the spirit of a true and genuine *Confucian,* for few ideas were more dear to him than the implementation of *cheng ming* (正名), or what in the West we have called the "rectification of names." On the other hand, in the way that he defended the independence and freedom of children and their *innate* ability to correct themselves without undue interference from either parents or teachers, he was being a true *Taoist* as well.

But, like any true *Taoist,* father was no mere libertine. Rather, he was against all extremes and excesses, and regarded each person a *sacred vessel* that, especially in the case of children with sensitive souls, ought not to be tampered nor meddled with, but rather let alone to grow as spontaneously as possible into itself. In a sense, his particular attitude toward the PTA reflected in miniature the way he approached the law and life.

To his insightful mind, the PTA was simply another of the countless meddlesome human institutions that, though possessed of noble principles and goals, in time spoil and interfere with the natural processes of life. To him, such institutions excessively fuss over persons and things that are often best left alone. Characteristically, father was always in favor of preserving whatever was natural through moderate nurturing. He could in good conscience say with Aristotle, "Perfection is the enemy of the Good," and with Lao Tzu, "To be overgrown is to decay" (#55).

I think what he said that evening—a kind of gentle admonition to his fellow educators—simply reflected the proper proportionality of nature and nurture, of what constitutes authentic human existence. Father was rarely content with anything short of the dynamic balancing of the two. Here he not only defended his own tradition, but the best traditions of East and West.

Years later, I was rather enthralled to find in Emerson's essay, "Education," the following words nearly mirroring father's thinking on the education of the young:

"I suffer whenever I see . . . a parent or senior imposing his opinion and way of thinking and being on a young soul to which they are totally unfit. Cannot we let people be themselves and enjoy life in their own way? You are trying to make that man another *you*. One's enough.

Emerson continues: "The secret of Education lies in respecting the pupil. It is not for you to choose what he shall know, what he shall do. It is chosen and foreordained, and he only holds the key to his own secret. By your tampering and thwarting and too much governing he may be hindered from his end and kept out of his own. Respect the child. Wait and see the new product of Nature. Nature loves analogies, but not repetitions. Respect the child. Be not too much his parent. Trespass not on his solitude."

It should not come as a surprise that the great Boston Brahman, along with Walt Whitman, were among father's favorite American men of letters. To him, there was a good deal more of Lao Tzu in Emerson (as Lin Yutang also felt) than many a Chinese *Taoist*. He would have been happy to be spoken of in the same breath as Emerson, who may have looked and dressed as neatly as a Confucian but whose Bostonian heart clearly and manifestly showed the ancient, time-honored Taoist palimpsest.

VIGNETTE #4: FILIAL PIETY AND JUSTICE

Besides finding perfect peace in being both a Confucian and a Taoist, father was also a defender of true justice. This should not surprise anyone familiar with his juristic writings and his practices as a judge in the Shanghai courts. In *Beyond East and West*, he tells us what made him most happy upon his completing the initial draft of the Constitution of the Republic of China was that, though many of the other sections were roundly criticized, some coming under even severe attack, his writings on *human rights* remained fundamentally intact. This fact is a part of the public record. However important such constitutional and legal matters were, it was his sense of fairness and equanimity as a father that struck me at least equally as deeply as a son.

I had just turned 19, a typical American freshman with a fledgling interest in intellectual life. Unlike children in other families, however, we had the benefit of father's extraordinary library. At times, to whet my curiosity, I would wander into his study—with or without him there—to browse his collection. He never regarded any child's presence intrusive and was quite happy when any of us took some interest in good books. Although they were in every part of the house, even cluttering the walls of the dining room, his choicest volumes were stacked high everywhere in his second-floor study in seeming disarray.

On this particular day in his presence, I noticed a thin, new book with a dark-green cover, a bilingual edition of *The Hsiao Ching*, or, *Book of Filial Piety*. Looking up from his desk, father noticed my interest.

"Ah, yes, that's a new translation from Hsieh Papa's (Hsueh Kwang-ch'ien's) St. John's University Press. You might be interested in knowing that little book has been so important to the Chinese that some scholars believe it's the basis of Chinese culture and ethics." Father's equanimity was such that whenever he spoke of anything Chinese I do not ever recall his saying "*our* Chinese culture." He was the least chauvinistic person I knew and he thought all cultures, including his own native culture, belonged to the entire world.

Later, while studying Chinese philosophy in Taiwan, I came under the tutelage of Professor Hsieh Yu-wei who indeed did regard *hsiao* as the basis from which all other virtues developed. Father did not think so, but that is beside the point here.

"If you like, just take it and look through it for yourself," he said. Then, coming towards me, he took the book in hand and flipped through its pages. He had already gone through it quite thoroughly, marking its pages with his characteristic red and blue underlining.

"Ah, yes, here it is." He had stopped on chapter 15. "Now, before you start on the first chapter, I want you to spend time reading this first." He handed the book back to me. The chapter heading was, "The Duty of Correction." I thought, well, it's about correction, something that wouldn't interest a nineteen-year-old. Must be on how parents ought to correct their children. Nothing different from what I understood filial piety to be.

My eyes, however, soon fell on words he had underlined in red. I read quickly, "Dare I ask if a son, by obeying all of his father's commands, can be called *filial?*" To which Confucius, perhaps irritated, answered, "What kind of talk is this? What kind of talk is this?" Living on the East Coast and not far from New York City, I naturally and whimsically imagined Confucius speaking these words with a nasal New York accent, and I might even have chuckled to myself thinking about it.

He took the book in his hands again and told me to listen carefully while he read what he felt were wonderful and important words: "If a father had one son to reason with him, he would not be engulfed in moral wrong. Thus, in case of contemplated moral wrong, a son must never fail to warn his father against it; nor must a minister of state fail to perform a like service for his prince. In short, when there is question of moral wrong, there should be correction." Then, with his usual deep sigh, as if he were directing the following question to me personally, he read slowly, enunciating each syllable, *"How can you say that filiality consists in simply obeying a father?"*

As he did not particularly like the word "correction," he felt that "remonstrate" would convey the meaning more fittingly.

While teaching in the ROC, I have brought up this incident on countless occasions to illustrate the broad, two-way dialogical ethics that many believe central to classical Confucianism. I cite it also to indicate our father's eagerness in showing his own flesh and blood the true and broad responsibilities of children towards parents, as well as of subordinates towards their superiors. Genuine filial piety and respect lie far deeper than in mere kowtowing or obsequious obedience to those above us.

He might have initially pointed out those particular passages to illustrate a critical and central feature of Chinese ethics, to wit, its strongly implied significance of finding one's place in the universe through personal dialectics as set forth by the ancients. He knew too that through the many centuries, such a basic ethics has been conveniently and disingenuously forgotten by parents, educators and others, by anyone in positions of power and authority.

The above incident captures well two important characteristics in father's life. The first was his natural bent for openness and objectivity, his steadfast insistence in getting to the heart of any matter, whether it was the Law or Zen or even something of seeming insignificance to the untrained eye. As children, we were often privy to seeing him reveal his thoughts and feelings to others. The professional status of those he directed his words seemed always secondary in importance, and I cannot remember him ever compromising his position because of the person he was addressing. He remained true to himself, being *his true self* in word and deed.

Secondly, his maturing years—perhaps, from age 35 onward—found him increasingly working to salvage basic universal cultural treasures which he felt were being preempted and overtaken by the juggernaut of modernity and a too strong emphasis on unchecked technological development. To a fault, he disliked any tendency to bisect and divide life into different parts and categories; he knew this contributed to the furthering of alienation within each person and among people and societies.

Even more so, he saw thick encrustation growing over much of ancient literature that held irreplaceable treasures. Consequently, he regarded his true vocation not as a rash and blind return to some slavish traditions, but as recapturing our collective habit of seeing the past as *living* moral and spiritual fibers needed to guide us back to our lost roots. Yet, differing from the mystical-oriented and solitaries with little or no faith in technological progress, he walked the middle path convinced that technology could be put to good use if its development is directed not by unthinking forces but by *illuminated* intelligence.

On the other hand, his wisdom informed him the only discerning guide would come from a fully-grown humanity that knew well where our societies were heading, and, most crucially, *why* it was going in that direction. As a champion of the Natural Law, he was never able or willing to see the universe as indifferent. By the time he had passed on, it was obvious the world, fixated on itself, was no longer asking the same essential questions so dear to his heart.

Intellectually and morally, he was simply unable to entertain the possibility of any world-view, which was neither *eschatological* nor *teleological*, that is, one that did not contain within itself a beginning and a final purpose. Here, again, he was drawing inspiration from some of the richest classical traditions including the *Holy Bible* and the *Four Books*, the latter the classic canon of the Chinese that school children as late as the first decades of the 20th century would put to memory.

In this harshest of centuries that has been driven by a strikingly wanton sense of pragmatism, ruthless social and political tyrannies of unimaginable tragic dimensions, and the ongoing absolutizing of undirected whirlwind progress, father's life and writings can be seen as a conciliatory effort to combat such vast and diversely impersonal and dehumanizing forces. Recovery of humanity and all that is essential to making the person truly human and noble had to begin, for him, with *metanoia*, the moral and spiritual transformation of the self, the recovery of what his Church was wont to call the temple of the Holy Spirit.

Metanoia is the transforming process in which each person is regarded not as a means toward some engineered social and political end but as a *sacred being* holy and incorruptible in and of itself. His underlying message is that we are after all no mere trash bins containing the throwaway and the ephemeral, but delicately made cisterns of unimaginable beauty, each uniquely fired for the purpose of holding sweet nectar *from* and *for* divinity.

To father, whatever is heavenly, because timeless, cannot undergo permanent loss; at worst, having become strangers to the habit of living in permanency and transcendence, we allow the empirical ego with its exhausting and interminable practical concerns to order our lives. He saw this illness plaguing even men and women of religion and institutions. In the meantime, our timeless treasures, temporarily mislaid, are forgotten, and we lose our way. Although a man of countless earthly enthusiasms, father rarely allowed himself to be made inebriated for long by the transient and impermanent, which, by themselves, he regarded as dead dry bones. With Lao Tzu, his soul brother of 2500 years ago, he understood well the priceless and the unassailable:

For a whirlwind does not last a whole morning,
Nor does a sudden shower last a whole day.

(故飄風不終朝,驟雨不終日。)

(TTC, #23)

He knew whirlwinds and showers are found in the unbounded regions of the universal heart through which the Divine, wholly free, come and go according to its will. Life had taught him the difficult and cautionary lesson of not placing excessive worth on anything other than what we each initially bring into the world. He believed in letting things simply *be*, so as to allow them to develop on their own accord with as little fuss as possible. His own words came from an unadorned heart, simple, direct and true, and affected other hearts that were open and receptive to *being*. Perhaps that is why the mere specialist or present-day academic has never been able to enjoy and understand fully either his life or writings.

To the professionals who knew him—the legal experts, philosophers, educators, politicians, even poets and people of religion—he would address and even match their expertise, their breadth of knowledge and intellectual concerns, all of which he himself possessed in large abundance. Yet, in truth, he regarded much of contemporary intellectualism more as chaff than kernel. In the end, he appealed to their *whole persons*, therefore, to their *silence, simplicity* and *interiority*. A marvelous sense of proportion—what the Greeks called moderation and temperance, the Chinese, *Chung Yung, "the middle way"* or *"centrality"* (中庸), and the Christian, prudence. This quality quietly and unfailingly informed whatever he wrote and did. The following translation, his own, from the last part of chapter 38 of the *Tao Teh Ching*, could very well summarize the man:

> Therefore, the full-grown man sets his heart upon
> the substance rather than the husk;
> Upon the fruit rather than the flower.
> Truly, he prefers what is within to what is without.

> (是以大丈夫處其厚,不居其薄;
> 處其實,不居其華.故去彼取此。)

There was such a *oneness* about him that you had to take him complete or not at all. Though thoroughly versed in the Law, he never could master, condone nor allow himself to fall victim to *compartmentalization*, surely one of the great scourges of the 20th century. He could never learn to live a split existence, nor could he be happy in alienation, especially being mired in some self-imposed prison.

There was something wonderfully *organic and whole* about

him; hence when you dissect the man, when you analyze him and his thought in any fine detail, you may somehow miss the mark, ending up with the *not quite*. This was despite the fact he himself was masterly in the art of analysis, which he learned at the foot of some of the truly great legal thinkers and philosophers of the 20th century. But one gets the feeling his analyses were keen only because they were organically connected to some great life force.

He never allowed his profession or, later, his academic interests to dictate the path of his life nor vision of reality. In fact, even in his approach to the Law, he appeared far less interested in furthering its so-called positivistic and evolutionary agendas than in uncovering the *spiritual* and *moral* dimensions of the Law. For without those dimensions giving it support, he knew law would degenerate into mere deadweight, a collection of gross manipulations of what is indelibly written in our hearts. Nothing in his writings is more evident than the conviction that all truly productive human knowledge is anchored on a *hidden source* and carries with it the hope of self-discovery, which, in turn, would help us return to that source. Here, he was wholly one with Lao Tzu who tells us, "To go far is to return."

Ultimately, he believed it was the universal human heart informed steadily and *inflamed ecstatically* by the unquenchable fire of love that brings us back to our True Home. We find him solidly secure in *The Great Learning* (one of the *Four Books*) where we are told that, for everything, there is *a beginning and an end*. His traditional education included being fully versed in the Chinese classics, his childhood Bible. Even as the buds of his Christianity later bloomed into gorgeous bouquets, the Chinese classics remained his ever constant and faithful guide.

VIGNETTE #5

"I WILL GO TO THE ALTAR OF GOD;
TO GOD WHO GIVES JOY TO MY YOUTH"

My parents' coming upon their Catholic faith is documented in *The Science of Love* and *Beyond East and West*. It can also be found in the writings, particularly, *From Confucius to Christ*, of Dr. Paul K. T. Sih, his beloved student and Godson, and *My Twenty Years With the Chinese*, by the Reverend Nicholas Maestrini. The latter first gave father formal instructions in the doctrines of his new faith and, later, urged him to write his autobiography.

To speak of my parents without addressing the question of from where their joy might have sprung would do a disservice to both. Not that I presume to know it profoundly, yet their daily lives offer clear-cut clues as to their motivation and strength.

As a teenager I began to have some intimation as to what made their individual and marital lives special. Through simple example and words, my siblings and I were given a clear glimpse of their piety and an understanding of what held their lives and our large family together. I cannot remember when I did not regard my parents spiritually, as two lives synchronously bound together on a continuous line progressing upward, guided by Providence. Perhaps it was primarily because of seeing them as such paradigms that I have never taken any other idea of progress seriously. I believe my brothers and sisters share these feelings too.

From my early twenties, as I became more familiar with spiritual literature—surely the deepest and most intimate of writings in any tradition—the couple whose piety reminded me of my own parents' were Jacques and Raissa Maritain, whom they had befriended in Rome, and who were also converts. Coincidentally, the French neo-Thomist was ambassador to Italy at the time father was ROC's Minister to the Vatican. Later, the Maritains would carefully chronicle their rich lives together in separate journals.

During their relatively short years together in New Jersey (1951-59), my parents attended daily Mass at a cozy chapel with a tastefully-and exquisitely-designed interior on the campus of Seton Hall University. There, father had first taught law, then Chinese studies. Each morning, hand-in-hand, they would stroll on a steady incline from our home to the Immaculate Conception Chapel for the 8 AM Mass. Ordinarily, the walk would take no more than 6 to 7 minutes, but given my mother's little feet that had been bound as a child and, later, at 12 or 13, unbound, the short walk must have been for her a daily trekking as physically difficult as the Stations of the Cross.

Yet, she ventured back and forth stoically, rarely complaining. A common sight upon her returning home was seeing her seated in an armchair quietly and ritualistically rubbing her sore, contorted feet. To this day, it amazes me that I never heard her use her feet as an excuse to miss this daily sacred ritual. And, in fact, whenever his flesh was not so willing, it was mother who would rouse father from pleasant sleep to make sure they got to the chapel that morning "rain or shine," and sometimes even braving a typically heavy Jersey snowfall as well.

On the subject of Mass and Communion and faith in general, I remember certain notions that in time became common food for my mind. What follow are composite ideas gleaned over little conversations I had with father over the years.

"You might wonder what is the sense of going to Mass each morning. Let me tell you that I literally thrill with joy just at the thought of being with Christ at the beginning of each day! Do you know what is the first thing your mommy and daddy do the moment we get to the little chapel? We kneel before the altar *in total silence and emptiness.* Now, what do I mean by this? Just this. We come to God empty-handed with loving and grateful hearts. Since the Mass is a banquet, a joyous celebration of a meal and remembrance of the life of Christ, what better way to start the day than to *feast* with our Lord and to thank him for this incomparable nourishment?

"We carry our burdens *and* joys daily to His altar to offer them to Him completely. He knows what to do with them. As we come to a deeper understanding of being Christ's disciples, we see ourselves no more than instruments our loving Father has somehow chosen in his mercy, *for yet another day,* to do *his* bidding, *his* chosen work on earth. We come to him not with any great offerings of which, in and through ourselves, we in fact have none and, even if, humanly speaking, our offerings were in the eyes of humans something noble and great, they after all *originate* and belong to Him in the first place."

"Frankly, aside from our unconditional love and gratefulness, Our Lord doesn't need any of the things we have or whatever else we could give him. You see, in offering our total selves to Him, we become *fully dead to the world,* for the only thing we have then is an *empty self* completely at His beck and call. He fills up whatever we lack so that our lives might even *lack a lack!* If we ever try to fulfill our lives in this way ourselves, psychologically we might end up totally neurotic, but *God makes up the difference.* He makes up for whatever we cannot do ourselves—if we would only allow Him this pleasure. The only wisdom mommy and I have is that we know when to and when not to let go, to play our little roles well and remember always *to let God play Himself,* and never allow ourselves to play God."

"In my case, I find myself much like a broken cistern, full of cracks. I am incapable, by my own ridiculously insignificant efforts, of sealing the cracks so that the cistern would be able to hold something valuable. But, in his mercy, he pities my broken-ness by sealing those cracks that would then be able to hold the treasures he has given me, thus making me *whole* again each morning."

"Or, sometimes, I see myself as water held in a crude pot anxiously awaiting transformation. In his hands, he not only cleanses the impure, stagnant water but, without my knowing it, I find myself suddenly swimming in and consuming the finest of His vintages. The intoxication can be thoroughly overwhelming! Without being conscious that it is Our Heavenly Father who is secretly at work within us, our lives could easily degenerate into one of pride. But once we are aware of his *presence* and the hidden work he does within us, our entire being becomes washed over with and cleansed by his grace."

"Mommy and I live in total gratefulness for the continuous, ever-recurring miracle that cannot for a second *not* be happening. In my case, I can only humbly fall on my knees and say with an overflowing heart, 'Imagine, dear Lord and Master, you can even make a decent man out of an unfit scoundrel like myself!'"

"When mommy and I approach the altar each new morning, when we offer our lives to Him, we let *Him* decide who and what will benefit from our earthly work. For, in fact, by going to Him in this simple way, as children might madly race toward the open arms of a loving parent, our sometimes laborious tasks of life He takes out of our hands, sanctifies them and lifts them to His divine level. And He does this without our knowing it. That is, it is *He who mercifully unburdens us*, and the question as to what is and is not *efficacious* in what we say and do is at once no longer a concern to us at all. Without this divine participation in which Our Lord unburdens us, we humans would simply be incapable of living even an iota of freedom."

"And you cannot imagine to what degree of freedom He is capable of granting us—just for our asking. And, since in truth God is both Father *and* Mother, how could any truly earnest requests not be granted? If even our own mothers and fathers can so easily be touched by our sincere entreaties, how could *God*—infinitely greater than our own dear parents—not be touched by what we seek?"

"*Don't you see*, when we are still concerned about what will and will not benefit us and others, when we are troubled by every little thing—as Martha and even some Apostles in the Gospels seem to be—we are not yet living in *simplicity* and *freedom*. I did not really understand the meaning of our working and living only for the glory of God until I understood it to mean that only when we are detached from *both* success and failure can we truly give to others in a *selfless* way, and thus concretely live our lives in joy, freedom and simplicity. The secret is to live without motives."

"But if we must live with some motive, then let it be in pleasing God, who has given us everything. For when we please him, nothing else matters, as He has promised to take care of everything else. So, you see, how could your mommy and daddy live their lives other than in *inexplicable joy*? Having such a large family, we realize even our burdens and sufferings are given to us as *rare gifts* that will help us attain the greatest of all possible good, which of course is reunion with our true Lover. In comparison, all other earthly goals and successes and achievements are no more than counterfeit and dross."

The hallmark of my parents' lives was the steadfast daily living out of their religious beliefs. More than any other aspect of their lives together, the day-to-day working out of their salvation was what defined them. They lived their faith to the bone, rarely allowing other concerns to interfere with what they recognized as God's personal work in their souls. As for father, the crowning deed of his life, beyond all worldly achievements, which included his fine writings, lay in the inseparability of his intellectual life and everyday existence.

In his late 30s, days following his religious conversion, father gradually discovered that all words and deeds are forms of prayer, likened to sacred cables, offerings of praise and, especially, *love letters* that we adoringly address and send to our Redeemer. He had embarked upon a way in which his entire life he perceived as a fragile string of prayers serving as steps that he earnestly hoped, with the grace of God, might help him reach the Gates of Heaven. He took the Incarnation—the appearance of God on earth in the person of Christ—quite literally, so much so that, to him, the Holy Trinity, in its love for humankind, could not help but insinuate itself upon our lives through its endless earthly epiphanies.

Might we not say, too, that the secret of the man lay in that his *life of reason* could not be seen apart from his *life of faith*? Here, he resoundingly echoes St. Augustine. Reason and faith, like the fluid, unlabored wings of a bird in jovial flight, existed in such nearly perfect symmetry that he was able to soar effortlessly, with perfect grace into some uncharted reaches of his soul. We can only imagine what bliss such joyful flight must have been to him!

VIGNETTE #6:

THE TEACHER, HIS HAVANA,

AND THE GENTLE BEAST

Sometimes father was quite capable of using downright earthy humor to drive home a point, even a philosophical one. To me it was in the classroom that he appeared most at home, where he could simply be himself. During 1967 or thereabouts, he was teaching a class on Zen Buddhism on the South Orange, NJ campus of Seton Hall University. Both Terry Wong, my future wife, and I just happened to be there that evening. Out of the blue, there occurred a rather rich, heated debate among several clever graduate students over some delicate point.

Perhaps it was on the question of what is of greater authenticity and value, *sudden or gradual enlightenment*, a historical controversy of some import in Zen. Or it could have been over the question of what it means or whether it is possible to "*sit oneself into a Buddha,*" or even why a particular Zen aspirant received a solid slap across the face or a kick in the derrière by his master.

It matters little what had brought about the animated exchanges among the normally docile and polite classmates. After all, it was a graduate class on Zen, usually defined by a good deal of meditative thought and smatterings of chuckles over cups of tea. Some students, in imitation of their Chinese mentor, perhaps hoping to find enlightenment, would bring along their own tumblers of bitter green tea. Ordinarily, if the class were small enough, father would instruct at home, where he would indulge himself by using a small porcelain teapot, which he could easily bring up to his mouth. An old quaint habit from China successfully transplanted to New Jersey.

In his fine, dark-blue Chinese silk robe that he often wore to class, and with a long Cuban cigar dangling precariously from his mouth—a rare sight indeed at an American university, and before smoking was outlawed in most classrooms—my father sat beaming and with a bemused look for much of the time the verbal and intellectual skirmishes were taking place. He allowed the discussions to go on for a good ten, fifteen minutes. Then, feeling a bit antsy and from the Havana drawing and exhaling a large puff of smoke that shot up towards the ceiling, he held out his left arm, a bit cocked at the elbow. As the class slowly came to order, he said in a clear, loud voice,

"Good, good, very good discussion, solid exchanges, excellent ideas! You really went at each other vigorously, as though you were in a court of law. Some of you don't know this, I used to be a judge, you know."

You could see the students looking pleased. At the same time you could also feel complacency setting in. Then, seeing that the cigar was about to go out, the teacher poked his right hand inside the robe past the delicately, hand-made Chinese cloth buttons and groped for some object in a hidden pocket. Pronto, there appeared his shiny Ronson lighter, a proud gift from my sister Terry. He then struck it forcibly, whereby a huge flame came up perfectly—as if he had rehearsed it a thousand times—to meet the foul-smelling Havana. He took a few strong quick puffs and, barely skipping a beat, in implacable rhythm, continued:

"I enjoyed everything you said. See here, everything made sense. You're very perceptive and each of you seems to have reasons that, so far as I can see, are airtight, no holes. For a time, I thought I was sitting back in a courtroom listening to future barristers, nearly *déjà vu* for me." Some chuckles echo in the classroom.

Then, still half-teasingly, he said, "I can tell, being trained in the best schools in the West, you are all Aristotelians, masters of logic and the syllogism. *But,*" and here his voice began to rise ever so slightly, "I have to confess one thing. Yes . . . yes. The main trouble I see in your words is that everything really *did* make sense. A lot of sense, in fact. Maybe too much sense." He hesitated, allowing time for this last remark to sink in. This suddenly brought quizzical looks, and he seemed to know exactly why.

"You see, despite your fine arguments, even heated verbal exchanges, nothing you said, indisputable as it all was, *has as much cosmic validity as a simple bowel movement.*" Now, except for a few barely audible, nervous snickers, near total silence greeted his words. Some embarrassing seconds followed. There was much squirming in seats, the mood in sharp contrast to that of a few minutes earlier.

Puffing now furiously on his cigar, the smoke rising and hover-ing heavily overhead, he gave his characteristically slow, sweeping gaze at the entire class, with one hand over his mouth chuckling impishly to himself as he did so, and, I might add, looking more than a little delighted at the confusion his words had generated. Then, nodding and smiling through his scholarly spectacles from one perplexed student to another, he added, his voice now even louder, "*Don't you see?!*"

Playing the Zen master in his fine Chinese silk robe, he had, without their least suspecting it, slapped the unassuming students ever so gently across the face. And, at that second, who could have doubted the instantaneous occurrence of an imperceptible and sensational bowel movement of a more spiritual nature as it rumbled through the stuffy campus?

* * *

On another occasion, this time in a class on the *Tao Teh Ching* at Columbia University, father asked a question related to the text to which, except for a few soft whispers, there was quite a different response—dumbfounded silence. Again, sipping bitter green tea and slowly glancing about the room from left to right, then from back to front, and seeing that there were no raised hands, my father's eyes settled on a large, forbidding-looking German shepherd near the raised podium. The dark, ominous creature was dozing away contentedly and had even been heard snoring intermittently. On that day father appeared to look more like an attorney-at-law than a teacher, being dressed sartorially in his gray business suit.

Pointing ever so gently at the dog lest he disturb it, he addressed the students. "Look at Lucky there, snoring away so blissfully." He called all German shepherds "Lucky," for my brother Stephen, an incurable lover of such creatures, had called his by that name. In fact, he had had two of them, one in Rome, the other in Newark, both of whom father had wisely done all he could to distance himself from. Like many philosophers and poets, he did not take well to dogs, being either fearful of them or finding them too obsequious to his liking. Like T. S. Eliot, he favored the independence of purring cats and enchanting songbirds. In fact, with canaries and parakeets he would spend long intervals enticing them to break into song before returning to work again. In the Columbia classroom, he continued:

"Look at Lucky, in a world of his own, *totally* unaware of what's going on." Those days were before we all became gender conscious and he could safely assume such a beast could only be male.

"I guarantee, in his deep unconscious state, it is practicing perfectly what each of you highly intelligent Ivy Leaguers ought to be mastering—the art of *wu-wei*. Observe him closely: *Tao* goes in, around and through him *effortlessly*. No doors or windows and none of his senses bar or interfere with the *Way* of that docile, sleeping creature. Isn't it marvelous that he lives the *Way* without having any consciousness of it? Most of us—even if we know something of the presence of *Tao*—only know it consciously, by our meddling minds that habitually will not leave things alone. Hence, we end up spoiling everything. *Don't you see*, Lucky is no *ordinary* Columbia scholar?"

His words were immediately greeted by loud, spontaneous laughter, chaotic hand clapping and even foot stomping, the last display imported from among some European students. Such a ruckus rudely jerked the beast from its slumber. Feeling slightly agitated, and looking irritated and hardly conscious it was the center of attention, "Lucky" gave a perfunctory bark, then took sweeping stock of the scene around it. It rose up to stretch, changed its position some 180 degrees, got down quickly again on its haunches, and solemnly weighed whether such an outburst was worth losing sleep and dream over. It made its decision quickly and without much fuss, the big, black-and-gray dog returned to its delicious dreams, letting the mostly unkempt, hippie-like creatures before it go on with their silly diversion. After all, it thought, humanoids regard such raucousness as "fun," but Lucky attending to more serious matters could not possibly have considered it as anything more than much ado about nothing.

* * *

Is there any doubt that my father has returned to Eternity, joining his many friends, among them the Little Flower, Thomas Merton and Dr. Suzuki and, most of all, my dear mother? And, wasn't it a lovely day of wind and moon he was to all of us?

LIST OF CONTRIBUTORS

BENJAMIN ("BEDE") BIDLACK is currently an Assistant Professor of Theology at Saint Anselm College. After completing his M.A. in Chinese Religion at Boston University, he completed his Ph.D. in comparative theology at Boston College. His research includes comparative theology, body theology, and Daoist and Christian anthropology with special interest in internal alchemy and the thought of Pierre Teilhard de Chardin, SJ. During his doctoral dissertation he worked with Teilhard scholar Thomas King and Daoist scholar Livia Kohn and from Boston College with Mary Ann Hinsdale and Catherine Cornille. He recently published "Alchemy and Martial Arts: Wang Yannian's Gold Mountain Daoism" in the *Journal of Daoist Studies* No. 5 (2012). He is currently working on a new comparative study between Teilhard and Xiao Yingsou. The tentative title for his scholarly work is, *In Good Company: The Body and Divinization in Pierre Teilhard de Chardin, SJ and Daoist Xiao Yingsou*. Bede was the former President of Still Mountain Tai Chi Center and Program Coordinator for the Boston College Interfaith Initiative.

LIVIA KOHN graduated from Bonn University, Germany, in 1980. After six years at Kyoto University in Japan, she joined Boston University as Professor of Religion and East Asian Studies. She has also worked variously as visiting professor and adjunct faculty at Eötvös Lorand University in Budapest, the Stanford Center for Japanese Studies in Kyoto, Union Institute in Cincinnati, Ohio, and San Francisco State University. Her specialty is the study of the Daoist religion and Chinese long life practices. She has written and edited thirty books, as well as numerous articles and reviews. Her books include *Taoist Meditation and Longevity Techniques* (1989), *Daoist Mystical Philosophy* (1991), *Laughing at the Dao* (1995), *God of the Dao* (1998), *Daoism Handbook* (2000), *Daoism and Chinese Culture* (2001), *Monastic Life in Medieval Daoism* (2003), *Cosmos and Community* (2004), *Daoist Body Cultivation* (2006), as well as *Meditation Works, Chinese Healing Exercises, Introducing Daoism* (2008), and—most recently—*Daoist Dietetics*

(2010) and *Sitting in Oblivion* (2010). She has served on numerous committees and editorial boards, and organized a series of major international conferences on Daoism. She retired from active teaching in 2006 and now lives in Florida, from where she runs various workshops and conferences, and serves as the executive editor of the *Journal of Daoist Studies*.

LUCIEN MILLER (B.A., 1961; M.A., 1963; Ph.D., 1970, University of California, Berkeley) is Professor Emeritus of Comparative Literature at the University of Massachusetts in Amherst. He has specialized in East-West literary relations and Chinese language and literature. His publications include studies and translations of Chinese fiction and minority folk literature—*South of the Clouds: Yunnan Tales*; *The Masks of Fiction in the Dream of the Red Chamber; Exiles at Home: Stories by Ch'en Ying-chen*; a biography, *Tony Walsh: Alone for Others*, and essays on Buddhist-Christian encounter, the Chinese written character, and Bai minority folktales. His studies of oral folk literature are based upon fieldwork conducted in China and India. Teaching specialties include Buddhism and American culture, contemplative literature, travel and literature, and theory and practice of translation. His Merton work encompasses Merton's encounter with Judaism, Buddhism and Taoism, and Merton's correspondence with John C. H. Wu. He is a Roman Catholic Deacon and Spiritual Director at the Newman Catholic Center at the University of Massachusetts, Amherst.

CRISTÓBAL SERRÁN-PAGÁN y FUENTES is currently an Assistant Professor of Philosophy and Religious Studies at Valdosta State University. Before joining VSU he taught at Goucher College, Illinois Wesleyan University, and Coker College. He received his Ph.D. in Religious Studies from Boston University. The title of his dissertation was, "Mystical Vision and Prophetic Voice in Saint John of the Cross: Towards a Mystical Theology of Final Integration." In this study he adds Merton as a major Sanjuanist commentator. He has a Masters degree in Sacred Theology from Boston University, a Masters degree in Philosophy from Boston College, a Bachelor of Liberal Arts and a Bachelor in Business Administration from St. Thomas University. He is a member of The International Thomas Merton Society and an advisor to the Robert Daggy Scholarship Program. He is a regular contributor to

Merton conferences in Europe and the United States. His publications include articles on Merton and the Spanish mystics in *Thomas Merton: A Mind Awake in the Dark* (Three Peaks Press, 2002) and in *Seeds of Hope: Thomas Merton's Contemplative Message* (Cistercium-Ciem, 2008), and Merton on Dr. King and D. T. Suzuki in *The Merton Seasonal*. He also teaches world religions and Spanish mysticism courses in his native country Spain as part of a study abroad summer program in Madrid.

DONALD P. ST. JOHN is Professor Emeritus of Religion at Moravian College, Bethlehem, PA. He earned his Ph.D. at Fordham University under Thomas Berry. He has served on the Board of Directors for several organizations including the American Teilhard Association. He is former editor of *Teilhard Studies* (1994-2007) and winner of a Catholic Press Association Award (2004) for *Teilhard in the 21st Century: The Emerging Spirit of Earth* which he co-edited. He has published articles on Thomas Merton, Native American Religions and ecological spirituality. He is completing two books, one on Merton as radical ecologist and the other a spirituality for elders based on early Taoist philosophers.

JOHN WU, Jr. is Professor Emeritus of English Language and Literature at Chinese Culture University, Taiwan, ROC. He earned his B.A. degree from Seton Hall University and an M.A. degree in Philosophy from Chinese Culture University. His Master's Thesis was titled, "Eternal Values as Found in Lao Tzu's Tao Teh Ching" (in Chinese). He has published numerous articles on Thomas Merton and Asia including the *Asian Quarterly*, *Chinese Culture Quarterly*, *Cistercian Quarterly*, *The Merton Seasonal*, *The Merton Annual*, *Cross Currents*, and *Inter-Religion Quarterly* in Hong Kong. He is in the process of publishing in Taiwan a Chinese-English dual-language commentary on selected Merton prayers. He is a regular contributor to Merton conferences in Europe and the United States. In 1993 he was invited as the keynote speaker for the Third General Meeting of the International Thomas Merton Society in Colorado Springs, Colorado. John Wu, Jr. was a correspondent with Merton and son of John Wu. He wrote "Gentle Dragon" a preface to *John Wu—Totally Catholic, Totally Chinese and Totally Himself.*

ACKNOWLEDGMENTS

The editor thanks the following persons for their assistance in the preparation of this volume:

- The Contributors for their generous gifts of time and scholarship to this collection.
- John C.H. Wu, Jr. for his guidance and generosity in insuring the publication of the extant correspondence between his father and Thomas Merton.
- Neville Blakemore, Jr. for his professional and patient skills in typesetting this volume.
- Dr. Paul M. Pearson, Director and Archivist of the Thomas Merton Center at Bellarmine University and the Trustees of the Thomas Merton Legacy Trust for their assistance with this volume.
- Danielle Costello, Secretary of the Philosophy and Religious Studies Department at Valdosta State University for her assistance in typesetting one article and to faculty members of my Department for granting me the academic support to work on this volume for the past three years.
- Jonathan Montaldo for his editorial comments and great assistance during the whole process of reviewing the manuscript. Without his help and wisdom this volume would have taken longer time to see the light.
- Livia Kohn for submitting her article in our volume and for the photos that she gave us permissions to print.
- Anne Ogden and Judi Rice for their dedicated, patient, and diligent proofreading.

Additional Credits:

- Unpublished material in the Correspondence between Thomas Merton and John C. H. Wu, and between Thomas Merton and John C.H. Wu, by Thomas Merton. Copyright © 2013 by The Trustees of the Thomas Merton Legacy Trust. Printed by permission of The Thomas Merton Legacy Trust.

- Unpublished Correspondence by John C.H. Wu to Thomas Merton, and by John C.H. Wu, Jr. to Thomas Merton. Printed by permission of the Estate of John C.H. Wu and by permission of John C.H. Wu, Jr., respectively.
- Letters between Thomas Merton and John C. H. Wu from *The Hidden Ground of Love: The Letters of Thomas Merton on Religious Experience and Social Concerns* by Thomas Merton, edited by William H. Shannon. Copyright © 1985 by the Merton Legacy Trust. Reprinted by permission of Farrar, Straus and Giroux, LLC.
- "Man is Born in Tao" by Thomas Merton, from *The Collected Poems of Thomas Merton*, copyright ©1977 by The Trustees of the Merton Legacy Trust. Reprinted by permission of New Directions Publishing Corp.
- "Cutting Up an Ox" by Thomas Merton, from *The Way of Chuang Tzu*, copyright ©1965 by The Abbey of Gethsemani. Reprinted by permission of New Directions Publishing Corp.
- Books and articles quoted or cited in the text under the usual fair use allowances are acknowledged with full publication credits in the footnotes of each chapter.

INDEX

115, 247, 261, 350
"Rain and the Rhinoceros" (Merton)
115, 267
Random House 179, 298
realistic view 118
re-Christianization 148, 189
rectification of names 196, 382
red-head 19
Reformation 89
Reinhardt, Ad 301
relativism 130
religion 1, 2, 3, 6, 17, 87, 88, 89, 91,
110, 130, 177, 246, 290, 375,
376, 387, 388, 401
reliques 215
Republic (Plato) 42
resources 17, 85, 111, 112, 114, 118,
290
respect xv, 15, 85, 109, 134, 157,
185, 192, 212, 220, 237, 256,
385
resurrection 41, 185
revelation 17, 78, 141
reverence 112
Rhenish mystics 223
Ricci, Matteo 87
Rice, Ed 301
Rich, Richard 377
Richard, I. A. 193
Richardson, Jane Marie 142
Rilke, Rainer Maria 318
Rinzai 166, 200, 206, 255
Ross, Nancy W. 298
Ruether, Rosemary Radford 51
Ruysbroeck, John 223

S

sacred vessel 113, 382
sage 1, 3, 6, 7, 9, 33, 35, 36, 39, 42,
52, 58, 59, 74, 77, 105, 198,
249
Said, Edward 89
saint 129, 136, 157, 180, 296, 310
St. John, Donald P. xiv, 103, 403
samadhi 152, 168, 263, 265, 266
sanity 50, 51, 60, 104, 156, 157, 240,
247
satori 158, 252, 256, 309

scandal 153, 335
Schipper, Kristofer 90
Schumacher, E. F. 121
Schwartz, Benjamin 5, 6, 33, 35, 36
Science of Love, The (Wu) 136, 192,
210, 389
Seeds of Contemplation (Merton)
165, 166, 167, 188, 193, 200,
298, 309
Seeds of Destruction (Merton) 92,
258, 265
seeing the essential 164, 176
Seeking Paradise: The Spirit of the
Shakers (Merton) 100, 102
Seidel, Anna 17, 87, 90
Sekiso 291
self and other xv, 75, 82, 150
self-cultivation 1, 2, 3, 5, 6, 8, 10, 11,
12, 15, 16, 17, 21, 25
selflessness 165, 189
Serrán-Pagán y Fuentes, Cristóbal
30, 402
Seton Hall xv, 138, 176, 197, 210,
214, 251, 261, 266, 272, 320,
342, 345, 354, 357, 390, 394,
403
Seven Mountains of Thomas Merton,
The (Mott) 90, 92, 93, 99,
100, 101, 142, 266
Seven Perfected 21
Seven Storey Mountain, The (Merton)
127, 150, 190, 256
sexism 108
Shakers 100, 101, 102
Shakertown 100, 101
Shang-Yin dynasty 237
Shannon, William xv, 48, 52, 53, 54,
57, 61, 85, 91, 99, 103, 104,
147, 311
Sharper, Philip 326
Sheed, Frank (Sheed and Ward) 130,
140, 150, 156, 182, 192, 194,
197, 208, 242, 326
shen 13, 24, 73, 99. See also pure
spirit
Shen Hsiu 249
Shigeto Oshida 160
shikan-taza 249